Robert Shoemaker was born in Boston, USA and studied in Oregon and California before moving to London twenty years ago. He is currently Professor of Eighteenth-Century British History and head of the History Department at the University of Sheffield. With Tim Hitchcock, he is director of the Old Bailey Proceedings Online (www.oldbaileyonline.org), a fully searchable edition of all printed trial accounts from 1674 to 1834; a current project will add the trials from 1834 to 1913 to the website.

Tim Hitchcock is Professor of Eighteenth-Century History at the University of Hertfordshire. He was educated at the University of California at Berkeley, and at Oxford. He lives in London and has written or edited books on the histories of eighteenth-century poverty, sexuality and masculinity.

Tales from the Hanging Court

Tim Hitchcock
& Robert Shoemaker

HODDER
EDUCATION
PART OF HACHETTE LIVRE UK

First published in Great Britain in 2006 by
Hodder Education,
part of Hachette Livre UK,
338 Euston Road, London NW1 3BH

Paperback edition published 2007

www. hoddereducation.com

If you have any comments to make about this, or any of our other titles,
please send them to educationenquiries@hodder.com

British Library Cataloguing in Publication Data
A catalogue record for this book is available from the British Library

Library of Congress Cataloguing-in-Publication Data
A catalog record of this book is available from the Library of Congress

ISBN: 978 0 340 91375 8

Impression number   10 9 8 7 6 5 4 3 2
Year   2011 2010 2009 2008

Front cover image: Fleet Street from John Rocque's 1746 map (Sheet D2)
© Motco Enterprises Limited, ref: www.motco.com and Edward Marcus Despard
being hung (detail from an engraving), after unknown artist, published 1804
© National Portrait Gallery, London

Back cover image: A public execution at Newgate, London, late 18th century
© Museum of London/HIP/Topham

Typeset in 11 on 13.5pt Caslon by Phoenix Photosetting, Chatham, Kent
Printed and bound in Great Britain by CPI Cox & Wyman, Reading, Berkshire

Contents

List of figures

Acknowledgements and note on editorial method

Most of the historical material reproduced in this volume has been taken from the *Old Bailey Proceedings Online* (www.oldbaileyonline.org, referred to in the endnotes as *OBP*). This website reproduces the full text of the *Old Bailey Proceedings* in a searchable format along with images of the original printed pages. In this book the spelling has been modernised throughout, and small changes, both elisions and insertions, have been made without comment. When quoting from this material, please refer to the original text available online rather than this modernised version. Individual trials can be located by searching for the trial reference number identified in the endnotes.

The authors would like to thank all those whose hard work contributed to the creation of the Old Bailey website, and the organisations which funded it: the Big Lottery Fund, the Arts and Humanities Research Council, and the Universities of Hertfordshire and Sheffield. We are grateful to the Humanities Research Institute, publishers of HRI Online, for permission to reproduce extensive quotations from the text of the *Proceedings*. For permission to reproduce images included in this volume we would also like to thank: Motco Enterprises Limited, www.motco.com; Guildhall Library, City of London; The Bridgeman Art Library; the British Library Board; City of Westminster Archives Centre; London Metropolitan Archives, City of London; National Gallery of Scotland; National Portrait Gallery,

London; The Trustees of The British Museum; The Lewis Walpole Library, Yale University; The Trustees of the Weston Park Foundation, UK; General Photographic Agency; Hulton Archive and Getty Images.

Prologue

Early on a cool Monday evening in January 1742, Susannah Nichols set off for home from Newgate Street, the bulk of St Paul's Cathedral looming above her in the darkness. She could feel the reassuring weight of 16 heavy silver shillings clinking in a green silk purse secreted in the pocket inside her dress as she walked purposefully into Blowbladder Street and then Cheapside. By 5 pm, when she set out, it was already dark, but there was a full moon and the shops on either side glowed gently with candle light. People rushed past her, flitting into and out of the light, hurrying on to the warmth of a coffeehouse or a domestic fireside. The streets through which she walked were well paved and orderly; filled with 'lofty buildings, well inhabited by goldsmiths, linen drapers, haberdashers and other great dealers'.[1] To her right, the small medieval lanes synonymous with the trades practised in them stretched down to the Thames: the Old Change and Bread Street, followed by Christopher Wren's towering parish church of St Mary Le Bow. On the hour, Bow Bells, in concert with those of 100 other churches, filled the air, making conversation temporarily impossible. When the bells were silent, she could hear the click of wooden pattens on pavement and the squeal of wood on wood, as wagons and coaches went by, punctuated in turn by the cries of ballad singers and mackerel sellers, purveyors of cabbage nets and shoelaces.

She walked eastward to where Cheapside narrowed into the Poultry with its crush of alehouses and taverns. Today the Poultry is just one more anonymous street at the heart of

financial London, around the corner from the Bank of
England and the Stock Exchange, but in 1742, as Susannah
walked on the north side of the roadway, she was confronted
by the narrow entrance to the Poultry Compter – one of the
half dozen holding prisons that littered the City – and
suddenly found herself jostled by four young men and a
woman:

> Just as I came to the apothecary's door, the woman
> came behind me, and held me fast down. I attempted to
> get from her into the middle of the highway, and some
> fellows jostled me, and kept me close to her.
> Immediately I felt a hand in my pocket.

Susannah struggled, and turned about to face her assailant.
The woman she saw in the moonlight was named Eleanor
Brown and as soon as Susannah realised what was
happening, she cried out 'murder!' When Londoners were
criminally attacked, their first instinct was to cry for help,
knowing that passers-by on the crowded city streets would
usually come to their assistance.

Eleanor Brown later claimed she had been on her way to
Wapping to meet a country cousin just arrived from
Newcastle. But when the cry of 'murder!' and 'stop thief!'
first went up she was observed trying to slip away through
the gathering crowd. John Garnal had just turned into the
Poultry from King Street when he heard the cry for help. He
later described how Eleanor Brown rapidly:

> Crossed the way on the other side of the Poultry. She
> went an exceeding pace, sometimes walked and
> sometimes ran, so that I could not keep pace with her
> without sometimes running myself. When she came to
> the corner of Walbrook Street she turned down and I
> believe might be a dozen yards before me. I followed
> her to see where she went and when I turned the corner
> I saw her take off her cloak and put it under her arm
> and run with full speed. I then thought she certainly had
> the purse about her, upon which I ran and grasped hold

> of her, and told her, she had stolen a purse. It was just
> by the poulterer's shop that I first seized her, and a man
> (George Lesley) came to my assistance, and took hold
> of her likewise.

Eighteenth-century London was a city policed by consent, and every member of the public was theoretically obliged to answer a call of 'stop thief' or 'murder'. George Lesley was walking up Walbrook Street towards Cheapside when he came across John Garnal trying to restrain Eleanor Brown just opposite the Mansion House. He stopped to watch. However, Eleanor had a confederate, James Robinson – probably one of the men who had originally jostled Susannah Nichols – who made matters more difficult:

> I saw this man [Garnal] holding that woman [Brown].
> He said, she had stole a watch and desired me to assist
> him. I was at a loss whether I should stop or go past,
> and just as I came up to them, a man rushed from
> Cheapside and struck me over the head. I asked him
> why he struck me? And he said, Eleanor was his wife,
> and he knew she was innocent. While he was repeating
> these words, he redoubled his blows, and struck me
> again.

In John Garnal's recollection:

> Immediately I heard two blows behind me and the
> person that had got hold of the prisoner's arm reeled a
> little on one side. Soon afterwards I received a blow
> myself on the side of my head, and turning about to see
> from whence it came, Eleanor Brown sprang out of my
> arms.

Following this escape, 'stop thief' was once again cried out. Eleanor and James ran up Bucklersbury – the small street leading back towards Cheapside, famous for its apothecary shops and strange smells. William Lesley later said:

> We pursued them, crying 'stop thief!' The other people
> ran faster than I, so that I was a little distanced, and saw

no more of them till I came to the upper end of
Bucklersbury, and perceiving the man using his stick as
smartly as before, I seized him. The woman was taken
by somebody else at the same time, and when they
came together they denied that they had ever seen each
other before.

Finally, at the top of Bucklersbury, John Garnal, William
Lesley and William Lambkin managed to wrestle Eleanor
and James Robinson to the ground. Adopting the role of a
detective, Garnal then:

Desired the person, at whose door I seized Eleanor
Brown, to let me bring her in, but he held the door
against me. I then took her into the house of one Mr
Bingham, a silk dyer, and searched her, and turned a
purse and other things out of her pocket. She pretended
that she was entirely innocent of the matter and that she
was going to the bottom of Walbrook to see a friend who
was going out of town. After we had stayed some time at
Mr Bingham's the person was brought in that followed us
[James Robinson] striking those that endeavored to take
the prisoner, and we carried them both to the
watchhouse, where Robinson pulled out a purse and
shook some silver out of it into his hand. They were
carried the next day before the Alderman at Guildhall
and ordered to be searched; and the woman then
produced a green purse and the man a light blue one.

Charges against James Robinson were dropped in the 11
days that elapsed between these events and Eleanor's trial at
the Old Bailey for robbery. At her trial on 15 January 1742
Eleanor tried every strategy in order to get off. She cross-
examined the witnesses and attempted to undermine
Susannah Nichol's account of events. She called character
witnesses who related a long and varied career as a
charwoman and servant and brought others to verify her
account of the innocent journey to Wapping to meet her
country cousin. But it did not work. The jury found her
guilty and she was sentenced to hang.

As the awful sentence was passed, Eleanor's expectation must have been that in just a few days she would be tumbled into a cart and drawn through the crowded streets from Newgate Prison – near where Susannah Nichols had set out for home – to Tyburn, where a noose would be placed around her neck and the cart driven from beneath her feet, leaving her slowly to strangle to death. In fact, this grisly punishment was never actually imposed. Instead, Eleanor Brown was taken back to Newgate Prison where she stayed for the next five months – the sentence of death hanging over her – while her friends and family petitioned the king for a pardon. She finally disappears from the records of Newgate in June of 1742, having been neither transported nor hanged. The likelihood is that she simply died of disease in the miserable prison conditions. Susannah Nichols, meanwhile, went on to collect part of the substantial reward offered by the government to encourage victims of crime to prosecute highway robbers. In the end she pocketed £17 2s, perhaps two years' wages for a female servant.

Eleanor Brown was one of 57,000 defendants tried at the Old Bailey in the eighteenth century and one of almost 6,000 individuals sentenced to death. But, while 1,644 men and women were actually hanged, Eleanor was one of the majority whose execution was never carried out.[2] Nevertheless, a report of her crime and her trial was published, like all the others, in the popular periodical, the *Proceedings of the Old Bailey*, and voraciously read by Londoners, who found entertainment, information and titillation in the details of these stories of true crime. Today these reports stand as stark testimony to the early history of our modern judicial system and to the unique and vibrant world of pre-industrial London. These stories from the Old Bailey courtroom evoke a lost world of violence and disorder in the world's first great modern city.[3]

Introduction

'One of the most diverting things a man can read in London'

Louis de Muralt (1726)

The eighteenth-century courtroom at the Old Bailey – the most important criminal court in the English-speaking world, and the place where the modern adversarial trial was created – witnessed all the tragedy of human life. Violence, sex, money and drugs; jealousy, love and hate were rehearsed by victims and criminals under the gaze of jaundiced judges and suspicious jurymen. The stories told here were then rendered into print in the *Proceedings of the Old Bailey*. Published eight times a year, after each court session, the *Proceedings* are the dam and sire of many published courtroom dramas and detective stories and contain in full measure the anger of a victim of a senseless crime and the stark terror of a man condemned to death. In 25 million words, they record the 100,000 trials held between 1674 and 1834. First created to entertain the generation of Samuel Pepys, the *Proceedings* were published decade after decade throughout the eighteenth century. Within their pages can be found pathetic tales of suffering and mendacious accusations of crimes never committed. There are chilling acknowledgements of violence perpetrated on the innocent, as well as impudent denials. Vivid accounts of murders and riots, robberies and rapes were published for an enthusiastic audience, keen to feast on the lurid details of crime.

Even two centuries later the emotions of the courtroom hold the reader's attention. But within these 25 million words of crime and courtroom drama, there is much, much more. Everyday life, down to the smallest gesture and most subtle emotion, is recorded: how to order a drink at an alehouse, how to empty a chamber pot or buy a leek; where to sit at the play, what to wear when setting out to beg. The *Proceedings* teach us how to speak to a hackney coachman, and what not to say when confronted by a highway robber. They introduce us to people like Mary 'Cut-and-Come-Again' who, when arrested for theft, took out her breasts and squirted mother's milk in the eyes of her accuser, who spat at the justice as he recorded her crime, and who went to the scaffold refusing almost to her last breath to give her proper name. They introduce us to Thomas De Veil, the sexually rapacious reforming magistrate who, along with his successors Henry and John Fielding, established the first modern police force. And to Princess Seraphina, the transvestite male prostitute who haunted the balls and masquerades of 1730s London in fine clothes and an elaborate wig; and William Garrow, the first and most eloquent Rumpole of the Bailey. Criminals, pathetic and vicious by turns, thieftakers breaking the law while claiming to enforce it, barristers sometimes brilliant and frequently pompous and foolish and, above them all, the officers of the court sitting in cold judgement, are all here.

Tales from the Hanging Court brings to a modern audience this world of characters, emotions and detail. It recreates the life and death dramas on which Daniel Defoe, Henry Fielding and Charles Dickens based their novels. It presents a few dozen of the most colourful and revealing trials from the 50,000 witnessed by the court in the eighteenth century; trials that evoke this place and time, these fears and emotions; trials that allow the modern reader to feel the grit and humanity of life in eighteenth-century London, its cruelty and its charms.

London was at turns beautiful and squalid, orderly and chaotic. Rebuilt following the disastrous fire of 1666, the City's medieval streets were now home to brick buildings in the classical style. The fire-damaged heart of the City was remade with houses fronted by serried ranks of sash windows; their structures made uniform by some of the most stringent building regulations ever imposed. The major thoroughfares, backstreets and side alleys were filled with houses in a style laid down in the crisp prose of a government commission, making London one of the architectural jewels of Europe. Equally impressive were the aristocratic urban palaces lining the new streets and formal squares of Westminster. Chains, iron railings and padlocks attempted to segregate the inhabitants of these new suburbs from their poorer neighbours, creating gated communities reserved for the powdered and bewigged. But as London spread into the open fields in every direction, other suburban developments, notably those to the east and north of the City, outside the areas governed by planning regulations, were haphazard and of poor quality. Here speculators threw up squalid houses made with poor materials and even poorer workmanship. Every jobbing carpenter who could scrape together a few pounds in capital tried to become a property developer. House collapses in these crowded neighbourhoods were common, with whole families occasionally crushed in their beds.

At the start of the century London had a population of just under 600,000; by 1800 it had reached nearly one million. It had become the largest city in the western world. This inexorable growth, this seemingly unstoppable urban bloat, was almost entirely the result of migration. High mortality rates and unhealthy living conditions, in combination with a relatively late age at marriage, ensured that Londoners could not rely on nature to fill the shoes of the dead. Instead, London depended on the thousands of immigrants, primarily young and predominantly female, who came to the capital each year.

They moved in order to escape poverty and exploitation back home, but as important was the prospect of jobs and adventure in the big city. London's economy grew and diversified over the course of the century. In the West End, the growing importance of the London season to Britain's aristocracy and gentry led to increasing demand for luxury goods and services, employing an army of servants, shopkeepers, coachmakers, dancing masters and an ever more finely graded set of other flunkies. At the other end of town, in the districts of the East End, jobs could be found in manufacturing, brewing and distilling, sugar processing and textile production. By the river, London's port served as the centre of a growing network of national and international trade, the home of thousands of sailors, dockworkers, shipbuilders and watermen, who in turn contributed to the livelihoods of fishwives, prostitutes and alehouse keepers. The City of London itself fed on all these activities. Its warehouses bulged with an ever expanding list of commodities. Its coffeehouses were filled with men raising cash and capital, while its courts adjudicated on an ever more complex set of business dealings. In most years, in most decades in the eighteenth century, London was booming. But its economy was vulnerable to sudden downturns and disastrous collapse. Mad speculation, the disruption of trade routes during wars, or the sudden drop in demand heralded by peace, regularly turned economic boom into bust.

Few people could know this vast metropolis in its full variety. Much as today, Londoners saw their world as a patchwork of competing communities and neighbourhoods. As Tom Brown wrote in 1700, 'We daily discover more new countries, and surprising singularities, than in all the universe besides. There are among the Londoners so many nations differing in manners, customs and religion, that the inhabitants themselves don't know a quarter of them.'[1] Immigrants came from England, Scotland, Wales and Ireland, and from every corner of the globe. Just as it is today, London was by far England's largest city, accounting for over 10 percent of the total population. When the circulation of migrants to and from the capital is included, historians have calculated that one in every six Englishmen and women lived in London at some point during their lives. But the city's attraction was not restricted to Britain alone. It provided a new home to Protestants fleeing repression in France, blacks fleeing slavery or discharged onto the streets from the armies of a growing empire, and Jews from Spain and eastern Europe. Each new group of immigrants found its own neighbourhoods, contributing to the cacophony of voices to be heard in the alleys and streets. When James Dawson Burns recollected his eighteenth-century London childhood, it was the different accents that came to mind. He recalled St Giles in the Fields, filled with the 'blackguard slang of landsmen of all nations, mixed up with the technicalities of prigs and professional beggars', while around the river he remembered 'the jargon of salt junk and the fo'-castle, refined with coal dust and the elegant vocabulary of Billingsgate'.[2] The wealth and complexity of this social geography left many visitors bewildered. Even that most knowledgeable of Londoners, Henry Fielding, was confused and a little frightened. For him London was 'a vast wood or forest, in which a thief may harbour with as great security as wild beasts do in the deserts of Africa or Arabia'.[3]

National origin, religion and class all marked the divisions between London's many communities. The largest Irish colony, dubbed 'little Dublin', was in St Giles in the Fields, just to the north and west of the medieval City. But by the end of the century, Irish communities could also be found in

Whitechapel and Saffron Hill, Poplar and Southwark and, perhaps most notoriously, in the Camel Buildings off Orchard Street in Marylebone. Twenty thousand Jews lived in London. The relatively wealthy Sephardim from Spain and Portugal came first and congregated around Aldgate, where they built the Great Synagogue in 1697. They were followed by Ashkenazi from central and eastern Europe, fleeing religious persecution, who found work in the disreputable used clothing market known as 'Rag Fair', by the Tower of London at the eastern boundary of the City. French Protestants, the Huguenots, established thriving communities in the silk-weaving district of Spitalfields in the east and at the Savoy in the west. Many young men about to set off for the grand tour spent a few weeks polishing their accent in the courts and coffeehouses of these districts. Blacks, from Africa, the Caribbean and North America could be found in all the neighbourhoods of the capital. Brought as personal servants and slaves by returning plantation owners, by the vagaries of international war and as refugees from the American Revolution, the black population of London numbered several thousand by the 1780s. Gypsies, working as hawkers and pedlars, fortune tellers and tinkers, wintered around Seven Dials in St Giles in the Fields, and occupied established encampments in the rural hinterlands of the capital.

Money and occupation divided and defined still other communities. At the beginning of the century, London was in many respects still a medieval city. The gentry could still be found living side by side with the poor. By the end of the century, London was increasingly subdivided between the rich, the poor and the middling sort. As the city spread out over the nearby fields, the elegant aristocratic squares of the West End, populated by lords, gentlemen, and the tradesmen and servants who catered for their needs, contrasted ever more starkly with the densely populated

East End, composed of men and women who worked in the weaving trades and on the docks. In between the City and the West End lay socially heterogeneous and conflict-ridden parishes like St Giles in the Fields, the parish that witnessed the largest number of crimes prosecuted at the Old Bailey. By 1800 a member of the gentry would no more consider leaving his West End haunts to walk to the East End, than he would consider walking to the moon. Neither would he consider living in the mercantile City. In 1808 Robert Southey noted sarcastically that: 'London is more remarkable for the distribution of its inhabitants than any city on the continent. A nobleman would not be found by any accident to live in that part which is properly called the City, unless he should be confined for treason or sedition in Newgate or the Tower.'[4]

But for most of the century the residential divisions of wealth and poverty, nationality and religion that divided Londoners were easily crossed. The city's narrow streets witnessed a disorderly co-mingling of pedestrians of all backgrounds, for whom these public spaces were much more than a means of getting from one place to another. For hawkers, ballad sellers, stall keepers and shoeblacks, the streets were their workplace, where they sold their wares and services. Beggars took up prominent positions from which to appeal to the charity of the better off, while prostitutes aggressively pursued their clients, often consummating the transaction in a side alley. Official and unofficial celebrations such as processions and bonfires took place in the streets, while working people used them for a host of recreational activities including throwing at cocks, football and boxing and wrestling matches. Picking their way through the hawkers and beggars, and the processions and fights, were shoppers and strollers, and men and women hurrying onto their next job, or to meet a friend, to go for dinner or to see a play.

Differences of wealth and status could be transcended, or at least so many Londoners believed. There was a high degree of social mobility as newly minted fortunes transformed the fortunate into gentry, while sudden debts or unemployment could throw just about anyone into prison or the workhouse. The definition of a gentleman, once strictly rooted in heredity, landholding and a coat of arms, loosened, so that by 1730 Nathaniel Bailey could claim: 'All are accounted gentlemen that have money, and if he has no coat of arms, the King of Arms can sell him one.'[5] Or indeed, if a man *looked and acted* like he had money, he would be regarded by many as a gentleman. Contemporaries fretted about the breakdown of the social order, as status was increasingly determined by ever deceptive appearances. 'Of all the follies and fallacies which reign in London,' one anonymous author complained, 'none is more glaring than affectation, of endeavouring to impose ourselves on the world, for what we are not.'[6] This uncertainty could be a source of amusement (the masquerade was a uniquely eighteenth-century entertainment), but as many novels testified, it could also lead to disaster when promised wealth failed to materialise. The problem of trust became ever more critical as traditional signs of class and wealth became less certain. It was impossible to conduct business without it, but it was difficult to know who to trust in this world where identities seemed to be taken up and discarded like so many coats and wigs. In this context, the independence and apparent lack of subservience of working people seemed ever more intolerable: servants dressed like their masters and mistresses, and journeymen and mechanics seemed to grow more ungovernable with every passing generation.

This fast paced and chaotic world formed the context for the crimes prosecuted at the Old Bailey. Almost all prosecutions recorded in the *Proceedings* were for felonies and therefore, in principle, shared the possibility of being punished with death. But much more than their legal status, the crimes of violence, property and immorality tried in the court shared a metropolitan wellspring. They grew from bigotry and prejudice, defensiveness, fear and greed; from all the emotions and insecurities unleashed when a traditional society was confronted with diversity and change. National and religious differences led to riots and attacks on immigrants, foreign visitors and non-conformists; attempts to defend men's honour and reputations resulted in swordfights among the gentry and boxing matches among working people; and attempts by men to maintain control over their wives in a city where women could aspire to financial independence resulted in domestic violence and spousal murders. And self-serving politicians, confronted with new opportunities for rabble rousing and populism, used the mob to press home their sectarian agendas.

Property crimes, by far the most common type of offence tried in the court, were motivated above all by the dire poverty experienced by those thrown out of work by sudden economic downturns and personal misfortune. Single women, whose employment opportunities were at the best of times limited to a narrow range of low-paid jobs, were the most vulnerable. But poverty was not the only cause of theft. At every turn in a city where new consumer goods were piled high in the newly invented shop windows, the poor were confronted by objects of desire and some men and women, desperate to follow the latest fashion, succumbed to temptation. Other prosecutions for theft arose out of workplace conflicts and more or less genuine differences of opinion about property rights. Moralists never tired of pointing out the vices of the metropolis and blamed crime on the personal failings of Londoners. But that immorality was itself driven by the opportunities created by London life. Alcohol was readily available in any of 10,000 drinking establishments, from the more respectable inns and coffeehouses to neighbourhood alehouses, spirit shops and even women selling shots of gin from a bottle on the streets. Drunkenness was frequently harmless, but it did occasionally lead to violent disputes. In contrast to the fears of contemporary commentators, however, the 'gin craze' of the 1730s and 1740s contributed to crime not because an inebriated population lost its moral compass and were driven to steal in order to pay for their addiction, but because drunken Londoners, often distracted by lust, provided an easy target for opportunistic but more sober thieves.

Only a tiny proportion of crime committed in London actually led to a trial. The vast majority of crimes went undetected or at least unpunished. Taking someone to court was both time consuming and costly and many victims accepted informal 'satisfaction' from the culprit, for example by securing the return of their stolen goods in exchange for dropping the charges. The relatively primitive forces of policing were simply not up to the task of preventing or effectively investigating crime, and the burden of detection and prosecution fell overwhelmingly on the victim. Those crimes that did end up at the Old Bailey did so either as a result of the zeal of individual prosecutors aided by the haphazard efforts of constables and watchmen, or the entrepreneurial activities of informers and 'thieftakers' motivated by the prospect of financial reward.

Even were the victim determined to prosecute, this did not ensure that the case would ever come to trial. It first had to be vetted by the propertied men of the Grand Jury, to determine whether there was a case to answer. If a 'true bill' was found it was only then allowed to proceed to a trial, held during one of the eight annual sittings of the court. Each trial lasted on average no more than 30 minutes, and was held at the Old Bailey courthouse, just 200 yards northwest of St Paul's Cathedral. The court was named after the original fortified wall, or 'bailey', marking the edge of the medieval City of London. The building was destroyed by the Great Fire and was rebuilt and rebuilt again on two more occasions during the course of the eighteenth century. Until 1737 the courtroom was open to the elements – both judges and defendants suffering the cold and the heat. The western wall was left open in order to increase the supply of fresh air and reduce the risk that prisoners with gaol fever (typhus) would infect others. In front of the courthouse was the Sessions House Yard, where litigants, witnesses, and spectators gathered to marshal their forces and observe the proceedings. In 1737 the building was remodelled and enclosed, purportedly in order to keep out the weather, but also to limit the influence of unruly spectators. In 1774 the court was rebuilt again by George Dance at a cost of £15,000 and this time included a semi-circular brick wall immediately in front of the courthouse – the bail dock. This wall provided better security for the prisoners awaiting trial and was intended to prevent communication between them and the public clamouring outside. The wall also obstructed views of the courtroom through its external windows, and provided a narrow and easily controlled entrance to the court, preventing a sudden influx of spectators. Gradually built into the fabric of the building was an increasingly fraught relationship between court and public. This came to a head during the Gordon riots in 1780 when the courtroom was badly damaged and crowds carried away the furniture and burned it on bonfires in the streets.

Until 1824 there was only one courtroom, in which carefully positioned seating was provided for the judges, jurors, officers of the court, legal counsel, and spectators. A semi-circle of seats surrounded the accused standing at the bar, with jurors and judges looking down from a raised position. Below, their papers spread before them, sat the lawyers and clerks who ran the machinery of justice. A large

Figure 0.01 Old Bailey Sessions House (circled), from John Rocque's 1746 Map of London. Credit: Motco Enterprises Limited, ref: www.motco.com

glass mirror was positioned to reflect daylight on to the face of the accused as they stood at the bar and pleaded for their lives – a bright light designed to help the jurors see into the motives and morality of the defendant. Spectators had to pay a fee of 6d or 1s to secure admittance. The trials attracted a mixed audience of London's more and less respectable inhabitants and it was alleged that criminals attended in order to devise strategies for when their turn would come to stand at the bar. The crowd's presence could influence or intimidate the jurors, who often reached a verdict without leaving the courtroom. There were two juries, one for crimes committed in Middlesex, and another for those originating in London. Both sat throughout each session, passing judgement, turn and turnabout.

Those who were unable to attend the trials at the Old Bailey read about them in the printed *Proceedings*. First published in serial form in 1674 as part of an explosion of popular literature about crime, the Mayor and Aldermen of the City moved to established control over their content from 1679. Early editions were between four and nine pages long and comprised the briefest trial summaries. In the 1710s the

Proceedings begin to include some verbatim reports, especially of trials thought to be salacious, amusing or otherwise entertaining. In December 1729, in the face of growing competition from daily newspapers and published collections of trials, the publisher introduced a number of changes to the format in order to make the *Proceedings* more attractive to readers. They were expanded to 24 pages, and included yearly indexes, cross-referencing between trials, and advertisements. But, most importantly, the growing sophistication of shorthand note taking allowed the publisher to include an increasing number of verbatim accounts of the testimonies of prosecutors, witnesses, and defendants, as well as judges' comments and questions. As the number of trials held at the Old Bailey grew and the City of London demanded ever higher standards of accuracy, the *Proceedings* increased in length, reaching, on average, over 100 pages per issue by the beginning of the nineteenth century.

As the *Proceedings* increased in cost and respectability over the course of the eighteenth century, readership actually declined. Londoners had plenty of other opportunities to read about the crimes tried at the Old Bailey, much of it written in a far more accessible and titillating style. With the expiration of press licensing in 1695 and the huge increase in popular literacy in the eighteenth century (male literacy rates in London reached over 70 percent), there was a large market for the cheap printed literature produced by 'Grub Street'. As the century passed, the *Proceedings* became just one of several types of publication designed to meet the demand for literature about crime. Some alternatives were relatively sober, including reports found in newspapers and the *Ordinary's Accounts* (biographies of condemned convicts written by the chaplain of Newgate Prison). But others, such as pamphlet accounts, single-page broadsides, and ballads, were often self-consciously scurrilous and sensational. This potpourri of publications certainly satisfied public demand, but the competing accounts of individual crimes were often contradictory, and Londoners were left to draw their own conclusions about whether the men and women forced to stand at the bar of the Old Bailey were guilty or innocent, heroes or villains.

In the tales that follow, stories of individual crimes have been pieced together from the *Proceedings* and a wide range of other sources in order to recreate for a modern readership the events Londoners first pored over more than two centuries ago.

1

Stop Thief!

Eighteenth-century Britain did not have a police force. The very word 'police' in its modern sense of an organised body of state officials did not emerge until the very end of the century. When Britons contemplated the possibility of creating such a force, it appeared to them to smack of arbitrary and tyrannical government of the sort they denigrated in France and which seemed ill suited to a Britain that endlessly congratulated itself on its liberty and balanced constitution. The price of this freedom was the expectation that individual Britons themselves would play a significant role in enforcing the law and detecting crime: legally, anyone who witnessed a serious crime in progress or who heard the cry of 'murder!' or 'stop thief!', was, as already observed, obliged to join in the pursuit. The parish constables and night watchmen, who were typically part-time, unpaid local officials, generally restricted their activities to arresting suspects once they had been captured by victims or the wider public. As a result, at the heart of eighteenth-century justice was a kind of vigilantism that ensured a relatively high proportion of men and women found themselves involved in the enforcement of the law.

It also ensured that many arrests were mistaken or malicious.

Some crimes were unlikely to be prosecuted in this 'do-it-yourself' manner. Those who committed victimless offences, including gambling, sodomy, prostitution, profane swearing and cursing and vagrancy (all considered crimes at this time) were prosecuted differently and more erratically. In these instances, the constables and night watchmen who normally stood idly by waiting for malefactors to be delivered up to their care were responsible for actively pursuing criminals. Unless pressured by zealous neighbours or specifically instructed to do so by a justice of the peace, however, they rarely took these duties too seriously. Only when officers and informers were motivated by the prospect of a financial reward or by a strong religious commitment, as was the case with the members of the Societies for the Reformation of Manners established in the wake of the Revolution of 1688, were any attempts made to prosecute vice systematically. At the height of their influence between the 1690s and the 1720s, the societies prosecuted thousands of minor criminals each year, employing informers to infiltrate the free and easy world of irregular London. Many crimes, sodomy for example, were prosecuted in large numbers only because of the religious fanaticism of men like those who promoted these societies.

This system of predominantly private arrest and prosecution had evolved in a rural society and by 1700 was creaking under the strain of trying to satisfy the needs of a rapidly growing metropolis. Fears of violent retribution and of criminal gangs made individual Londoners wary of getting involved or making an arrest. And unless criminals were caught in the act, it became ever more difficult to chase them down in the streets and alleys of Europe's largest city. Frustrated by the small number of criminals arrested and prosecuted, in the 1690s parliament and the crown began to offer substantial rewards (initially up to £40) to those responsible for the arrest and conviction of anyone guilty of certain serious crimes. These rewards encouraged the development of thief taking as a profession. Thieftakers lived on the borders of the criminal underworld, but they were seen as providing a useful service to the state. In addition to earning money from official rewards, these men also profited from a second source of income, derived from their knowledge of criminal networks.

Facilitated by the expansion of the newspaper press in the early eighteenth century, victims of theft in London resorted to advertising in an attempt to recover their lost goods, offering a reward with no questions asked. Prosecutors at the Old Bailey had to pay their own legal costs and even on conviction frequently failed to recover their stolen property. As a result many victims chose to bypass the judicial system altogether and advertise their goods. By responding to these advertisements, which were appearing regularly in the press by the 1710s, thieftakers acted as intermediaries in arranging the return of stolen goods and they received a portion of the rewards offered by the victims. Some, most notoriously Jonathan Wild, combined returning stolen goods and thief taking to create an extensive criminal network, using the threat (and occasional reality) of punishment by the criminal justice system to discipline their underlings. Wild himself went even further and engaged in thief making, growing his own thieves and then profiting from the rewards doled out when he stage managed their arrest and conviction, often leading to their execution.

As distasteful as the activities of thieftakers were, they rapidly became an essential part of the law enforcement system – without them, too much crime would go unpunished. So when the novelist Henry Fielding became a justice of the peace in 1748, shortly followed by his blind half-brother John, they set out to control thieftakers and make them respectable by hiring them on retainers and giving them a base of operations at their house in Bow Street. (Henry died in 1754, but John carried on as a justice until his death in 1780.) By advertising their services in the newspapers, the Fieldings hoped to make these men (and the Fieldings themselves) an indispensable part of the judicial system, encouraging victims to report crimes to Bow Street immediately so that they could send out their men in search of the culprits. The Fieldings even gave these men a new, less pejorative, name – 'runners' – and in the process created one of the key foundations of modern policing in Britain: a body of experienced detectives.

Once arrested, those accused of felonies had to be kept imprisoned until they could be brought before a justice of the peace for a preliminary hearing. London was full of lockups, variously called watchhouses, roundhouses, compters, and prisons, which were used to hold suspected criminals for short periods of time until the legal process took its course. Like Newgate Prison, where both prisoners committed for trial and convicts awaiting transportation or execution were kept, lockups were run on an essentially commercial basis. For prisoners with money, keepers often provided services including a comfortable bed and good food and drink. Running London's prisons was such a lucrative business that the position of keeper was normally purchased only for a substantial sum. In contrast, prisoners without money were kept in squalid conditions and expected to survive on the county ration of a penny loaf per day, supplemented by charity and doles.

The preliminary hearing in front of a justice of the peace was a key feature of the judicial process. Typically, it took place in the parlour of the justice's own home and was often a very public event, conducted in front of spectators. According to the letter of the law, suspected felons should have been automatically forwarded to the Old Bailey for trial, but in practice preliminary hearings were used to filter out cases where the facts were insufficient to warrant a prosecution. Where the case was stronger, the hearing provided an opportunity to marshal the evidence against the accused in preparation for the trial. The use of the preliminary hearing in this way gave huge power to individual justices, sitting alone in almost God-like judgement. Some, including the Fieldings and their predecessor at Bow Street, Sir Thomas De Veil, used these hearings as a platform from which to build an extensive reputation as crime-fighting magistrates, establishing both a new resource for victims of crime and the model for the magistrates' courts of the next century and beyond.

Ye Dogs, Do You Rob at this Time o' Day?

Thousands of Old Bailey trials only took place because the culprit was arrested by passers-by who, responding to the cry of 'stop thief!', apprehended the suspect. As a method of policing, the 'hue and cry', as it was called, was open to error and abuse. Those making the arrest could easily be misled by either the supposed victim or the perpetrator, and defendants on trial for their lives frequently claimed that this is precisely what had happened in their case. One arrest made in response to a cry of this sort was reported in the London Evening Post *in the late Spring of 1735:*

> Tuesday, about five in the afternoon, a gentleman was knocked down by one footpad in the long field by Pancras, who took from him his gold watch and ten guineas. But being closely pursued by a man who was at some distance when the robbery was committed, he took to a pond and stood in the middle, and bid defiance to his pursuer. But the latter calling three men who were passing by to assist him, the rogue was taken and carried to St Giles Roundhouse, and he proves to be one of the Suttons.[1]

In 1734 and 1735 John Sutton, a former apprentice to a
tobacconist, together with his brother George, was
suspected of committing a series of robberies in London and
its suburbs. John Sutton spent that particular Tuesday
afternoon in May with three friends drinking, first at a
public house, later moving on to a brandy shop and then an
alehouse in one of the more disreputable neighbourhoods on
the edge of the City. According to his later, possibly
drunken, confession the four young men agreed to go out
and find someone to rob. He told Justice John Poulson that:

> I and Godson, Stockton and Benyan, met about two in the
> afternoon at Lloyd's, the Sun and Horseshoe in Dyer's
> Street, and there agreed to go into the fields and rob. From
> Lloyd's we went to an opposite brandy shop, and thence to
> an infamous house, the Two Fighting Cocks at the Brill,
> kept by Taylor alias Pritchard. Going from thence we met
> with William Power. One of us (who was in a black cap)
> fell upon Power. I took his watch and put it into my
> waistcoat pocket, but people coming up, and the watch
> string hanging out, I threw the watch on the ground.

'The fields' where these events took place were Lamb's
Conduit Fields, named after an Elizabethan system built to
supply fresh drinking water to London's poor. In 1735 the
fields stretched from just north of Great Ormond Street
towards St Pancras and Highgate. Interspersed among the
meadows were a bowling green and a burying ground for the
new parish of St George Bloomsbury.

William Power, the victim of this robbery, set out that
afternoon to meet William Howson, a servant or apprentice,
in Red Lyon Street. According to Howson, Power was
already inebriated when he offered the young man a drink at
an alehouse across the fields:

> My Master [James Brook, a poulterer in Holborn] sent me
> into Red Lyon Street to see for this gentleman. I found
> him there, and he said if I'd go to the Three Tuns, he'd

make me drink. I went with him, and coming to a pond, we met four fellows who said to one another, 'He's drunk'. Power replied, 'Damn 'em'. 'What would they be at? Damn ye', says he in the black cap, 'Will ye fight?' And so stripping back his coat, he struck at Power on the breast. Then Sutton took Power's watch and put it into his own pocket. I desired them not to hurt the gentleman because he was in drink, though he was not quite drunk, for he could walk very well.

Power's account of the altercation leading up to the theft of his watch skated over the issue of his own drunkenness, but was otherwise consistent:

Figure 1.01 Lambs Conduit Fields, from John Rocque's 1746 Map of London. Credit: Motco Enterprises Limited, ref: www.motco.com

> On Tuesday the thirteenth of this month, between five and
> six in the evening, as I was walking in the fields not far
> from Lamb's Conduit with a neighbour's lad [William
> Howson] a little behind me, I was met by the prisoners
> and other fellows. One of them (in a jockey's black cap)
> struck me on the breast and collared me; and just as I was
> falling George Sutton came up and took out my watch.

Upon missing his watch, Power immediately cried out,
and Howson immediately ran to secure help, shouting out
some variant of the typical cry, 'stop thief!' Power later
explained to the court:

> I missed it immediately, and said, he has got my watch.
> Thereupon Howson went to the end of Red Lyon Street
> and called for help. When I was down, Sutton beat me
> violently.

In total five men answered Howson's call. Their testimony at
the subsequent trial varied in some details from the
newspaper report of the arrest. One of the first to arrive on
the scene was Mr Elkins, a bricklayer. Elkins told the Old
Bailey that:

> Going into Lamb's Conduit Fields, I stood up a little for a
> shower of rain when William Power went by me. I
> followed and saw four men about him. A man and a
> woman came by and said, 'There's a man has been
> robbed, and will be murdered.' I ran towards them with
> my trowel in my hand and called to Thomas Plunket to
> come along with the pistols. When we came up two of
> them got away, but the two prisoners stayed and Sutton
> collared Power and threw him on the grass.

According to Power, when Elkins arrived he said, 'Ye dogs,
do you rob at this time o' day? I'll run my trowel in your guts'.
   Thomas Plunket, another actor in this drama, told the
court:

> Going with Mr Elkins towards Pancras, we heard a
> gentleman had lost his watch. We ran up to the place.

William Power said Sutton had robbed him. Sutton
damned Power and struck him for saying so. Thomas
Godson stood by and endeavoured to part them. I asked
Sutton what he meant by abusing the man? He answered
he would serve me the same, and so he and I had two or
three struggles. I was sorry Sutton fell in my way, because
I had some knowledge of his family.

Thomas Holloway and Alexander Christopher also ran to the
scene. Both saw the struggle and witnessed Sutton's attempt to
escape. Holloway recorded how:

Coming by the New Burying Ground, a little on this side
of the bowling green, I saw five people in contest. Two
had hold of each other's collar. Power said, 'For God's
sake help me, for I am barbarously used, and robbed'. A
man came up with a trowel, and Sutton ran away, but fell
into a ditch, where he was taken.

Christopher backed up this version of events:

I was at my master's stables next to the fields and hearing
a noise of a robbery I ran out with other servants, and saw
five or six men together, and one sneaking along by a
hedge, and when he came over the ditch he looked pale
and frightened, and we stopped him.

Power ran to call a constable, but it was only *after* the
victims, aided by the five men who came to their assistance,
had chased Sutton down and wrestled him into submission
that official help in the form of a constable arrived. As so often
happened in the eighteenth century the role of the constable
was confined to carrying the suspect to a holding prison, in
this case St Giles Roundhouse, to be held until he could be
examined by a justice of the peace. But this approach of relying
on ordinary Londoners to make arrests had its drawbacks.
Frequently the men and women who apprehended suspects on
the streets proved to be unreliable witnesses, while the absence
of any figure of authority to verify their accounts allowed many
defendants to plead false arrest.

The next day, Wednesday, John Sutton was brought before Justice John Poulson, who induced him to sign a confession, and on the strength of this, both Sutton and Thomas Godson were transferred to Newgate to await trial. Following up its earlier report of the arrest, *The London Evening Post* also reported on the trial:

> Thursday the Sessions began at the Old Bailey, when 21 prisoners were tried, four whereof were capitally convicted, viz. William Hughes for the murder of his mother; Elton Lewis, for the murder of Mary Robinson; Charles Peele, for stealing a bill exchange of £170 out of the house of the Honourable Edward Carteret, Esq.; and John Sutton, for robbing of William Power on the highway of a silver watch.[2]

Sutton and Godson were indicted for 'assaulting William Power in an open field near the highway, putting him in fear, and taking from him a silver watch, a chain, and seal, value £3 9s'. The victim and Howson, plus the five men who helped arrest Sutton, testified for the prosecution.

The accused had two lines of defence. The first was to attempt to discredit Sutton's written confession. Sutton claimed: 'I was drunk when I made that confession, and the thieftakers persuaded me to say any thing'. In calling the men who apprehended him 'thieftakers', Sutton was attempting to cast doubt on their testimony, implying that they were motivated by the prospect of a financial reward and were probably corrupt. Unfortunately for Sutton, this claim was ignored by the court after Justice Poulson directly refuted his assertion that the confession was improperly obtained: 'He was sober – I bid him not be deceived, for it was an examination, and not an information. He read it over himself before he signed it'. An information provided evidence against others and would have ensured that the prosecution against Sutton would be dropped, but an examination meant that Sutton himself had been identified as the focus of the prosecution in this case.

Thomas Godson introduced a more effective argument, which questioned in a different way the motives of those who came to Power's assistance. He claimed that the altercation was not a robbery at all but a fight prompted by an argument. He told the court:

> I am a shoemaker and lived at Rochester. I came to
> London on the Sunday night, and on the Tuesday
> following I went to see a brother-craft in Phoenix Street,
> but did not meet with him. As I was coming back I met
> Sutton and he asked me to drink, for I had some
> knowledge of him, having formerly done work for some
> of his family. We went to the Sun and Horseshoe where I
> found two more of his acquaintance. We drank together
> there and when we came out I was going towards
> Houndsditch, but by their persuasions I went with them to
> a house across the fields. I don't know the house for I was
> never there before. But I was in haste to go home and so
> we came away, and had not gone far before we met
> William Power with whom one of Sutton's acquaintance
> (in a black cap) had some words, upon which, Sutton
> stepped up and said, 'Damn ye, will you fight'. Presently
> Power said he had lost his watch, at hearing which I was
> frightened and trembled, but seeing a watch upon the
> ground I took it up and gave it to him.

As all the parties involved readily admitted to having been drinking, this story was plausible enough, and the testimony about the fight and returning the watch was confirmed by other witnesses. Thomas Godson, unsurprisingly, was acquitted.

In contrast, Sutton was convicted and sentenced to death. He had been tried and acquitted on a charge of robbery at the Old Bailey the previous December,[3] and had also been charged with several robberies at the Surrey Assizes during the course of the spring, although these had been thrown out by the grand jury and did not go to trial. Eighteenth-century juries were frequently aware of previous accusations and Sutton's notorious reputation almost certainly contributed to their verdict, despite the ambiguity of much of the evidence presented against him. His reputation must also account for his failure to obtain a pardon. On 5 June the *London Evening Post* once again picked up the story:

> Yesterday morning between nine and ten, Sutton and Gregory (convicted of robbery, burglary and rape) in one cart, and Hughes and Lewis (both convicted of murder) in another, were carried under a strong guard to Tyburn. Sutton appeared not much concerned, but just before he was turned off shed a few tears, and made a speech to the spectators, his brother George Sutton was in the cart with him, to whom he spoke in private, and kissed him.[4]

After the hanging John Sutton's body was handed over to his friends, who arranged for the burial.[5]

Mother Clap's Molly House

While passers-by provided vital assistance in arresting those suspected of crime, typically they did so at the request of the

victims, who normally provided the key prosecution evidence at the subsequent trial. But who was to provide the lead in the arrest and prosecution of those accused of victimless crimes such as sodomy? For the prosecution of this type of crime the English judicial system relied on informers, men who, for financial or other reasons, deliberately sought out offenders and brought them before the court. Such men were often reviled for profiting from the misery of others, and were believed to be, and often were,

Figure 1.02 Field Lane, c. 1800. Credit: Guildhall Library, City of London

corrupt. But when their activities resulted in the prosecution of deeply unpopular groups such as homosexual men, they received a sympathetic hearing at the Old Bailey.

One Sunday in late June 1726 Gabriel Lawrence was caught up in a raid mounted against the 'molly houses', places where homosexual men socialised together. He was among the 40 or 50 men who congregated that night at Margaret Clap's house next to the Bunch of Grapes tavern in Field Lane, parallel to the still open sewer of Fleet Ditch, and near the modern site of the Holborn Viaduct. A few decades later Field Lane was described as:

> A sort of distinct town, or district calculated for the reception of the darkest and most dangerous enemies to society; in which when pursued for the commission of crimes they easily conceal themselves and readily escape.[6]

As described in testimony at the Old Bailey, Mother Clap's, as it was known, was infamous as a place of rendezvous for London's vibrant male homosexual subculture:

> The house bore the public character of a place of entertainment for sodomites. For the better convenience of her customers Margaret Clap had provided beds in every room in her house. She usually had 30 or 40 of such persons there every night, but more especially on a Sunday.

Molly houses were not new in the 1720s, but in 1726 they came under sustained attack by the Societies for the Reformation of Manners. These Societies were originally established following the Revolution in 1688 in an attempt to shore up the new government by eliminating vice and irreligiosity from public life. Many Londoners supported these aims, but the Societies' use of paid informers to gain convictions made them increasingly unpopular. In the decades before the 1720s the vast majority of the people the

Societies prosecuted were prostitutes and Sabbath breakers, with informers and reforming constables cruising the public streets in search of offenders, but by 1726 they had turned their attention to homosexual men.

Thomas Newton was one of the most active agents provocateur. But in his testimony at the Old Bailey, explaining how Gabriel Lawrence was arrested, he presented himself as a victim rather than a policeman. Newton went to Mother Clap's that night and:

> Was conducted up one pair of stairs, and by the
> persuasions of Peter Bavidge (who was present all the
> time) he suffered the prisoner to commit the said crime of
> sodomy. He has attempted the same since that time, but I
> never would permit him any more. When Mrs Clap was
> taken up in February I went to put in bail for her; at which
> time Mr Williams and Mr Willis told me they believed I
> could give information, which I promised to do. I went the
> next day, and gave information accordingly.

But most of the evidence at this trial came from another agent of the Societies for the Reformation of Manners, Samuel Stephens. He had been quietly infiltrating the world of the molly houses for months. He told the court that he observed the mollies that night:

> Making love to one another as they called it. Sometimes
> they'd sit in one another's laps, use their hands indecently,
> dance and make curtsies and mimic the language of women
> – O Sir! – Pray Sir! – Dear Sir! Lord how can you serve
> me so! – Ah you little dear toad! Then they would go by
> couples into a room on the same floor to be married as they
> called it. The door at that room was kept closed by
> Ecclestone, to prevent any body from balking their
> diversions. When they came out, they used to brag in plain
> terms of what they had been doing, and Margaret Clap was
> present all the time, except when she went out to fetch
> liquor. There was William Griffin among them, who was
> since hanged for sodomy, and Derwin who had been
> carried before Sir George Martins for sodomitical practices

with a link boy. I went thither 2 or 3 Sundays following, and found much the same practices as before. They talked all manner of the most vile obscenity in Margaret Clap's presence, and she appeared wonderfully pleased with it.

On some nights discussion could be even more animated. Several months before his arrest at Margaret Clap's, Gabriel Lawrence spent an evening at the Tobacco Roll and Crown, another molly house. At the trial of Martin Mackintosh for attempted sodomy, Joseph Sellers, a constable and another agent of the Societies, described Lawrence's behaviour. He:

> Began to scold at Mark Partridge, calling him vile dog, a blowing up bitch and other ill names because Partridge had blabbed out something about one Harrington's being concerned with him in sodomy. Partridge excused himself by telling the company that Harrington first divulged the secret and that what he said was only to be even with him. Upon this they seemed to be pretty well reconciled.

The same evening Lawrence also met up with Mackintosh, who:

> Sold oranges and for that reason he went by the maiden name as they called it Orange Deb. He and Lawrence appeared very fond of one another, they hugged and kissed and employed their hands in a very vile manner.

Sellers also portrayed himself as a victim. He recounted how, on that same evening, 'Orange Deb' had:

> Put his hands in my breeches, thrust his tongue into my mouth, swore that he would go 40 miles to enjoy me and begged of me to go backward, and let him – but I refusing, he offered to sit bare in my lap, upon which Partridge snatched a red hot poker out the fire and then run it into his arse.

Lawrence called his friends to give evidence at his trial about his character as a respectable heterosexual. Henry Hoxton described how he had:

> Served him with milk these 18 years, for he is a milkman
> and I am a cow-keeper. I have been with him at the
> Oxfordshire Feast, and there we have both got drunk and
> come home together in a coach, and yet he never offered
> any such thing to me.

And his father-in-law, Thomas Fuller, said Lawrence, 'married his daughter 18 years ago. She has been dead these 7 years and he has a girl by her that is 13 years old'. In addition, the *Proceedings* reported that: 'Several others deposed that he was a very sober man and that they had often been in his company when he was drunk, but never found him inclinable to such practices'.

Despite this evidence of his good character, Lawrence was convicted on the evidence of Thomas Newton and Samuel Stephens and sentenced to death. He was executed on 14 May, along with two other men convicted on Newton's evidence. Executions of homosexual men were intended to send a dire warning to the wider populace, but in this instance the lesson was overshadowed by the collapse of the scaffolding erected for the audience and the concurrent gruesome execution of Catherine Hayes by burning alive for the murder of her husband John.[7]

In total, seven men were convicted of sodomy in 1726, five of whom were convicted on the evidence of the informers Newton, Stephens and Sellers. Despite the notoriously poor reputation of informers, these men were able to secure convictions in these cases owing to the deeply rooted hostility to 'sodomites'. This hostility was equally evident when, three months later, Margaret Clap was convicted of running a brothel and procuring and sentenced to the pillory. According to a report in the *London Journal*, she 'stood in the pillory last Tuesday in Smithfield for keeping an house for the entertainment of sodomites. The populace treated her with so much severity that she fell once off of the pillory and fainted upon it several times'. And in rather more florid language, the *Weekly Journal: or, The British Gazetteer*, described how, 'Being unable to bear the salutes of the rabble, she swooned away twice, and was carried off in convulsion fits to Newgate'.[8]

Thief-Catcher General

The difficulty of locating and convicting thieves in an ever growing city meant that new methods were constantly being sought. Informers, long used for the prosecution of vice, began to play a new and increasingly important role in the prosecution of theft. Their activities were encouraged by large rewards offered for the prosecution and conviction of the most serious offenders. Although this system of rewards meant the authorities frequently paid large sums to members of the criminal underworld, in the absence of a detective police force, there seemed to be few alternatives. By combining thief taking with the seemingly contradictory activity of facilitating the return of stolen goods by paying rewards to the thieves who stole them, Jonathan Wild managed to control much of London's criminal underworld in the early 1720s. Ultimately, his methods threatened the very integrity of the judicial system and the authorities were forced to act against him.

Katharine Stetham, an old blind woman who kept a lace shop near Holborn Bridge on the main road between the City and the West End, became a victim of theft on 22 January 1725. She testified to her experience at the Old Bailey four months later:

> Between three and four in the afternoon a man and woman
> came into my shop, under a pretence of buying some lace.
> They were so very difficult that I had none below that
> would please them and so, leaving my daughter in the shop,
> I stepped upstairs and brought down another box. We could

> not agree about the price and so they went away together;
> and in about half an hour after I missed a tin box of lace,
> that I valued at £50.

The painstaking labour that went into its production ensured that lace was incredibly valuable. After discovering the theft and believing she had little chance of finding the culprits once they had escaped into a city of half a million inhabitants, Stetham did what many victims in similar circumstances did. She went to see Jonathan Wild, a man well known as someone who could secure the return of stolen goods in exchange for a reward and no questions asked.

Taking advantage of Londoners' willingness to pay such rewards, Wild built up an extensive network of thieves and confederates whose stolen goods he redeemed. At the same time, he kept this coterie of criminals in check by the simple expedient of occasionally turning a few over to the authorities for prosecution in exchange for even more substantial rewards. Between the 1690s and 1725, the maximum reward available for securing a felony conviction grew to £140. At a time when even a relatively skilled artisan such as a carpenter or bricklayer could expect to earn between £20 and £30 a year, this was a huge amount of money. It was Wild's activities in claiming rewards for convicting his own confederates that led him immodestly to style himself the 'Thief-Catcher General of Great Britain'. In a sense, he was – between 1716 and 1725, Wild served as a witness in at least 36 Old Bailey trials, and claimed his evidence was instrumental in the conviction and execution of at least 67 individuals. Wild thus lived on the boundaries of illegality. He performed a service for the state, but he was also master of a criminal underworld.

Jonathan Wild cleverly manipulated not just the thieves in his control, but also the victims who used his services. His first response to Stetham's plea for help was to avoid her altogether, thereby increasing her desire to make use of his services. She told the court, 'The same night as the theft, and the next, I went to Jonathan Wild's house', but he was not available. Consequently, she 'advertised the lace', which means she placed an advertisement in a newspaper offering a 15 guinea reward for the return of the stolen goods (a guinea was worth 21s, or just over £1). This advertisement threatened to cut Wild out of the case, so the next time she went to see him, he agreed to speak to her:

> He desired me to give him a description of the persons
> that I suspected, which I did as near as I could. And then
> he told me that he'd make enquiry, and bade me call again
> in two or three days. I did so, and then he said that he had
> heard something of my lace, and expected to know more
> of the matter in a little time.

Wild was in no rush to solve this case and did nothing for about two weeks, until Stetham visited him again, offering an even higher reward: 'I came to him again on the 15th of February. I told him that though I had advertised but 15 guineas reward yet I'd give 20 or 25 rather than not have my goods'. Wild's response was to present himself as an honest broker, disinterested in the extra money:

> Don't be in such a hurry, says he, I don't know but I may
> help you to it for less, and if I can, I will. The persons that
> have it are gone out of town. I shall set them to
> quarrelling about it and then I shall get it the cheaper.

That same day Wild was arrested on another charge and committed to Newgate. His specific offence was assisting one of his thieves in escaping arrest, but the authorities were aware he was involved in a much wider range of illegal activities, as the 'warrant of detainer' issued against him listed 11 different sorts of crime.[9] Wild had become too big for the authorities and it was time to bring him to book, but they did not yet have the evidence to secure a conviction.

Eighteenth-century prisons were in many ways remarkably casual institutions. Visitors could more or less come and go as they pleased, and as a result Wild was able to continue running his empire from Newgate. According to Elizabeth Stetham, 'On the 10th of March he sent me word that if I would come to him in Newgate, and bring 10 guineas in my pocket, he could help me to my lace'. In arranging for the exchange of the reward for the goods, Wild tried to ensure that he was not seen to visibly profit from the theft. Accepting a reward without attempting to prosecute the thief was a felony under a clause of the 1718 Transportation Act, a provision which was popularly known as 'Jonathan Wild's Act', since it represented an early attempt to stop his activities. Stetham described the transaction:

> He desired me to call a porter; but I not knowing where to find one, he sent a person who brought one that appeared to be a ticket-porter. Wild gave me a letter, which he said was sent him as a direction where to go for the lace; but I could not read, and so I delivered it to the porter. Then he desired me to give the porter ten guineas, or else (he said) the persons that had the lace would not deliver it. I gave the porter the money. He went away and in a little time returned and brought me a box that was sealed up, but not the same that was lost. I opened it and found all my lace but one piece. Now, Mr Wild, (says I) what must you have for your trouble? Not a farthing, says he, not a farthing for me. I don't do these things for worldly interest, but only for the good of poor people that have met with misfortunes.

Although pretending to be charitable, Wild actually had his eye on a further bit of business. He told Stetham:

> As for the piece of lace that is missing, I hope to get it for you e'er be long; and I don't know but that I may help you not only to your money again, but to the thief too; and if I can, much good may it do you. And as you're a good woman

and a widow, and a Christian, I desire nothing of you but
your prayers, and for them I shall be thankful. I have a great
many enemies and God knows what may be the consequence
of this imprisonment.

By conducting this transaction within the walls of Newgate,
however, Wild played directly into the hands of the
authorities, and provided them with the evidence they
needed to prosecute him for a specific criminal act. He was
indicted in May 1725 on two charges: the theft of Mrs
Stetham's lace, and arranging the return of the stolen goods
without attempting to prosecute the thieves. During the
trial his illegal practices, long known but never proven, were
exposed in the cruel light of the Old Bailey courtroom. The
'man and woman' who had stolen the lace were Henry Kelly
and Margaret Murphy, and it emerged that it was only
under Wild's prompting that they had actually committed
the crime. Kelly testified first. He explained that on 22
January he had gone to visit Mr and Mrs Jonathan Wild in
their house.

Wild was in company. We drank two or three more
quarterns of Holland gin, and then I and Mrs Murphy got
up to go away together. Wild asked me which way I was
going? I told him to my lodgings at the Seven Dials. I
suppose you go Holborn Way, says he. We answered, Yes.
Why then, says he, I'll tell you what, There's an old blind
bitch that sells fine Flanders lace just by Holborn Bridge.
Her daughter is as blind as herself, and if you call there,
you may speak with a box of lace [that is, steal a box]. I'll
go along with you and show you the door. So Wild and I
and Murphy went together, till we came within sight of
the door. He pointed and showed us which it was, and
said he would wait for us, and bring us off, if any
disturbance should happen. Murphy and I went to, and
turned over a great deal of lace, but could see none that
would please us, not a piece that was broad enough and
fine enough, for it was our business to be very nice and
difficult. At last the old woman stepped upstairs to fetch

another piece, and as people of our profession are seldom
guilty of losing an opportunity, I made use of this. I took
a tin box of lace, gave it to Mrs Murphy, and she hid it
under her cloak. The old woman came down with another
box, and showed us several pieces, for which she asked
6s. a yard. We offered her 4s. and not being likely to
agree about the price, we came away and found Wild
waiting where we left him. We told him what success we
had had, and so went back with him to his house. There
we opened the box and found eleven pieces in it. He
asked us if we would have ready money, or stay till an
advertisement came out. Stock being pretty low with us at
that time, we chose the first, and so he gave us three
guineas and four broad pieces. I took for my share three
guineas and a Crown, and Mrs Murphy had the rest. I
can't afford to give you any more, (says he) for though I
have got some influence over her, by helping her to goods
two or three times before, yet I know her to be a stingy
hard-mouthed old bitch, and I shan't get above ten
guineas out of her.

Margaret Murphy confirmed this evidence, as did Katharine
Stetham with respect to what had occurred in the shop.

As the *Proceedings* reported, 'The evidence was full and
positive against the prisoner'. Jonathan Wild was caught
with his metaphorical pants down. He was not only a
thieftaker, he was a thief*maker*. He had encouraged thieves
to steal, purchased the stolen goods and then (indirectly)
received a reward for their return. In other cases he had gone
on to collect rewards for convicting the very persons he had
encouraged to steal in the first place. The only real defence
Wild could come up with was to appeal to his supposed
record of public service. He mentioned the dozens of thieves
he had been instrumental in convicting (and hanging) over
the years. He also attempted to use this history of
prosecution as a means of questioning the integrity and
motives of the witnesses brought against him. When these
arguments failed, his counsel (paid for, no doubt, by the

profits of his illegal practices) attempted to secure an acquittal on a technicality.

Early on the day of his trial Wild employed the first tactic. He:

> Dispersed about the court a considerable number of printed lists of the felons that he had apprehended, which concluded in these words: In regard therefore of the numbers above convicted, some that have yet escaped justice are endeavouring to take away the life of the said Jonathan Wild.

This was not a ridiculous argument. Wild had been useful to the authorities, and he did have many enemies, who would not have hesitated to perjure themselves to get rid of him. This strategy, however, backfired when the prosecution counsel (probably funded by a government keen to be rid of Wild) used it as an excuse to launch an attack on his character. The prosecuting lawyer noted with some glee that the circulation of the list constituted an improper attempt to influence the jury. He observed:

> That such practices were unwarrantable and not to be suffered in any court of justice. That this was apparently intended to take off the credit of the King's witnesses, and to prepossess and influence the jury. But as he believed them to be men of integrity he was under no apprehensions that it would have such an effect, nor, on the contrary, could he suppose that they would give any other than a conscientious verdict, according to evidence.

And he suggested:

> That if a strict enquiry was to be made after the motives of Wild apprehending those criminals named in his list, we should find that they were private interest, old grudges, or fresh quarrels, and not the least regard to justice and his country, etc.

After the first prosecution witnesses had testified, Wild's second tactic was brought into play. His counsel, who as the

Proceedings sarcastically observed, 'waited in readiness if any point of law should arise', stood to his feet and objected that Wild had been indicted for theft, but it had not been proved that he had actually entered the shop. The court, conscious that a second indictment, on 'Jonathan Wild's Act', had also been laid against him for receiving the stolen goods, accepted the argument and the charge of theft was essentially dropped. Stetham's testimony in support of the second charge of failing to prosecute a known felon was then heard.

It was now time for Wild to make his case for the defence, which essentially rested on a claim that the indictment against him was flawed in its specification of who had stolen the lace. Wild:

> Said nothing in his defence, but that he had convicted a
> great number of criminals; only he desired that Murphy
> and Kelly might be called in again, which was granted.
> Then (this Indictment being laid for helping Katharine
> Stetham to goods that had been stole from her by persons
> UNKNOWN) he prayed, that Murphy might be asked who
> stole the lace? In expectation that she would unwarily
> swear, that herself and Kelly were the persons (for though
> such evidence was given in the former trial, the law could
> take no notice of it in this, except it had been sworn over
> again). But the court informed him that as Murphy was an
> evidence upon oath nobody could require her to answer
> any questions to accuse herself. Then he prayed the court
> would ask her, if he Wild stole the lace? To which she
> answered, No, but he was concerned with those that did
> steal it, and he received it after it was stolen.

Once again, Wild's tactics had backfired, as it had led Murphy to confirm his role in receiving the stolen goods.

Wild and his counsel made one last desperate argument. They suggested that because Murphy had testified that Wild was guilty of a felony, and Jonathan Wild's Act was intended to punish those who were *not* felons, but who were guilty only of assisting felons, Wild could not be found guilty on that statute. The court peremptorily rejected the argument and ruled:

> That felons were so far from being excepted in that Act, that it was principally intended against them; for it particularly mentions, 'Those that make it their business to help people to stolen goods'. And that the case of the prisoner came within almost every circumstance of the Act; it being evident that he was a person that had secret acquaintance with felons, who made it his business to help people to stolen goods, and by that means gained money from them.

The jury concurred and Wild was found guilty of the charge of receiving stolen goods without attempting to prosecute the thieves. He was sentenced to hang.

Ordinary Londoners were delighted at this turn of events. Wild had become deeply unpopular since his participation in the arrest and conviction of the highwayman and escape artist Jack Sheppard the previous year. He had many enemies, particularly the friends and families of those who he had helped convict and have executed. A mock invitation celebrating the fact of his execution was published; it was directed to all the 'thieves, whores, pickpockets, family felons etc.' in Great Britain and Ireland.

The traditional procession from Newgate to Tyburn on the day of his execution became an occasion of vocal public celebration. The *London Journal* claimed:

> Never was there a greater crowd assembled on any occasion, than to see this unhappy person; and so outrageous were the mob in their joy to behold him on the road to the gallows that they huzza'd him along to the Triple Tree, and showed a temper very uncommon on such a melancholy occasion, for they threw stones at him; with some of which his head was broke.[10]

When he reached the gallows, the executioner, as tradition demanded, allowed Wild some time for reflection before he

Figure 1.03 A 'Ticket' to
Jonathan Wild's Hanging (1725)

was turned off. But, as Daniel Defoe reported, the crowd grew impatient: 'The mob called furiously upon the hangman to dispatch him, and at last threatened to tear him to pieces, if he did not tie him up immediately'.[11] Following the hanging, his corpse was in danger of being seized by the crowd, but it was surrendered when the mob was told (falsely) that it would be dissected by the surgeons, thereby contributing further to Wild's ignominy. In the end the body was buried in St Pancras churchyard, only to be stolen from its grave a few days later.

As the most notorious criminal of his day, Wild's reputation long outlasted him. After his death, the profound ambiguity of his role and his corrupt manipulation of the criminal justice system were used in parallels drawn with prime minister Robert Walpole and many subsequent politicians, and formed the basis for the odious 'Peachum' in John Gay's *Beggar's Opera* (1728).[12]

Sir John Fielding's Runners

At mid-century, as well as being a successful novelist and essayist, Henry Fielding and his half-brother John were London's most active magistrates. As a part of an ambitious programme of reform, they attempted to rehabilitate the thieftakers by bringing them under their wing. The Fieldings

employed ex-constables and former thieftakers on a retainer,
sending them out from their house in Bow Street on missions to
search for stolen goods and make arrests. To attract business,
Londoners were encouraged to report all crimes to the Bow Street
'rotation office'. Since much of this activity was still funded by the
rewards offered for successful convictions, the Fieldings faced the
challenge of convincing the public that their officers could be
trusted. They tried to solve this problem by giving them a new
name: 'runners'.

At 1 o'clock in the morning of 31 October 1774 thieves
broke in through a window into the Surgeons' Hall, on
Monkwell Street near the churchyard of St Giles,
Cripplegate, and stole several pieces of the Surgeons'
Company's ceremonial silver (a soup ladle, tablespoons,
teaspoons, a pint mug, two salvers, a coffee pot, and a cream
pot), as well as some clothes and money. The Hall was not
only the meeting place of the Surgeons' Company, but also
the home of Joseph Cruttendon, clerk to the company,
whose quarters formed an integral part of the Hall.

Cruttendon told the court at the Old Bailey how he
discovered the theft:

> I have the whole dwelling, there is no one resides in it but
> myself. On the first of November, when we were going to
> breakfast about nine o'clock we missed the milk pot. The
> maid servant then went into the back room, and missed
> most of the things mentioned in the indictment upon
> which I went up into my office, and found the drawers in
> which I keep my money broke open with a chisel, in a
> rough and clumsy manner. I took all the money out of it a
> day or two before, except three shillings in halfpence,
> which was gone. I missed a shirt out of a drawer that is
> always left open for the washerwoman, and two silk
> handkerchiefs that I laid the night before upon the desk in
> the store room, out of which the plate was taken. I saw the
> mark of a dirty foot upon the table. There is a square
> window to that room and it appeared plainly that

somebody had entered in at this window, and shut it down
again. The window looks upon the steps in the main street
that goes up to the hall. I concluded from the
circumstances of the robbery, the drawer being broke
where I kept my money, and no other, and a pair of
candlesticks being left, which were not silver, but plated,
that William Pritchard who had lived with me four
months, and had the care of my plate, and knew the
drawers where I kept my money, must be concerned in
this business. Pritchard left me on the 10th of September
last and he perfectly knew the situation of the plate.

Along with Peter Thane and Edward Parker, Pritchard had
indeed been responsible for the robbery. The three of them

Figure 1.04 'Barber Surgeons' Hall, from the Churchyard of St Giles,
Cripplegate' (1791) © British Library Board. All Rights Reserved.
Shelfmark 679.h.5, folio 92

were poor and down on their luck. Pritchard told an
acquaintance that 'he had pawned his shirt the night before,
and not one of them had a farthing'. 'Two or three days
before, Thane had hardly any clothes to his back.' Another
witness at the trial said 'all three of them had very ragged
clothes'.

Although Pritchard was suspected, Cruttendon was
unable to find him or recover the stolen goods. Instead, it
was information provided by John Vince, a copperplate
music printer living in Parker's Lane, off Drury Lane,
which led to the arrest of the thieves. Vince told the
court:

> On the Tuesday after Mr Cruttenden's house was robbed,
> Thane came into my room. He had good clothes on, and
> silver shoe and knee buckles. I asked him how he came
> by them. He was a long while before he would say any
> thing, and at last he said he had been concerned with
> Parker and Pritchard in a robbery at Surgeons' Hall.
> I asked him how he came by the buckles. He said, he
> bought them with part of the money he got for the plate.

When Vince met the thieves the next morning at the
Chequer's pub in Shire Lane, near Lincoln's Inn Fields, they
were spending the proceeds of the theft with abandon.
Vince:

> Found Pritchard reading the paper. He had a pair of
> stockings and a pair of shoes tied up in a handkerchief,
> and a hat on, which he said, he had bought with the
> money he sold the plate for. We sat down there and he
> asked us if we would have any breakfast? I said we were
> going to have some. He said, no my lads, you have no
> money, I have money, therefore call for what you like. We
> got some herrings and a loaf and butter. I asked where
> Thane was? He said that he had bought a great coat in
> Monmouth Street, and was waiting while the collar was
> altering, and would be with us in about half an hour. He
> came in about that time. He was dressed in a great coat.

Later that evening the blow-out continued:

> Pritchard asked us if we would have any supper. We made
> answer, it was rather late-ish, we would have a pot of beer,
> or so. No, says he, we will have something to eat, and he
> sent Thane for some pork. He brought both roast and
> boiled. We ate it together, and had two or three pots of
> beer; and about ten o'clock we went from the house,
> because Thane was in a hurry. He was going to lie with a
> girl he knew. He said he was in a hurry, he could not stay
> any longer. We parted with Thane at the door. Pritchard
> and Grigg and Shields and I, went all together to the
> Noah's Ark, at St Giles's. Pritchard there treated ever so
> many people with aniseed, to the amount of about a
> shilling's worth.

In the course of their conversations, it became clear that
Pritchard and Thane were deeply suspicious of Parker, their
partner in the theft:

> There was a great deal of talk among them. They said,
> Parker was a great rogue, that he had slanged them, that
> they were to have but five pounds a piece, and they were
> sure the plate was worth forty pounds.

When the money was divided up, Thane worried that the
coins he was given had been clipped and were thus of
reduced value:

> I think my half guinea looks light. Pritchard said, I think
> mine does too, we will have them both weighed.
> Accordingly they went to the bar, and had them weighed.
> They came back, and said, they were both rather too good
> weight.

At the same time, Pritchard also distrusted Thane because
of his youth. While in the pub, he told Samuel Wade: 'I
ventured my life last night for the plate which many a one
would not have done with that lad'. But it was not just their
mutual distrust which began to make the thieves uneasy.
Pritchard was deeply concerned that they might be

apprehended by the Bow Street runners. After some drinks at the Noah's Ark, Pritchard confided to Vince that 'He believed it was all over with him, for the traps were all after him – meaning Sir John Fielding's runners'. Fielding's self-publicity had made Londoners fully aware of the runners and while this semi-official police force maintained some dubious links with the criminal underworld, it still struck fear in the hearts of many thieves. Later, as they walked through the streets towards Piccadilly, Pritchard said: 'If I am taken, I am a dead man, and he cried almost all the way'. Fear of arrest may explain why Thane used some of the profits from the crime to purchase a pair of pistols, although according to Samuel Wade, Pritchard and Thane told him they intended to commit further crimes. They reportedly said 'now they got tools [meaning the pistols] that would get money and money they would have for they would go upon the scamp [meaning to go upon the highway]'.[13]

Powerful as the runners were, they could not arrest criminals until they obtained information about their identity and whereabouts. In order to attract business, the Fieldings placed advertisements in the newspapers encouraging Londoners to make use of the runners' services. One advertisement in the *Public Advertiser* in 1754 read:

> Whereas many thieves and robbers daily escape justice
> for want of immediate pursuit, it is therefore
> recommended to all persons who shall henceforth be
> robbed on the highway or in the streets, or whose shops or
> houses shall be broke open, that they give immediate
> notice thereof, together with as accurate a description of
> the offenders as possible, to *John Fielding*, esq. at his
> house in Bow Street, Covent Garden.

Upon receiving a report, Fielding promised he 'would immediately despatch a set of brave fellows in pursuit'.[14] In this case, John Vince provided the runners with the information because he bore a grudge against Parker. Vince went to Justice Saunders Welch, a former high constable who manned one of the 'rotation offices' established by the Middlesex magistracy to complement the Fieldings' office in Bow Street. Open at regular hours, these offices provided Londoners with a place to report crimes and seek assistance. There Vince encountered Charles Jealous, one of the Bow Street runners and a man whose extensive activities as a thieftaker are documented in the *Proceedings*, his name appearing in 127 trials between 1774 and 1794. Vince informed Jealous and two other runners (James Jenkins and John Evans) of the theft and where they could find the culprits, Parker, Pritchard and Thane. Evans later told the court:

> The last hanging day but one Vince came to my house,
> and said, some people that were concerned in robbing Mr
> Cruttenden's house were going to Tyburn in a coach and
> mentioned the prisoners at the bar.

On the morning of 7 November 1774, a day when seven men were due to be hanged at Tyburn, the three thieves went to watch the spectacle. They went perhaps out of some subconscious knowledge that their own destiny lay at Tyburn, but more likely simply because executions were treated as a form of entertainment by the London mob. Pritchard and Thane took a coach. At nine o'clock, the three runners, accompanied by Vince, set out to catch them. According to Evans:

> I and Jenkins and Jealous went to the bottom of Wells
> Street and took a coach to meet these people. When we
> came to Tyburn Turnpike, as we stopped to pay, a coach
> came up, which Vince informed us was the coach. They
> were in that coach.

The runners approached the coach gingerly, fearing that the culprits were armed:

> I went to one door and opened it, and desired Mr Jenkins
> to jump into the coach at the other door. We found
> Pritchard and Thane in the coach. Pritchard put his hand
> inside his coat and took out a handkerchief. I snatched it
> out of his hand, and said, if I saw him put his hand there
> again I would blow his brains out. Then I told them, I
> insisted upon every man in the coach putting his hands on
> his knees, and the first that refused I would make a couple
> of eyelet holes in his body. They did put their hands on
> their knees. There were only Pritchard and Thane in the
> coach, Parker was afterwards taken at the gallows by
> Charles Jealous.

Following the arrests, the three prisoners, dressed in the
fine clothes they had purchased with the proceeds of the
theft, were brought to the office of Justice Welch. As Evans
later told the court:

> I searched Pritchard and found this pistol (producing it)
> upon him was loaded, and he had powder and balls. In his
> coat pocket I found this chisel (producing it). He had
> another pistol but by some means they handed it from one
> to another, and it is gone. These buckles (producing a pair
> of shoe and a pair of knee buckles) I took out of Thane's
> shoes and knees. They are new. I was informed they were
> bought with part of the money received for the plate stole
> from Mr Cruttenden.

Jenkins took the chisel and went to Cruttendon's house to
see if it matched the marks that had been made in prising
open the set of drawers, and discovered that it did. Justice
Welch then examined the prisoners, and satisfied that they
had a case to answer, he committed them to Newgate Prison
to await trial.

At the Old Bailey, the witnesses for the prosecution
included Cruttendon (the victim), his wife and servant, John
Vince, the three runners, and Dennis Shields, a drinking
companion of the defendants. The defence attempted to
discredit the runners, calling them 'thief-catchers', evoking
memories of the corrupt practices of earlier thieftakers such

as Jonathan Wild and more recently the McDaniel Gang (broken up in 1754), and claiming they had bribed the witnesses. Parker charged: 'These men have been with the thief-catchers, and they have fed them up, and said, if they would not swear against me in particular – I beg your lordship will ask Shields, whether he has not been maintained by the thief-catchers'. Shields denied this, saying he had been in prison ever since the defendants were arrested.

Unable to discredit the runners, the prisoners' defence rested on explanations for why they had suddenly acquired so much spending money, and on attacking the character of John Vince. Pritchard claimed that an acquaintance had lent him 35s, and Thane explained that he had won about a guinea and a half gambling. Neither provided witnesses to corroborate their evidence. Parker attacked the prosecution:

> The witnesses are men of very bad characters. Vince was
> tried here for robbing his master two or three sessions
> ago, and I was a witness against him. Jealous came up to
> me and shook his fist at me, and said, he should do for
> me now. I have no friends in the world only God and
> myself.

Vince had indeed been tried and acquitted the previous September, but for receiving stolen goods, not theft, and although Parker had been involved in the case he had not been a witness against him.[15] In fact the prosecution evidence had implicated Parker heavily in selling the stolen goods. The fact that witness testimony in that trial accused Parker of cheating his accomplices of much of the proceeds may explain why Vince was willing to inform against him in this instance.

All three defendants were convicted and sentenced to death. As if to justify the sentence, the *Proceedings* reported that Pritchard had been tried for a highway robbery the previous session, 'when the good character given him by Mr Cruttenden, conduced in great measure to his acquittal'.[16]

This time he received no sympathy. The three were hanged at Tyburn five weeks later, on Tuesday 10 January 1775.[17]

The Roundhouse

When Londoners were arrested for a crime, whether the offence was petty or serious, they had to be interviewed by a justice of the peace. If no justice were available, or the arrest took place at night, the accused were temporarily kept in a lockup, such as the St Martin's Roundhouse. In some cases large numbers of suspected petty criminals could be incarcerated at once. Like all eighteenth-century prisons, conditions for those unable to pay for special treatment were primitive. Those with money, however, provided a business opportunity for the keepers.

The watchhouse, or roundhouse as it was normally called, belonging to St Martin in the Fields stood almost opposite the parish church on St Martin's Lane, just south of Duke's Court on what is now part of Trafalgar Square. It was made up of three floors, and a set of stocks capped by an ornate wooden carving of one man flogging another stood in the street outside. On the lower ground floor there were two cells, called 'the holes', one each for men and women:

> You go up four stone steps into the roundhouse, and this place is below these steps. The height of it is six foot two inches; the length and breadth six foot six, by six foot two; the window is two foot six, by one foot six. There are some iron bars, but no glass. There is a shutter which puts up with three slits, about a quarter of an inch wide, and about eighteen inches long. There is a door to the passage leading to the hole, and opens into the hole, two foot wide. The door does not go up to the top by nine inches or thereabouts, and there is another room for the men which is eight foot five, by six foot three, and there is a passage nine foot three by four foot ten, which leads from the women's hole to the men's hole; and there is a door at the head of the stairs.

Above the cells, on the upper ground floor was the drinking room, where in the years before July 1742 watchmen, constables and prisoners sat through the long nights, fortified by a constant stream of beer and gin sold by Eleanor Bird, the watchhouse keeper's wife. Above this was a floor with two rooms, where William Bird and Eleanor lived with their four children. At his later trial for murder, William Bird cut a sorry figure. His papers were in disarray and his witnesses failed to arrive; while Eleanor was harried and jeered by an angry crowd at the Old Bailey. But, on any day prior to 15 July 1742, William and Eleanor would have counted themselves lucky. They had made a successful life for themselves as servants of the parish, William as constable and Eleanor assisting him in running the watchhouse, and they had risen from the insecure status of working-class artisans to that of literate functionaries in a growing bureaucracy.

The watchhouse was the centre from which the policing of the parish was organised. The constable of the night and the watchhouse keeper oversaw the work of 43 watchmen employed by the parish and six beadles appointed by the City of Westminster. Each night they set out from the watchhouse alternatively to sit in their watch boxes, or to do the rounds of their beat, calling out the hour as they went.

Thursday night, 15 July 1742, was hot and humid, and the watchhouse at St Martins was set to play host to an aggressive sweep of prostitutes and beggars from the streets. Booker Holden, a 'midnight reformer' and the High Constable of Westminster, had decided to clear the parish of these undesirables. And on the authority of a general warrant issued by Sir Thomas De Veil, Britain's most powerful justice and the Fieldings' immediate predecessor, and with the aid of an army of constables, beadles and watchmen, he swept through the streets in the hours after the watch was set at 11 pm, entering homes and shops and bathhouses, picking up both pre-selected individuals and anyone who had the misfortune to present a suspicious appearance by wandering in the wrong clothes or in the wrong place. Those arrested were to be kept at the roundhouse until they could be brought before Justice De Veil in the morning.

A washerwoman, Elizabeth Surridge, was one of those arrested:

> I was carried to St Martin's Roundhouse between twelve and one, and I stayed drinking till about three o'clock in the watchhouse up stairs. Then I happened to fall asleep by the fire side and Mr Bird came to me, and said, Come, you Bitch, you shall not sleep here. And then he put me and two other women into the hole. Mr Bird himself put us down.

So was Elizabeth Amey. She was a prostitute who had previously worked at a notorious brothel, The Rose in Oxenden Street just west of Leicester Fields, and was arrested in a cook shop:

> I was taken up about twelve o'clock at night. We went up stairs and staid there till between two and three in the morning. We drank three or four pots of beer, and some shrub [a mixture of rum, sugar and lemon]. I went down into the hole on my occasions. Bird followed me down, pulled my cap off and beat me with a key. I cried and screamed and desired to go up and pay my reckoning, and he said I should not. The air on opening the door was as that of an oven.

And Sarah Starks:

> I was carried to the roundhouse about half an hour after eleven and put into the hole by Mr Bird.

The vast majority of the people taken up that evening were the poorest of London's women, dressed in what cheap finery they could afford, or if past prostitution, in the rags of a beggar. Between 11 at night and 4 in the morning more and more women were brought in, so that by the time the constable of the night set off for bed, there were 26 people being held in the women's hole, and nine men in the cell next door.

The conditions quickly became intolerable. Elizabeth Surridge later described the situation:

> It was very hot, not fit for so many people to be there, and there was the stench of a necessary house. The door was fastened presently after we were put in. Some of us sat in our shifts, one woman sat naked for it was so hot.

But at first, there was something of a party atmosphere:

> Some of the prisoners joined to get a dram. There was a poor woman brought it in a bottle, and William Bird's son Thomas said, You will all get drunk before morning, and shut the window up, to prevent our having a dram, but he opened it himself again, in about ten minutes.

In her testimony at the Old Bailey, Mary Cosier described the conditions in the hole:

Cosier.	I was taken up the 15th between eleven and twelve at night.
Question.	What place were you carried to?
Cosier.	To the watchhouse in St Martin's.
Q.	What room were you put into?
Cosier.	I was put into the hole directly.
Q.	Who put you down?
Cosier.	The man of the watchhouse.
Q.	Look round and see whether you know the person that put you down?
Cosier.	It was that man, the man with a paper in his hand [that was the prisoner at the bar, William Bird].
Q.	How many people do you reckon were there when you were first put in?

Cosier.	I cannot say exactly – there might be about twenty people. The place was almost full.
Jury.	You say it was almost full; how near was it being full?
Cosier.	I cannot say how many more it would hold, for I think the place was full when I went down, but they crowded in more afterwards till four o'clock in the morning. It was so dark I could not well tell how many were there; but in the whole I believe there were twenty-seven or twenty-eight.
Q.	Was there any complaint of heat in the place?
Cosier.	Yes, and we cried out, Fire, Murder, for Christ's sake let us have water, for the Lord's sake a little water, for we are stifled with heat. I would have given four shillings for a gallon of water.
Q.	Did you say so to any body that came down stairs from the roundhouse?
Cosier.	I cannot say that. We cried out as loud as we could cry out. When the window was open a woman came and brought her sister-in-law a quartern of gin, and Bird's son told his father and Bird came out and pushed her down, and shut up the window of the hole himself and said they should have nothing at all.
Q.	Did you hear him say so?
Cosier.	Yes, I did. It was between four and five o'clock in the morning and the window was shut up from that time till a quarter of an hour after ten. It was that time when I went out.
Q.	How were you forced to sit?
Cosier.	We were very much crowded, I never have been my self since. (The witness appeared to be in a weak condition, and soon after she had given her evidence fainted away.) My thighs were so black I could not tell what to do with them. This handkerchief was as stiff as buckram with sweat from the heat of the place.

Q.	Were any of the poor creatures in fits?
Cosier.	In the time I was there, there were four or five in fits from the heat of the place. But Ann Branch, the little crooked body in the red cloak, died on this side of me, about seven o'clock in the morning. I held her up as long as I could, for I was very weak myself.
Q.	Were there any people lying dead upon the ground?
Cosier.	Yes, but I did not know they were dead for I strove to awake them, thinking they were asleep. I was the last that came out alive but three and I shook two of them to awake them.
Q.	How many were found dead when you were let out?
Cosier.	Four, sir.
Q.	If that door had been open that leads to the stairs would there have been room enough for you?
Cosier.	Yes, I believe there would. I would have given a shilling for a little air for half an hour.

The sweep of London's streets was finished by four in the morning and William Bird went to bed, while one after the other the women in the hole fainted, four dying of dehydration and alcohol poisoning.

The door to the hole was finally opened at 10 o'clock the next morning by one of the parish beadles, William Anderson:

> There was a particular acquaintance of mine taken up and put in the hole. I went about ten o'clock and asked for Bird. They said he was in bed, and I went up and called him, and he came down. I opened the door in order to let her out. As soon as the door was open, the people bounced out directly upon us. The place was very nauseous, and the smell so strong that I thought it would have struck me down. They called out for water, for they

were quite stifled. I fetched some water from the pump. They drank that up, and I got them some more.

Elizabeth Surridge recalled how:

St Martin's clock had struck ten before the window was opened. I thought every minute an hour. Then a watchman came and opened the window. I took hold of a woman's arm that was dead. Said I, Here is one woman dead, and the rest are a-dying, and they took no notice of that. But Mr Bird hurried us before the justice. When I came out of the place, I drank a pint of dirty water myself, and said, For God Almighty's sake, to Mrs Bird, give me a little water for I am almost perished, and at last she gave me a pint of fresh water.

And Mary Cosier later said:

I was so thirsty by the confinement and heat of the place that I drank four pints of dirty water, and then I drank all the water out of a tea kettle which stood in the corner of the place. I do not know whether that was clean water or not. A gentleman brought three pails of water and I drank three quarts of that, but I brought it up again.

George Colclough, a barber, periwig maker, and surgeon, who lived nearby was called at about 10 or 11 o'clock:

The person that came, said, For God's sake, Mr Colclough, come and bleed one who is very ill. I went to the roundhouse and when I went down the stairs, I saw a young woman lying upon the ground. I blooded them first who were in the most danger. One Mr Perkins was there, said he, Mr Colclough, shall I come to your assistance? I said, there is need enough of it, so he assisted me. There was one of the women, I believe, had been dead two hours. When I came to this woman that I saw first, she was got up to the ground-floor. I blooded her, sent for a chair, and put her into it, and gave her wine and water. Then I went and blooded another woman at the door in the street, and took others to the workhouse. One of those in the workhouse was two days before she spoke to me. One was quite dead when I went in, another was near expiring, and two more died.

At the end of a long night four women were dead and several, including Sarah Starks and Sarah Bland had been admitted into the parish workhouse for treatment. Thirteen others were marched through the streets south of Covent Garden to the house of Sir Thomas De Veil.

In 1742, at the age of 58, De Veil was at the height of his power and from his recently acquired house in Bow Street (later to be taken over by the Fieldings) just east of Covent Garden, he ran an extensive network of informers, thieftakers and spies. His study was the centre of the administration of local government and justice for Westminster, and it was he who had signed the general warrant that led to the roundup of the night before. In many ways De Veil was responsible for the resulting deaths, but he quickly made sure that it was William Bird, the watchhouse keeper, who eventually stood trial for murder. On Saturday the 17th, De Veil published an advertisement in the *London Evening Post* in which he prominently named Booker Holden as the originator of the warrant and downplayed his own role. The advertisement went on to blame the constables for having 'greatly misbehaved' themselves, before successfully offering up William Bird as a possible scapegoat.

A coroner's inquest on the four deaths was held on Saturday morning and Bird was bound over on a charge of wilful murder. Later that night an angry crowd gathered at the watchhouse. 'Stones, bricks and other things were flung into and against the house by the mob' and the whole brick front of the building collapsed. The eventual cost of repairing the watchhouse came to £84 10s. While awaiting trial, Bird was confined first in the Gatehouse Prison and later in Newgate. On the occasion of his transfer between prisons a few days after the tragedy, a loud and boisterous mob of several thousand people followed his progress, jeering and catcalling as he went. Eleanor Bird and their four children, Thomas aged 12, Hannah aged 7, Eleanor 4 and John, a babe in arms at five weeks, were forced to enter the parish workhouse, where they shared house room with several victims of the disaster.

Eight weeks later on 9 September, William Bird was delivered to the Old Bailey in chains to the jeers and insults of the crowded courtroom. The watchmen, beadles, and constables, the women themselves, and even Sir Thomas De Veil were called to give evidence, with Bird making ineffectual interjections along the way. At the end of an almost unprecedented ten hour trial, the jury declared a verdict of 'special', essentially refusing to pass judgment on a technicality. As soon as this was announced the Grand Jury processed indictments on two further deaths and a second trial was arranged for the next sessions. On this occasion the indictment was drawn up more carefully, avoiding any possibility Bird would get off. After seven more hours of evidence, he was found guilty and sentenced to hang.

Bird's life, however, did not end on the gallows. Instead, perhaps because of his status as an employee of the parish, his sentence was commuted to 14 years' transportation, and he was shipped to Maryland on 13 April the following year. The ship, the *Justitia*, was under the command of Barnett Bond and, on his orders, Bird was denied food and water. He died, some might say appropriately, of starvation and dehydration before the ship reached Maryland. Eventually Bond himself stood trial for murder at the Court of Admiralty held at the Old Bailey and was acquitted. A year later, Bird's widow, Eleanor, married a neighbour, Thomas Pettart, a shoe closer at the Fleet, and in the early 1750s was once again admitted with her four children to the parish workhouse.[18]

The Justice's Parlour

When suspected criminals were brought before them, justices of the peace conducted a preliminary hearing in order to determine if the case was strong enough to be sent to the Grand Jury for possible trial at the Old Bailey or a lower court. Although these hearings were conducted in the justice's home, they often took place before an audience. They gave self-promoting justices like Sir Thomas De Veil considerable power, and De Veil seems to have relished the opportunity of publicly demonstrating his activity and skill in shaping the outcomes of the judicial process.

On a busy Sunday evening in the summer of 1735, the Hoop Tavern was crowded with drinkers. Located in a courtyard off the Strand, one of London's busiest thoroughfares, the keeper of the Hoop, Phillip Shirley, kept a watchful eye on his clients. He paid particular attention to two new arrivals who acted suspiciously:

> On Sunday the 29th of June at about a quarter before ten at night, my house being very full of company, two young gentlemen came up my passage and went into a ground room in the yard, and rung the bell. I went my self with a candle. One of them turned his face aside under pretence of wiping it, and then laid his head down on the table, which gave me some suspicion. The other called for half a pint of red, which being carried in they bid the drawer send for a coach. Do they take this for a coffeehouse? says I, Do they think it is worth my while to keep servants to run on their errands? Let them walk.

The drinks were brought, as was conventional in the more upmarket London pubs, in fashionable (and valuable) silver tankards:

> In two minutes my drawer, Giles Wilton, came with a pint of Lisbon in a cool tankard. I bid him take care of the tankard for I did not like my customers. He said he'd warrant the tankard should be safe and so he carried it in. They afterwards ordered twelve pennyworth of beef steaks, some of which were set by the fire to keep warm for another person, whom as they pretended they waited for. They bid Joseph Fisher, another of my servants, bring

them a tankard of oat ale, and thereupon he carried in
another tankard. They sent my porter on three errands,
and while he was gone the last time they made off with
both the tankards. A little before this I saw one of them
looking out. The large tankard weighed sixty nine ounces
twelve penny-weight, the other cost me ten pound.

The next day Phillip Shirley went to a printer and
commissioned a handbill offering a reward for the return of
the stolen tankards. The 'printed advertisement' asking
pawnbrokers to apprehend anyone who attempted to sell the
stolen goods was distributed by a messenger from the
Goldsmith's Company. One was given to James Barthelemi,
a goldsmith.

The advertisement, however, was not the instrument that
led Patrick Gaffney, a 22-year-old Irishman who had served
with the army in Scotland, to be identified as one of the
thieves, leading to his trial for theft, and Barthelemi's trial
for receiving stolen goods, at the Old Bailey in September.
Indeed, the two were not the first to be tried for the theft.
On the basis of Phillip Shirley's suspicions, one of his
servants, John Dun, was arrested for the crime and tried at
the Old Bailey in July. But the evidence against him was
uncertain. He also had a solid alibi and good character
references and as a result was acquitted.[19] Instead, it was
information provided the next month by Gaffney's alleged
accomplice and fellow Irishman, John Ratcliff, and the
detective work of Thomas De Veil which made the second
trial possible.

De Veil became a justice in 1729 and was extraordinarily
active in carrying out his duties – attracting both the
attention of the government, which rewarded him financially,
and also the poor. Londoners flocked to his house in
Leicester Fields (now Leicester Square) both to make
criminal accusations and to watch him conduct the
preliminary hearings which would decide whether or not

accused criminals would face trial. A few years after the events described here, he moved to Bow Street, and his habit of holding public criminal hearings in his front room formed the basis of the more formal tribunals later conducted by Henry and John Fielding in the same building. De Veil was also renowned for his qualities as a detective. He once solved a burglary case by pretending to have a sudden need for a penknife and asking a suspect if he could lend him one. When the penknife was handed over, its broken blade matched the point of a knife found at the scene of the crime.[20] But he was also well known for his philandering, frequently conducting private interviews in a small room in his house where he allegedly offered suspects clemency in return for sexual favours. He was also suspected of protecting brothel keepers and others in return for their services. De Veil was a man with many enemies, among whom could be numbered the women he exploited for sex, the members of the criminal gangs which he broke up, and even some of his fellow justices. The last group complained that he stole their business and they feared that his willingness to hear the complaints of the poor diminished the standing of the office of justice of the peace. De Veil was a vain and self-promoting man who rarely missed a trick to further his reputation.

In the middle of August, Ratcliff was brought to Justice De Veil's house charged with an entirely different crime, the capital offence of stealing a mare. In this predicament Ratcliff did what many accused felons did in the same situation and attempted to turn king's evidence by informing on an alleged fellow criminal – in this case Gaffney. Ratcliff told De Veil about the theft of the tankards and explained how he and Gaffney had used Frances Charnock, Ratcliffe's common-law wife, to dispose of them:

> Next day about three in the afternoon I sent Frances
> Charnock with the least tankard to Barthelemi, a
> goldsmith at Charing Cross. She stayed till the evening,

and when she returned she said she had sold it to him for
six pound.

Ratcliff explained that he had chosen Barthelemi because he
knew he would not ask any awkward questions about the
source of the tankards. He explained that the other tankard:

> Was melted down in three or four lumps in Gaffney's
> room while he was present, and three or four days
> afterwards I carried it myself to Barthelemi. He weighed
> it and gave me nine guineas, but I said it came to nineteen
> shillings more. He reckoned it at four shillings and nine
> pence or four shillings and ten pence an ounce, I cannot
> say which. He asked me if I dealt in the country, and I
> answered, Yes, I deal in small wares. I sent Charnock next
> day for the nineteen shillings, and he gave it her.

This information was taken down in writing and De Veil
summoned Charnock and Shirley to his house, who
confirmed the story.

Why De Veil chose to prosecute this crime, in return for
letting Ratcliff off the more serious offence of horse theft, is
unclear. Perhaps he had long suspected that Barthelemi was
a receiver of stolen goods and shared the view of many
Londoners at the time that such receivers bore a major
responsibility for encouraging theft in the city. Barthelemi
was probably a Jew and there is more than a hint of anti-
Semitism in De Veil's actions. Jews were frequently
suspected of being heavily involved in trading stolen goods
and popular prejudice labelled them as devious and
untrustworthy. In any case, De Veil accepted Ratcliff's
information and signed a warrant for Barthelemi's arrest.

When Barthelemi was brought before De Veil, the justice
secreted Ratcliff and Charnock in a separate room and
confronted him with the evidence. De Veil described the
confrontation in his testimony at the Old Bailey:

> When he came I read Ratcliff's whole information to him,
> and he absolutely denied that he knew any thing of the

matter. But when I brought out Ratcliff and Charnock to confront him, he owned that he bought the tankards, and said he gave ten pound seven shillings for one of them.

De Veil's explanation of what happened next confirms his view of Barthelemi as a shifty, untrustworthy character and illustrates De Veil's ability to manipulate the publicity of the magistrate's preliminary examination for his own ends:

> After I had brought him to own that he bought the
> tankards, he took me aside into another room and told me
> this matter might prove very troublesome to him, but it
> was in my power to make it more agreeable, and if I
> would go to his shop he would make it easy to me, or
> words to that effect. When I came back with him into the
> other room, I asked him before twenty or thirty people, if
> he was not ashamed to offer to bribe me? He answered
> that what he intended to give me was only his prayers.

But Phillip Shirley, the tavern keeper, reported a similar experience with Barthelemi: 'He sent for me into the same room, and offered me twenty, twenty-five, and then thirty guineas if I would be easy'.

At Barthelemi's trial, Frances Charnock described Barthelemi's purchase of the first tankard:

> On Monday, about three in the afternoon, I went to
> Barthelemi's house with the small tankard. He was not at
> home, but his wife desired me to stay, which I did, and
> soon after he came in. He lighted candles and shut up the
> shop. He asked me no questions how I came by it, but I
> told him without asking, that I came from Mr Ratcliff.
> Then he weighed the tankard in a room behind the shop,
> and cast it up on a piece of paper, and told me how many
> ounces it weighed, and how much it was an ounce, but I
> have forgot both, only I remember he said it came to six
> pound three shillings, or wanting three shillings, I do not
> know which.

In cross-examining Charnock, Barthelemi's attempt to discredit her evidence only made him appear less credible:

Barthelemi.	Did not I ask you how you came by it?
Charnock.	No, not a word.
Barthelemi.	Did not you pass for the wife of one Johnson, and bring a note?
Charnock.	No.
Barthelemi.	You did, and you said your husband had had a suit of law in the country, and on that account you was forced to sell the tankard. What letters was it marked with?
Charnock.	I do not know.
Barthelemi.	It was not on Monday that you brought it, but on Thursday.
Court.	Produce your books and contradict her if you can, by showing a regular entry.
Barthelemi.	I keep no books. I cannot write. (As this was hardly spoke loud enough for the court to hear him distinctly, he dropt this pretence and said): I set it down so in my book, and that I gave her six pound nineteen shillings.

Despite the fact that, as Gaffney pointed out, Ratcliffe testified 'to save his own life' and despite the witnesses provided by Barthelemi who confirmed that he had paid the true value of the tankard (and therefore must have assumed the seller was bona fide), that he was a hard-working shopkeeper with a good reputation, and that he had once stopped a woman trying to sell a teapot that he thought might have been stolen, he was convicted and sentenced to be transported for 14 years. Patrick Gaffney, who had been acquitted of pickpocketing at the same sessions and only testified briefly in this trial, was sentenced to death. He was hanged on 21 September, still protesting his innocence.[21] De Veil, whose reputation was constantly under attack, must have enjoyed this opportunity to present himself publicly as a good detective and an incorruptible magistrate, though London's Jewish community no doubt thought differently.[22]

Mary Cut-and-Come-Again

Despite the power of justices like Sir Thomas De Veil, some criminals were not afraid to stand up to them, as is evident in the case of this ballad seller accused of theft. Ballads were a common feature of street life in eighteenth-century London and the crowds they attracted provided rich opportunities for pickpockets and other thieves.

A good ballad singer could always gather a crowd and in the dusk of a Saturday evening in late March 1745, a motley collection of singers and music lovers converged on Leicester Square, or Leicester Fields as it was known in the eighteenth century. The square was the well-heeled home of a rich community. William Hogarth lived here, as did Joshua Reynolds and, prior to 1742, Sir Thomas De Veil. But despite its wealthy inhabitants, the square also formed an important public space for poorer people.[23]

By late March the long evenings of a northern spring had only recently taken hold and Londoners were eager to stay out late, after the confines of a long winter.[24] In the early nineteenth century Francis Place recalled that a lustily sung street ballad provided a perfect excuse to linger.

> There was always a considerable crowd of fools, idlers and pickpockets to hear them. There were many such groups in different parts of London in proportion to the vileness of the songs and the flash manner of singing.

Many of the songs were religious or historical in nature, but most, as Place complained, were about sex and crime. Among the songs he recalled hearing was 'Bawl Away', which he remembered 'was sung by two women at the end of Swan Yard opposite Somerset House in the Strand, every evening'. This particular ballad was accompanied with an exhibitionist cancan, made all the more outrageous by the absence of undergarments. The lyrics went:

> My smock's above my knee she did say, she did say
> My smock's above my knee she did say.
> My smock's above my knee and you may plainly see
> You may have a smack at me. Bawl away, Bawl away.[25]

But, even more popular than the sexually charged songs like 'Bawl Away' were the tales of gentlemen highwaymen and criminal heroes. Dick Turpin and Jack Rann, or 'Sixteen-String Jack' as he was known, were immortalised in popular ballads that celebrated their lives, crimes, adventures and 'game' deaths on the gallows at Tyburn. Songs such as these could be heard even in the respectable confines of Leicester Fields.

On this particular evening, between 7 and 8 o'clock, Elizabeth Turner 'Was going along Leicester Fields. There were some people singing ballads, and I stopped to hear the ballad singing'. And as she did so, another woman sidled up beside her:

> There was some talk of her being a ballad singer, but then she only stood to hear. And as I was standing there, she cut my apron off my sides and took my bundle that was in my apron from me, and she hit me a slap on the face and run away. It was a violent blow, my mouth was in a gore of blood, and she knocked me down and put me in fear of my life.

Elizabeth's apron, tied up around her waist, contained another apron, a shift, and a mob cap, altogether worth only around 4s 3d. But, Elizabeth's attacker was poor enough to make even this small sum seem worth risking her life to steal. Her assailant only provided her proper name, Mary White, to the Ordinary of Newgate Prison a few days before her death. She was tried under her slang name, Mary Cut-and-Come-Again. She was born to poor parents in St James's parish, and had only the most rudimentary charity school education. By 1745 she was living on the streets, making money as a prostitute and ballad singer, having garnered her nickname, 'for her dexterity in cutting off women's pockets'.[26] In the eighteenth century pockets did not form an integral part of a dress or pair of breeches, but were cloth sacks secured inside one's clothes with a long string. They were a tempting target for thieves.

After the assault, Mary fled. First, she ran towards Cranbourne Alley, opening just to the northeast corner of the square and then through Ryder's Court and Bearbone Square, until finally she reached Grafton Street and then Monmouth Street, one of the centres of the second-hand clothes trade, where she perhaps hoped to quickly sell on her ill-gotten goods. Dickens would later describe Monmouth Street as 'the burial place of the fashions',[27] but more importantly it was a marketplace in which no one enquired too carefully about the ownership of the goods on sale.

Mary thought she had escaped, but in fact Elizabeth had followed her and, as she reached the corner of Grafton Street and Monmouth Street, Elizabeth grabbed Mary and wrestled her for the bundled apron of clothes, calling for help as she did so. This time Elizabeth was the more powerful. Henry Juratt and Mary McPherson, who were standing near by, came to Elizabeth's assistance and between them secured both the bundle and Mary.

Mary's first response was anger. She cried out:

> The bitch wants to take my life away. And said, the things were her own. She wished the blessed God Almighty would shut heaven's gate against her, and as her mouth was open, she wished it might never shut again, if the apron was not hers; and to her accuser she said, Damn her eyes, she should not have the apron.

Henry Juratt replied:

> I dare say they are not yours, how can you say the things
> are yours? I have seen many a ballad singer, and I never
> saw one with two aprons.

Mary seems to have believed that her time was up. She
fulminated and screamed at her accusers, defiant to the last.
Like many of the characters in the ballads she sang about
the streets, Mary seems to have decided to play the 'game'
criminal in the face of an unfair criminal justice system. To
Mary McPherson, who helped subdue her, Mary said:

> She would not be taken away till a proper officer came.
> Mary then pulled her breasts out, and spurted milk in the
> fellows' faces, and said, Damn your eyes, what do you
> want to take my life away?

The watchmen finally arrived, and holding Mary firmly,
escorted her and the small band of witnesses to the nearest
justice of the peace, probably Thomas De Veil. By the time
they arrived, her blood was up and her behaviour almost
mad:

> She licked Elizabeth Turner before the justice and said,
> she longed for it; and said she would spit upon the
> justice's seat, and she did so. The justice said he would
> send her to Newgate, and she said, Damn my eyes then I
> shall have a ride for the money. Then the justice ordered
> her to be fettered and handcuffed; and she said, if he
> would take the handcuffs off, she would tell him her right
> name, otherwise she would not.

Later, in court, Mary claimed that she and Elizabeth Turner
had been drinking together:

> Mrs Turner asked me to drink a dram, and I told her, I had
> rather have a pint of beer, and she tied the apron upon me
> herself, and said, she wanted to tie her garter; so I run
> away with the things and she run after me and cried out
> stop thief.

Mary pointed out the quarter-mile distance that separated Monmouth Street and the scene of the crime and asked why she had not been challenged sooner. She asked to see the apron Elizabeth had been wearing in hopes of being able to demonstrate that the strings had not been cut at all. But when it was produced in court, 'one of the strings was a quarter of a yard shorter than the other'. In the end she was found guilty of 'highway robbery', an offence whose legal definition included violent thefts committed on the streets of London as well as on country highways. When it came to the sentencing, the court may well have been aware of her previous convictions for theft, under the name of Mary White, in 1741, 1743 and 1744. Like the subject of so many ballads, she went to her death at Tyburn, asking that 'the spectators would pray for her' and declaring that 'she bore no body any spite'.[28]

A Dismal Prison

Anyone waiting to be tried for a felony at the Old Bailey was incarcerated in nearby Newgate Prison. Like the roundhouse, Newgate was run as a business by its keeper, and those who could afford to pay for special treatment could find luxurious accommodation on the 'keeper's side'. The poor, by the same token, were confined in the squalid conditions of the 'common side', where the prisoners were left to run prison life according to their own autocratic rules.

The furnished lodgings Elizabeth Bennet rented from Mary Bakewell on Thursday 15 March 1742 were basic. They comprised little more than a small room, with a bed, a mattress, a blanket and a few sticks of furniture. But to rent even this tiny corner of London, Elizabeth had to spin a tale to convince her landlady that she could afford it. She claimed 'that she was married and that her husband was butler to a gentleman in Bloomsbury'.

This helped to explain why she was alone and at least temporarily assured Mary Bakewell that her furnishings were safe. But something did not seem quite right and Mary became suspicious. When Elizabeth returned home late the next day, she demanded to be allowed into the room so she could check that nothing was amiss. Elizabeth claimed to have mislaid the key, but Mary, with the assistance of another lodger, Thomas Test, searched her clothes, found the key and pushed in to the room. A blanket was missing and Elizabeth was arrested.

In the first instance, she was taken to one of London's miscellaneous lockups to await a preliminary hearing. But all prisoners who were to stand trial at the Old Bailey were eventually transferred to Newgate Prison, just north of the courthouse. On Sunday 22 April, a few days before her trial, Elizabeth Bennet was escorted there in possession of nothing more than the clothes she stood up in. Newgate stood at the junction of Holborn and Newgate Street and incorporated a gate through the City walls. The passageway underneath was a favourite haunt of pickpockets. In 1748, as he was 'going under Newgate', Benjamin Johnson 'felt something bobbing against my pocket, and saw John Kates with my handkerchief in his hand'. As he explained to the court, 'as I had lost three handkerchiefs before, it made me the more cautious'.[29] Open grates in the walls of the passageway allowed the prisoners to beg for money from the passers-by, and eight times a year the area outside the prison filled with a ghoulish crowd of onlookers as condemned men and women were shunted into carts for their last journey through London to Tyburn.

The prison itself was five storeys high, and had been substantially rebuilt after the Great Fire of 1666 and would be rebuilt again in 1770, only to be badly damaged in the Gordon riots a decade later. In 1742, however, it was run down and overcrowded. On hot days the stench of

Figure 1.06 View of Newgate prison and adjacent buildings, engraving
c. 1750. Credit: Guildhall Library, City of London

unwashed bodies and human suffering filled the neighbourhood, while the population of the prison was regularly scoured by waves of typhus. In 1750 half the court officers at the Old Bailey, including the Lord Mayor and two judges, died, along with some 40 others, when prisoners brought the contagion into the courtroom.

The world that Elizabeth entered that Sunday was a place apart, governed by its own rules and its own logic. The ward she was conducted to was little more than a bare room, but it played witness to a complex hierarchy, at the top of which stood Elizabeth Newbury, who had been imprisoned until she was able to pay a fine. Elizabeth Bennet's first encounter with Newbury proved frightening and difficult:

> When I was brought to Newgate, Elizabeth Newbury demanded a shilling for ward dues. I told her I had no money, but if she would please to stay till my friends came, I would give it to her. She said that would not do, for she must have something in pledge. I told her I had nothing to give her but my gown, and I was not willing to part with that. Upon that she and two more fell a swearing at me, and she said she would take it off by violence if I would not give it her. I asked her whether she could answer for stripping people? She said, – yes, who could hinder her? And then she took my gown off my back by force, and I have never seen it since. I demanded it again once since that time; and she said she could not give it me without I gave her the shilling.

Elizabeth Bennet had come up against the system of prisoner-financed and prisoner-run government by which Newgate was managed. At her trial for the theft of Bennet's gown, Elizabeth Newbury explained the system:

> I was made a ward-woman by the partners, and when I got a shilling I always gave them 9 pence out of it, and they told me if people had no money, I must make it, or else I must pay it myself; and as for this gown, Bennet was starving with cold and hunger, and pulled it off and I lent her 7 pence half penny upon it.

The practice of asking the prisoners to manage their own affairs was centuries old and had originated in the City's other gate prison, Ludgate, being extended to Newgate at the request of the Court of Aldermen in 1633. Originally, the prisoners were meant to hold a monthly meeting where they would elect a steward and wardsmen and discuss their problems. By the mid-eighteenth century this system had degenerated into a more autocratic one, in which four 'partners' were simply appointed by the keeper of the prison and these partners in turn appointed the wardsmen and women. Together these prisoner trustees ensured that each of the 18 wards of Newgate was cleaned daily and that the regular routines of prison life were adhered to – the monotonous rituals of locking and unlocking, of cleaning up and slopping out. And the whole system was greased by the liberal application of ward dues or 'garnish'.

Bennet was housed in one of the prison's 13 'common side' wards, reserved for those too poor to afford the more comfortable accommodation and ample provisions available on the 'keeper's side'. For food she received only the most basic allowance of a penny loaf of bread a day, supplemented by charitable donations. If she was lucky she might be allowed to beg at the grate from passers-by, although with so many prisoners all seeking this privilege, it was available to only the most needy or most insistent. Fourteen years after Bennet's incarceration Thomas Gresham was killed by William Thornton in a dispute over the right to beg at the grate.[30]

The ward Bennet shared with as many as 30 other women was only 26 by 32 feet, and crammed with hammocks and rough bedding. Her fellow prisoners included a ragtag collection of debtors and vagrants, as well as a much rougher element, all of whom seemed to owe some allegiance to Bennet's persecutor, Elizabeth Newbury. One of the prisoners was Mary Smith, who later gave evidence at Newbury's trial in an attempt to undermine Bennet's complaint:

> I am a prisoner, and saw Bennet when she was going to
> pay her dues. She said she had no money, but she would
> pawn her gown and apron for them. Newbury offered to
> stay till her friends came, but Bennet immediately took
> off her gown and coloured apron, and insisted on
> pledging them. What became of them afterwards I
> can't tell, but we all paid 1s. for ward dues at our first
> coming in.

Smith was little more than a girl. She was not very bright and seems to have adapted well to prison life. She had been in Newgate for at least nine months awaiting transportation to North America. Along with her younger sister, Mall, she had lured 5-year-old Elizabeth Minton from her home in Albemarle Street with the promise of a piece of plum cake. They dragged her by the hand to Tottenham Court Road and stripped her of a quilted calamanco coat and a set of stays, before leaving her 'sitting on a dung hill'.

The two sisters were eventually run to ground, and the coat and stays found in a nearby ditch. Taken before Thomas De Veil, Mary as good as admitted the theft. Everyone in the room heard her say to her younger sister: 'Mall, if it had not been to buy you a new gown, I had not committed this robbery'.[31] By the time of Bennet's trial nine months later she was clearly under the influence of the older and more experienced, and altogether smarter, Elizabeth Newbury.

The ward also housed two other women who gave evidence at Newbury's trial – Margaret Wheatley and Margaret Clark. Aware that she might have to return to Newgate and co-exist with the prisoners following the trial, Wheatley chose to keep her head down. She testified:

> I heard the ward woman ask Bennet to pull off her gown
> for the ward dues; she said she would not, but Newbury
> bid her strip for she must have her ward dues, and she
> accordingly had the gown, but I could not see whether she
> took it off herself, for I was a-bed.

Margaret Clark also studiously avoided committing herself:

> I know nothing at all but that Newbury behaved in a civil
> manner. I saw nothing of it. Newbury never stripped me
> of any thing, but demanded eight pence, which was her
> due, and I paid it.

Perhaps ironically, the person who navigated the
treacherous waters of Newgate and the Old Bailey most
successfully was the apparent victim in this crime, Elizabeth
Bennet. At her own trial for the theft of the blanket, her
only defence was the bitter complaint that:

> She had been very ill used in gaol by a woman who lay
> for a fine, and that she had taken her gown from her by
> violence because she had not money to pay the ward dues.

Despite hearing clear evidence of her earlier theft of a
blanket, the jury acquitted Bennet, while the court brought
Elizabeth Newbury to book for stealing the gown, finding
her guilty of theft and sentencing her to be branded in the
thumb. The rules of the wider society did occasionally apply
to Newgate prisoners.[32]

Conclusion

In modern Britain, despite the occasional 'have-a-go hero'
and private prosecution, we expect crime to be dealt with by
the police and prosecution to be led by the state. In
eighteenth-century London there were no professional
policemen and there was no public prosecution service. As a
result private individuals were forced to take on a much
more active role in the arrest and prosecution of criminals.
From the first cry of 'murder!' and 'stop thief!' to the final
prosecution at the Old Bailey, ordinary men and women
were expected to take the lead. It was down to the victim
and anyone they could corral off the streets to secure the
suspect and deliver them up to the constable. And it was

again down to the victim to make a credible case in court. For these reasons, the vast majority of criminals escaped prosecution. Those arrested by informers and vigilantes or by thieftakers playing the system against itself could be forgiven for cursing their luck as they whiled away the hours in London's commercially run prisons awaiting their trials.

In part, this made for an arbitrary and brutal system in which wealth, zealotry and prejudice weighed more heavily in the scales of justice than did truth. Your chances of prosecution rested as much on whether your victim had the spare time and the spare cash to see it done as on your actual guilt. But it is also clear that this was a form of policing requiring consent. Criminal justice was the result of negotiated understandings of what was acceptable behaviour and what ought to be punished. Where the general public saw no crime, no crime could be prosecuted. And where public anger focused attention on an individual or a specific offence, the forces of the state were largely powerless to shape the outcome. Even justices of the peace such as Thomas De Veil and Henry Fielding, sitting smugly in their parlours, wavered in the face of public outrage. Many historians have seen in eighteenth-century justice the workings of a 'Bloody Code' in which raw and arbitrary power were visited on working people by an unfeeling aristocracy. There is no doubt about the arbitrary and bloodthirsty nature of the system. But at the same time it is important to remember that every prosecutor and witness, every informer and juryman, many of whom came from modest social backgrounds, was implicated in the final outcome.

2

Crimes of Blood

Violence – both real and threatened – was endemic to eighteenth-century London. In the home, discipline was maintained with blows – husbands beat their wives and masters and mistresses beat their servants. On the public stage it was used to punish crime: felons were routinely hanged, whipped and branded to the applause or derision of the public, or pelted with rotten eggs, vegetables and even stones on the pillory by their neighbours. On the streets, violence was a normal way to settle a dispute – men fought duels and boxing matches or, more crudely, brawled outside pubs. It was also frequently used in popular protest. Crowds regularly marched through the streets, shouting, breaking windows and occasionally pulling down a house. But violence was rarely indiscriminate and these practices were accepted, within limits, as a part of the theatre of public life. It was commonly believed (although not technically true) that a husband could use a stick to beat his wife as long as it was no thicker than a man's thumb; while in the eighteenth century few doubted that sparing the rod would spoil the child. Despite this backdrop of everyday violence, however, some things remained beyond the pale. Violent killing in all its guises normally led to criminal proceedings at the Old Bailey.

With the exception of infanticide, homicide was a largely male phenomenon, with men accounting for 90 percent of those put on trial. During arguments, and especially when their point of view was contradicted, men were quick to defend their honour by challenging their detractors to a fight. In the early eighteenth century gentlemen frequently carried swords and were quick to draw them, while lower class men simply raised their fists. In many cases the parties would simply step outside the alehouse or coffeehouse where they were drinking to settle the matter. The resulting fights, conducted more or less according to accepted rules of fair play, normally ended when someone was injured or conceded defeat. Death was not the intended outcome, but given the crude state of contemporary medicine, injuries often proved mortal. When formal duels were arranged between gentlemen they normally took place the next day. In the first half of the century duels were fought with swords and were frequently fatal. But as the century wore on, the pistol replaced the sword, making duelling both more formal and, ironically, safer, owing to the clear rules which limited their use. Unlike duels, which normally took place in private (since they were illegal), boxing matches took place in public and attracted large audiences. Spectators' interest in betting on the outcome often prolonged the matches beyond endurance and sometimes led to fatalities. Those responsible for causing deaths in fights and duels were always tried for murder, but sympathetic juries normally gave a verdict of manslaughter, under the pretence that the killing was not premeditated.

Whereas most male violence happened in public and involved other men, female violence typically occurred in or around the home, and claimed its victims from members of the household, both male and female. Women did not carry weapons, but there were plenty of possible instruments ready at hand, not least kitchen knives and pots and pans. Whereas male violence was circumscribed by unwritten rules, female violence was unexpected and therefore unregulated. As a result, while such violence was relatively rare, it occasionally led to brutal injuries and death.

Crowd protest was commonplace. Londoners were accustomed to taking to the streets to voice their grievances on issues as varied as politics, religion, working conditions and the sexual misdemeanours of their neighbours. By staging bonfires, shouting and chanting and marching through the streets, they called attention to their views. More aggressively, some crowds demanded that householders show support for their grievances by placing lighted candles in their windows. Those who failed to do so found their expensive panes of hand-made glass shattered by bricks and rocks. Where the target of mob hostility was associated with a particular place, such as a brothel, the house could be attacked and the entire fabric with the exception of the brickwork dismantled and burned in bonfires on the street. The violence of the crowd was typically focused on property, rather than individuals, but the sense of threat and fear felt by those who were the objects of mob attacks was nonetheless very real.

Riot was a misdemeanour and very rarely prosecuted at the Old Bailey. It could, however, be tried under specific statutes, notably the 1715 Riot Act, which made it a felony for 12 or more people to remain at the scene of a riot an hour after a command to disperse was read out by a magistrate, but prosecutions under this act were rare. The riots which generated the most trials were the Gordon riots in 1780, the most destructive in London's history. Crowds roamed the city streets for almost a week, initially in protest against a Catholic Relief Act, but the demonstration quickly degenerated into an uncontrolled melée. Dozens of houses, chapels and public buildings, including Newgate Prison and the Old Bailey Courthouse itself, were damaged or destroyed, causing at least £100,000 worth of property damage. But although hundreds died in the riots, most were killed by soldiers attempting to suppress the disorder – once again, the crowds attacked property, not people.

Despite the chaos of the Gordon riots, the general trend over the course of the eighteenth century was for public violence in London to decline. Cultural acceptance of violence became problematic as male honour was redefined and linked to qualities other than the ability to knock someone else's brains out. The homicide rate declined by a factor of six, to below modern levels, by the first decade of the nineteenth century. The development of the pistol duel, with its carefully orchestrated procedures and the mediating role of seconds, led to a significant reduction in fatalities, while boxing matches became more of a spectator sport, with the violence of the street transferred onto the stage. Crowd protest, fundamentally discredited by the excesses of the Gordon riots, became less common, and was largely replaced by new methods of publicising grievances, such as public meetings and lobbying conducted by clubs and societies. The increasing intolerance of violence can also be seen in changes in official punishments. Branding fell into decline and, together with burning at the stake, was eventually abolished. At the same time, new punishments such as transportation and imprisonment made corporal punishment seem less necessary. Wife beating became increasingly unacceptable, while sports involving violence to animals (such as throwing at cocks) were viewed as unnecessarily cruel. At the Old Bailey there was a growing desire to bring everyone responsible for violent deaths to trial, even when the death manifestly resulted from an accident.

Despite this trend, violence remained a fundamental feature of London life, although it gradually became more hidden. Homicides were increasingly confined to the home and wife beating continued unabated, although less frequently discussed. Pistol duels were more popular than ever, but now took place at dawn in out of the way places and with no spectators. In 1790, in the first scandal of its sort in British history, London was convulsed by a panic over the activities of a serial attacker. The 'Monster' was a man who cruised the streets at night insulting women and stabbing them with sharp instruments, usually in the buttocks. Over 50 attacks were reported. The huge public interest in these attacks, more than the crimes themselves, reflects the continuing place of violence at the forefront of the public imagination and indicates that the modern world of sex crimes had arrived.

Regardless of these changes, there remained plenty of business for the Old Bailey.

She Came out Through the Casement Window

The rules, both unwritten and written, which governed violence between men assumed that the two parties were essentially equals. Violence between the sexes had no such rules, with one exception. Men were entitled to 'discipline' their wives by beating them, as long as the violence did not cause serious injury. But as this was an unequal relationship the violence was difficult to police. Men did not appreciate interference in their relationships with their wives, and unsurprisingly this violence often got out of hand. Almost 10 percent of the killings committed by men and recorded in the Old Bailey Proceedings *were of their own wives.*

When Thomas and Sarah Daniels quarrelled on the evening of 28 August 1761 in a house in Hare Court off Aldersgate Street and the neighbours heard Sarah scream, they did not respond immediately. They knew that the couple often

Figure 2.01 Hare Court, Spitalfields, eighteenth-century weavers' cottages. 1914 watercolour, by Edward Arthur Phipson (it is signed using his adopted name of Evacustees A. Phipson). Credit: City of London, London Metropolitan Archives

argued and they assumed that Thomas regularly beat his wife. They continued to listen, however, and were able to hear what happened – to be, in eighteenth-century terms, an 'ear-witness' to the events that followed.

As the daylight faded Mary Allen, who lived three doors away from the house in which the Daniels rented a second-floor room, was eating supper when the screaming started. Soon the noises became more puzzling. She 'heard a noise like unto the knocking of a hammer as if nailing up a door' and heard Sarah screaming 'my life, never no more, my dear soul, never no more'. Mary went down into the street, where she heard more shouting. The next thing she knew Sarah came tumbling out of the half-open casement window and fell face first into the gutter. She was totally naked, blood ran from her left breast and she was speechless. She was taken up and carried back into the house and a surgeon was called. She died the next morning.

Did Thomas Daniels kill his wife? This was difficult to prove, because no one had seen Thomas actually push her out the window, but it is clear from the witness statements at the trial that Mary Allen and the other neighbours quickly jumped to the conclusion that this was a case of wife beating run out of control. Thomas, however, conducted a strong defence and both the cross-examinations and his own testimony made these initial assumptions look less and less plausible.

Mary Allen was the principal witness for the prosecution. She told the court:

> About a quarter after ten o'clock on a Friday evening, in
> the month of August last, I was eating my supper, I heard
> a woman scream. I got up, and went to the window, and
> when I came there, she had done screaming. I thought it
> was Daniels beating his wife, but I could not be sure. I
> came down stairs, and went to the end of the court. I
> heard Daniels say (I believe it to be him), I heard a man
> say, Damn you, you bitch, will you ever come after me
> more. She said, My dear life, never no more. She
> then gave another violent scream and came out of the
> window, and as she came out she was bent double, I saw
> her head first.

She elaborated her story under questioning from the judge and was later cross-examined by Thomas Daniels:

Question.	Could you observe any body behind her?
Mary Allen.	There was no light in the room, and as she was coming out, she said O! save me, save me.
Q.	Did it appear to be her own voluntary act to come out of the window, or that she was forced out?
Allen.	I believe she was forced out, by the violent force she came out with, and as she was coming out, she said these words. She fell face-downwards stretched, her full length into the kennel, quite naked, not a thread upon her, no shift, no cap. At my screaming out, the people came out at the next door. I then ran and called Mr Clark the constable.
Q.	For what purpose did you call a constable?
Allen.	Because I believed the woman to be murdered.
Q.	By whom?

Allen.	By her husband.
Q.	Did you hear a man's voice offering to throw her out at the window?
Allen.	No, I heard nothing more than what I have said.

The constable was George Clark:

> Mrs Allen came and knocked at my door, and said, For
> God's sake come out, for Daniels has throwed his wife out
> at the window. When we got into the house, we went up
> into the two pair of stairs room that looks into the street.
> There we found the prisoner alone, without hat or wig,
> coat or waistcoat. I laid hold of his arm and asked him
> how he could be guilty of such a rash action, of throwing
> his wife out of the window, and asked how she came to be
> naked. He said, she pulled her shift off, and tore his shirt,
> and then threw herself out at the window. There was the
> shift torn all down before, and all at the wrists. I bid him
> put on his clothes, and said, he must go to the compter.
> I could hardly tell whether the shift was a shift or not, it
> was torn so. He looked about the room, and seemed
> to be a little confused. Then some more people came
> up-stairs. He put on his clothes and we took him to
> the compter.

Thomas Daniels appears to have conducted his own
defence. His initial statement told a rather different story
than that related by his neighbours:

> That Friday evening I happened to be out till about ten at
> night at the Nag's Head in Houndsditch. I had three pints
> of beer, and a pint of beer along with a young man of my
> acquaintance. When I came home my wife had locked me
> out. I found she was awake in the room and she would not
> let me in. I went down stairs and came up again, very
> serious and good-natured, and said, Sally, my dear, let me
> in. I took and put my back against the door, and broke it
> open. She came out of bed and flew upon me, and tore my
> shirt from my back almost. She hit me several blows. I
> said, Sally, what makes you do so? What do you use me
> so for? She tore her shift all off her back and cap from her

head, and pulled and tore every thing from her back, and
tore all to pieces. I said, Sally, be easy, don't do so. I was
sitting on the bed unbuttoning my breeches. She took up
something, as my back was towards her, and struck me
over the side of my head, which perfectly stunned me.
With that she flew out of the window directly, and cried
out as she went down, Save me, save me, the last words
she said. She was gone in an instant. There I sat upon the
bed as Mr Clark found me. The door was open, just as I
broke it open, when he came up. I never offered to nail
the door, or put any thing to the door. When he came up,
he said, How came you to throw your wife out of the
window? I said, No, I did not, she throwed herself out, as
I am a living man. God Almighty is my witness.

The principal witness he called in his defence was Joseph
Holmes, churchwarden of the parish. Holmes raised some
awkward questions for those who thought Sarah had been
thrown from the window:

In the morning, about half an hour after six somebody
came and said, there was a murder committed. Now I will
tell about the room. I went about half an hour after six; I
do not know whether I did not see her expire myself.
There was the mother and a great number of people
crying and yowling; saying, she was murdered. I said, for
God's sake, good people, let the door appear open. I went
to see if any blood appeared under the window. There was
none. I looked to see the situation of the room. There was
a chest of drawers, a table, a low chair. The window is as
high a window as is common. I saw no blood at all, and if
there had been any struggle, by a man's forcing a woman
out at the window, the window must be broke. There were
garden pots standing on the outside of the window.

Question.   What window do you speak of?

Holmes.   I speak of a two pair of stairs window, there is
               but one window in the front. It opens with a
               double casement.

Q.   Did the garden pots stand in that part of the
               window that was open?

Holmes.	It may be a foot on the left-hand side, the side that was not open.
Q.	Did it appear to you practicable for a man, with a table standing under the window, to throw her out at that window?
Holmes.	There was a chair. I rather think she must go to the window, to call out for assistance, and over balance herself in the hurry, and so tumble. I apprehend the chair was always standing there.
Q.	What size woman was she?
Holmes.	She was a shortish sort of a woman. I think it is impossible to throw her out without breaking the glass, and there is but one pane broke now.

Other witnesses confirmed that it would have been impossible to throw her out of the window without a struggle, and that there was no evidence of a disturbance. Sarah Frances testified that, although the couple were prone to quarrel, Thomas was not usually the aggressor:

> I have heard her threaten several times, she would kill him. I have heard her cry out several times. Once I carried a pot of beer up, I looked through the key hole; and at that time, he was not near her when she cried out, Pray, dear Daniels, let me alone, he did not meddle with her. The key hole was so large I could see from the chest of drawers to the window.

Others testified that Thomas was a 'good-natured' man and that his wife had frequently abused him.

When the jury met to consider its verdict it must have been aware that, with no eye witnesses to the actual events in the room apart from Daniels himself, it was impossible to establish with any certainty what actually happened. But, unable to imagine a situation in which a wife might mistreat a husband, the jury could only see these events in the light of a man attacking his wife. As a result the jury found him guilty of murder. The seriousness of the crime meant that the court immediately sentenced him 'to be executed on the Monday following, and his body to be dissected and anatomised'. To increase the shame of his punishment, Daniels's body would be handed over to the surgeons and be cut up for medical instruction in front of an audience in the Surgeons' Hall.

Despite the limited time available, Daniels's friends managed to get the hanging postponed while they petitioned for a pardon. On 10 October the execution was formally respited, owing to the fact that 'several favourable circumstances have appeared in this case since his trial, which tend even to render doubtful the truth of the fact of which he was convicted'. On 26 October, following further investigation, he received an unconditional royal pardon.[1] Nonetheless, Daniels's reputation was in tatters and on 23 November he published a 24-page pamphlet, *The Affecting Case of the Unfortunate Thomas Daniels*, in which he tried to convince the public, and particularly women, of his innocence (he seems to have wanted to remarry). He argued that, atypically, *he* was the mistreated spouse in their marriage. He reported that Sarah was frequently drunk and beat him. She had taken up with another man and was in the habit of wounding herself and then telling the neighbours that he had mistreated her. On the evening of her death, he claimed, she had struck him several times with a hand brush, but then because she thought she had killed him she jumped out of the window in despair.[2] Whether his readers were convinced by these claims is impossible to tell, but if they had read the *Old Bailey Proceedings* they would have already been aware that there were two sides to this story.[3]

He was None the Best of Husbands

Women could *be as cruel and violent as men, or perhaps even more so, since there were no equivalent unwritten cultural*

*expectations governing how they should use violence. Most
female violence took place in the home, and was directed against
members of their own families and households.*

In March 1726 the residents of Westminster were shocked
by the discovery of a man's decapitated head floating in the
Thames near the horse ferry. The head was cleaned up and
placed on a pole in St Margaret's churchyard, abutting
Westminster Abbey, in the hope that someone would
identify it. Although it was viewed by a large number of
people, after four days still no one had identified it. The
smell became offensive, so it was placed in a bottle of spirits.
A few days later, suspicion began to fall on Catherine Hayes.
Her explanation for the recent disappearance of her husband
John seemed suspicious and the head shared many of his
features. A warrant was issued for her arrest and when the
constables arrived, Catherine was found in her darkened
room with Thomas Billings sitting on her bedside, without
his shoes and stockings on. The press later interpreted this
as clear evidence of a sexual relationship.

Both Hayes and Billings were committed to prison, as was
Thomas Wood, who had been drinking with them the night
John Hayes disappeared. Wood was the first to confess that
they had murdered him. Billings followed and finally
Catherine acknowledged the crime. But when she learned
that she could be found guilty of petty treason and burned at
the stake for killing her husband (since he was legally her
master), she changed her mind and resolved to plead
innocent, resting her case on the claim that she had not
actually committed the murder herself. When they came up
for trial at the Old Bailey, Wood and Billings pleaded guilty.
Only Catherine Hayes was tried, for the offence of 'being
traitorously present, comforting and maintaining the said
Thomas Billings in the murder of the said John Hayes, her
husband', an offence which was legally deemed to be as

serious as the actual killing. At the trial her earlier confessions provided the strongest evidence of her guilt. Richard Bromage and Leonard Myring provided damning testimony.

> Richard Bromage. After Catherine Hayes was committed to Newgate, I and Robert Wilkins, and Leonard Myring went to visit her. I am sorry, says I, to see you here on this account. And so am I too, says she. For God's sake, says I, what could put it into your head to commit such a barbarous murder upon your own husband? Why, says she, the devil put it into my head. But however, John Hayes was none of the best of husbands, for I have been half starved ever since I was married to him. I don't in the least repent of any thing that I have done, but only in drawing those two poor men into this misfortune. I was six weeks in importuning them to do it. They denied it 2 or 3 times, but at last they agreed. My husband was made so drunk that he fell out of his chair, and then Billings (who was a tailor) and Wood carried him into the back room, and laid him upon the bed. I was not in that room, but in the fore room on the same floor when he was killed. But they told me that Billings struck him twice on the head with a pole axe, and then Wood cut his throat.
>
> When he was dead I went in and held the candle while Wood cut his head quite off, and afterwards they chopped off his legs and arms. And why, says I, did you use your husband in such an inhumane manner. Because, says she, we wanted to get him into an old chest, but he was too long and too big. We thought to have done it with only cutting off his head and his legs, but we were forced to cut off his thighs and his arms, and then the chest would not hold them all. The body and limbs were put into blankets and carried out at several times the next night, and thrown into a pond. But what, says I, could induce the men to be guilty of all this? Was it for the sake of money?
>
> No, says she, the devil was in us all, and we were all got drunk. And what, says I, can you say for your self when you come before the judge? Why, says she, it will signify nothing to make a long preamble. I will hold up my hand and say that I am guilty, for nothing can save me, nobody can forgive me.

Leonard Myring's account of her confession, however, was less explicit:

> I was with the prisoner 2 or 3 times before this; one of
> those times was I think on the Sunday after she was
> committed. I am glad you are come, says she, for the men
> that did the murder are taken and have confessed it. I was
> not with them when they did it, for I was sitting upon a
> stool by the fire in the shop, but I heard the blow given
> and heard somebody stamp. And why did not you cry out,
> says I, because I was afraid they would kill me, says she.
> And after his head was cut off, it was put into a pail, and
> Wood carried it out. Billings sat down by me and cried,
> and would lie all the rest of the night in the room with the
> dead body. But what, says I, was the first occasion of your
> contriving to do this? Why, says she, my husband came
> home drunk one night and beat me, upon which says
> Billings, this fellow deserves to be killed, and says Wood,
> I would be his butcher for a penny, and I told them they
> might do as they would, and so they made a contrivance
> to kill him. But I did not know that they would do it the
> night that it was done on. And why, says I, did not you tell
> your husband of this design to murder him? Because says
> she, I was afraid that he would beat me.

John Blakesby, who lived at a nearby alehouse, the Brown's Head in New Bond Street, testified to the purchase of the substantial quantities of wine used to make John Hayes drunk:

> On the 1st of March last, about 4 in the afternoon, the
> prisoner and 2 men that pleaded guilty came to our house
> for 6 quarts of mountain [strong Malaga wine], which she
> paid for at the bar, and saw it put into bottles. I sent a
> porter home with her that he might know where to fetch
> the bottles when they were empty. But about 9 the same
> night, one of those two men brought back the empty
> bottles and had another quart of wine away with him in a
> bottle which he brought besides ours.

The final prosecution witness was the Hayes's upstairs neighbour, Mary Springet, who, despite closely monitoring the strange noises and comings and goings which occurred on the floor below her that night, failed to detect the murder. Rather, she thought a different crime was being committed (a 'midnight flit' – moving out in the middle of the night in order to avoid having to pay rent) and she sought to prevent it. When she asked Catherine to explain the strange noises, Catherine asked her why she was so uneasy. Mary replied: 'Truly, Mrs Hayes I believe you're a going to move your goods by night, and I think it's a shame you should do so when you have got money that lies by you'.

Catherine rested her slim hopes of an acquittal on making a limited confession:

> The prisoner in her defence acknowledged that 3 or 4
> days before her husband was killed, she knew that there
> was a design against his life, and that she was in the next
> room when the murder was done, but said that she had no
> hand in it, and therefore she was clear of his blood.

The jury thought otherwise, and found her guilty. She was convicted of the heinous crime of petty treason and was sentenced to be drawn on a hurdle to the place of execution, there to be burned alive. Billings and Wood were sentenced to death by hanging, but Wood fell ill and died in prison before execution day.

The *British Journal* reported not only the gruesome details of Catherine's execution on 14 May, but also some astonishing new facts about the case which rendered the crime even more sensational:

> Catherine Hayes was drawn to Tyburn on a hurdle, and
> there burnt alive, without the indulgence of being first
> strangled, as is customary in such cases; for which a
> special order was sent to the sheriff. She was fastened to
> the stake by an iron chain round her body, having a halter
> also about her neck (running through the stake) which the
> executioner pulled at when she first began to shriek. She
> affirmed in Newgate that Billings was her own son, got by

Figure 2.02 Catherine Hayes, Thomas Billings and Thomas Wood Decapitating the Body of John Hayes (1726). © British Library Board. All Rights Reserved. Shelfmark 1131.h.33 (1), frontispiece

> Mr Hayes, tis supposed before her marriage with him. If
> so, Billings murdered his own father, assisted in
> quartering him, and then lay with his own mother, while
> his father's mangled limbs were under the bed. A most
> horrible scene of wickedness![4]

The crowds pressing to see the execution were so large that a scaffold erected for the spectators collapsed. The same afternoon Thomas Billings was hanged along with three thieves and three 'sodomites'. Hayes's gruesome death, however, stole the show.[5]

In order to satisfy public interest, at least three pamphlet accounts of the murder were published, as well as one ballad. As he did following every execution day, the Ordinary of Newgate Prison, James Guthrie, published biographies of the executed convicts in his *Ordinary's Account*. If prisoners testified to their repentance, Guthrie willingly included accounts of their lives and crimes more or less in their own words. This allowed a more complicated picture of this crime to emerge, reflecting the murderers' own disagreement over whose idea it had been to commit the crime in the first place. While Billings blamed Catherine, she denied it, and claimed that her only prior knowledge of plans to murder her husband came from overhearing a conversation between him and Wood in which Wood told him: 'I think it no more a sin to kill you than a dog and a cat, because you are so cruel to that poor industrious woman, and because you are so atheistical and wicked'. She also reported that:

> Mr Hayes was a very unkind husband, beating and
> mortifying her upon every trivial occasion in a cruel
> manner; and when she was with child, he would never
> suffer a midwife to be called but once which with his
> other ill usages proved the cause of an abortion, and
> commonly put her in hazard of her life.

When asked to explain why she concealed the murder, she said 'that the ill usage he always gave her cooled her

Figure 2.03 'The Manner of Burning a Woman Convicted of Treason' (1777). © British Library Board. All Rights Reserved. Shelfmark 1485.p.8 (2), folio 124–5

affection towards him, and her only son being concerned, she could not think of delivering him up to public justice'.[6]

No doubt alarmed by these insults to the murdered man, the friends of John Hayes printed an alternative narrative of the killing in a 32-page pamphlet. This focused the blame for the crime firmly on 'the monstrous perfidy and cruelty of a woman'; and argued that the young men had been led astray by Catherine. The pamphlet also contained allegations of prior acts of deception and disloyalty committed by Catherine.[7]

A popular ballad, full of inaccuracies, further heaped responsibility for the crime onto her. 'A Song, on the Murder of Mr Hayes, by his Wife', sung to the popular tune of 'Chevy Chase', was sold on the city streets:

> In Tyburn Road a Man there lived
>> A just and honest life,
>
> And there he might have lived still
>> If so had pleased his wife.
>
> But she to vicious ways inclined
>> A life most wicked led
>
> With tailors and with tinkers too
>> She oft defiled his bed.

(Billings was a tailor.) Now labelled a religious zealot (rather than an atheist), the song alleged Hayes went to church twice a day:

> This vexed his wife unto the heart
>> She was of wrath so full,
>
> That finding no hole in his coat,
>> She picked one in his skull.

Having killed him, she cut up the body and disposed of it, and, when the body parts were discovered, she confessed the crime. Billings and Wood were not even mentioned in this account.[8]

These were just the first of many retellings of the story of this barbaric murder published in the ensuing decades. With each retelling it was increasingly Catherine who was held responsible, even though by all accounts she did not commit the actual murder. No doubt it was the shocking claim that she had encouraged her son to kill and brutally dismember his father and her husband, in combination with the belief that she had committed incest with him, that focused popular ire onto her. Catherine embodied popular fears of the chaos and disorder that women could create when they strayed from their prescribed social roles.[9]

He Behaved Honourably Enough

To be considered a proper man, you had to be willing to fight whenever you were insulted or challenged. In defence of their honour, many working men participated in boxing matches, while gentlemen fought duels. From the middle of the eighteenth century, pistols replaced swords as the weapons of choice in duels. Their introduction, the result of the large number of duellists with military training and access to firearms, was accompanied by accelerating criticism of duelling as a custom. Public opinion increasingly declared that it was based on a false concept of honour. Contributing to this perception was the fact that pistols were potentially more lethal than swords and at first there were no agreed rules for how to conduct a duel with these new weapons.

On 11 December 1749 Admiral Charles Knowles faced a court martial on the charge of failing to fully engage the enemy in an action off the coast of Cuba with a Spanish squadron during the War of the Austrian Succession.[10] One of Knowles' accusers was Edward Clark, captain of the

Canterbury, one of the ships that made up Admiral Knowles's fleet. Also present at the court martial was Thomas Innes, captain of the *Warwick*, part of the same fleet. Innes was an inveterate enemy of Clark. The court martial was dominated by charges and counter-charges voiced by these two captains and their supporters. In his testimony, Clark allegedly 'swore very hard' against Innes. In response, Innes suggested that Clark had been acting under the influence of an admiral other than Knowles. This was a suggestion even the court found shameful. Afterwards, a fellow captain told Innes, 'he had said so severe a thing of Captain Clark, which he could never forget, and that he must be obliged to resent it'. Undaunted, Innes replied: 'His sensations are so callous that I have long endeavoured to affront him, and cannot, adding, I look upon him to be a scoundrel and a coward; saying, I meant every word I said'.[11]

This atttack on Clark's reputation, which Innes unguardedly repeated to several other officers, was bound to reach Clark's ears. As an eighteenth-century gentleman, Clark could not allow the insult to stand. At 8 o'clock on the morning of 11 March 1750 Clark went to Innes's lodgings in Leicester Fields to confront him. As Innes's servant, William Newman, subsequently told the Old Bailey:

> I heard a great knock at the door, I came down stairs, and met Captain Clark at the dining-room door. He asked me if Captain Innes was up? I said no, but I would call him, which I did. Captain Clark stayed in the dining room all the time. My master got up very soon. He asked me if it was Captain Clark, I said it was. After my master got up, and came into the dining-room, he ordered me out of the room. I went into the next room, and when I was there, I heard Captain Clark say to Captain Innes, Sir, you have used me very ill. I think Captain Innes's answer was, I have not used you ill. There was some discourse, which I could not distinctly hear; after that I heard somebody speak, insisting on his fighting sword and pistol (the voice I took to be

> Captain Clark's voice). After that there were some words
> passed, and Captain Clark came out of the room. He was
> there but a little while; he came down part of the stairs,
> then he went back again, and went to Captain Innes and
> desired him to call on him in the morning, and said,
> remember, tis sword and pistol. Then Captain Clark came
> down, and went away directly. After he was gone, I went up
> to the people of the house, and said to them, Captain Clark
> has been here and has challenged my master.

Another servant, Edward Welton, testified as to Newman's
reaction to this news:

> Newman came up stairs in a great fright (my wife and I
> were in bed). He told us, Captain Clark had been there,
> and challenged his master. I said, Lord no! Be sure to let
> me know when it will be. Said he, that I will, and at night
> he came up again, and said his master had ordered him to
> black his shoes, and set them by him; adding, he believed
> it would be tomorrow morning.

Duels customarily took place early in the morning in out-
of-the-way places, in order to avoid attracting the attention
of anyone who might try to interfere. But those who knew a
duel was about to take place, particularly when it involved a
close acquaintance, often tried to stop the duel. Innes
attempted to prevent his friends and servant from attending
by ordering Newman to invite two captains to come to his
lodgings for breakfast. They were not fooled, however, and
Welton later reported the events of the following morning
to the court:

> I heard the captain walking in his room, and heard him go
> down, and the door clap. I jumped out of bed and got to
> the window, and saw him go up Castle Street. I heard the
> door shut again and saw William Newman run towards
> Leicester Fields. I made haste to the back of Montague
> House, and looked about on every spot of high ground I
> could find, quite to Marylebone. I not finding them, made
> haste home again.

Newman, however, had heard that duels were often fought in Hyde Park, and on going there between 6 and 7 o'clock in the morning he found the duellists:

> Captain Innes, with my master, was going down from Grosvenor's Gate. Captain Innes was on Captain Clark's right hand, not a great way from where the duel was fought. At my first seeing him I believe I was about 500 yards from him, being just got into the park. They walked down to the place where the duel was fought, then I came very near them – I believe within about twenty yards. I had a very clear sight of them, and as they parted the trees hindered me from seeing the position they were in, but then I moved so as to see them. Captain Clark was standing with his pistol in his hand, and Captain Innes was getting himself in a posture to be ready. They were about five or six yards asunder. As Captain Innes was reaching out his arm towards Captain Clark, Captain Clark fired his pistol. There was Captain Clark's servant at a distance and a mourning coach with two servants at some distance. My master turned round at the explosion of the pistol and dropt on his left knee. Captain Innes did not fire at all (his pistols were produced in court both charged, and the ball that was taken out of Captain Innes's side). Captain Clark's servant took the pistols up and gave them to me. The bullet penetrated on the right side and was taken out on the left. It had gone almost through him. I attended my master to his death.

Fighting by sword and pistol normally meant that the parties exchanged shots first before switching to swords. As this was one of the first duels involving the use of pistols, the unwritten rules which would later govern the use of these weapons were not yet fixed. This may explain why Clark fired too soon, but what is remarkable is the fact that Innes, although clearly unhappy at the way the duel had been conducted, was willing to forgive his killer. Part of the code which men of honour followed dictated that those injured in duels were expected to forgive their attackers, and that is just what Innes did. According to Newman, Captain Innes:

> Bade me tell every body that should enquire about it, that
> Captain Clark behaved very well, but he did not think he
> behaved very honourable, for he took full aim at him,
> saying, he fired before he was ready. This he said as soon
> as his wound was dressed. He several times said, He
> forgave Captain Clark, and hoped God would forgive him.
> Captain Innes died about eleven that night. These words
> were spoke about 11 or 12 at noon. He did not think of
> surviving his wound. He said, in my hearing, this will be a
> long night with me, if please God to spare my life till
> morning; seemingly in great pain.

The words of a dying man were thought to possess a unique
spiritual truth and were freighted with great emotional
authority. Innes's forgiveness of his killer, demanded by the
code of honour, was mentioned by more than one witness at
the trial, and was held to be particularly significant. Innes
was also reported to have told one of his servants: 'Never let
my enemies know what I feel, and what I suffer'.[12] Even in
death, he wished to defend his reputation.

Edward Welton testified to what happened when the
fatally injured Innes was brought back to his lodgings:

> Newman came running home with his master's sword in
> his hand. This was about nine in the morning. The captain
> was brought home in a chair wounded. We got a surgeon
> and he was dressed. I held his hands in mine, I believe
> about six hours; they were cold, seeming almost dead.
> About eight at night he asked my wife and I how we did,
> and bid us take notice of what he said, and declare it
> when asked by any: As he was a dying man, he forgave
> Captain Clark with all his heart, and all the world; saying,
> he behaved like a gentleman, but he fired too soon. My
> wife asked him, how he could go to fight such a
> gentleman as Captain Clark? He said, God's will must be
> done, though he strove to take away my life at the court
> martial, it must be done, and is done.

Edward Wood was the surgeon called to Innes's side. As was
customary, he asked Innes about how he had received his

wound. Innes's response reveals a further problem with the way the duel had been conducted: the parties had stood too close together.

> I am a surgeon, and extracted the ball. It entered close to the false ribs on the right side, about a hand's breadth from the pit of the stomach, and it had broke one of the false ribs on the left side, and there it was taken out. This wound, no doubt, was the occasion of his death. He told me, on my asking him, he got the wound in a duel with Captain Clark in Hyde Park; saying, he believed they stood about four yards from each other. Said I, that was murder to stand so close; but, said he, I was obliged to do it, because my pistols were small.

During the second half of the eighteenth century, men fighting pistol duels normally stood ten paces, or about eight to ten yards, apart. In this case, however, Innes's pistols were three-and-a-half inch 'common' pocket pistols which could not kill at that distance. It would also become customary for both duellists to fight with the same types of pistol, but in this case the weapons employed were quite unequal. Captain Clark's pistols were longer, seven-inch 'horse' pistols, and were 'screwbarrelled' or rifled to improve accuracy. Clark's weapon thus gave him a distinct advantage. Indeed, the impact of rifling on the accuracy of duelling pistols, and hence the death rate among duellists, ensured that later weapons were manufactured without this refinement in an attempt to save lives and increase the role of chance in the encounter.

Six weeks after the duel Clark was tried at the Old Bailey for murder. The high status of the defendant, the seriousness of the charge and the presence of two counsel each for the prosecution and the defence meant that this would be a long trial. Serjeant Hayward opened the case for the prosecution, telling the jury that this was no ordinary killing, but the result of the:

Wicked practice of dueling, in which the public seems to
be greatly concerned, that the utmost endeavours ought to
be used to stop it, as the motives to it, as well as the
practices of it, are pregnant with danger to civil society. It
would almost shock a man to think that human nature can
be so depraved as to venture on practices of this kind;
practices that can arise from nothing but implacable
malice and revenge, which we are strongly enjoined to
forbear, and to calm and govern our unruly passions. It is
said, by the military gentlemen, that it is inconsistent with
their honour to put up with affronts and injuries, and that
there is no way for them to resent any insult committed
on their honour, but by dipping their hands in the blood of
their adversary (an excellent doctrine this to gain ground
in civil society!) and if ever this nation should be so
unhappy as to have such a notion prevail, I think there
would be an end of all civil society. It is a false and
imaginary honour that is the occasion of it and it is
against all principles of virtue and religion whatsoever.
The principles on which it is founded are unchristian and
thus the practice of it diabolical.[13]

Witnesses for the prosecution included Innes's servants,
who had been present in the house when the challenge was
issued, witnesses to the duel itself and the surgeon who
treated Innes.

The substantial case for the defence was very incompletely
reported in the *Old Bailey Proceedings*. All that was recorded
was the bald fact that several prominent figures had testified
to Clark's good character, saying that he was not the sort of
person who would readily engage in a fight:

Lord Southwell, Admiral Martin, Admiral Byng, Admiral
Faukes, Lord Montague Bertie, Captain West, Captain
Wickham, Colonel Lee, Captain Dent, Sir John Cross, the
Revd Dr Hale, the Revd Mr Horton, Mr Stanley, Captain
Forrest, Colonel Durand, all, and each of them, gave
Captain Clark an exceeding good character, for that of a
gentleman's behaviour, not easily moved to passion, willing
to reconcile differences, and one of a peaceable disposition.

But as was stated at the end of the trial, the publisher had
been forced to abridge the report in order to make room for
the other trials in that session, and in this special case the
Lord Mayor had authorised the publication of a separate
account.

From this additional pamphlet, we learn that the case for
the defence rested on three further points. First, officers who
had been present at the court martial testified to Innes
having made highly dishonourable comments about Clark,
thereby justifying Clark's attempt to restore his honour.
Second, it was claimed that what was said in Innes's dining
room did not amount to a challenge, since the words 'of
sword and pistol' were not heard by all the witnesses, but the
word 'satisfaction' was. It was claimed that what Clark
demanded was only an explanation, not a fight. In response
the prosecution argued that everyone had clearly understood
that a challenge had been issued. Finally, other witnesses,
who had been present at the duel, testified to Innes's
magnanimous behaviour afterwards, suggesting that Innes
did not think Clark guilty of any crime. Witnesses had
secured Clark, to ensure he could not escape, but Innes
reportedly said, slowly and distinctly: 'I desire you to release
him, for what he has done was of my own seeking. He has
behaved like a man of honour'.[14]

Although he called many witnesses, Clark himself did not
testify in his own defence. Instead, his counsel spoke for
him, telling the court that Clark could only be found guilty
of manslaughter, since there was no premeditated malice:
Clark was under a simple obligation to defend his honour.
The language Innes had used was such that 'must have
raised a passion in any person whatsoever that was subject to
the infirmities of human nature; it was hardly possible for
flesh and blood to forbear'.[15] As one witness reported,
following the duel Clark said, 'What I have done I was
obliged to do, and I am very sorry for it'.

In contrast, Mr Serjeant Hayward, counsel for the prosecution, argued that this was a case of murder, since there *was* clear evidence of premeditated malice:

> I own, I cannot at present see of what use this can be to the prisoner: I should rather think it a proof, that there was an inveterate hatred and implacable resentment subsisting between them, and would be taken to be an evidence of express malice. A challenge is an appointment to meet at a future time in order to fight with and take away the life of an adversary, and has always been considered as a deliberate and determinate act of the mind, and consequently carries malice along with it.

Hayward, waxing ever more eloquent and ever more pompous, then launched into another diatribe against the practice of duelling:

> See here the melancholy consequences of this pernicious and abominable practice of duelling. One brave man lost to his friends, lost to his relations, lost to the community; another equally brave in great danger likewise of being lost, in all the before mentioned respects, as he seems now to me to stand on the very brink of eternity. Is not this enough to strike a horror into the most sanguine mind, and prevent for the future such pernicious practices that can arise from nothing but the practices of false honour, practices that tend so greatly to the prejudice, if not the destruction of civil society? Let me earnestly recommend patience and forgiveness of injuries; and take my word, that a time will come, when a compliance with this divine precept will be deemed meritorious in us, and looked upon as an act of righteousness. And then, amidst all affronts and wrongs done us, we may make ourselves easy with that comfortable assurance, that verily there is a reward for the righteous; doubtless there is a God that judgeth the earth.

No doubt influenced by this closing peroration, the jury found Clark guilty of murder. This was a highly unusual verdict, for murder cases resulting from duels almost invariably resulted in manslaughter verdicts, where the punishment was typically branding. But in this case:

> When the jury brought in their verdict, the foreman
> acquainted the court that they could not by law do
> otherwise than find him guilty. But the provocation given
> by the deceased to the prisoner was so extraordinary, that
> they begged the court would please to recommend him to
> his Majesty's mercy.[16]

Once the trials were completed at each session, and before sentencing, convicts were customarily allowed to address the court and plead for leniency. In Clark's case, no doubt owing to his high social status, he was allowed to do this immediately following his trial, rather than wait until the conclusion of the sessions. He gave the following speech:

> My Lords, I am very sensible of the great indulgence of
> your lordships, in this early passing the sentence of the
> law upon me, though tis the last of all human favours I
> could have hoped to have received from your lordships
> hands.
>   As the jury, my lords, were pleased to show their
> compassion to the failings of human nature, in
> recommending me to the royal mercy, I hope there have
> appeared some circumstances in my case, which may not
> render me altogether unworthy of the recommendations of
> your lordships also.
>   Far, my lords, shall it be from me to endeavour, by the
> rules of law, to justify the crime I have been convicted of,
> nor can I express the affliction I am under for that
> unfortunate gentleman whose death has occasioned this
> trouble to your lordships, and misfortune to myself; but if
> through the mediation of your lordships, the royal mercy
> should be extended to me, the remainder of my life shall
> be employed in preventing other gentlemen from falling
> into those unhappy circumstances I now appear in.

The court ignored Clark's plea and sentenced him to death. Like juries, judges rarely explained the reasons behind their decisions and we can only speculate as to why Clark received such a severe sentence. Perhaps the judges had been persuaded by Serjeant Hayward's concerns about the pernicious effects of duelling. Or perhaps the court, concerned by the crime wave which appeared to be sweeping London following the end of the war, was determined to demonstrate its willingness to punish serious crime with the full rigour of the law.

In any case, Clark was not executed. No doubt repeating the arguments used in his defence, he, or his friends, was able to petition the Lords Justices to respite his sentence and eventually pardon him. In the end, this unfortunate and awkwardly conducted duel led to the death of only one of the participants.[17]

They Set Them To Like Two Cocks

Gentlemen were not the only men who settled their differences and defended their honour through fights conducted according to agreed rules. But the lower class version of the duel, the boxing match, had distinctive characteristics. Rather than fighting with swords or pistols, men used their fists. And while duels were typically conducted in secret, boxing matches took place in public, attracting large crowds and becoming the subject of furious betting. This sometimes led the audience to encourage the fighters to continue the fight long after they were ready to stop. As a result, what should have been a safer form of combat, given the lack of weapons, could easily become fatal.

On 13 June 1751 a group of old shopmates, both carvers and sawyers, were drinking together in the Crown Alehouse (also known as the King's Head) in Compton Street, Soho, when an argument broke out. As one of the carvers, Charles Troop, later testified:

> George Bartholomew and Thomas Prince came into the
> company both very much disguised in liquor; they called

> for six pennyworth of rumbo [rum punch]. The people let
> them have it; then they called for another; they would not
> let them have any more; then they called for a pot of beer.
> I offered to go away, they both insisted on my staying.
> Prince lent Bartholomew two shillings; Bartholomew said
> afterwards he had not got it; words ensuing, they threw
> the beer about the house. Then George Bartholomew gave
> him half a crown, and Thomas Prince gave him sixpence
> out of it. Then Bartholomew fell upon me about this
> money I saw him borrow, and said I ought to be beat, and
> he would lick me; then Bartholomew pulled out a crown,
> and said he'd fight me for it; then he took a handful of
> silver and threw it upon the table, and said he'd fight me
> for a shilling; then I said I'd fight for only a dozen of beer,
> so we went to fight for that shilling.

A dispute about borrowed money escalated into a challenge
to Charles Troop's masculinity, which could only be settled
by a fight, and, as was conventional with boxing matches,
they agreed to fight for a small prize. George Smith, a
sawyer, agreed to hold the money, and Prince, a carver, was
to be Bartholomew's second. (It is not clear who acted as
Troop's second.) According to Smith, the assembled men
tried to prevent the fight:

> I and three more were at the King's Head; we were on one
> side of the house, and Prince, Troop, and Bartholomew on
> the other; they had some words so as to come to fighting,
> I cannot tell what about. We begged they would be easy
> and not fight. They continued wrangling some time; at
> last they were to fight for a dozen of beer, the money was
> put down, I took it up. They wanted to fight in the house,
> the people desired them to be quiet; then they agreed to
> go and fight in the field.

From Compton Street, the men walked up Wardour
Street, past Oxford Street, and into Marybone Fields, an
open space on the edge of the metropolis which at this date
was littered with debris from the construction of nearby

houses. Smith's description of the fight suggests that it was conducted according to the rules of 'fair play':

> They stripped and shook hands (they had both shook
> hands several times in the public house before, and
> declared no animosity). A lemon was bought and divided
> and each of them had half to suck before they began. I
> took up Bartholomew's clothes, and called out for a friend
> of mine to take care of the other's. They fought as near as
> I can guess about half an hour; a great many falls they
> had on both sides, sometimes one uppermost, sometimes
> the other. They both received blows, but the falls were a
> great deal worse than the blows.

By sucking on the lemon, the boxers would reduce the bleeding from any facial injuries they might receive. Other witnesses reported that they had 'three set-tos', meaning that the fight was restarted three times after the parties had fallen. While Prince reported that the two 'fought fair boxing, what we call so, about twenty minutes', another witness, Thomas Bugden, reported an incident where Troop attacked Bartholomew after he had fallen, but he did not attach much importance to it:

> I had not an opportunity of seeing the whole of it, but I
> saw two falls. Once Troop fell upon Bartholomew with
> his knee in his guts, which the company cried out shame
> on; but they fought a long time after that.

What all the witnesses agreed on was that Bartholomew and Troop were very drunk, lending a somewhat comical character to the fight. When they attempted to shake hands at the start, they staggered and missed and had to try again. During the fight, according to Charles Lucas, a sawyer, 'The two men were so drunk that as they went to strike at each other they missed their blows, and sometimes pitched on their heads or fell away.'

The fight took place on a Thursday and attracted a considerable crowd, consisting of passers-by and men working on the nearby construction sites. Thomas Bugden, for example, who was at work in Marybone Fields, saw the two men going to fight and recognised them as fellow workmen and went to watch. John Doller, a 16- or 17-year-old son of a bucklemaker who lived nearby on Tyburn Road, appears to have just been walking by when he 'saw a mob, and went up to them'. James Simpson, a japanner, had been sitting in the parlour of his house on Wardour Street when he saw the crowd heading towards the fields. He asked what was the matter, was told that two carvers were going to fight, and went with a neighbour to watch them.

The presence of a large crowd interfered with the fight and kept it going longer than the combatants wished. Lucas reported that they barely had room to swing their arms:

> Thomas Prince, in assisting his friend, got one eye almost
> knocked out, and there were so many strangers come
> about that he and others were afraid to go nigh almost.

As James Simpson reported, the crowd shouted encouragement from the sidelines, maximising their enjoyment of the match by prolonging it:

> After they had fought a minute, or a minute and a half,
> one of them lay down, he was taken up and set to, they
> fought the space of another minute, then there was
> another fall. There came a parcel of fellows from making
> bricks, I believe there were 20 of them, and said, you will
> not leave yet. Troop seemed sick one time and lay down.
> These people by main strength got them up again and set
> them to like two cocks, and made people afraid to attempt
> to part them.

The match ended after one of the falls when George Bartholomew could not get up.

At this point the crowd left. George Smith reported that 'After the battle was over Bartholomew lay alone on the ground; I lifted him up, he desired me to let him alone; I helped to put on his shirt and waistcoat'. Three men carried him to the nearby White Hart alehouse in Windmill Street, off Tottenham Court Road. John Doller helped wash Bartholomew's face, which was covered with blood. Bartholomew then drank a glass of brandy and vomited blood. He was having difficulty speaking and a coach was called to take him home. Bartholomew's wife, Jane, was present when he arrived:

> On the 13th of June my husband was brought home in a
> coach, and never spoke after. He was put to bed, and there
> died between four and five the next morning. He was
> bruised in every part from head to foot, not a place in him
> was free, his private parts also. He was as black as a
> Negro.

As a suspicious death, the case was investigated by the coroner. He held his inquisition three days later and heard testimony from seven witnesses, including Thomas Tipping, a surgeon who inspected the body after death. Despite the fact that all that the key events of this story had been witnessed by several persons, the witnesses, perhaps in an attempt to ensure Troop was not charged with murder, provided very little evidence about the cause of the quarrel or the possible cause of death, simply stating that the participants were drunk and had fought fairly. At the inquest Smith testified that:

> They had several falls and fought for about half an hour
> and they boxed fairly. When they gave out he took up the
> deceased. But he can't tell who gave out first. They shook
> hands before they began and when they gave out they
> shook hands again.

With similar brevity and emphasis on the handshake, James Simpson described the fight as follows:

> Charles Troop stripped and trembled very much and when
> the deceased and he came together they shook hands, but

both seemed to be very drunk. Then they attacked each
other and Bartholomew endeavouring to make a blow, he
fell down. They had several falls, but did not seem to hurt
one another. There was a brick bat near where the
deceased fell, but he did not see him fall on it.

It was the surgeon, Thomas Tipping, who provided the key
evidence, suggesting (as hinted by Simpson) that the death
was caused by one of Bartholomew's falls:

He opened the head of the deceased George Bartholomew
and found a fracture on the *oss planum* near the left eye
which he apprehends could not have been done with the
fist. But it might have been done either by a stick or a
violent weapon or a fall on a stone. There was another
wound on the forehead but not mortal in its nature. But
the first was. He then opened the body and found some
extravasated blood and the liver putrefied.[18]

We have no information about the deliberations conducted
by the coroner's jury, but their verdict was manslaughter.
Troop, they ruled, should be held responsible for
Bartholomew's death, although the verdict judged that the
killing had not been premeditated or with malicious intent.

When the City of London grand jury met about two
weeks later they came to a different view and indicted Troop
for murder. He was therefore put on trial at the Old Bailey
on 3 July on charges of both murder and manslaughter. With
the witnesses at the trial providing very similar evidence to
that provided to the coroner, however, no prosecution
evidence was presented to suggest that the killing was either
premeditated or malicious. In his defence, Troop testified (in
a passage cited at the start of this account) that although the
dispute originated in an argument, the reason it ended up in
a fight was because they had mutually decided to fight for a
prize of some beer money. Key additional evidence was once
again provided by Tipping, who now seemed more certain
about the cause of death:

> I opened his body by the desire of the coroner's jury, but
> did not open his skull. The parts of the body were all
> sound and well, only putrified by the extravasated blood.
> There were some external bruises, but none but the
> fracture had gone far in. There was a large contusion on
> the scrotum; his head was contused violently, and there
> were two great wounds upon it. I imagine the fracture was
> owing to the fall, as it seemed to be done by the round
> end of a stone about the breadth of a shilling, which
> fracture I look upon to be the cause of his death.

Charles Colwell, a witness for the defence who had not
testified at the coroner's inquest, confirmed this theory:

> I was the first that came into the field. I gathered the loose
> bricks that lay about and threw them at a distance, and
> cleared a place to fight in; the ground was dry and
> prodigious hard. When they first engaged Troop made a
> blow at Bartholomew and retired I believe near ten or
> twelve yards, staggered and fell. The deceased followed
> him up and waited for his getting up again. My opinion is
> that by this means they might get amongst more
> brickbats, and by the fall he might receive his damage.

Accepting this explanation, the jury found Troop guilty of
manslaughter and he was sentenced to branding. More than
250 years later, this seems a justifiable verdict in the case of
a death that was clearly the result of the public enthusiasm
for conducting, and watching, boxing matches. These were
fights intended to settle disputes and provide entertainment,
not result in death.[19]

Down With the Irish

*Crowd protest was a common and largely accepted feature of
daily street life in London. Riots rarely involved violence against
people; it was their houses that bore the brunt of the crowd's
anger, with the new sash windows found in Georgian houses
providing a tempting target for stones and rubbish. The popular
expression 'to pull down a house' did not normally mean*

demolition down to its foundations, but everything but the
brickwork was vulnerable to damage. While the violence was
thus circumscribed, the underlying threat to personal safety as
well as property should not be underestimated.

The streets, pubs and coffeehouses of London were
simmering with fear and discontent in the summer of 1736.
The threat of a Jacobite rebellion lurked in the background
and the government, led by the long-serving Prime Minister
Robert Walpole, continued to pass unpopular legislation.
The Gin Act, which attempted to reduce consumption of
this popular drink by imposing a duty of 20s per gallon and
requiring all vendors to take out a licence costing the huge
sum of £50, was set to take effect on 29 September. In July, a
small bomb (containing phosphorous) went off in
Westminster Hall. No one was injured, but it threw about
the hall a parcel of handbills with a list of laws deemed
injurious to the lives and trade of the country. Top of the list
was the Gin Act. Although Jacobites were behind the
explosion, they were not the only ones who were dissatisfied.
An act against smuggling imposed harsh penalties on those
trading in untaxed goods and an act authorising the building
of a second bridge across the Thames, Westminster Bridge,
threatened to put many watermen out of work. As J. Furnell,
a government agent working in Shoreditch in the East End
of London reported:

> It is evident that there are great discontents and
> murmurings through all this mobbish part of town. The
> Gin Act and the Smuggling Act sticks hard in the
> stomachs of the meaner sort of people and the Bridge Act
> greatly exasperates the watermen insomuch that they
> make no scruple of declaring publicly that they will join
> in any mischief that can be set on foot.[20]

On top of all this, an influx of Irish workmen who were
willing to accept lower wages than their English

counterparts threatened the jobs of weavers and building workers, particularly in Spitalfields and Shoreditch. Always the subject of racial and religious prejudice, the Irish constituted an obvious lightning rod for popular hostility.

Twenty years earlier, in 1716, the tower of the medieval church at St Leonard's Shoreditch fell down during a service. It was only in 1736 that the rebuilding finally began to a design by the city architect, George Dance the elder, in imitation of Christopher Wren's more famous St Mary le Bow. During the demolition of the old church that summer, the contractor, William Goswell, a vestryman, faced a strike by his English workmen demanding higher wages. He dismissed them and engaged Irish labour from the area for half or two-thirds the wages he paid his English workers. When the English workers complained, fights broke out. Shortly thereafter a broadside was distributed throughout the neighbouring streets, whipping up hatred against the Irish by evoking their alleged violent temperament. It claimed that a female Irish cook had sworn 'it was nothing to cut up an English man's heart', while her husband allegedly offered 'ten guineas for a pint of English blood'.[21]

The broadside had the desired effect. On Monday 26 July hundreds gathered in Shoreditch, shouting 'Down with the Irish'. The next evening the crowd reached 4,000 and attacked and gutted a pub where the Irish ate and drank. According to the *London Evening Post*, the crowd 'pulled down the house almost to the ground in a few minutes, drank up all the beer in the cellar, and carried away and destroyed the goods in triumph'.[22] The City authorities unsuccessfully attempted to disperse the crowds by reading the Riot Act. The militia was called and played cat and mouse with the mob all evening, with the crowds only dispersing at daybreak. Thursday witnessed similar scenes. Asked by a militia lieutenant to explain their grievances, the 'captain of the mob' answered:

> Mr Goswell had paid off his English labourers and
> employed Irish because they worked cheaper and several
> of the master weavers employed none but Irish by which
> means the English manufacturers were starving and that
> they now chose to be hanged than starved.[23]

The lieutenant promised to redress their grievances and the crowd dispersed, shouting two or three huzzas.

But the crowds formed again on Friday evening, starting in Spitalfields around 7 pm, at the beginning of what was to become the worst night of violence. They moved down Brick Lane towards the poorer districts of Whitechapel where many Irish men and women lived. Looking eastward up Whitechapel Street, Richard Burton saw them coming:

> I was at the end of Red Lion Street, and I saw the mob
> coming down Bell Yard, with sticks and lighted links
> [torches]. One of them made a sort of a speech directing
> the rest to go down Church Lane, to the Gentleman and
> Porter. There was about 50 or 60 of them then, and they
> had 2 or 3 links with them. One read from a paper the
> signs of the Gentleman and Porter, the Bull and Butcher,
> and the Tavern in Well Street. I did not hear them make
> any declaration what was to be done, but I went directly to
> Mr Allen's to inform him they had great sticks, like stakes.

Having warned Allen, Richard Burton resorted to subterfuge in an attempt to save his house:

> While I was standing at Allen's door, the mob came down.
> I told them the house had been mine for a fortnight, and
> that the man who kept it before was gone. One of them
> was called Captain Tom the Barber, and was in a striped
> Banjan [loose flannel shirt]. I desired him to use me
> favourably, and told him it was my house. They said they
> knew I was not Irish by my tongue, and I should not be
> hurt. I made them set up candles in the windows, and
> pacified the mob seemingly well, but a woman telling
> them it was a sham, and that I was only the brewer's
> cooper, the sticks flew immediately and beat the candle
> out of my hand, as I stood at the door.

Graves Aikin, who lived nearby in Lemon Street, also heard that the mob was coming:

> July 30, at night, my child came to me about 10 o'clock
> and told me there was a great mob gone by. I went home
> and a lodger told me the great cry was, put up your lights.
> My wife was very much frightened and begged me to get
> out. I told her I would stay, but she insisting upon my
> leaving the house. I went out and heard the mob at Mr
> Allen's. I went thither and heard them cry, Down with the
> Irish – down with the Irish. I saw them breaking Allen's
> windows, and raking in the kennel, I suppose for stones,
> but I cannot say I saw them take any up. Then I heard
> them enquire for my house. A woman directed them to it,
> and they fell immediately upon it.

Two of the houses that were hardest hit were the Rose and Crown, off Church Lane, and the Bull and Butcher, at the end of Church Lane on Cable Street. Their owners later testified to the damage in court:

> James Farrel. I live in Rose and Crown Alley in Church
> Lane. On the 30th of July I was at home. My wife was
> gone to bed with my godchild, and I was undressed and in
> my shirt when the noise came down the alley. I opened
> my window and looked out, and heard them knocking at
> the next house. Hall and Kelly cried out, Damn you that is
> not the house, and then they came to my house. I had a
> candle in my hand, and saw that Page and Kelly were the
> first that attacked my windows with their clubs. Kelly's
> wife opened her door, gave them a candle, and cried,
> Damn them, have their heart's blood. I was at the window
> with a candle in my hand, and saw Robert Page break my
> windows, and the middle panel of the door.

By this stage Farrel had begun to fear for his life:

> When the door was broke, I thought it high time to get
> away, so I opened a back casement and got out in my shirt
> from the first story. I said to my wife, you can't get out,
> you must be at their mercy. I had no sooner spoke, but a

board was thrown in which hit her on the thigh. I jumped
out of the window into Hog Yard, and heard the mob
crying, Damn it, which are Irish houses?

John Waldon kept the Bull and Butcher in Cable Street:

I have a great number of country shopkeepers lodge in my
house when they come to town. We have some 60 or 70
people in the house, but that night we had but 18. The
30th of July every one in the house was gone to bed but
myself, and I was stripped to all but my stockings and
breeches; but hearing the mob come down, and crying,
Down with the Irish, and seeing all the houses
illuminated, I bid all my lodgers get up and shift for their
lives. I got over a wall 8 feet high, and some of the
neighbours helped the lodgers off. I left the house to their
mercy (for my wife was out at a woman's labour) and they
stole and broke every thing I had. I stayed in the house,
till the shutters and glass all flew in together. Six of my
shutters were broke, and 70 odd panes of glass, which
damage cost me £3 13s. to repair.

Frightened residents summoned help from Justice
Phillips, the local magistrate, who immediately demanded
military assistance, telling his neighbours:

Reading the proclamation [the Riot Act] will signify
nothing. If you will go to the Tower and give my service
to the governor, and desire his assistance, I will venture
my person. They went, and the governor sent 30 men to
my door, and the captain told me, they had orders to go
with me and follow my directions.

The mob, however, had learned how to evade the military,
and so special tactics were called for:

I desired him that his men might march quietly without
beat of drum and in the dark and when we came to the
end of Lemon Street the houses were all illuminated and
we heard a great noise, as if they were knocking the
houses to pieces.

Justice Philips's intention was to arrest the largest number possible:

> The street was very light, and I could see (at a distance) the mob beating against the shutters with their clubs and could hear the glass fly. So I said to the captain, now let us be upon them at once. I drew my sword and ran to the house they were attacking, and that man Page, I took him with his club breaking the windows. I could not tell whether he might not make use of it upon me, therefore I told him, if you don't surrender I'll run you through. The soldiers at the word of command had stretched themselves into a line and then enclosed as many of them as they could. Page I took myself, driving furiously at the windows.

Captain Joseph Hudson had direct command of the troops:

> As the mob were beating against the front of the house, Mr Phillips and I at the front of our men, with our swords drawn, struck at one or two of them, and two or three of those who were attacking the house we seized immediately.

In the process of wielding their swords and making arrests, the soldiers inflicted several injuries, as one of them, Daniel Barnes, later admitted:

> I was indeed at the taking of William Orman Rod. He was cut in the head and was then very much disguised with his own blood. I remember I took Orman Rod out of the mob, and that either my captain or Mr Phillips cut him over the head. He was within 4 or 5 yards of the door, but I did not see him strike, nor did I see any thing in his hand.

At this point, according to Richard Burton, the rest of the mob instantly dispersed:

> Justice Phillips coming down, and the captain with his soldiers, they took some of them and the rest made off immediately, and were gone as suddenly as if a hole had

been ready dug in the bottom of the street, and they had
all dropped into it at once.

Nine were apprehended and taken to the watchhouse,
located in the middle of Cable Street near the entrance to
Lemon Street – the site of the Cable Street riots 200 years
later. Given its proximity to the scene of the riots, however,
there were considerable fears that the crowd might try to
rescue the prisoners. As Justice Phillips told the court:

> Those we had taken were carried to the watchhouse, and
> that I might be more sure of the prisoners I called them
> over at the watchhouse and took down their names. Then
> we posted 12 soldiers with their bayonets on their muskets
> round the watchhouse, because we were apprehensive the
> mob would rescue the prisoners.

Five were put on trial for riot at the Old Bailey, but not
until the October sessions, two and a half months after the
events in question. It may be that popular opposition to the
Gin Act, which came into force in late September,
prompted the government to press ahead with the trials
despite the relatively weak prosecution case. All five
defendants claimed that they were innocent bystanders who
had been swept up by the soldiers in the commotion of the
riot. William Orman Rod, a blacksmith from Church Lane,
told the court that 'hearing the soldiers were come, I went
out to see the sight, and was taken'. Thomas Putrode went
outside to look for his wife, and 'the mob came past me, and
the soldiers took me'. Joshua Hall claimed that the soldiers
had mistook some wood which he was carrying home from
his job for a weapon:

> I worked at Mr Sharp's, a sawyer and lath render. As I
> came home from work I stayed half an hour, as others did,
> to look on. The people that swore I had a club in my hand
> are mistaken. Tis common for lath-renders to bring home
> a bit of a chip or a lath in their hands.

Witnesses testified that they had only seen Robert Page and Robert Mickey actually causing damage, though Putrode and Joshua Hall were seen shouting 'Down with the Irish'. The only testimony against William Orman Rod was that he had been taken 'out of the mob'. Nonetheless, in a climate of fear about a breakdown of public order, all five were found guilty. They were sentenced to between one and two years imprisonment, an unusually harsh punishment for rioters, and they were required to find sureties for their good behaviour.[24]

Pull Down All the Bawdy Houses

Brothels were a traditional target of popular hostility – in the seventeenth century, crowds of apprentices demolished them annually on Shrove Tuesday to reduce the temptations of sin during Lent. Eighteenth-century rioters occasionally continued the custom, but with different motives. Owing to worries about rising crime, the government attempted to suppress one riot of this sort in 1749 with particular vigour. But in this case prosecuting the rioters was not easy, since the authorities had difficulty proving that they had apprehended the right men.

When the Grand Jury for the City and Liberty of Westminster met on Thursday 29 June 1749 to decide whether pending criminal prosecutions should proceed to trial, the session began, as was traditional, by an address ('the charge') from the chairman of the Westminster justices of the peace. Henry Fielding, who had just been appointed to this role after having become a justice of the peace the previous November, delivered a reasonably conventional speech on this occasion. He provided an outline of the key principles of the criminal law before moving on to the more topical part of his speech, where he identified the most threatening offences of the day which merited the special attention of the grand jury. With the recent arrival in the city of large numbers of demobilised sailors and soldiers with money in their pockets and sex on their minds, Fielding reminded jurors of their duty to indict bawdy house keepers 'as a matter of serious and weighty consideration'. Brothels were the cause of 'many mischiefs, the fairest end whereof is beggary; and tend directly to the overthrow of men's bodies, to the wasting of their livelihoods, and to the endangering of their souls'.[25]

Coincidentally, two days later the *London Evening Post* reported that a brothel had been destroyed in a riot:

> On Saturday two sailors thinking themselves ill used at a house, the sign of The Crown, near the New Church in the Strand, went out, denouncing vengeance, and in a little time returned with a great number of armed sailors, who entirely demolished all the goods, cut all the feather beds to pieces, and strewed the feathers in the street; demolished all the wearing apparel, and turned the women they found in the house naked into the street. They then broke all the windows and considerably damaged another house adjoining. A guard of soldiers was sent for from the Tilt Yard, but they came too late to prevent the destruction of everything in the house.[26]

During a visit to The Crown, three sailors had been robbed of 30 guineas, four Portuguese coins (moidores), a banknote worth £20 and two watches. When they complained to the keeper, they were met with 'foul language and blows' and so decided to seek revenge. The following night, another brothel, The Bunch of Grapes, was burned to the ground, and the mob broke open two watchhouses and rescued those who had been arrested for rioting.

Shortly after midnight the sailors started work on a third house, The Star. Around 100 spectators gathered to watch the sailors, and 'expressed their satisfaction by continuing huzzas'.[27] The arrival of a body of soldiers, announced by a beating drum, brought an abrupt halt to the proceedings and

Figure 2.04 'The Mob Assembled to Pull Down the Bawdy-House Kept by Peter Wood in the Strand, 1st July, 1749'. Credit: City of Westminster Archives Centre

the mob fled, leaving the destruction half-completed. Many furnishings remained undisturbed and, although goods had been thrown into the street, the rioters had not yet had the opportunity to set them on fire. Several men were arrested.

Around one in the morning another man was arrested in a nearby alley. Edward Fritter, a watchman, testified in a sworn deposition:

> As he was at his stand at the upper end of Bell Yard,
> Samuel Marsh, another watchman, called out to him,
> 'stop that man before you', upon which this informant ran
> after him, and at about a hundred yards distance overtook
> him, and pushed him up against the rails of Carey Street.
> And this informant then said to him, 'so, brother, what is
> all this you have got here?' To which the man answered, 'I
> am an unfortunate young man, and have married one of
> the women of the town, who hath pawned all my clothes,
> and I have got all her linen for it'.

The man, who was drunk, was Bosavern Penlez, a journeyman barber and peruke maker and son of a clergyman. Inside his shirt he had stuffed a bundle of linen, consisting of 10 laced caps, four laced handkerchiefs, three pairs of laced ruffles, two laced clouts (pieces of cloth), five plain handkerchiefs, five plain aprons and one laced apron. He was taken to the watchhouse, where he offered a different explanation, claiming that he had picked up the bundle in the street. The next day, he and the bundle were brought before Henry Fielding, where the linen was identified by Jane Wood, wife of the keeper of The Star, as her property.[28]

Penlez was one of several prisoners who were examined that Monday in Henry Fielding's house in Bow Street as a mob gathered outside. As the interview with Penlez and the others continued, the mob rescued one of the prisoners and threatened to break into the house. Although hostile to brothels, Fielding was more concerned about public order and so committed the rioters to prison to await trial, charging them with the serious offence of 'high treason in levying war against his majesty by riotously and tumultuously assembling themselves together in order to suppress and pull down all bawdy houses'.[29]

James Cecil, a constable, described the difficulties he had
in conveying the prisoners to Newgate:

> Though an officer with a very large guard of soldiers
> attended upon the said occasion, it was not without the
> utmost difficulty that the prisoners were conveyed in
> coaches through the street, the mob frequently
> endeavouring to break in upon the soldiers and crowding
> towards the coach doors.

As Cecil passed the Old Bailey, 'He saw a great mob there,
who had been breaking the windows of some house or
houses there; several of the said mob were in sailor's habits,
but upon the approach of the soldiers they all ran away.'[30]
Meanwhile Fielding received information that a body of
about 4,000 sailors had assembled on Tower Hill and
intended to march to Temple Bar that evening. With
speculation that the sailors would raid the armoury at the
Tower for arms, Fielding felt justified in requesting more
troops to patrol the West End. But the outbreak of rioting
was now over.

Following several rescues and the death of one the
prisoners, only five men remained in custody as the Old
Bailey sessions approached. The decision to charge all five
under the terms of the 1715 Riot Act was controversial: the
act, which mandated the death penalty, had long been seen
as an example of Whig tyranny and had rarely been used.
Instead, most riotous behaviour was tried under the common
law as a misdemeanour and those convicted were normally
only fined. Moreover, a key stipulation of the Riot Act, that
a proclamation to disperse the riot had to be read by a
magistrate, had never actually been carried out during these
disturbances. As in 1715 when the Act was originally passed,
it appears to have been the government's fear of more serious
unrest which led the act to be invoked in this case.

Two of the charges were rejected by the grand jury before
the case came to court, and only three men, Bosavern

Penlez, John Wilson, and Benjamin Lander actually stood
trial at the Old Bailey on 6 September 'for that they,
together with divers other persons to the number of forty
and upwards, being feloniously and riotously assembled to
the disturbance of the public peace, did begin to demolish
the dwelling house of Peter Wood'. The chief witness for the
prosecution was Wood, keeper of The Star:

> I live at The Star in the Strand. I saw these prisoners at
> the bar at my house, in the night betwixt the 2d and 3d of
> July. They came betwixt 12 and 1 o'clock; there were I
> believe about 400 of them; they came ringing a bell, and
> calling out, the host, the host. The watchman came
> running over the way, and said, Mr Wood, they are
> coming, they are coming. About fifty of them passed by
> the door. I was in great hopes they would have gone by; I
> made them a bow and said good night, till such time as
> the bell came opposite my door. Then they that were past
> my door wheeled about and fell back towards George's
> coffeehouse door, then they all surrounded the whole
> place. The first stroke that was given was at the lamp at
> my door. I advanced from the door directly and begged
> for mercy; saying, Gentlemen, if I have done any thing
> wrong, take me to the watchhouse or any place of safety.
> Then they all fell to breaking my windows; upon that I
> fell upon my knees. They broke the shutters, sashes and
> the glass of my windows. Said I, I'll give you 10 nay 20
> pounds if you will desist; with that they seemed to stop a
> little. Somebody amongst them called out here is 10 here
> is 20 pounds offered, but upon this there was a grave
> gentleman came jumping from over the way.

This man, whose name was Wrench, was indicted for
promoting the riot, but the grand jury rejected the charge.
According to Wood's wife, Jane:

> There was an elderly man came from over the way and
> said, pull away, my boys, take no money, down with the
> bawdy-houses, down with the bawdy-houses. Then they
> cried out where are your whores?

Eight or 10 men entered the house through the window.
According to Peter Wood:

> Wilson and Penlez were among them. They fell to
> breaking between the passage and the parlour. I saw the
> two prisoners break the partition with their sticks, and
> pull the pieces out with their hands. All the furniture in
> the parlour was destroyed; they threw all into the street. I
> was knocked down with a stick on the stairs, and there I
> lay. Some of them called out, and said the man is killed. I
> hearing that thought I would lie a little longer, thinking by
> that to raise their compassion. Then they went into the
> back parlour; I cannot immediately say what they did
> there; then they went up stairs. I was on the stairs; Penlez
> and Wilson said, You dog, are you not dead yet? They
> cried, all up, all up, all up; then I kneeled down on my
> knees, kissed their hands and begged for mercy.

Wood was saved by the arrival of the soldiers:

> Then came the guard with a drum beating, then they all
> took to flight. They rang the bell and cried out, the guards,
> the guards; so they went all away that could directly.
> Lander was taken upstairs.

He then went to inspect the damage:

> In the dining room, which had before in it a bed, pictures,
> chairs, a mahogany table and other furniture. Every thing
> was gone out of the room except a little marble slab,
> which I had put in a corner of the room. The windows
> were all torn to pieces, the frames all pulled down.

Peter Wood's testimony was corroborated by his wife
Jane, and servant James Reeves. All three were then cross-
examined by the defence counsel, who tried to suggest that
none had actually seen the three defendants in the house
causing damage:

> Question.   Was Lander one of them at their first coming
>   up?

Peter Wood.	I did not see him then.
Q.	Did you see him any time before the guards came?
Wood.	Yes, I saw him in the passage.
Q.	How long before the guards came?
Wood.	About half an hour before.
Jane Wood.	Lander knocked me down, and I was beaten almost to a jelly.
James Reeves.	I saw Lander there about a quarter of an hour before the guards came; I saw him strike Mr Wood over the head, as his back was towards him. I saw him push one of the partition boards down in the passage. I did not see him in the parlour. I never saw him do any farther mischief than with his shoulder.
Q.	As to Wilson, can you mark any particular thing that he did?
Peter Wood.	Yes, he broke the shutters, and after the place was laid open, I saw him come into the parlour.
Q.	Did any others besides him break the shutters?
Wood.	Yes, many.
Q.	How come you to be so positive of the prisoners among so many?
Wood.	Upon my kissing their hands.
Q.	Did you kiss the hands of all three?
Wood.	No, Sir.
Jane Wood.	I held Wilson by the face and stroked him, and begged they would desist.
James Reeves.	I saw Wilson in the parlour just as the settee bed was going to be thrown out; I saw him help to lift the bed out.
Q.	How could you distinguish Penlez, when you say you was knocked down upon the stairs?

Peter Wood.	I was upon my legs when I saw him, there was nobody betwixt me and him, and I had hold of him by the hand two or three times, begging of him to desist. They cried out, they would destroy all the bawdy-houses in general. I believe he was a little in liquor.
Q.	Did you see him before the guards came?
Wood.	Yes, I did, sir, I saw him at the beginning of the riot at the outside.
Jane Wood.	Penlez broke the clock with a stick, and the inside partition in the entry.
James Reeves.	The first man that came to the door was Penlez, he came in at the door, then he came in at the window, and was the first man that struck at the clock. I saw him break the window shutter. When he came into the fore parlour he began to play away at the things, the glasses, the pictures. He beat down the bird-cages; the partition that parts the entry from the parlour; he was there the whole time; he was the first man that went up stairs; he was the greatest rascal amongst them all. I saw Mr Wood lying on the stairs, and heard Penlez say to him, You dog, are you not dead yet?

Defence counsel was more successful in trapping Reeves and Jane Wood into giving contradictory evidence about the size of the stick Penlez allegedly carried:

Question.	What had Penlez in his hand?
James Reeves.	He had a large stick, three foot and a half, or four foot long.
Q. to Mrs Wood.	What did Penlez break the clock with?
Jane Wood.	He had a short stick with which he struck it.
Q.	How long was it do you think?
Jane Wood.	Not long enough to walk with.

Witnesses for the defence testified to Peter Wood's bad reputation and the much more respectable character of the defendants. In cross-examination, Wood was asked why neither he nor his landlord had paid the scavenger's rate for removing rubbish. Wood was forced to say: 'The reason of it is upon the account of what some people say, it is a disorderly house. He never paid it'. Instead the tax was paid by John Thompson, who did not live there but 'has come sometimes to cut the ladies' hair in the parlour'. Wood was also forced to explain that he had been fined £20 for selling liquor without a licence. The defence then called John Nixon, the collector of the scavenger's rate. Asked if he believed that Wood and his wife were to be believed on their oaths, he said:

> Upon my word, I think not. For my part I would not hang
> a dog or a cat upon their evidence, they keep such a bad
> house and other things. They have threatened my life, and
> my neighbours are afraid to appear against him.

Perhaps believing that this was sufficient to discredit the testimony against them, Wilson and Penlez offered no further evidence beyond several witnesses who testified to their good character.

Lander, however, also had an alibi. Going home shortly after midnight with some friends, he had met the soldiers who were going to suppress the riot. One of his companions, Edward Ives, told the court that a soldier told them:

> They were going to disperse a mob in the Strand, and that
> was the third time they had been doing it that night. He
> told us, he would be obliged to us if we could get a pint
> of beer, saying he was very dry.

They obliged, and then Lander followed the soldiers to The Star. While inside the house, he was arrested. This evidence directly contradicted prosecution testimony that Lander had been present causing damage *before* the soldiers arrived. On this basis, Lander was acquitted. Wilson and Penlez, however, were convicted and sentenced to death, but with a recommendation to mercy.

News of the sentences caused public outrage and hundreds of Londoners petitioned the king for a reprieve. Petitions came not only from nearby parishioners, who had long suffered from the presence of bawdy houses in their neighbourhoods and who felt the riots were not that big a crime, but also from many respectable gentlemen. Newspapers reported that petitions were submitted from over 300 'principal inhabitants' of the parish of St Clement Danes, a group of 'worthy and honourable gentlemen', 'a worthy society of gentlemen of distinction', and 'several gentlemen of great repute'.[31] Even more surprisingly, the 12 jurors who had convicted Wilson and Penlez petitioned for a reprieve, both on the grounds of 'humanity and compassion' and because they had come to the conclusion that Peter Wood's testimony at the trial could not be trusted. They also felt that the case for the defence had not been as strong as it could have been, noting the 'fatal neglect' to produce witnesses to contradict Wood's evidence.[32]

At 10 pm on the evening before the execution a messenger arrived at Newgate Prison with the news that Wilson, but not Penlez, was to be reprieved. Why was Penlez left to hang? Days before the execution, the circumstances concerning his original arrest came to light. As the Ordinary of Newgate reported:

> There was a circumstance started a day or two before the execution which carried a bad face with it, and which no doubt was a great means of preventing mercy being extended towards him; which is, that when he was taken, there was a bundle of linen found upon him, tied up in a handkerchief. When this came to light, twas thought necessary to ask him particularly as to this fact. To this, his reply to me and others was that it was true, he had such a bundle, but how he came by it, he did not

remember, nor could he recollect whether he himself tied
it up, or any body else.[33]

In fact, Penlez had originally been indicted for burglary as
well as riot, but once convicted on one capital charge the
judge had ruled that he could not be tried again on another
charge relating to the same incident. Most people were
unaware of the circumstances of his arrest and the second
indictment, but Henry Fielding himself appears to have
brought this evidence to the attention of the crown. Faced
with the contradictory demands of a desire to demonstrate
mercy and the need for an exemplary punishment to address
the current crime problem and dissuade the mob from
further rioting, the king took the obvious step of pardoning
one of the convicts and executing the other. With the
additional charge of theft laid at Penlez's door, he was the
obvious candidate for hanging.

Penlez would not be the only person to suffer on
18 October. He was joined on the scaffold by 14 others,
13 sailors and a sailor's wife. Paradoxically, although he
was hanged for participating in a riot instigated by sailors,
he was not a sailor, while all the others condemned to die
that day for other crimes were sailors (or related to one).
That morning, as the *London Evening Post* reported, a
procession formed outside Newgate Prison:

> Between nine and ten the fifteen malefactors were put into
> six carts; the sheriff was preceded by the warden of Wood
> Street Compter, and his own livery servants in due order;
> next the sheriff alone, with his gold chain round his neck,
> and a white wand in his hand, the proper tokens of his
> office, followed by the City Marshall, and several
> attendants two and two; and the procession closed with
> the criminals, guarded by legal officers.

At Holborn Bar, where the carefully ordered procession
moved from the City of London into Middlesex, it was met
by an officer and a party of soldiers, who offered to

accompany the procession to preserve order. In the light of the immense public opposition to the hanging of Penlez, this may seem a reasonable request. The sheriff, however, conscious that use of the military was more likely to foment than prevent disorder, rejected the offer, much to the satisfaction of the newspapers. The sheriff:

> Genteelly dismissed the officer from any further attendance, as not apprehending any necessity for the support of the *military power* in the due execution of the law.

The paper then painted a very orderly picture of the executions:

> At the place of execution the criminals appeared all to behave very penitent; and the carts drew off about twelve o'clock. The spectators were infinitely more numerous than ever were seen on the like occasion, but without the least tumult or disorder. Tis hoped that the great and remarkable example set by Mr Sheriff Janssen, in executing (agreeable to our constitution and ancient custom) his office without the aid of a *military force* will be productive of the most happy circumstances in many other instances, and prevent the soldiers from being called in to quell every little disorder.[34]

In fact, order had only barely been maintained. The crowd included thousands of sailors armed with bludgeons and cutlasses. There were widespread fears of an attempted rescue or that, as often occurred, there would be a violent struggle after the hangings for possession of the bodies between friends of the deceased and surgeons who wished to use the bodies for dissection. To defuse tensions, the sheriff spoke to the mob, promising that he would hand over the bodies following the executions, but he also threatened to read the Riot Act if any disorder occurred. This carrot and stick strategy worked. Later than evening Penlez was buried in the churchyard of St Clement's. The funeral was paid for by a subscription raised among the parishioners. The *London Evening Post* reported that 'the corpse was attended by an infinite number of persons, much lamenting the unhappy fate of the sufferer'.

Public opposition to the hanging of Penlez carried on throughout the autumn, as the case became caught up in a by-election campaign to elect a member of parliament for Westminster, a constituency with a notoriously radical and tumultuous electorate. The failure of Lord Trentham, the government candidate, to intervene to secure a pardon for Penlez was a major feature of the opposition campaign, and allowed the government's handling of the affair (including the use of the Riot Act and the summoning of the military) to be characterised as a typical government attack on the liberties of the subject. A number of letters and broadsides printed during the campaign raised the case of Penlez. Late in October a 'monumental inscription' to him was published, describing his execution as 'violent and ignominious', and noting that of 400 persons involved in the riot, 'he only suffered, though neither principal, nor contriver'.[35] The ghost of Penlez even appeared in an election procession:

> A person was carried about in a coffin dressed in a
> shroud, attended by a number of lights (candles), etc.
> designed to represent Penlez who was executed for the
> riot at the bawdy house in the Strand. He frequently sat up
> and harangued the populace for his unhappy fate.[36]

According to one observer, this ghost 'carried about in triumph' was 'surely a high insult on the government' and 'had raised more people to vote in St Clements than there are houses in the parish'.[37]

The ghost of Penlez proved hard to lay to rest. On 7 November 'a gentleman concerned' published a 55-page polemical pamphlet, *The Case of the Unfortunate Bosavern Penlez*, which claimed that the execution had been entirely unjustified. Attacking bawdy house keepers as parasites on young women, the author described Peter Wood's testimony as a pack of lies, pointing out that his testimony concerning Lander had been directly refuted during the trial, leading to his acquittal. If he lied about Lander, how could you trust his evidence concerning Penlez? Penlez was described as a 'silly unthinking lad', but of 'unblemished character', who, fuelled by drink, had unintentionally and innocently been caught up in the riot. To use him as 'an example of severity', therefore, was 'overstrained and unnecessary'.[38]

Henry Fielding, faced with criticisms of his own conduct (including the allegation that he had been bribed to protect the bawdy houses), and intending not only to shore up his own reputation as a novice justice but also to support the government (and his patron), published a defence of the handling of this case in *A True State of the Case of Bosavern Penlez* on 18 November, four days before polling began. Complaining that Penlez had been 'transformed into a hero', Fielding sought to justify the Riot Act as an essential tool for the maintenance of order and to characterise the destruction of bawdy houses as a serious threat to public order. An example was called for and Penlez, as a thief as well as a rioter, 'deserved his fate'.[39]

In the end, with Penlez executed and a government victory in the election (albeit with a narrow majority), Fielding prevailed, although public resentment lingered. Even today historians still argue over this case, with some claiming that the execution was unwarranted and carried out simply in order to shore up Fielding's authority, while others believe Fielding's version of the events was essentially accurate.[40]

Newgate, A-Hoy!

The nadir of public order in eighteenth-century London came with the spasm of anti-Catholic violence that erupted in the hot

days of early June 1780. The Gordon riots took Londoners by
surprise and drove the city to the point of civil collapse. The
streets were overrun with rioters moving from house to house,
attacking Catholic houses and chapels and the houses of
magistrates who opposed the will of the mob. Although almost no
one was killed by the rioters, it took over a week, and the deaths
of 285 men and women at the hands of the army, before a
sepulchral peace could be reclaimed. In the aftermath of those days
of destruction, the court at the Old Bailey (itself damaged in the
riots) was called upon to mete out justice to the perpetrators. In
the end only 160 of the tens of thousands involved were actually
charged and only 25 eventually executed. To find yourself before
the court you literally had to stand out from the crowd. James
Jackson, Thomas Haycock, George Sims and Benjamin Bowsey
did just that.

Lord George Gordon's 'Monster Petition' was so large it
could not be carried by even the strongest man. Filled with
40,000 signatures,[41] and composed of hundreds of sheets of
parchment rolled up into a huge bundle, it demanded the
immediate repeal of the almost entirely innocuous 'Catholic
Relief Act' of 1778. This act had removed some technical
bars to inheritance and property holding for Catholics and
lifted the threat of life imprisonment for priests. It also
obliged Catholics to take an oath of loyalty to the crown. For
many Londoners, however, the Catholic Relief Act was a
wedge issue that appealed to a centuries' long tradition of
anti-Catholic sentiment. Few could resist an appeal to rally
in defence of the Protestant religion, which seemed to many
to stand as much for traditional English liberties as for a
body of religious beliefs.

By 10 in the morning on 2 June it was already hot and
St George's Fields, to the south of the river, began to fill
with supporters of Lord Gordon, his 'Monster Petition'
and the Protestant Association he led. The intention was

to deliver the petition to parliament and force the repeal of the act. Thousands of blue cockades were issued to the crowd, which was then divided into four companies. In the lead a Scottish division set the pace to the sound of bagpipes. It was led by a kilted Highlander, with drawn sword. Following behind were divisions from the City, Westminster and Southwark. In martial order the protesters marched across London Bridge, and up Fish Street Hill and Grace Church Street to Cheapside. Some contemporaries put their number at upwards of 100,000, although more conservative (and better informed) commentators estimated it at 14,000.[42] Historians have argued about the precise social mix of the petitioners who set out from St George's Fields, but it is clear that as this army of protest marched through the London streets, many of the poor and unemployed joined its number. As this first group travelled along the traditional medieval procession route through London (from St Paul's to the Palace of Westminster), others took the shorter route across Westminster Bridge, to meet their fellows with an ear-splitting cheer in Parliament Street and New Palace Yard.

There followed hours of milling about as Lord Gordon tried to use the threat of public clamour to force parliament to his anti-Catholic will. A few days later, a young law student, Samuel Romilly, wrote to his brother describing the scene:

> They seemed to consist in a great measure of the lowest
> rabble. A miserable fanatic accosted me to question where
> my cockade was, and told me that the reign of the
> Romans had lasted too long. I mingled in a circle which I
> saw assembled around a female preacher, who, by her
> gestures and actions seemed to be well persuaded that she
> was animated by some supernatural spirit. The want of a
> cockade was a sure indication of a want of the true faith,
> and I did not long remain unquestioned as to my religious
> principles. My joining, however, in the cry of 'No

Popery!' soon pacified my inquisitors, or rather, indeed,
gained me their favour; for a very devout butcher insisted
upon shaking hands with me as a token of friendship.[43]

Members of Parliament and the House of Lords were
manhandled and threatened, and above the whole Lord
Gordon played the demagogue. In the end, the vote was
deferred in the hope of dispersing the crowd. But
disappointed of an immediate repeal, after a long hot day
milling about and awaiting news, this Protestant melée
slowly turned into a riotous assembly. In the hours after
midnight, the Catholic chapel of the Sardinian ambassador
was broken into and set alight, the moveable furniture
fuelling one of the tens of bonfires that sprang up
throughout the city. By the next morning the chapel
belonging to the Bavarian Embassy in Warwick Street had
been similarly looted, and the streets were full of the dead
embers of countless bonfires.

In the days that followed, the homes of prominent
Catholics were attacked, and groups of men and women
roamed the streets, extorting money to support the cause –
many with an iron bar in one hand and a hat held 'in a
begging way' in the other, demanding what they called 'mob
money'. At night, lights were put in the front windows of
houses in a general illumination. The lack of a candle was
likely to result in the unwelcome attention of the crowds.
Political prevarication and uncertainty fuelled the crisis,
which grew ever more violent as Saturday turned to Sunday
and then Monday.

Ann Candler, a pauper with child to her breast – who had
recently come to London to join her alcoholic husband –
spent that week cowering at home in a rented room, too
frightened to go out. The experience destroyed the last
vestige of her marriage and left her 'exposed to the horrors
of extreme poverty in the midst of strangers'.[44] Francis
Place's father, the owner of a 'sponging house' where men

and women were held as security for their debts, spent that week similarly paralysed with fear.

By Tuesday 6 June, and after another disappointed attempt to force parliament to repeal the act, the violence of the crowds turned from chapels and the homes of prominent Catholics to those of the magistrates who authorised the arrest of rioters, and then to the prisons of the capital, most notably to Newgate Prison.

That Tuesday afternoon outside the Houses of Parliament, James Jackson was in the thick of the crowd. A sailor, Jackson was dressed in 'a brown coat, a round hat, a checked shirt, and a pair of long trousers'. He had recently returned from sea and was observed lifting his closed fist to the air and egging on the crowd. John Lucy, a hairdresser who worked in Clerkenwell was also in the crowd that day. At Jackson's later trial, Lucy described the scene:

> About the hour of five o'clock, as near as I can recollect, I observed a very large mob in Palace Yard and a very great tumult. A party of horse rode amongst them; as I was informed, by the order of Justice Hyde. Jackson hoisted a black and red flag, which was upon a pole. He stood the next man to me, or next but one. He cried 'Hyde's house, a-hoy'. He was seconded by several of the mob. They proceeded immediately there. I followed at a distance.
>
> I saw the flag at Charing-Cross. I followed into St Martin's Street, where I understood Justice Hyde's house was, and the mob followed the flag to Mr Hyde's house. They stayed there near an hour, as near as I can recollect. Jackson still had the flag. Then he cried out 'Newgate, a-hoy'. That was about six o'clock, as near as I can recollect. He went down Orange Street coming towards Newgate. Great numbers of the mob followed him.[45]

Justice Hyde's furniture was piled high in the street and consumed in several bonfires. Even before the mob had started to move towards Newgate, the prison keeper, Richard Akerman, feared that his house would suffer a similar fate. As a place where several rioters were imprisoned, Newgate was an obvious target for the rioters, and Akerman held the keys. By 5 o'clock he was already 'agitated a good deal, having had an information that the mob was coming to visit me'. He packed up his plate and asked Mary Clark, a servant, to help secure his substantial house next door to and interconnected with the prison. She later described how she 'barred the door, chained, and bolted it with two bolts and put up the shutters'.[46]

In the meantime, the crowd moved deliberately from Justice Hyde's house, just south of Leicester Fields, past St Martin's Churchyard, down the Strand, and towards Newgate. A small boy, John Steel, on an errand for his father, saw the crowd surging up the Old Bailey, 'with great sticks in their hands and great spokes of wheels' which had been pilfered from a shop. Rose Jennings also saw the crowd:

> The mob approached three abreast, some with paving mattocks, others with iron crows and chisels; and then followed an innumerable company with bludgeons. They seemed to be the spokes of coach-wheels. They divided; some went to Mr Akerman's door with the mattocks, some to the felon's door, and some to the debtor's door.
>
> They attacked Mr Akerman's house precisely at seven o'clock; they were preceded by a man better dressed than the rest who went up to Mr Akerman's door. He rapped three times, and I believe pulled the bell as often. Mr Akerman had barricaded his house. When the man found that no one came, he went down the steps, made his obeisance to the mob, and pointed to the door, and then retired.[47]

The paviour's mattocks wielded by many in the crowd were heavy picks, shaped like an adze at one end, and a chisel at the other. Anyone carrying a mattock through the streets of London must have appeared uniquely threatening. Jennings was also:

Struck with the formidable appearance and order in which
they divided and proceeded to destroy the place. The men
threw their sticks up at the windows, which they broke
and demolished, yet notwithstanding these sticks were
coming down in showers, two men with a bar, such as
brewers servants carry on their shoulders, attacked the
parlour window to force it open. The window shutters
were exceedingly tough. They at last forced them partly
open, but not quite. I then saw a man in a sailor's jacket
helped up [possibly James Jackson]. He forced himself
neck and heels into the window. They found the house
door still difficult to get open. Before it was got open the
other parlour window was opened and the mob were
throwing the goods out at the window. At last the house
door gave way. About the same time some of the goods
and furniture having been thrown out into the street, a fire
was kindled.

Later that evening, drunk on both alcohol and the
burning of Newgate, Thomas Haycock dropped into The
Bell tavern in St James's Market flushed and proud.
Haycock was a waiter and poor. A friend said of him, 'When
you have lost that coat on your back you have lost all you are
worth'. He also had a history of mental illness. But on this
evening he was the centre of attention as he described his
role in taking Newgate earlier that evening to an incredulous
audience:

> He related his heading the mob from the Parliament
> House to Justice Hyde's house. That after leaving a party
> to complete the business at Justice Hyde's, he marched
> them to the end of Drury Lane. How he went into some
> shops in Long Acre; that there they got spokes of wheels,
> crows, pickaxes, and iron bars, and then went to Newgate.

One of his audience, John Lambert, asked him: 'What could
induce him to do all this?'

> He said the cause. (And Lambert replied) Do you mean a
> religious cause? He said no; for he was of no religion. He
> said, there should not be a prison standing on the morrow

in London. He said, the Bishop of London's house as well
as the Duke of Norfolk's house should come down that
night.

Haycock went on to describe what happened when the mob
came to Richard Akerman's house next to the prison. He
said:

> Damn my blood I have done the business! He said, He
> had pulled down Akerman's house and let out all the
> prisoners. That there was a short man there with broad
> shoulders; a tall man got upon his shoulders and butted
> his head against the windows, and in four or five times he
> shoved the window in, and so got in. He said he was the
> first man who entered Newgate and after demanding the
> keys they gave Mr Akerman five minutes time to consider
> of it. With the sheets and furniture of Mr Akerman they
> set fire to the door, with a bureau he particularly
> mentioned they set fire to the door.

As some of the crowd were battling for entry to Akerman's
house, others assaulted the main gate of the prison. Rebuilt
only a few years earlier in an imposing classical style
designed by George Dance the Younger, Newgate was, in
the words of the poet George Crabbe, 'very large, strong and
beautiful'.[48] Built to hold prisoners, it was a formidable task
even for a large crowd to break in.

At the head of the crowd which included James Jackson
and Thomas Haycock was George Sims, a tripe seller from
St James's Market, where Thomas Haycock also worked.
John Pitt recalled:

> On the 6th of June, at about seven o'clock at night we saw
> a vast concourse of people coming down to Newgate.
> They hallooed Newgate a-hoy. Sims and some others
> came up to the great gate, down the Old Bailey. He swore
> a desperate oath that he would have the gates down. He
> either damned his eyes, or damned his blood, he would
> have the gates down. Then they began at the gates, some
> with sledge hammers, and others with pick-axes. Sims

> had a large stick. I called to him because I had known him
> for some years. I said, 'Very well, George the tripe man, I
> shall mark you in particular'. I had known him six or
> seven years. Then he went towards Mr Akerman's house.

From his vantage point behind the grate, Pitt could see the
front of Akerman's house:

> I saw the feathers fly. They had got some of Mr
> Akerman's goods out, and they continued throwing them
> out. Then they set them against the gate and set them on
> fire, and they would have burnt those gates down, but we
> kept throwing water against them to cool them, to keep
> the lead from melting, and letting the hinges out. Then Mr
> Akerman's house was set on fire. That burnt into our fore
> lodge and into the chapel, and set the different wards on
> fire.

One way or another, Jackson, Haycock and Sims drew
attention to themselves by their actions at the head of the
mob. Benjamin Bowsey, a black man who had emigrated
from America six years earlier, was the object of the court's
attention almost solely because of his colour. He was an
active participant in the looting of Akerman's house, but the
witnesses who appeared at his trial emphasised his race more
than his actions. Later depictions of the scene outside
Newgate included two clearly drawn black figures at the centre of the action, one of whom was meant to represent
Bowsey. He had been a footman to General Honeywood,
but, at least according to the General, he was 'a very honest
and very foolish fellow that got into idle company' while
employed in the kitchens of St Alban's Tavern. This is the
same tavern where Thomas Haycock was employed as a
waiter, and it was located in St James's Market, where George
Sims worked as a tripe man.[49] All three, Bowsley, Haycock
and Sims, almost certainly knew each other, and it is entirely
possible that they conspired to promote the riot. But, more
importantly, despite differences in race and occupation, they

Figure 2.06 'An Exact Representation of the Burning, Plundering and Destruction of Newgate on the Memorable 7th of June 1780' (detail). Note the audience in the windows on the left and the black man wielding an axe in the foreground. © City of London, London Metropolitan Archives

were all part of a broader male culture of working Londoners for whom prisons and the court represented the power of the state.

Rose Jennings was sitting on the first floor of his brother's house across from the prison, and prided himself on his clear observation of the participants:

> When the conflagration took place I applied my mind to the mob, and endeavoured to form a distinction between the active and inactive people. I thought I did so. The inactive people seemed to form a circle. I observed a person better dressed than the rest among those within the circle, who did not meddle, but seemed to be exciting and encouraging others. I saw several genteel looking men, and amongst them a black. When I first saw the black I turned to a lady and said, 'this is a motley crew, and of

every colour'. Near nine o'clock I heard a cry and a
jingling of keys in the hands of some persons. Amongst
them was the prisoner at the bar, Benjamin Bowsey. He
was without his hat, and his hands were down.

Jennings was particularly cross-examined at the Old Bailey
about Bowsey's race, and Jenning's ability to make a positive
identification:

Question. There were I believe other blacks in the mob?

Answer. I never saw but one; I saw a black at first, but did
not remark him so as to swear to him.

Q. You could not swear to him I suppose from the
difficulty every man has in his mind to swear to
any black?

A. Yes.

Q. There is more difficulty to swear to a black than to a
white man?

A. No. The second time I made my remark too
judiciously to err.

Q. When was it you first saw the black?

A. After the goods were first set on fire, which was
about a quarter after seven o'clock.

Q. What dress had the black on?

A. Something of a dark colour, but my remark was on
his face.

Q. What was remarkable in that man's face more than
another black?

A. The make of his hair was one thing. The curls were
out if he had had any, and his hair smooth on his
head. His face was so exposed to my view the
second time that I could not be better situated to
make any remark on his face.

Ann Wood was watching the same scene from the 'three-pair-of-stairs room' across the way – the third-floor window – and took particular note of Bowsey:

> It was a little after seven o'clock. I saw him in Mr
> Akerman's two-pair-of-stairs room. He stood against the
> window with something in his hand and looked at me for
> some time before I observed particularly what he was
> doing. I looked at him then, and he took up something off
> the ground and held it up to me. When he held it up, I
> went down from the window into the dining-room. I came
> up again, and he was there still. He seemed to be looking
> in a drawer upon the floor, and seemed to be doing some
> thing up into a bundle.

Like Rose Jennings, Ann Wood was positive she could identify Benjamin Bowsey, and like Jennings was vigorously cross-examined:

Q.   What makes you so positive that this is the man?

A.   I know his face perfectly again by his standing and looking at me so long.

Q.   You recollect him only by his face?

A.   His face and his hair.

Q.   Did you see any other black there?

A.   Yes, I did; not in the house but in the mob.

In some measure it was not just Bowsey's riotous behaviour and appearance that led to his trial. Unlike most of the people involved that night, more intent on burning Akerman's goods than stealing them, Bowsey made away with a number of items which were later found in his possession and produced in court. Bowsey's room in cheap lodgings was eventually searched by a constable, Percival Phillips, and three pairs of stockings, a pocketbook and a handkerchief were discovered in a locked trunk. Most damning of all, however, and on a shelf nearby, Phillips

found a large ornate key, figured with a crown. Richard
Akerman, keeper of Newgate Prison, identified the goods:

> This pocketbook, I believe, has been in my possession
> thirty years. It was, I believe, in one of the drawers
> belonging to my wife. Here are several of my banker's
> cheques which had my name to them.

The stockings were equally distinctive:

> Here is a very remarkable pair which I had made for me,
> and the maker wove the initials of my name in them in
> open work. Bowsey has put the initials of his name (B B)
> over it. They were in the drawers in a one-pair-of-stairs
> room. Here are several others that were marked by my
> sister. They are mine. I believe the handkerchiefs to be
> mine, but there are no particular marks on them.

And as for the key:

> This is a remarkable key; it is a key of the park, it has a
> crown and my name at length upon it.

While Bowsey was pilfering Akerman's goods, the crowd,
having broken in to Newgate and set fire to the building,
had to rush to save the prisoners. George Crabbe was in the
crowd and recorded the events in his diary:

> They broke the gates with crows and other instruments,
> and climbed up the outside of the cell part, which joins
> the two great wings of the building where the felons were
> confined. They broke the roof, tore away the rafters, and
> having got ladders they descended. Not Orpheus himself
> had more courage or better luck; flames all around them,
> and a body of soldiers expected, they defied and laughed
> at all opposition. The prisoners escaped. I stood and saw
> above twelve women and eight men ascend from their
> confinement to the open air, and they were conducted
> through the streets in their chains. Three of them were to
> be hanged on Friday. This being done, and Akerman's
> house now a mere shell of brickwork, they kept a store of
> flame there for other purposes. It became red-hot and the

doors and windows appeared like the entrance to so many volcanoes.[50]

From Newgate alone some 300 prisoners, both felons and debtors, were released.[51]

Henry Angelo was also watching. He paid six pence for a place at a garret window above the scene. He saw 'The captives marched out, with all the honours of war, accompanied by a musical band of rattling fetters'.[52] As the prisoners had their chains knocked off, wine and gin liberated from Akerman's cellar was distributed through the crowd. As the fire grew, it began to threaten surrounding buildings, and to rage out of control. Eventually fire engines were let through, and the flames were doused.[53]

The firing of Newgate was just the first event of a long night of destruction. The neighbouring Old Bailey courthouse was invaded and furniture from the courtroom was burned in the street. Part of the crowd marched off to Bloomsbury Square, ringing a loud bell they had discovered in Akerman's cellar, declaring their intention to roast alive the Archbishop of York and the Lord Chief Justice, Lord Mansfield. At the same time, others set off for Bridewell, the New Prison and Clerkenwell Prison. A crowd later attacked the Fleet Prison as well, forcing reluctant debtors from their beds. By the end of the night there was barely a prisoner or prison left in the capital. One estimate suggests that some 1,600 prisoners were released. The rioters 'insisted upon lights being put up at every window in joy for the destruction of Newgate; the illumination accordingly was general, the sky glowing on every side with the light of different conflagrations'.[54]

Until 3.30 in the morning the streets belonged to the rioters alone. But then the authorities changed their tactics. Up until this point, justices had been unwilling to order the army to fire on the crowds, fearing that in the event of any deaths the soldiers would be charged with murder. Now the king stepped in and ordered the soldiers to act directly without waiting for orders from the magistrates and the word was given for a small command of soldiers to open fire on the crowd. Five people, four men and a woman, were killed outright and seven more were wounded. This set off a running battle that carried on throughout the night and continued the next day.

On Wednesday little had changed. Although attacks on the Bank of England were repulsed, the King's Bench prison was fired, as was the Fleet, the Borough Clink and Surrey Bridewell. One of the largest distilleries in London, Langdale's, was attacked, and thousands of gallons of gin was appropriated by the rioters. The building was set on fire and as the flames took hold, drunken men and women rushed to the cellars to claim more gin. Many died, soaked in raw spirits and burned to death.

Battles broke out throughout the city. Hastily marshalled troops were force-marched up from provincial towns and the channel ports. And while the violence continued through Thursday, on Friday, by opening fire and by sheer force of numbers, the army regained control of the streets. Writing to his brother, Samuel Romilly claimed that by Friday afternoon 'the most profound tranquillity reigned in every part of London'.[55]

This tranquillity had been bought at a high price. As well as the 285 rioters killed by soldiers, a further 173 were wounded. Four hundred and fifty individuals were under arrest, including Lord George Gordon himself, who was eventually tried for treason. Contemporary estimates put a price of £180,000 on the damage to property.

As for James Jackson, George Sims, Thomas Haycock and Benjamin Bowsey, they were among the 85 people tried at the Old Bailey for their part in the riots. Jackson was found guilty and hanged before the Old Bailey itself. George Sims, the tripe man, called several character witnesses, was found innocent and walked from the courtroom; while Thomas Haycock was found guilty and joined Jackson on the gibbet. Benjamin Bowsey was also found guilty and sentenced to death, but he escaped the noose. The king eventually granted him a full pardon.

As a 9 year old, Francis Place was soundly beaten by his father for skipping church to explore 'the ruins of the places burned by the rioters',[56] but neither the army's bullets, nor the court's terrible judgment, or even the blows of an angry father, could remove the Gordon riots from the popular imagination of Londoners. At the least, the riots raised mixed emotions. For propertied Londoners, they represented a world gone mad and a warning for the future. Politicians (even radicals) would never again appeal so recklessly for the support of the mob. After the events of 1780 most no longer considered rioting a legitimate form of protest. But for others, the leaders who marshalled this seeming 'phrensy of the multitude' became heroes.[57] A ballad sung about the streets in the years after 1780 captures the admiration that many felt. 'Jack Chance' celebrated the life of a foundling child discovered on the steps of Newgate, who 'learn'd to curse, to swear and fight, And everything but read and write'. According to the ballad, he was a natural for the mob:

> With blue cockade proclaimed for war
>
> With bludgeon, strut or iron bar
>
> No head, a mob he never would fail
>
> At gutting the mass house or burning a gaol.

Like James Jackson and Thomas Haycock, however:

> But a victim he fell to his country's laws
>
> And died at last in religion's cause
>
> No popery made the blade to swing
>
> And when tucked up he was, just the thing.[58]

Rejoicing to See the Lights

*Violence took many forms, and not all were the result of passion
or malice. Coroners were required to investigate all deaths that
occurred in suspicious circumstances, and inquest verdicts that
blamed deaths on the actions of others, regardless of motive,
regularly led to trials at the Old Bailey. As the century progressed
there was a growing intolerance of all sorts of violence, and an
increasing desire to hold to account even those responsible for
accidental deaths.*

Tuesday 16 August 1796 was the Duke of York's birthday,
and a fine excuse for an illumination, an elaborate display of
candles formed into a dramatic shape. By a little after 8
o'clock that evening the gang of children living around
Bishopsgate Street were 'making a great noise, huzzaing'.
They were excited and happy as candles and lamps were lit
opposite the church:

> When the man began to light up the lights, three or four
> children ran across the way clapping their hands, rejoicing
> like to see the lights.

A few minutes earlier, however, the Newmarket mail coach
had set out from one of London's great inns, on the much
more serious business of delivering the post. It turned up
Bishopsgate Street heading out on its overnight journey
through the English countryside to East Anglia. The
schedule was precise. The mail contractor later explained:

> I am compelled to go to Newmarket in eight hours; 63
> miles; they must go full ten miles an hour; government
> compels us to do that. There are five changes of horses in
> the night, and stopping for passengers to refresh; I am
> sure they must go full ten miles an hour.

Turning into the wide roadway of Bishopsgate Street, the
coachman, William Clark, picked up speed. The guard, Bolt
White, sat behind him, over the coach boot at the rear. A

locked mailbox at his feet, he had a pistol ready in case they encountered highwaymen. White was dressed in the scarlet frock coat trimmed with gold braid that declared his employment by the Post Office, and he was meant to blow a regular warning to pedestrians on a three-foot tin horn. On that evening, however, no one could remember hearing him play. Lamb Beazley sold fish about the streets and was in Bishopsgate Street. Although she saw the coach 'coming on very fast', she did not hear 'the horn blow before the coach came up'. Neither did James Shakeshaft, who was returning home to Sun Street. He was a retired Post Office worker himself and knew how a mail coach was meant to behave:

> I was on my return home from a little beyond Bishopsgate Church. I perceived a mail coach coming very furiously along, galloping; when I first saw it, it might be forty or fifty yards from the place where they were illuminating. I heard no horn blow, but at the rate that it was coming at, any one that stood in the way must have been killed, it was then in the middle of the road.

Mail coaches first appeared on the streets of London in 1784. They were light and fast – a technological marvel. The body of this particular coach was made up of maroon and black panels and rolled on bright red wheels. On each door the words London and Newmarket were stencilled above 'Royal Mail' and the royal coat of arms. On the boot a unique registration number was displayed. It had space for four passengers inside and a further two on the roof and was pulled by four fresh horses. The service was so regular that some people had even begun to commute into and out of London by coach.

On this evening, as on many others, John Morris caught the Newmarket coach:

> I sleep out of town, and frequently get a lift by it. I leave the office about the time that the mail goes off; coming down Houndsditch I saw the mail go past and ran after.

Ten-year-old Michael Connel was one of the children excitedly waiting for the lamplighter to begin the illuminations. Lamb Beazley later recalled that Michael was one of four children who ran across the roadway:

> I turned my head round to see if my little boy was among them. I then saw the mail coach coming very fast. I immediately stamped my foot, and hallooed to the children immediately to get out of the way. They got away as well as they could, and as the little boy that was killed was making his escape over to the other side, the horse's feet came rearing up, and the right side foot knocked the child down, and the horse behind him trampled over him as he lay upon his belly. The two wheels went over his back.

At the same moment, Esther Wise set off:

> I sat at the corner of New Street with fruit in a barrow, and I was going to cross over for a candle. The mail coach was going by at the same time. I made a stop for it to pass me. I ran directly behind the coach as it passed me and I saw the horses rear up, and I saw the child under the fore-horses' feet, and the child turned upon its side as if trying to get up, and the other horse trampled upon him. I don't know whether the wheel went over him or not. It was done in an instant, and the mob gathered, and I saw no more of it.

Dennis Brames was also waiting for the illuminations:

> I was standing to see the lamps lighting and I saw the mail coach coming along at a very great rate indeed. Just as it came to the spot, the man came out to light the lamps with a ladder, and the boys set up a great hallooing in the road. The fore-horses reared up and knocked the boy down, and the off hind horse trampled over him. The off fore-wheel and off hind-wheel went over his back and loins. I saw the boy taken up and in a few minutes after brought in to the doctor's and the coach went on at a very great rate afterwards.

Just a few moments earlier, John Morris had seen the coach go by and had chased after it:

> It might be forty or fifty yards before me. I went after it,
> and overtook it at the time of the accident. I saw the
> wheel go over the deceased, I saw it was a boy, and as I
> was following the coach I jumped over the boy, and
> overtook the coach immediately after. I stopped the coach
> and got upon the box with the coachman.

Ignoring the crowd that was quickly assembling over the now dead body of Michael Connel, and having collected a paying passenger, the coachman, William Clark, whipped his horses and rode on. At Clark's subsequent trial for murder, the guard, Bolt White, explained what happened next in response to the staccato questioning of first the prosecuting attorney, Newman Knowlys, and then the defence counsel, William Fielding:

Bolt White.	I was guard to the Newmarket Mail-coach on the evening of the accident.
Question.	Who was the driver of the coach that evening?
A.	William Clark, the prisoner.
Q.	Your place is behind the coach, not upon the box?
A.	Yes.

Cross-examined by Mr Fielding.

Q.	You were the guard?
A.	Yes.
Q.	You had a horn, I take it for granted?
A.	Yes.
Q.	Did you blow the horn frequently as you came along Bishopsgate Street?
A.	Yes.

Q.   This horn of yours was as a warning that you were coming along?

A.   Yes.

Q.   Do you remember when you were coming near a spot where illuminations were preparing?

A.   Yes.

Q.   Do you recollect whether you there blew the horn?

A.   Yes; all through the crowd of people.

Q.   Was there a noise, huzzaing and shouting, when you came near this place?

A.   Yes; just as we went through it.

Q.   Do you recollect at which side the coach was going, at this time?

A.   Rather nearer to the church side of the road.

Q.   Were you going at more than the usual pace that you go down Bishopsgate Street?

A.   Much the same that we commonly go.

Q.   How long has that poor fellow driven the mail coach?

A.   About seven months.

Q.   What is his character?

A.   A very good character.

Q.   Is he a good natured fellow?

A.   Yes.

Q.   He would not do a mischief to his fellow creatures, I hope?

A.   No.

Q.   Was he sober at that time?

A.   Very.

Q.	When was it that you knew of the accident having happened?
A.	I did not know of it till we got to the Bald Faced Stag upon Epping Forest.
Q.	When it was made known to him did Clark express his sorrow?
A.	He told me of it when we got there; a passenger that had got up afterwards, told him that he had run over a boy.
Q.	Did he accompany this declaration to you with a proper feeling?
A.	He said he did not know whether he was hurt, he hoped not.

Mr Knowlys.

Q.	Did you hear the cries of the people at all as you passed by?
A.	No.

William Clark himself let his defence counsel and his employer, George Boulton, speak on his behalf. Boulton, in particular, who claimed to have known Clark 'from his infancy', gave him the strongest support he could, saying he was 'a lad of remarkable good disposition':

> I never knew him in liquor in my life. He was brought up
> by my father, and has lived with me ever since. He has
> drove this mail from the first day I had it.

Clark's temperament was discussed, as was his treatment of animals and his 'heart' and 'character'. Finally, William Fielding felt he had done enough:

> I have a number of witnesses from the Post Office, but I
> will not trouble the court with any more.

The jury retired, and spent an unusually long time – two hours – arguing over the case. It was a hit and run accident with a tragic outcome. In the end, they brought in a verdict of 'not guilty' and William Clark walked free.[59]

The Monster

The eighteenth century witnessed the birth of the criminal celebrity – notorious criminals whose exploits were publicised in the media and who became the subject of public fascination. At the end of the century this phenomenon took a disturbing new turn when public attention focused on an apparently psychopathic serial attacker. In this instance the moral panic created by media attention to 'The Monster' encouraged the very crimes the public was so concerned to stop. His trial, moreover, called into question the fragile system of justice meted out at the Old Bailey.

On 12 May 1790 a German visitor, Georg Forster, noted in his diary that London was in an uproar. A 'Monster' was terrorising the streets, insulting women and stabbing them with sharp instruments, usually in their buttocks. This man 'goes about in various different guises wounding beautiful women with specially invented instruments, with hooks hidden in bouquets of flowers, with knitting pins, etc.' Londoners, he reported, talked about little else:

> The newspapers are full of him; the playwrights entertain audiences with his exploits from the stage; the ladies are afraid of him. The mob gives every pedestrian a keen look in case he is the Monster; all the walls are covered with posters advertising a reward for the apprehension of the Monster; a fund has been opened to finance the hunt.[60]

Between May 1788 and June 1790 there were reports of over 50 attacks on women in public by unidentified men wielding sharp implements. Although the details varied, the assaults shared many characteristics. They were generally unprovoked and carried out by men unknown to the victim.

The culprit used insulting and threatening language and a sharp object to cut through the victim's clothes and into her flesh, typically in the thigh or bottom, but sometimes the face. He then lingered, clearly enjoying watching his victim suffer. The instruments, which were often disguised and sometimes designed to cause particularly horrific injuries, included knives hidden in canes or attached to shoes (for use when kicking), sharp pins disguised inside bouquets (which the victim was urged to smell) and claws with several sharp prongs. Some women were also kicked or punched on the breast or head.

RENWICK WILLIAMS
commonly called
THE MONSTER.

Figure 2.07 'Renwick Williams, Commonly Called the Monster' (1790). Credit: Guildhall Library, City of London

It was not until April 1790 that organised efforts to apprehend the culprit began. Newspapers, the Bow Street runners, neighbourhood associations, and an anonymous private philanthropist offering a reward, all joined the campaign. After several false arrests, in June a suspect, Rhynwick (or Renwick) Williams, a 23-year-old artificial-flower maker, was arrested and identified by several victims. Although assault was a petty crime, the desire to see the 'Monster' severely punished ensured that he was charged with a felony, under an obscure 1720 statute against cutting up women's clothes. With an angry mob outside the courtroom demanding vengeance (as well as a hostile audience inside), he was tried at the Old Bailey in July for an attack on Ann Porter which had occurred in the previous January.

Arthur Pigott (or Pigot), counsel for the prosecution, opened the trial:

> May it please your lordship, and you gentlemen of the
> jury, this is the most extraordinary case that ever called for
> the attention of a court of justice. It is an unpleasant task
> to call your minds to a scene so new in the annals of
> mankind; a scene so unaccountable; a scene so unnatural
> to the honour of human nature, that it could not have been
> believed ever to have existed, unless it had been
> demonstrated by that proof which the senses cannot resist.
> It must appear unaccountable to us that any human being,
> unless impelled by some impulse which cannot be
> explained, should have committed an act, to which no
> hope of reward, no inclination of revenge, excited by a real
> or supposed injury, no idea of concealing an atrocious
> offence, nor any natural propensity which has hitherto
> been supposed to actuate a human creature, could have
> urged him. Thus acting apparently and visibly, without a
> motive for the commission of the deed, the prisoner at the
> bar has made a wanton, wilful, cruel, and inhuman attack
> upon the most beautiful! The most innocent! The most
> lovely! And perhaps I shall not trespass upon the truth,
> when I say the best work of nature!

That divine creation was Ann Porter, one of four daughters of Thomas Porter, keeper of an establishment called Pero's Bagnio, an apparently respectable hotel, tavern and bathhouse in St James.

Ann was attacked while returning home from the Queen's Birthday ball on 18 January. Appearing in the courtroom wearing a veil to protect her from Williams's gaze, she told the court that as she approached her house on St James's Street at 11.15 pm:

> My sister desired me to make haste; and we went as fast
> as we could; she said something else, but I did not
> distinguish the words. Just as I was passing the corner of
> the rails I felt a violent blow on my hip; I turned round to
> see from whence it proceeded, and I saw that man
> (pointing at the prisoner at the bar) stoop down.

Her testimony to the court was frequently interrupted by questions from prosecution counsel:

Question. Had you ever seen that man before, madam?

Answer. Yes, sir.

Q. Oftener than once?

A. Three or four times.

Q. When you had seen him before had he said any thing to you?

A. Yes, he had.

Q. Did you know him as an acquaintance, or were you under the necessity of meeting him?

A. I know no more of him than walking in the middle of the day; he insulted me and my sisters with very gross and indelicate language; he walked behind me and muttered.

Q. I do not ask you to repeat what he said to you, but in what manner had he spoke, and what sort of language?

A. Very gross, and very abusive.

Q. Had that happened to you more than once?

A. Yes, sir, three or four times.

The questioning returned to the events on the evening of 18 January:

Q. When you was standing at the door of your father's house, and received this blow, and turned round, and saw the man stooping down, did you at that time recognise that man to be the same that had spoken to you before?

A. It struck me immediately to be the same man; I knew him the moment. He did not run away. I was very much shocked at the sight of him; I endeavoured to pass on the side of the door: I felt

a very strange sensation; and I fancy he must have
passed at the same time I did. He stood opposite to
me, and stared in my face: he walked up to the top
of the steps, on the opposite side of the door I was
of, and he stood as close to me as he possibly
could.

Q.   Look at him, as he stands there; have you any
doubt of that being the person that struck you the
blow?

A.   No, sir, I have not the smallest doubt; I could not
have been positive, but I saw him three or four
times before. I suffered so much from the insults
I received, that it is impossible I could be mistaken.
I could never forget him.

Q.   In what manner were your clothes cut?

A.   They are here, sir.

Q.   Did they appear to be cut with a sharp
instrument?

A.   Yes, a very sharp one.

Sarah Porter, Ann's sister, had also encountered Williams
before, and heard 'the most dreadful language that can be
imagined'. She was also asked to describe the encounter
with him on the evening of the 18th:

Some chairman was passing by who said, by your leave; upon
which he started round, stared in my face, and looked again, and
said, oh! oh! and instantly gave me a violent blow on my head,
the back of my head.

Q.   Upon that what did you do?

A.   I requested my sister to run. I said, Nancy, for
God's sake make haste, do not you see the wretch
is behind us; a name we always distinguish him by.

Q.   There was another lady with you I understand: did
you all run?

A.   Yes, as fast as we could. I ran first to ring at the
            door; while I was ringing at the door I turned
            round to see if he was coming, and I saw him run
            past, across the stable yard; he was close to my
            sister; and he dropped down. I was so terrified, and
            I looked again; the words were half uttered when
            he rushed between Mrs Mead and me; and I saw
            him strike with the greatest violence, and I heard
            the silk rent. His hand was shut, I observed
            particularly.

John Coleman, a fishmonger, then testified concerning
the circumstances which led to the arrest of Williams
exactly five months later. A second counsel for the
prosecution, Mr Shepherd, led the questioning:

Q.   Do you remember being with Miss Porter on the
            18th of June last, in St. James's Park, in the
            evening?

A.   Yes; I perceived her very much agitated, indeed;
            and she told me the wretch had just passed her; she
            pointed him out to me.

Q.   (Pointing to Williams sitting in the dock) Was that
            the person she pointed out to you?

A.   That was the person.

Q.   Did you follow him?

A.   I followed him, and he walked exceedingly fast.

Coleman then told an extraordinary tale of his pursuit of
Williams, following him at a distance of between one and
five yards, out of the park, through Whitehall and into St
James, without actually accosting him. When he entered a
house, Coleman simply waited until he came out again.
Finally, in Bond Street, Coleman plucked up his courage
and tried to engage Williams's attention:

> I did every thing that laid in my power to insult him, by
> walking behind him, and walking before him, looking at
> him very full in the face, and making a noise behind him.
> I used every art I could to insult him; he would not take
> any insult; he never said a word. I followed him behind;
> and I behaved in this kind of way (peeping over his
> shoulder, and making a clapping with his hands) and I
> was going to knock him down once or twice. He crossed
> Oxford Road, and went into Vere Street.

When they reached South Moulton Street, Williams
went into the house of a Mr Smith. Coleman asked and was
allowed to follow him in, where he was finally able to
confront Williams:

> I began to make an apology for my rude behaviour to this
> gentleman; and I told him I thought it was very odd he did
> not take any notice of my manner of proceeding. I told him
> I had come to a resolution to know his address, and would
> give him mine. He said he thought it was very proper that I
> should assign some reason for my wishing to know his
> address. I did not know what reason to assign; I was a little
> agitated; I did not like to say, Sir, you are supposed to be
> this Monster; and I told him at last that he had insulted
> some ladies that I was very intimate with, that I was
> walking in the park with one of the ladies, and she had
> pointed him out to me, and that as far as lay in my power I
> would have satisfaction for that insult. He said, good God! I
> never insulted any ladies in my life. I told him I could not
> then proceed any farther with him, for I was not sure he
> was the man; but he must favour the ladies with a sight of
> him. Mr Smith said that I talked very fair, and that he
> thought it was very proper to give his address to me.

They exchanged addresses and parted company, but then
Coleman had second thoughts and returned to Williams,
and asked him to go directly to see the Porters that evening.
He agreed and they went to the house:

> I introduced the gentleman to the ladies in the parlour, and two
> of the Miss Porters immediately fainted away; that was Miss

Sarah Porter, and Miss Ann Porter, exclaiming 'Oh my God!
Coleman, that is the wretch'.

Q.	Did he say or do any thing when the Miss Porters cried out, that is the wretch?
A.	He said, the ladies' behaviour is extremely odd; he said, good God! they do not take me for this person, about whom there has been so many publications? I answered, it really is so, sir; I do not recollect he made me any answer to it.
Q.	How long did he stay there?
A.	He was there an hour. Miss Porter thought proper to send for some ladies: I heard him say once or twice that the ladies were prejudiced.

Having established the Porters' identification of Williams as
the culprit, the case for the prosecution concluded with testimony from Mr Tomkins, the surgeon:

Mr Shepherd.	I believe you attended Miss Ann Porter after she was hurt?
A.	I did.
Q.	From the nature of the wound which she had, must it have been made with a sharp instrument?
A.	A very sharp instrument.
Q.	Did you examine the clothes?
A.	I did; I examined the gown, which was considerably cut, and the petticoat too; I am not sure whether I saw the shift; I believe I did not.
Q.	Did it appear to be done with the same instrument, and at the same time?
A.	Certainly.
Q.	How deep was the wound?
A.	The first part of the wound was only through the skin, the middle part was at least three inches or four inches deep; and then it ran about three inches more through the skin only.

Court.	What was the whole length of the wound?
A.	I believe between nine and ten inches.
Mr Knowlys.	Whether a cut with a sharp instrument, merely to cut the clothes, would have wounded so deep as that?
A.	No; that I do not know. It must have been with great violence; part of the blow was below the bow of the stays; if not it would probably have pierced even the abdomen.

Renwick Williams opened the case for the defence by reading a statement to the court:

My lord and gentlemen of the jury, I stand here an object deserving your most serious attention and compassion. From conscious innocence of the very shocking accusations made against me, I cannot but hope that just and really liberal minds will have reason to commiserate my situation, and must feel me deserving pity and compassion. As my case has been multiplied in horror, though with submission I think, in comparison, far beyond even the sufferings of my accusers. I must reprobate the cruelty with which the public prints have abounded in the most scandalous paragraphs, containing malicious exaggerations of the charges preferred, so much to my prejudice, that I already lie under premature conviction, by almost an universal voice. I rest my case to the decision of an English jury; and in hopes of being able to establish my innocence in your opinion, I most seriously appeal to the Great Author of Truth, that I have the strongest affection for the happiness and comfort of the superior part of this creation, the fair sex, to whom I have in every circumstance that occurred in my life endeavoured to render assistance and protection. I have nothing, my lord and gentlemen, farther to say, but that however strange and aggravated this case may appear to you, I solemnly, and with the utmost sincerity declare to you all, that this prosecution of me is founded in a dreadful mistake, which I hope the evidence I shall bring will prove to your satisfaction.

Several witnesses then testified to Renwick Williams's alibi – he had been at work at the time of the attack. His employer, Armarvel Mitchell (or Aimable Michelle; a Frenchman who gave his evidence through an interpreter), testified that Williams had been working for him in his workshop on 18 January, and owing to the press of work (a large order from Ireland, and a last-minute order for some fabric for a Mrs Abingdon) he stayed at work till 12.30 in the morning. Other women who worked with him corroborated this testimony, but they found it difficult to prove the time at which he left work. Several stated that:

> The maid came in, and said, that when she opened the
> door, the watchman went by crying half past twelve; and
> she made a remark, that the clock went extremely right,
> for it agreed with the watchman.

But under cross-examination one witness admitted that this remark had not been made at the time:

Q.   Do you mean that the maid stated that at that
            time?

A.   I do not recollect that the maid mentioned the
            circumstance at that time; but since that time
            she came and told us of it, and made the
            remark voluntarily. We sent to the maid, to
            know if she could recollect the circumstance;
            and then it was that the maid stated the fact
            about the watchman and the clock.

Q.   How long ago was it?

A.   Since the prisoner was apprehended.

Several witnesses also testified to Williams's good character, including Armarvel Mitchell, who said that he had always behaved with civility and good nature to the young ladies that worked with him in the house. More shockingly, several 'beautiful' women testified to Williams's 'habits of fond, constant, and manly intercourse with them'. One woman even testified that he had once saved her life! Perhaps because it was so incongruent with popular expectations, the testimony of these women was omitted from the published *Proceedings*.[61]

The judge, Sir Francis Buller, then summed up the evidence in a long speech to the jury. He began by supporting Williams's plea that the jury should ignore 'popular prejudice' and concentrate on the evidence presented in the courtroom. He then set out 'material points for you to discuss', but told the jury that owing to the fact that the offence Williams had been charged with was possibly inappropriate (he thought this was the first prosecution under this obscure statute), he had doubts about the form of the indictment. Consequently, should the jury find him guilty, he said he would refer the case to the opinion of senior judges.

The first question for the jury to consider was, had Williams been correctly identified as Porter's attacker? Here the judge seemed convinced:

> Gentlemen, this is the whole of the evidence on the part of the prosecution; first you find that the four young ladies have all sworn very positively to the person of the prisoner; you will naturally examine what opportunities they had of knowing the prisoner, and whether they were likely to be mistaken; they had seen the prisoner several times before, and in the day time, and the manner in which they had seen him certainly called upon them to pay particular attention to his person. And upon no occasion did they entertain the smallest doubt; but when they saw him in St James's Park, they said most positively that he was the person, and challenged him likewise at their house.

Second, the jurymen were invited to consider how Williams had behaved when Coleman followed him, suggesting that Williams must have been aware of the pursuit, and that his failure to respond suggested he had something to hide. Similarly, the judge called attention to Williams's silence when he was brought before the Porters and accused of being the Monster. Finally, he called the alibi into question, noting missing details and contradictions in the evidence presented.

In summary, the jury was given a very clear steer:

> Gentlemen, it is for you to say which side you give credit to. If you believe the witnesses on the part of the prisoner; and that he continued in Mitchell's house from two or three that afternoon, till half past twelve, he could not be the person that committed this injury; and of course you will acquit him. If on the other hand, you are satisfied from the testimony, and the very positive testimony, of the four Miss Porters, that he was the man, and that they knew his person so well before, that they could not be mistaken; if you see from his conduct at the time he was brought back, and in the moment he spoke to Miss Sarah Porter, that he was the man; if you believe her evidence when put together, you must give the effect to it, and pronounce that the prisoner was the man.

The jury, apparently without even retiring, immediately fulfilled the judge's expectations and pronounced a verdict of guilty. But owing to the legal uncertainty about the charge, sentencing was put off to the December sessions.

Following the trial, doubts about Williams's guilt were raised in several newspapers, and, most substantially, in a pamphlet published in September by the polemicist Theophilus Swift, who identified several procedural defects in the trial and claimed Williams was not the Monster. The pamphlet caused an uproar and led some to question whether the Monster had ever really existed. In November the case was reviewed by the 12 senior judges of England, who quashed the indictment and ruled (as Buller had feared) that Williams had been charged with the wrong offence. He would therefore have to be retried on a new indictment.

Williams stood trial for a second time on 8 December, this time in the new Sessions House on Clerkenwell Green, on misdemeanour charges of assaulting with intent to murder three women, Ann Porter, Elizabeth Davis and Elizabeth Vaughan. At the start of the trial Williams was again allowed to address the court. He made a 'pathetic speech' in which he solemnly swore to his innocence and appealed to the candour and impartiality of the jury. Mr Pigott, counsel for the prosecution, then addressed the jurors and asked them to do the impossible, to forget everything they had previously heard about this case. He then once again outlined the horrible, unprecedented nature of the crime, declaring:

> He had not words to express the dreadful injury, the
> shocking barbarity, the brutality, the ferocity of the
> prisoner, who in total want of all morality, of all
> humanity, and of all the claims of manhood, had made
> this attack on the person of Miss Porter.

The case for the prosecution was similar to that presented at the first trial, but with the addition of evidence of Williams's alleged previous insulting language given to the sisters. Mr Tomkins, the surgeon, also made Porter's injuries seem worse than he had in his testimony in the first trial. He:

> Described the wound given to Miss Porter, as in the
> former trial; and added, that he had been in many scenes
> of horror, but never saw any thing that affected him so
> much before; that the room was full of blood, and the
> poor girl laying like a dead corpse. He said that if he had
> been to have made an incision as a surgeon, he could not
> have made a clearer wound; the instrument must be very
> sharp; she had a fever, and was five or six weeks before
> she could walk.

Notably, although Williams's insulting language seemed important to the prosecution, counsel refused to ask the Porter sisters what Williams had actually said to them.

Pigott stated that he did not wish the 'young women to pollute their mouths with the repetition of that language which issued from him', but assured the jury that 'it was the most horrid, and the least sufferable to human ears'.

Williams had dismissed the counsel he used in the first trial, whose performance had been ineffective, and instead at the last minute secured the services of the pamphleteer who had come to his defence in print, Theophilus Swift. Having already vigorously cross-examined the prosecution witnesses, Swift commenced the case for the defence with a very long speech, in which he attempted to discredit the prosecution evidence by making a number of arguments that had not been made in the first trial.

First, he pointed to the existence of the offer of a £100 reward for the arrest and conviction of the Monster, which he said had the potential to lead to untrustworthy evidence. Although the Porters had refused to accept any portion of the reward, Coleman had received £50. And indeed, Coleman's evidence was full of errors: 'Of all the witnesses I ever beheld, Coleman is the most extraordinary'. Earlier, Swift suggested Coleman had been engaged to marry Porter. Although she denied it, they were in fact married the next April.

Second, Swift called into question the identification of Williams as the man who attacked Ann and Sarah Porter. He argued that the Porters had allowed their previous interactions with Williams (which the latter admitted) to shape their belief, and that of two other prosecution witnesses, that he was their attacker: 'I call it bolstering up of the evidence'. He questioned whether there had been enough light for them to see Williams's face, since the street lamps had been obstructed by bow windows on either side of the door.

Third, and most extraordinarily, he argued that the previous conversations between Porter and Williams had

been of a very different nature from the insults described by
the prosecution:

> There has been indisputably an acquaintance between the
> prisoner and the witnesses, and the conversation and the
> knowledge which the prisoner and the witnesses have was
> of a very different nature indeed. I will not stain the word
> justice, by saying that there were private motives behind
> the curtain, but there were conversations of a very
> different nature, such as excited the present prosecution.

In a word, Williams had courted, and been rejected by, Ann
Porter, and in subsequent encounters they had exchanged
insults, including allegations from Williams that Porter had
slept with a Captain Crowder, 'with whom you went off
from a bagnio'.[62] This is why the prosecution had been so
unwilling to explain precisely what had been said when
Williams had insulted Porter. Swift's raising the question of
Porter's sexual virtue in the courtroom was considered
scandalous and evoked loud disapproval from the audience.

Finally, and perhaps most damningly, Swift argued that
Williams could not be the Monster because the attacks had
continued after he was arrested and the recent attacker
matched the description of the culprit that Ann Porter had
given at Bow Street:

> Gentlemen, I could tell you of a lady that has been most
> barbarously and cruelly wounded. I was with her at the
> moment it happened, on the 20th of August; and a most
> cruel business it was; and I am sorry to say that was the
> seventh time she had been assaulted since Williams was
> committed. I could not get the lady here today; her father-
> in-law is a very old man, and he is dangerously ill, but I
> hope you will give credit to the fact; if not I will be sworn
> to the truth of it.

Either copycat attackers had responded to the huge
publicity this case received or Williams was not the
Monster. This potentially damning evidence, however, was
not mentioned again.

Following this speech, the defence returned to its 'indisputable alibi', and the same fellow workers were called to testify, but according to the *Proceedings* they were even less convincing than at the first trial. Nonetheless, overconfident of his own persuasive powers, Theophilus Swift did not allow Williams to testify in his defence.

According to the account in the *Proceedings*, the trial ended as follows, starting with a rebuttal to the defence case from the prosecution counsel:

> Mr Pigot replied at considerable length, in a very forcible manner to Mr Swift's observations, and concluded with reminding the jury of the situation some of their families might be in, if by their verdict the wretch should be set at liberty again. After which the chairman summed up the case, recapitulating the whole evidence very minutely, with many pertinent observations, and begging the jury, for God's sake! to divest themselves of all prejudice. At one o'clock the jury retired for half an hour, doubting only whether they should find the prisoner guilty of an assault with an intent to murder, or only of a common assault, when they returned with a verdict, guilty of the whole indictment.

Williams was also found guilty of assaults on the other two women.

Justice William Mainwearing, chairman of the court, then addressed Williams:

> Renwick Williams, you have been indicted for an assault on Ann Porter. You have been tried and found guilty by a cool, impartial, dispassionate, and deliberating jury, much to the satisfaction of the court, and much to their honour; for I must again say, that I never saw a jury conduct themselves with more propriety in all the experience I have had of courts of justice. They seemed to have divested themselves of all prejudice, and to be unconnected with the general mass of people.

Williams was sentenced to two years' imprisonment in Newgate for each of the attacks on the three women, six years in total. This was an unusually long prison sentence for the time, reflecting both popular outrage and judicial perception of the seriousness of the offence.

Although initially Williams, as a celebrity, was visited by many Londoners in his Newgate cell (and there was even a waxwork model exhibited of him attacking the Porters),[63] the case was quickly forgotten. The last recorded Monster attack took place in August 1790, while Williams was imprisoned awaiting the second trial. He remained in prison until his sentence expired in 1796. In the year after his release he married and promptly disappeared from the historical record. He died in the same obscurity in which he had lived until the astonishing events of 1790 threw him so reluctantly into the limelight.[64]

Conclusion

The delicate balance between the legitimised violence of the individual and the authority of the mob, on the one hand, and the demands of public opinion and the brutal power of the state, on the other, changed only very gradually over the course of the eighteenth century. Men defending their honour with swords, pistols and fists became both less acceptable and more clearly limited by the bonds of customary behaviour. The deadly threat of a rapier's thrust, or the sudden blow of a fist outside a pub, was reduced by the introduction of almost courtly rituals. And while domestic assault continued, it too became less tolerated. By the end of the century violent deaths of all sorts caused a new disquiet, even when they clearly resulted from tragic accidents. Similarly, the mob, which had ruled the streets of early eighteenth-century London, became ever less trusted. The middling sort merchants and artisans who willingly put up lights in their windows in support of the anti-Irish riots of 1736 thought better of their actions in the years following the Gordon riots of 1780. In part, the driving force behind these developments was a new public opinion made manifest in the pamphlets and newspapers of Grub Street. The baying crowd demanding retribution and 'justice' did not so much go away, as go into print.

In so many ways, eighteenth-century London witnessed the creation of a recognisably modern world. Its declining violence, its rising tide of public opinion expressed in print and its growing intolerance and distrust of the mob seem oddly familiar. But, with these developments came distinctly modern problems. If the 'Monster' was Britain's first serial sex offender, on trial just as the Marquis de Sade was inventing violent pornography from his prison cell in the Bastille, he was a talisman of developments to come. And if his treatment, both at the Old Bailey and at the bar of public opinion, strikes a niggling note of distrust at this distance, this too seems remarkably modern and painfully familiar.

3

The Trial

As a prisoner, whiling away the hours and days until the next meeting of the court, you had plenty of reasons for both despair and hope. Life in prison was miserable if you were unable to pay for special treatment and although you probably knew why you had been arrested, you often did not know whether you would be tried on a capital charge and face death or a lesser charge. On the plus side, you could reflect on the many opportunities the several stages of the judicial process offered to escape the noose. The charge could be framed as a non-capital offence, the grand jury could throw out the indictment, the prosecutor could fail to appear (which would mean the trial could not proceed), the trial jury could acquit you (as it did in two-fifths of all cases) or you could be found only part guilty (as occurred in another fifth of the cases), thus ensuring a lesser punishment. Even leaving aside the possibility that the judges might exercise mercy in the sentencing process and the very real chance of obtaining a pardon from the king, the likelihood of actually being hanged was relatively low.

Before the sessions commenced, the clerk of the court drew up the indictment, relying on information provided by the victim and written depositions taken by the justice of the peace who conducted the preliminary hearing. Decisions taken at this stage of the legal process were important, since the definition of the offence determined the possible punishment. The grand jury, a body of respectable elite and upper middle-class men including gentlemen, merchants, professionals and wealthy shopkeepers, then met to examine the indictment and decide whether there was sufficient evidence to proceed to trial. If so, it was approved as a 'true bill'; rejected indictments were labelled 'ignoramus' (or 'not found') and the case was immediately dropped.

It was only at this point that you were formally arraigned and asked to plead to the charge. The vast majority pleaded not guilty. Indeed, the court encouraged this plea because if you confessed to a crime there was little flexibility in the punishment meted out, whereas if a trial took place, mitigating evidence could be introduced that might lead to a lesser sentence or a pardon. The small number of defendants who refused to enter a plea were, unless they were found mute 'by visitation of God', subject to the ordeal of *peine forte et dure*, in which they were forced to lie down and have weights placed on them until they either relented or died.

Although the basic format remains the same, eighteenth-century Old Bailey trials share few characteristics with their modern counterparts. The differences are epitomised by their length: eighteenth-century trials were very short, averaging around half an hour per case. On a typical day in the early eighteenth century the court heard between 15 and 20 cases. Some took even less time: in 1833 it was calculated that the average trial took only eight and a half minutes. It is likely that the rapidity with which trials were held severely disadvantaged defendants, who had little time to accustom themselves to the courtroom environment before they were forced to plead their case.

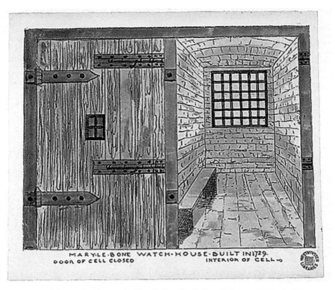

Figure 1.05 The Holding Cell of the St Marylebone Watch House.
Credit: City of Westminster Archives Centre

Figure 2.05 'The Devastations Occasioned by the Rioters of London
Firing the New Gaol of Newgate and Burning Mr Akerman's
Furniture, etc. June 6, 1780'. Credit: City of London, London
Metropolitan Archives

Figure 3.01 'The Old Bailey' by Thomas Rowlandson (1809). From Rudolph Ackermann, *The Microcosm of London* (1808–1810). © Guildhall Library, City of London/The Bridgeman Art Library

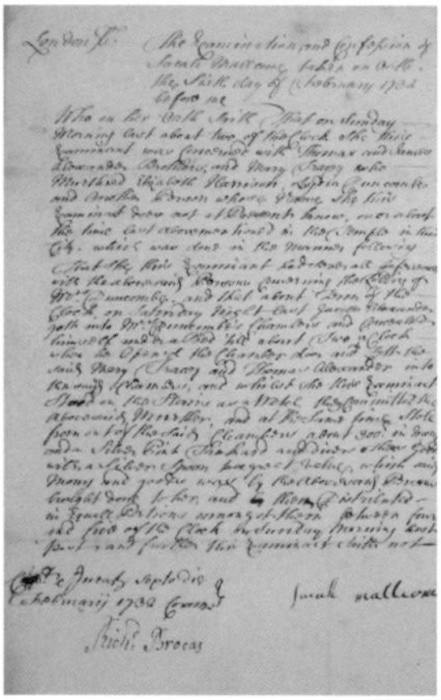

Figure 3.05 Joseph Baretti, after Sir Joshua Reynolds (1773). Credit: National Portrait Gallery, London

Figure 3.03 Sarah Malcolm's Confession (1733). Credit: City of London, London Metropolitan Archives

Figure 3.04 'Sarah Malcolm in Prison', by William Hogarth (1733). William Hogarth, Sarah Malcolm. Detail. © National Gallery of Scotland

Figure 3.06 'Being Nervous and Cross Examined by Mr Garrow', by Thomas Rowlandson (1806). British Museum 10841. © The Trustees of the British Museum

Figure 4.05 William Dodd, by John Russell (1769). National Portrait Gallery, 251. Credit: National Portrait Gallery, London

Figure 4.04 'A Shoplifter Detected' (1787). Courtesy of The Lewis Walpole Library, Yale University

Figure 5.01 'View of an Execution at Tyburn' by John Hamilton (1767). © The Trustees of The British Museum

Figure 5.03 'The Pillory at Charing Cross' by Thomas Rowlandson (1809). From Rudolph Ackermann, *The Microcosm of London* (1808–1810). © Guildhall Library, City of London/The Bridgeman Art Library

The majority of a trial was spent hearing prosecution witness testimony, with the judges frequently intervening to ask questions or make comments. As the defendant, you were then asked to speak. In many cases, particularly where the evidence was clear, defendants chose to say little or nothing. Juries could draw their own conclusions from such behaviour. There was no presumption of innocence and no right to remain silent. Defendants hoping to be acquitted needed to disprove the evidence presented against them and to positively establish their innocence. The presumption was that if you were innocent, you should be able to prove it. Defendants could cross-examine prosecution witnesses and call their own witnesses but, unlike prosecutors, they could not compel witnesses to attend and, since trials were not scheduled, they did not know when witnesses needed to appear in court. Witnesses who could testify to the defendant's good character were especially helpful, since many verdicts were decided by the appearance of trustworthiness presented by each side. And even if you were found guilty, evidence of a good character might lead to a lesser punishment.

The introduction of lawyers fundamentally altered the character of trials. Very few lawyers participated in Old Bailey trials before the 1730s, and for many decades thereafter they were the exception rather than the rule. In the 1690s the government began to hire lawyers to prosecute the most serious offences, including cases of seditious words and libel, treason, coining, and violent offences such as murder, rape, and robbery. Once the role of lawyers for the prosecution was established, they were increasingly hired by victims pursuing private prosecutions to ensure cases were handled properly. As a defendant in misdemeanour and treason cases (from 1696) you could also have a lawyer represent you, but they were excluded in felony cases (except for the purpose of raising narrow points of law) until the mid-1730s. In relation to felonies, lawyers were thought to be unnecessary and possibly even harmful: you should not need help to tell the truth. Moreover, judges were explicitly charged with looking out for defendants' interests, and to admit defence lawyers would be to admit that they were failing in this duty. By the 1730s, however, the growing number of lawyers appearing for the prosecution led the courts to allow counsel for the defence as a way of establishing a more level playing field. Even so, defence lawyers were not allowed to address the jury until 1836 and they were, in any case, rarely used until the late eighteenth century. Even in 1800 only one-quarter to one-third of defendants in property cases had counsel.

Defence lawyers became actively involved in the cross-examination of prosecution witnesses and they frequently suggested that the prosecutor or his witnesses had ulterior motives. They pointed to the rewards witnesses might expect after a successful conviction, as was the case with thieftakers, and they repeatedly accused accomplices who turned king's evidence of perjuring themselves to save their own lives. It was the close questioning of prosecution witnesses in this way that led to the court becoming increasingly sceptical of evidence provided by accomplices, where this was not corroborated by another witness. Defence lawyers also contributed to judicial distrust of hearsay evidence and pre-trial confessions. Their participation also meant that defendants sometimes no longer testified at all (this eventually led to defendants acquiring the right to remain silent). Consequently, prosecution cases gradually became subject to higher standards of proof, tipping the balance of power in the courtroom, which had been heavily weighted against defendants at the beginning of the century, towards them as the century progressed. This shift, however, only occurred for defendants who were able to afford the cost of counsel (no state assistance was available except in cases of murder). In most cases, where the defendant was too poor to hire a lawyer, the prosecution retained the upper hand. The presence of lawyers (on both sides) also led to a reduction in the role of the judge. In the absence of lawyers, judges played a major role in conducting trials. They examined witnesses and the accused and often clearly stated their own views on the merits of the case. Although after 1670 judges were no longer allowed to punish juries who failed to produce the verdict they wanted, judges continued to put pressure on juries, by asking them, for example, why they had reached a particular verdict or by requesting them to reconsider their decision.

Trial juries were composed exclusively of men, and of men only marginally less respectable than those included in the grand jury. Often having considerable prior experience of jury service, they rarely took long to make their decisions. Until 1737 they typically heard several trials in a row before they retired to consider the verdicts. With the rebuilding of the courtroom in that year, space was provided for the first time for the jury to sit together and from then on verdicts were pronounced after each trial, frequently after simply huddling together in the courtroom. The speed with which verdicts were arrived at suggests that the views of the foreman and the most experienced jurors tended to predominate. But jurors may have also been influenced by the spectators almost at their elbows, watching their deliberations. The jury could declare the defendant innocent or guilty or could deliver a partial verdict. In the last case, defendants were found guilty of part of the charges against them or of a lesser offence, such as theft but not with violence, manslaughter rather than murder or the theft of goods to the value of only 39s. Because the nature of the charge determined the possible punishments, the choice between guilty or part guilty was vital; partial verdicts often saved the convict's life. Such decisions were made taking into account the defendant's age, sex and character as well as the actual evidence. Indeed, this last was often explicitly ignored, as juries often committed 'pious perjury', for example by valuing goods manifestly worth more than 40s (such as coins to a higher value) at only 39s. This ensured that the convict could not be sentenced to death (theft of goods worth 40s or more from a house was a capital offence).

In reading the trial accounts published in the *Proceedings*, it is frequently difficult to understand why a particular verdict was reached. Many people were declared innocent when the trial evidence appears to suggest a guilty verdict, while many others, against whom the evidence was considerably weaker, were nonetheless found guilty. In part, this impression of inconsistency reflects the importance the eighteenth-century court put on aspects of judgment that could not be recorded in words on the published page. The appearance and demeanour of the defendant and prosecutor; the unstated local knowledge of jurymen; and the subtle role of contemporary prejudices about the nature of crime all contributed to the final verdict.

Trials placed defendants at a huge disadvantage. Typically without the benefit of legal assistance, they had to organise their defence on their own while in prison. Unaware of the specific evidence that would be presented against them until they stood at the bar, they had to respond spontaneously to statements made in court. This was thought to be the best way of ascertaining the truth, but it put the accused under immense pressure. At the same time, prosecutors also suffered under this system. They too often lacked legal counsel and judges were sometimes partial to the defendant. But at least prosecutors had the advantage of being able to plan the case in advance, while at liberty. Although at the end of the century the increasing use of defence counsel restored some of the balance, most defendants were unable to afford legal assistance. Their hopes rested on the mercy of the judge and the sympathy of the jury.

He was a Frightful Corpse

Coroner's inquests were summoned in response to almost every unusual death. Held in the front room of an alehouse as near the scene as possible, most inquests resulted in a verdict of accidental death or suicide or one of several versions of death by misadventure. In the minority of cases where an individual was held responsible for the killing, a verdict of manslaughter or murder was returned and the case was referred to the Old Bailey for trial. By the eighteenth century medical doctors were taking a growing role in determining the cause of death, but the most important element of a coroner's inquest was its ability to construct a consistent story. Where the evidence was confused and contradictory, where, as in this case, the micro-politics of poverty led to blame and distrust, there was little option but to take the case forward to the grand jury and, finally, to trial.

Catherine Constable and her husband ran a low lodging house – home to the itinerant, the ill and the desperate. Located in St Sepulchre's just south of Smithfield Market, it witnessed the rough-scrabble poverty of Londoners on the edge of destitution. Perhaps half a dozen lodgers and sub-tenants were living there in the autumn of 1739, and Richard Challenger, Dick to his friends, was among the poorest of them. He paid just a few pence a night, perhaps 1s 6d per week and lodged in the cellar. He spent very little time there, however. Like many poor men and women, he lived primarily in public, eating and drinking from street stalls and in gin shops. The streets also provided him with employment: according to an acquaintance, 'He used to sell greens about the streets o'mornings, and fish o'nights.' His health was bad. His skin was 'all over scabs and sores' and

there were blotches all over his body, the exterior signs of
venereal disease. But it was not so bad as to cause his friends
concern. Venereal disease was almost endemic among the
poor, and while it resulted in scabs and scars, in the gradual
erosion of the bone and cartilage that gave shape to your
nose and forehead, it could take decades to kill you.

On the morning of Saturday 10 November 1739
Challenger was out at work when he met James Powel, who
later testified that:

> Between ten and eleven in the morning, I was at Casey's
> in the Old Bailey, and Challenger came in to sell greens.
> He was then as hearty as any one in this court; and if I
> had had a hundred pounds to have laid out in the
> insurance of any man's life, I would have insured Dick's.

That same day, just after noon, however, Mary Belville had
a drink with Challenger:

> At the Lion and Ball, at the corner of Fleet Lane. He told
> me he was not exceeding well – not so well as he should
> be. I am so cold, says he, that I am like a post. I told him
> we would have a pint of beer and it should be warmed.
> After which I asked the woman of the house if she wanted
> any greens, if she did, Dick would bring her some? She
> said, he might if he pleased, and he went out and brought
> her his greens, and she bought four Savoy cabbages and
> six cauliflowers.

No one knows where Challenger spent the rest of the
afternoon and evening, but he arrived home in his cups
sometime after ten o'clock to find one of his fellow lodgers,
Elizabeth Bradshaw, waiting for him. Down on his luck,
Challenger had borrowed six pence from her to buy greens
to sell, and owed a further few pence to a local shop.
Elizabeth Tranter witnessed the scene:

> On Saturday night, November the 10th, Dick came home
> between ten and eleven and Bradshaw said to him, So
> Dick, where's the ten-pence halfpenny you owe me? Dick

said, Mrs Bradshaw, I can't give it you tonight, but if
you'll stay till morning, when I have sold my greens, by
God you shall have it. She told him she'd stay no longer,
and if he did not pay her that night, he should not come
in; he should come in there no more, till he brought the
money. There are four steps at the door, and he was upon
the top of the steps when he told her he could not pay her
that night. I saw Bradshaw give him a push down all the
four steps. He stood with his face toward hers. She
pushed him down backwards and he fell down all the
steps.

What happened next is a confused jumble of claim and
counter-claim. Tranter recalled that Challenger:

Was shut out for half an hour, in which time I heard him
call out, Mr Constable! Mr Constable! [the landlord of the
house]. Is a poor man to be murdered because he has got
no money? He spoke this very faintly, and I hearing him,
let him in in the dark, so I can't tell what condition he
was then in, but he complained of his head, and went
down to his cellar. I did not see him again till seven
o'clock the next morning. He was then sitting upright in
the bed, with his clothes on and he had bled a vast deal.
His shirt and pillow were very bloody and his hair was
matted with the blood that came from his head. He
hallooed out, Thieves! Thieves were come to rob him!
That was the occasion of my going down. I asked him
how he did? He said he was very ill, very cold. There was
no surgeon or apothecary called to help him, but
somebody got him a hot pot, which he could not drink, he
was so weak. There was a woman washing in the cellar
and she saw all this as well as I. The accident happened
on Saturday night, and on Sunday night, about six, he
died.
    I was present when the body was washed. A woman
who lived at Constable's washed him, but she is not here.
I saw his head was bloody, and the blood came from the
back part of his head, but the hair was not cut off so near
as that I could see any wound. There was no coroner
called, and but one searcher; and when she came, Mr

Constable called me up stairs, and bid me take no notice
of the cut in his head. The deceased was drunk when he
fell down, but not so much as to be insensible of what he
said, or did; and I don't believe Bradshaw pushed him
down wilfully; she did not do it with any great force.

Elizabeth Bradshaw presented herself as even less
responsible for Constable's death. Challenger:

Came home between eleven and twelve on Saturday night.
I asked him for my money and swore he should not come
in till he paid me; and I argued some time with him for it.
Then I put my hand to his shoulder and he turned down
the steps and tumbled. After this I let him in myself and
he went into the kitchen and sat two hours by the fire
without making any complaint, and paid me five farthings
of my money.

Margaret Atkins also lodged at the Constable's. She:

Came home on Saturday night, between ten and eleven
and found Challenger sitting in the chimney corner. He
called for hot drink. Tranter warmed it for him, and he
seemed brisk. I sat up in his company till between one
and two. At one, I told him t'was time to go to bed, but he
desired to stay longer. At last he took a candle and went
down to bed. I followed him down to see he did no
mischief with his candle. He stood sea-sawing upon the
stairs and told me, he was so drunk that he could not get
into his bed. I desired him to take care of his candle, for,
says I, if we should all be burned in our beds, what shall
we do. So I came up, and desired Tranter to look after
him. In the morning, Elizabeth Tranter went down and
gave him a dram of aniseed. He complained of no wound,
nor did I see any blood.

The day after the incident Mary Belville arrived on the
scene: 'On Sunday I sent to Challenger's cellar for a head of
celery and heard that Dick was fuddled, and was not up'.
She was followed by Challenger's friend and business
partner, Joseph Taylor:

We were partners and sold fish and greens together. He
was the first that let me into the business. On Sunday
morning I went to his cellar and served Belville a
halfpennyworth of greens. I called, Dick! Dick! But
nobody answering, I pushed open the cellar door and went
down, and found him lying stark naked on the ground,
with his knees up to his mouth. I lifted him up and put
him in bed, and called Mr Constable. He came down with
another friend and gave him part of a pint of hot liquor
with gin or brandy or something, put into it. I saw no
blood on him. There was a scar upon his head, just upon
his crown. You may call it a scratch and I believe the
pebble stones behind him might do that, for I found him
lying upon them. When the hot pint came down, he
looked very hard at me, but could only say, Joe! very
cold! very cold, Joe! I stayed with him till four o'clock,
then I left him.

Taylor was then followed by the landlady, Catherine
Constable:

I went down into the cellar on Sunday morning and saw
Challenger leaning on his elbow. I asked him, what ailed
him? Mrs Constable, says he, I am so cold, I am like a
post, feel me! I took hold of him and found him very cold
and chilled down all one side of him, upon which I bid
Tranter give him a glass of aniseed, and I supported his
head while he drank it. God bless you, Mrs Constable,
said he, I am cold as a post. He made no complaints, and
as for blood – I saw none.

Dick Challenger died on Sunday evening, and the cares of
life and health were replaced by the rituals of death.
Elizabeth Tranter 'warmed two pots of water and brought
them down'. Tranter did not touch the body herself, and
later said to a neighbour, Hester Barber: 'I am surprised how
they can touch him, he's all over scabs and sores'.
Nevertheless, Catherine Constable and Mary Melville
washed the body and laid it out ready for burial. By Monday
morning Dick Challenger was in the ground.

To some, however, the rapidity of the burial seemed suspicious. No coroner's inquest had been called and no enquiries made. Of course, an inquest was expensive, and the Constables were likely to find themselves lumbered with the bill, but even so, burying a body, however humble, within just a few hours of death when neither the weather nor disease made it imperative, just looked suspicious. The local justice of the peace, Sir William Billers, got wind of the death and instructed his clerk to make enquiries. He 'sent a letter to the coroner, who ordered the body to be taken up, and a proper inquiry to be made'. A formal inquest was called and John Row, a surgeon:

> Was sent for to inspect the body the night the jury sat on it, which was the Thursday after the accident. Mr Snow scalped him and I examined the head and brain. There was no contusion through the flesh, only through the skin, or in the way of rubbing, as by a brick.

Despite inconclusive and contradictory evidence from this and other witnesses, the coroner's jury had to choose a verdict. Although the evidence was largely based on rumour and suspicion, Elizabeth Bradshaw was charged with the killing.

Just under a month later, on 5 December, she stood trial for her life at the Old Bailey. Witness after witness was called and the last poverty-soaked days of Dick Challenger's life were rehearsed. In the end the jury decided that, drunk and riddled with disease, Challenger was just one more victim of the streets, and that while a wrong may have been committed, it was so commonplace a wrong that no punishment could be extracted from its perpetrators.[1]

Refusing to Plead

Defendants who refused to enter a plea effectively rejected the authority of the court. This subversive behaviour could not be tolerated, and judges responded by first threatening and then

ordering the terrible practice of placing crushing weights on the
accused until either they relented or death intervened. While it
seems incredible that anyone would willingly undergo such a
procedure, refusal to plead provided almost the last opportunity
for criminals to demonstrate their bravery and defiance of
established authority.

In a letter home, César de Saussure, a Swiss traveller who
visited London in 1725–29, described a bizarre judicial
practice:

> There is a sort of question called the 'press', which is
> made use of when an accused person refuses to plead or
> contest the authority of the tribunal over him. In these
> cases he is stretched on the ground, his feet and hands are
> tied to stakes, and on his stomach is placed a plank with
> weights, more weights being added every four hours. The
> accused remains without food in this position until he
> consents to plead his cause and to recognise the validity
> of the tribunal. Cases have been known of criminals
> preferring to die in this fashion after two or three days of
> atrocious suffering, rather than by the hands of the
> executioner, and this in order not to leave a mark of
> infamy on their families, and to save their possessions
> from going to the crown according to the law.[2]

This procedure was *peine forte et dure*, a corruption of the
medieval practice of 'hard and severe punishment' imposed
on defendants who refused trial by jury after trial by ordeal
was abolished in 1215.[3] There are a handful of cases of
defendants refusing to plead at the Old Bailey in the 1670s
and 1680s, but by 1700 most people assumed that the
practice had been abandoned. In 1721, however, while
London was in the grip of an epidemic of highway robbery,
it was revived. In that year there were three cases recorded at
the Old Bailey, and a further case in neighbouring Surrey.
Together, they generated substantial publicity, which is
probably how de Saussure became aware of the practice.

William Spiggot (or Spigget) had been a highwayman for
over seven years and led a gang of at least eight men.[4] He
claimed to have committed numerous robberies, chiefly on
the roads leading from London out to Hounslow Heath,
Kingston and Ware. In January 1721 the gang was cornered
by some of Jonathan Wild's men in a Westminster tavern,
The Blue Boar, and several were arrested. One, Joseph
Lindsey, a clergyman sunk from religion to gambling and
highway robbery, turned king's evidence in return for a
pardon and testified against the others. On 13 January
Spiggot, Thomas Cross and William Heater were brought
to the Old Bailey to be tried. As the *Proceedings* report:

> William Spigget alias Spiggot, and Thomas Phillips alias
> Cross, having had several bills of indictment for robbing
> on the highway found against them by the grand jury,
> were brought to the bar to be arraigned and take their
> trials, but they stood mute and refused to plead till they
> should have the money, horses, accoutrements, and other
> things which were taken from them when they were
> apprehended returned to them.

But as the court reminded them, their goods had been
seized and given to those who apprehended them as a
reward under the terms of an act of parliament 'for
encouraging the apprehending of highwaymen' passed in
1692. The relevant part of the statute was read out:

> And it is hereby further enacted that all and every person
> or persons who shall so take, apprehend, prosecute, or
> commit such robber or robbers, as a further reward shall
> have and enjoy to his and their proper use and behoof the
> horse, furniture and arms, money, or other goods of the
> said robber or robbers that shall be taken with him or
> them.

In increasingly sensational language, the *Proceedings*
provided a full report of what followed:

But they still refusing to plead, the court acquainted them with the ill consequences of their refusal, and what a heavy judgment they would draw down upon themselves if they persisted in their obstinacy; and the more effectually to convince them of their folly and error, ordered the judgment to be read to them, which if they continued mute must be pronounced against them, and put in execution, which judgment was to the effect following:

That the prisoner shall be sent to the prison from whence he came, and put into a mean house, stopped from light, and there shall be laid upon the bare ground without any litter, straw or other covering, and without any garment about him, saving something to cover his privy members and that he shall lie upon his back, and his head shall be covered, and his feet bare, and that one of his arms shall be drawn with a cord to one side of the house, and the other arm to the other side, and that his legs shall be used in the same manner, and that upon his body shall be laid so much iron and stone as he can bear, and more, and that the first day after he shall have three morsels of barley bread, without any drink, and the second day he shall drink so much as he can three times of the water which is next the prison door, saving running water, without any bread: and this shall be his diet until he dies. And he against whom this judgment shall be given, forfeits to the king his goods.

All this having no effect upon them, the executioner was called and ordered to tie their thumbs, as usual in such cases; but all being in vain, and they still peremptorily refusing, and declaring that they would not plead notwithstanding all the admonition that could be given them; the court proceeded to pass sentence against them to be pressed to death, as the law directs. Whereupon they were carried back to Newgate in order to undergo that judgment the law had inflicted on them; but when they came to the press, Thomas Phillips alias Cross desired to be carried again to the bar, saying he would plead.

When Thomas Cross, a 33-year-old former seaman who could neither read nor write, was brought back to the

Figure 3.02 'William Spiggot
being Pressed in Newgate'.
Credit: British Library Board. All
Rights Reserved. Shelfmark
1485.p.8

bar after he agreed to plead, Spiggot, a 29-year-old father of three, was brought with him in the hope that he, too, would change his mind. He did not, and instead 'remained inflexible, and insulted the court'. Therefore he was brought back to the press room in Newgate and forced to lie naked spread-eagled on the ground, while iron weighing a total of 350 pounds was placed on his chest. Before he was put into the press, Thomas Purney, the Ordinary of Newgate, tried to 'dissuade him from being the author and occasion of his own death; and from cutting himself off from that space and time which the law allowed him, to repent in, for his vicious course of life'. He replied, 'if he came to take care of his soul, he would regard him, but if he came about his body, he desired to be excused, he could not hear one word', and submitted to the press. In his *Ordinary's Account*, Purney reported what followed:

> I there prayed by him, and at times asked him, why he
> would destroy his soul as well as body, by such an
> obstinate kind of self murder. All his answer was, pray for
> me, pray for me! In the midst of his groans, he sometimes
> lay silent, as if insensible of pain; then would fetch his
> breath very quick and fast. Two or three times, he
> complained that they had laid a cruel weight on his face,
> though nothing was upon his face, but just a thin cloth;
> that was however removed and laid more light and hollow,

but he still complained of the prodigious weight they had
laid upon his face; which might be occasioned by the
blood being flushed and forced up into his face; and
pressing as violently against the veins and small tendrils
there, as if the pressure upon them had been externally on
his face.

After half an hour of this 'torture', as Purney called it, an
extra 50 pounds was added, which finally caused Spiggot to
recant and tell those present, including a justice of the peace
and Purney, that he would plead:

> Accordingly, the weights were at once taken off, the cords
> that stretched out his hands were cut, and he was lifted
> up, and held by two men, while some brandy was put into
> his mouth to revive him. He was very faint and almost
> speechless, for two days.[5]

Few were actually pressed to death; most defendants gave up
before even seeing the press, after the first step of the
procedure was completed when their thumbs were tied
tightly together with whipcord in open court. Spiggot
remained defiant far longer than most.

Spiggot was brought back to the Old Bailey, where he and
Cross pleaded not guilty to indictments for the robberies of
John Watkins and John Turner. William Heater, who had not
refused to plead, was also indicted as an accessory to this
second robbery, for harbouring Spiggot and Cross and
receiving the stolen goods. The evidence against the two
principals was strong. Watkins positively identified Cross and
Spiggot as two of the thieves who had robbed him on
Hounslow Heath and Turner's stolen goods had been found
in Spiggot's lodgings. The testimony against Heater, however,
was only circumstantial: several witnesses testified that they
had seen him leading the horses which were used in the
robberies. Perhaps unsurprisingly given the strength of the
evidence against them and their previous behaviour, Spiggot
and Cross offered no defence, other than to exonerate Heater:

> The prisoners Spiggot and Cross both declared that
> Heater was innocent of the matter, and only acted as a
> porter in fetching and carrying their horses.

The jury had little trouble reaching a verdict, and the punishment was inevitable, given the severity of the crime:

> The evidence not being sufficient against Heater, the jury
> acquitted him, and found Spiggot and Phillips alias Cross
> guilty of these indictments, who had also several other
> indictments found against them. Death.

Both were executed at Tyburn on 8 February 1721 and the crowd, perhaps impressed with Spiggot's heroism in having experienced the ordeal of the press, carried off his body so it could not be dissected by the surgeons.

Why had Cross and Spiggot even contemplated facing such a horrific procedure? According to Purney:

> The reasons, as far I could learn from Spiggot, of his
> enduring the press, were, that he might preserve his
> effects, for the use of his family; that it might not be
> urged to his children, that their father was hanged; and
> that Lindsey should not triumph over him, by saying he
> had sent him to Tyburn.[6]

The first point is unconvincing, since those dying under the press forfeited their goods to the crown. It does not appear that the material well-being of Spiggot's family was his primary concern. Rather, as the second and third points suggest, he sought to maintain his reputation as a man of courage and resolution, as the leader of a gang, not a victim.

In telling their life stories to the Ordinary as they awaited their executions, both Cross and Spiggot bragged about their crimes, with Spiggot saying, 'It was in vain to mention his numerous robberies on the highway, being perhaps about a hundred'. Cross:

> Seemed to glory in the robberies he had committed, and
> said that Spiggot and he once robbed at ten o'clock at

night one hundred passengers, whom they took out of
several wagons that followed in a train; and that they set
the passengers in a row along the road, and robbed and
counted them.[7]

The Ordinary, Thomas Purney, went out of his way to try
and refute these men's idea of courage, giving a sermon to all
10 prisoners awaiting execution on 'the nature of Christian
courage'. No doubt particularly with Cross and Spiggot in
mind, he included a passage discussing two kinds of 'false
courage':

> 1st. That it was a false courage, for malefactors sentenced
> to die, to appear wholly careless and unconcerned at the
> great change of nature; which rather shows obdurateness
> and insensibility than a manly and becoming resolution.
> 2dly, That it was a false courage for malefactors assured
> that they shall die, to lay violent hands upon themselves,
> to prevent the effects of the law; as there is something
> cowardly and base in cutting off our lives, for fear of pain
> and shame.

Purney further commented that:

> We had instances of men of uncommon impiety who so
> much more valued the good opinion of men, than the
> praise of God and angels; and had endeavoured to
> preserve the honour of their families, even at the expense
> of throwing themselves into hell.[8]

Purney was right: by defying the court in refusing to plead,
Cross and Spiggot sought to cement their reputations as
men of courage and resolution, reputations which had been
established during their substantial careers as highwaymen.
In doing so, they were clearly playing to the gallery. Popular
opinion valued criminals who challenged the authorities,
such as those who died 'game' (steadfastly and defiantly) at
Tyburn.[9]

After this case, however, very few defendants at the Old
Bailey refused to enter a plea, perhaps because the growing

use of transportation meant that the accused had greater hopes of avoiding the death penalty. Although the procedure of *peine forte et dure* remained on the books until 1772, it was increasingly viewed by enlightened opinion as irrational and barbaric. After it was finally abolished, refusal to plead was deemed to be the equivalent of pleading guilty. In 1827, by which time many defendants were saying very little and leaving their defence entirely to their counsel, this presumption of guilt was reversed and refusal to plead was deemed the same as pleading innocent. This legacy of the medieval trial by ordeal had finally been erased.[10]

The Irish Prosecutor

In the absence of lawyers most trials began with testimony from the victim, who usually provided the most damning evidence against the defendant. Although the court normally treated such testimony with respect, the prosecutor occasionally became the butt of the proceedings. This happened most frequently when the supposed victim of a theft was visiting a prostitute at the time. There was a strong belief that the libidinous men, usually drunk, who found themselves in this position deserved everything they got. In this case, the published Proceedings *reinforced this humiliation of the prosecutor by reproducing the peculiarities of his accent and voice in print.*

At 11 pm on 25 February 1725 an Irishman, James Fitzgerald, was walking under Newgate near the courthouse at the Old Bailey when he met Susan Grimes, a prostitute from St Giles in the Fields. When he described this encounter in his testimony at the Old Bailey, his heavy Irish accent was reported phonetically in the *Proceedings*, as the publisher played to traditional anti-Irish prejudices and sought to exploit the entertainment value of the case.

Fitzgerald's 's's were transformed into 'sh's, making him
appear both ridiculous and possibly still drunk:

> James Fitzgerald deposed to this effect. On the 25th of
> February last, about 11 at night, O' my shoul, I wash got
> pretty drunk, and wash going very shoberly along the Old
> Bailey, and there I met the preeshoner upon the bar, as
> she wash going before me. I wash after asking her which
> way she wash walking, and she made a laugh upon my
> faush, and took me to Newtoner's Lane.

Here the negotiations commenced:

> Arrah joy (shaid I) you should always have somebody
> with you, when you go sho far alone. She told me she
> would be after taking me with her, if I would give her any
> thing. Arrah, my dear shoul (said I) you shall never fear
> but I will give you shome thing, if I have got nothing
> myself.

They walked together a considerable distance to her
lodgings (across Holborn Bridge, down Holborn Hill and
along High Holborn and Broad St Giles to Oxford Street),
before finally arriving at her lodgings on Charles Street.
Fitzgerald denied, however, that he intended to have sex
with Grimes:

> Sho we went together; but not having any deshign to be
> consherned with her, I paid her landlady a shilling for a
> bed. For it ish my way to make love upon a woman in the
> street, and go home with her, whenshoever I intend to lie
> alone.

Portraying himself as the passive actor in this case, he said
Grimes became aggressive once they got to the bedroom. As
his testimony proceeded, however, it sounded ever more
ridiculous to his English audience:

> But ash to the preceshoner, she wash after making me shit
> upon the bed with her, and sho tumble together; but I
> wash after shitting in the chair, and then she was coming

> to shit in my lap; but I would not let her, and sho she shit
> beside me; and then I wash hoping that she would be
> eashy; but for all that she would not let me shit at quiet,
> for she wash after being concerned with my breeches, and
> got away my watch whether I would or no; and I pulled,
> and she pulled; and sho for fear she should get it from
> me, I let go my hold.

Having, by his account, lost his watch, he told the court:

> I went for a constable, and he carried her to the
> watchhouse, where he took the watch upon her.
> He found it in a plaushe that my modesty won't suffer
> me to name; for ash I am a living Chreestian, she had
> put it into her ****.

The constable confirmed that he had found the watch on
Grimes, but with uncharacteristic modesty, the *Proceedings*
did not reveal precisely where the watch had been concealed.

In her defence, Grimes no doubt spoke in a heavy
cockney accent, but the *Proceedings* reported it with
conventional English spellings, rendering her testimony
much more believable than that of her prosecutor – at least
for the reading public. According to her, Fitzgerald was the
one seeking sex, and she was the one who called for
assistance:

> I met the prosecutor under Newgate; he took hold of me,
> and asked where I was going? I told him to my lodging in
> Charles Street and bid him go about his business; but he
> would follow me home. My landlady opened the door,
> and then I desired him to leave me; but he catched hold of
> her hand, and said he would come in and drink for he was
> as well acquainted there as I was. So he called for two or
> three quatterns of brandy, and having no money to pay for
> it, he pawned his watch to her for 5 shillings. He was so
> impudent that we were both forced to fall upon our knees
> to keep his hands from under our petticoats. Then he
> would have gone up to bed with me; which I refusing, he
> threatened to swear my life away; for he said he was an

Irishman, and could swear farther than ten Englishmen.
Whereupon I called in a watchman, and so we were both
taken into custody.

Faced with this contradictory evidence and two witnesses
(an apparently drunken Irishman and a prostitute) who were
no doubt both considered of dubious character, the jury may
have found it difficult to decide which to believe. In the end,
possibly instructed by the judge, they acquitted Grimes on a
technicality. She had been indicted on the wrong charge. As
the *Proceedings* report:

It appearing upon the prosecutor's oath that she took the
watch from him violently, and with his knowledge; and
she being indicted for stealing it privately, and without his
knowledge, the jury acquitted her.

But this was not the end of the story. A few months later
the publisher of the *Proceedings* was summoned to appear
before the Court of Aldermen, and 'to bring with him at the
same time the person who takes the minutes at the sessions
house and transcribes the same for the press'. When they
appeared they were censured for 'the lewd and indecent
manner of printing the last sessions paper' and ordered to
acknowledge their offence and ask the pardon of the court.
They agreed, and their apology was published by order of
the court in the weekly newspaper, the *Post Boy*. For the
future, the court also ordered:

That Mr Town Clerk do for the future give notice to such
persons as shall from time to time be authorised to print
and publish the proceedings of the sessions that they take
care to publish the same in such a manner as may give no
cause of offence.[11]

Henceforth, readers of the *Proceedings* would encounter a
more sober tone. But given the large number of trials which
featured prostitutes picking their clients' pockets, readers
could continue to rely on the *Proceedings* for lewd

entertainment; and no doubt continued to enjoy reading about prosecutors struggling to present themselves as wholly innocent victims in circumstances where their own behaviour might well be questioned.[12]

Sarah Malcolm's Defence

Until the mid-1730s, defendants were never represented by lawyers at the Old Bailey; they were expected to make their own defence. Nor were they warned in advance of the evidence that was to be presented against them. It was believed that confronting the accused directly with the evidence and demanding an unmediated response was the best means of ascertaining the truth. In the words of one legal authority, it took 'no manner of skill to make a plain and honest defence'. Often caught red handed, many defendants had little or nothing to say. Others, despite their innocence, found it difficult to make a convincing case in the few short minutes available to them. But in this extraordinary trial, the defendant mounted a resolute and surprisingly powerful case, even though she was a poor young woman accused of a heinous offence, and she was pleading for her life in front of an all-male court and jury.

On 6 February 1733 the London newspapers reported a terrible crime:

> On Sunday morning, a most horrid murder was
> committed in the Temple, upon three women, by persons
> unknown. The case was one Mrs Duncomb, a widow,
> upwards of 70 years of age, who lived up four pair of
> stairs, and there also lived with her another elderly person
> as a companion, and she kept a maid about seventeen
> years of age. Some persons got in as supposed at the top
> of the house, and so into the chambers, and murdered the
> three persons in their beds. They lay in three different
> rooms, and it is supposed they murdered the maid first,
> her throat being cut from ear to ear; but by her cap being
> off, and her hair much entangled, it is supposed she

struggled. The companion seemed to have been strangled, though there are two or three wounds in her throat supposed to have been done by a nail; and the old gentlewoman it's thought was smothered, and killed last of all, she lying across the bed with a gown on, though the others were in bed. A trunk in the room was broke open and rifled.[13]

The following day Sarah Malcolm was arrested and charged with the crime. Examined by Sir Richard Brocas, Alderman of London and future Lord Mayor, she made a limited confession under oath:

> On Sunday morning last about two of the clock she was concerned with Thomas and James Alexander, brothers, and Mary Tracey who murdered Elizabeth Harrison, Lydia Duncomb and another person whose name she does not know, in the Temple in this City, which was done in the manner following. That she had several conferences with the above named persons concerning the robbing of Mrs Duncomb and that about ten of the clock on Saturday night last James Alexander got into Mrs Duncomb's chambers and concealed himself under a bed till about two o'clock when he opened the chamber door and let the said Mary Tracey and Thomas Alexander into the said chambers, and whilst she stood on the stairs as a watch they committed the above said murder, and at the same time stole from out of the chambers about £300 in money and a silver pint tankard and diverse other goods with a silver spoon to a great value, which money and goods was by the above persons brought down to her, and then distributed in equal portions amongst them between four and five of the clock on Sunday morning last past.[14]

Malcolm signed the confession and was committed to Newgate to await trial. The allegations she levelled against her accomplices were initially dismissed by the authorities. At the coroner's inquest on 8 February the jury:

> Brought in their verdict of wilful murder, and committed Sarah Malcolm only, it not then appearing that any other

person was concerned. As to her confession, they gave no
regard to it, none knowing any such persons she
pretended to be her accomplices.

Nonetheless, the next day Mary Tracey and Thomas and
James Alexander were arrested and brought before Richard
Brocas for examination. As the *London Magazine* reported:

Nothing appeared before him to found a suspicion upon
of their being guilty; nonetheless Malcolm insisting on it,
they were committed to Newgate. But it being thought
that she accused them only in order to save her own life,
they were allowed one shilling per day each, by the
Society of the Temple, during their confinement.[15]

The newspapers adopted a similar position, characterising
Malcolm as a cunning murderess and dismissing her claim
that she had not carried out the murders as a crude attempt
to turn king's evidence in order to avoid prosecution.[16]

At her trial on 21 February for the murders of Ann Price,
Elizabeth Harrison and Lydia Duncomb, as well as the
burglary of Duncomb's room, Malcolm was in an almost
impossible position. Not only had she already confessed to a
limited role in the crime, but public opinion had essentially
convicted her of the rest. Furthermore, while the
prosecution was conducted by a lawyer, she had to defend
herself unaided.

The trial lasted five hours, many times longer than most.
It began with a summary of the case presented by
prosecution counsel:

Mrs Lydia Duncomb was a widow lady, about 80 years of
age. She had one maid, Elizabeth Harrison, who had lived
with her many years, and was grown old in her service,
for she was about 60, and very infirm withal. But though
she was now past her labour, the good lady retained her
still, and hired others to do her work. Sarah Malcolm had
formerly been employed on such occasions as a
charwoman, and by that means had an opportunity of

becoming acquainted with Mrs Duncomb's circumstances. But about three months ago Mrs Duncomb hired Ann Price (the unhappy creature, for the murder of whom the prisoner stands indicted) to be a constant servant. She was a young maid not above 17. Mrs Duncomb had a middling fortune left her by her husband, and thus she lived with her two maids contented and in peace, till this night, this fatal night, the 4th of February! When (if my instructions are right) Sarah Malcolm entered the chambers of this little family and cruelly deprived them both of their lives and their money.

The prosecutor went on to explain how this 'barbarous fact' came to light the following day when a friend of Mrs Duncomb went visiting. When no one answered the door, she began to fear something was wrong, and with the help of a second friend and a laundress who worked in the apartment next door, eventually got in through a window.

They entered. But the surprise, the horror they were in, is not to be expressed, when the first object they fixed their eyes on was the poor unhappy young maid murdered! Inhumanely murdered! and lying weltering in her own blood, her hands clenched, her hair loose, and her throat cut from ear to ear! A terrible spectacle. But this was not all, the tragical scene did not close here. The honest old servant lay strangled on her bed, and a little farther, her good old lady robbed of her life in the same manner.

The eloquent prosecutor then described the circumstances which led to the arrest of Sarah Malcolm:

About twelve the same night Mr Kerrel coming home, found the prisoner (who was his laundress) in his chambers. He little expected to see her there at such an hour. He had heard of these murders and knew that she had formerly charred for Mrs Duncomb. He asked her if any body was taken up for the murders. She said, no. He told her, it was suspected the fact must have been done by somebody that was acquainted with the deceased. And as he had heard that she had formerly done business there,

she should continue no longer in his service, and
therefore bid her look up his things and go. Upon
examining he missed some of his clothes, and she
confessed she had pawned them. This made him still more
uneasy, and he resolved she should stay no longer; upon
which she went down stairs. His suspicion caused him to
search further, and in the close stool he found some linen,
and a silver tankard, with the handle bloody. Looking
under his bed, he found a shift and an apron all bloody.
These discoveries gave him an extraordinary concern. He
called the watch, and sent them after her. Such was the
providence of God that she had not power to go beyond
the Inner Temple gate. There she was found sitting
between two watchmen and she was brought back to him.
He showed her the tankard and the linen bloody as they
were, and asked her if they were hers. She said yes, and
that the tankard was left her by her mother. The officers of
the Temple carried her to the constable, by whom she was
taken before Alderman Brocas.

The principal witnesses for the prosecution were John
Kerrel, his neighbour in the Temple, two watchmen, and the
women who discovered the bodies. Acting much as a
defence lawyer might do today, Malcolm cross-examined
each of them carefully, focusing principally on the evidence
of the bloody linen:

Malcolm.	Was the linen you found in the close stool bloody?
Kerrel.	I am not sure whether it was that, or the linen I found under my bed that was bloody, for I was very much surprised, and I brought one parcel down, and Mr Gehagan brought another, and we threw them down in the watchman's box, and so they were mixed together.
Court.	Shew the tankard to the jury, and unseal the linen, and let them see that too, and the other things.
Kerrel.	This is the green silk purse that was found upon her in the watchhouse. She said she found it in the street; but some body taking notice that it was clean, she then said, she had washed it since. This

is the gown that some of the linen was wrapped in, and this is the bloody apron that was found under my bed, and which, she said, was not bloody, but the marks of a disorder.

Malcolm.   Was the linen wet or dry?

Kerrel.   I can't say which, but it was bloody.

Malcolm.   Was the gown bloody, or the shift bloody in the sleeves, or the bosom, or any where but in the lower part?

Kerrel.   I cannot say.

Court.   Is the shift here?

Kerrel.   Yes.

Court.   Produce it then, and let some body look on it.

Oliphant.   (Looking on it). I think here's a little blood on the upper part of the bosom.

Malcolm.   Upon your oath is it blood or a stain?

Oliphant.   I cannot be positive; but it seems like the rest.

The next to testify was John Gehagen, whose chambers were across the landing from Kerrel's and who was present when the bloody linen and tankard were found. Malcolm questioned Gehagen on the same topics:

Malcolm.   Was the blood on the tankard dry?

Gehagan.   It appeared then to be fresh.

Malcolm.   Was the blood on the shift and apron wet or dry?

Gehagan.   I don't know certainly.

Malcolm.   Who took the shift up?

Gehagan.   I had it in my hand; the blood on it was like that on the tankard, which I thought was wet.

Malcolm.   It has been folded up ever since, till now, and if it was wet then, it must be damp still if no air has come to it.

Malcolm then introduced another line of questioning, about whether there was any blood on the dress she had been wearing at the time.

Malcolm.   What gown had I on?

Gehagan.   I don't know.

Malcolm.   I would ask Mr Kerrel the same question.

Kerrel.   You came up in that blue riding hood you have on now, but I did not mind what gown.

Malcolm.   Had I any blood on my clothes, or was I clean dressed?

Court.   Why it was Monday morning when you was taken, you had 24 hours' time to shift your clothes.

The court, recognising the effectiveness of Malcolm's questioning, felt compelled to intervene on the prosecution's behalf. But Malcolm continued to argue, now directly with the judge:

Malcolm.   It's hard that people can swear positively to so many things, and yet could not perceive what clothes I had on.

Court.   They tell you their thoughts were taken up with other things.

Malcolm.   The watchman searched me, but did they find any blood about me?

Court.   You have been told already, that you had 24 hours' time to change your clothes, and that they did not mind what clothes you had on.

When a watchman, John Mastreter, testified, Malcolm managed to detect a small inconsistency in the evidence:

Malcolm.   Was the blood on the tankard wet or dry?

Mastreter. I can't tell; but I believe it was dry, because it did not bloody me when I took hold of it.

| Malcolm. | Mr Gehagan swore it was wet. |
| John Gehagan. | She rubbed it, and I thought it was. |

When Frances Rhymer, one of the friends of Mrs Duncomb who discovered the bodies that Sunday afternoon, took the stand, Malcolm introduced another possible line of defence, suggesting perhaps that Price had murdered the others and then committed suicide:

Malcolm.	Was the door locked or bolted before Mrs Oliphant opened it?
Frances Rhymer.	I don't know.
Malcolm.	Did you see any way that a person could possibly get out and leave the door bolted?
Court.	Somebody did get in and out too, that's plain to a demonstration.

In fact, a subsequent witness testified that it was possible for someone standing outside the door to bolt it from the inside.

Finally the surgeon who examined the corpses, Thomas Bigg, took the stand. Among other things, he testified that Malcolm's apron strings had been bloody at both ends. This allowed Malcolm to return to her principal line of questioning.

Malcolm.	Might they have been murdered with those strings and no blood appear in the middle?
Bigg.	They might have been strangled without making the strings bloody at all. But the strings being bloody only at the ends, which when the apron was tied on, would hang before, the blood might come upon them in the same manner as upon the rest of the apron, or it might be by folding the apron up before it was dry.
Malcolm.	If I had this apron and did the murder in it, how is it possible that my shift should be bloody both behind and before?

No response was recorded.

Then the court turned to Malcolm for her defence. With growing confidence she proceeded to address the court for half an hour. She started with her explanation for the bloody linen, explaining that it was a product of menstruation, a subject not normally discussed in mixed company and certainly not in a courtroom. This accounts for her keenness to establish that some of the blood had been dry:

> Modesty might compel a woman to conceal her own
> secrets if necessity did not oblige her to the contrary; and
> 'tis necessity that obliges me to say that what has been
> taken for the blood of the murdered person is nothing but
> the free gift of nature.
>
> This was all that appeared on my shift, and it was the
> same on my apron, for I wore the apron under me next to
> my shift. My master going out of town desired me to lye
> in his chamber, and that was the occasion of my foul linen
> being found there. The woman that washed the sheets I
> then lay in can testify that the same was upon them, and
> Mr Johnson who searched me in Newgate has sworn that
> he found my linen in the like condition. That this was the
> case is plain, for how is it possible that it could be the
> blood of the murdered person?
>
> If it is supposed that I killed her with my clothes on,
> my apron indeed might be bloody, but how should the
> blood come upon my shift? If I did it in my shift, how
> should my apron be bloody, or the back part of my shift?
> And whether I did it dressed or undressed, why was not
> the neck and sleeves of my shift bloody as well as the
> lower parts?
>
> I freely own that my crimes deserve death. I own that I
> was accessory to the robbery, but I was innocent of the
> murder, and I'll give an account of the whole affair.

She then provided a narrative of the crime which corresponded with the account she had given in her initial confession. She described how she had plotted the robbery, first with Tracey and then with the Alexander brothers. On the Saturday evening she met up with her accomplices, and the door to Mrs Duncomb's room being found open, she ordered James Alexander to go in and hide under the bed. At two o'clock in the morning:

> James Alexander came out and said, now is the time. Then Mary Tracey and Thomas Alexander went in, but I stayed upon the stairs to watch. I had told them where Mrs Duncomb's box stood. They came out between 4 and 5, and one of them called to me softly, and said hip! How shall I shut the door? Says I, 'tis a spring-lock; pull it to, and it will be fast; and so one of them did. They would have shared the money and goods upon the stairs, but I told them we had better go down; so we went under the arch by Fig Tree Court, where there was a lamp. I asked them how much they had got. They said they had found 50 guineas, and some silver in the maid's purse; above 100 pounds in the chest of drawers, besides the silver tankard, and the money in the box, and several other things, so that in all they had got to the value of about 300 pounds in money and goods. They told me they had been forced to gag the people. They gave me the tankard with what was in it, and some linen, for my share, and they had a silver spoon and a ring, and the rest of the money among themselves.

She then described her arrest, and admitted she had lied about the tankard:

> I own that I said the tankard was mine, and that it was left me by my mother. Several witnesses have sworn what account I gave of the tankard being bloody; I had hurt my finger, and that was the occasion of it. I am sure of death, and therefore have no occasion to speak any thing but the truth.

She also admitted that while in Newgate she had conspired with Will Gibbs to establish an alibi. But when she was examined by Mr Alstone, the turnkey, about the substantial amount of money that was found hidden in her hair, she decided she had to confess:

> I denied all till I found he had heard of the money, and
> then I knew my life was gone, and therefore, I confessed
> all that I knew. I gave him the same account of the
> robbery as I have given now. I described Tracey and the
> two Alexanders.

She then concluded:

> All that I have now declared is fact, and I have no
> occasion to murder three innocent persons by a false
> accusation, for I know I am a condemned woman. I know
> I must suffer an ignominious death which my crimes
> deserve, and I shall suffer willingly. I thank God that he
> has granted me time to repent, when I might have been
> snatched off in the midst of my crimes and without having
> an opportunity of preparing myself for another world.

It was an impressive performance by a woman who had
been universally convicted and traduced in the papers and
who faced a courtroom full of unsympathetic men. Malcolm
stuck with her story throughout and refused to admit, for
even a moment, any participation in the murders themselves.
It is surprising, however, that she called no witnesses in her
support, not even character witnesses. Perhaps as a poor
laundress, there were few respectable acquaintances on whom
she could call. In the end, the trial came down to the word of
one woman (who had admitted to various lies in attempting
to cover up the theft) against that of a phalanx of prosecution
witnesses. Perhaps it is significant that the jury took as long as
15 minutes to reach their verdict of guilty. By special order she
was to be hanged near the scene of the crime in Fleet Street,
to terrify 'other wickedly disposed people',[17] and demonstrate
to the world that the crime had been solved. Although Tracey
and the Alexanders remained in prison until the next sessions,
they were never tried for the crime.

Nonetheless, Malcolm continued publicly to maintain her
innocence of the murders. The night before her execution
she delivered a paper to Reverend Piddington, lecturer in

the parish of St Bartholomew the Great, 'with a desire that it might be published', which it was. Her story was the same: she had been involved in planning the robbery, but had not gone in the room and knew nothing about the murders until they were discovered the next day.[18]

It is difficult to know whether Malcolm managed to convince anyone. Certainly the predominant view remained entirely negative, not helped by the fact that she was Irish and Catholic. The report of the trial in the *London Magazine* was particularly hostile:

> She behaved in a very extraordinary manner on her trial, often times requesting the court for the witnesses to speak louder, and she spoke upwards of half an hour in her own defence, but in a trifling manner.[19]

Neither was the Ordinary of Newgate convinced. Adopting a far more hostile tone than he normally did towards his charges (probably owing to her Catholicism, and because she refused to confess), he described her as a:

> Most obdurate, impenitent sinner, who gave no reasonable satisfaction, with respect to her own particular case. She was certainly of a most bold, daring, boisterous, and wilful spirit, void of all virtue and the grace of God; which disposition led her from one sin to another, till at last she was so far deserted by God, by forsaking him and his ways, that she fell into those abominable and vile crimes, for which she deservedly suffered.

In his account of her final hours, he described her sincerity 'as at least pretended' and added:

> If there be anything contradictory, or what may seem disingenuous in this account, it is owing to the unhappy temper of this unfortunate wretch, who often varied in her declarations concerning this barbarous murder.[20]

Reinforced by William Hogarth's rather severe portrait of her (painted while she was in Newgate awaiting execution), this was the impression of Sarah Malcolm that endured: as an evil, barbaric and stubborn woman. Hogarth himself was reputed to have observed to a companion 'I see by this woman's features that she is capable of any wickedness'.[21] She was hanged on 7 March. A few weeks later an effigy of Malcolm was burned alongside those of the unpopular Robert Walpole and Queen Caroline, during celebrations of the withdrawal of the Excise Bill.[22] And in 1751 Henry Fielding included her in a list of the most treacherous women in history, alongside Lady Macbeth and Catherine Hayes.[23]

The Ordinary's comments notwithstanding, Malcolm's defence had been consistent in its basic tenets from the moment she admitted the theft in Newgate to her execution. It may even have been true. The only evidence directly linking her to the murders was the bloody linen, for which she had an explanation. Since she was likely to be executed anyway for her participation in the burglary, especially as the crime was linked to a triple murder, her determination to stick with her story before, during and after her trial is remarkable. The opportunities she took advantage of in her trial to present her side of the story are evidence of the substantial role defendants could (and indeed were expected to) play in eighteenth-century trials, even if the odds remained stacked against them.[24]

A Man of my Age, Character and Way of Life

Trials at the Old Bailey were only in part about establishing the facts of the case. Almost as important was the character of the victim, defendant and witnesses. Frequently those who testified were badgered about their immorality and demeanour and stories of their criminality and low circumstances were paraded before a sceptical jury. All evidence was judged in light of the character of those who gave it. Defendants especially were expected (if they were able) to call friends and neighbours to vouch for their good behaviour and quiet ways. Even if it could not change the verdict, this testimony could influence the court's choice of punishment.

On the evening before the Italian scholar Joseph Baretti stood trial for murder, his friend and fellow lexicographer Dr Johnson sat quietly with James Boswell discussing the correct way to respond to the execution of a friend:

> Boswell: But suppose now, sir, that one of your intimate friends were apprehended for an offence for which he might be hanged.
>
> Johnson: I should do what I could to bail him, and give him any other assistance; but if he were once fairly hanged, I should not suffer.
>
> Boswell: Would you eat your dinner that day, sir?
>
> Johnson: Yes, sir; and eat it as if he were eating with me. Why, there's Baretti, who is to be tried for his life tomorrow, friends have risen up for him on every side; yet if he should be hanged, none of them will eat a slice of plumb pudding the less.

The events that led to the trial of Joseph Baretti took place in the Haymarket some two weeks earlier, between 9 and 10 o'clock on a Friday night, 6 October 1769. The Haymarket, still an active market for hay and straw, was by the 1760s more important as the site of the Haymarket Theatre and a long string of coffeehouses, inns and shops catering for a prosperous clientele. It was also a notorious resort of prostitutes and footpads.

On this particular evening, Elizabeth Ward sat herself down in a doorway, next to a short woman in a brown dress about 20 or 30 feet from the corner of Panton Street at the north end of Haymarket. It was already quite dark and the shadows at the edge of the thoroughfare were full to bursting with the ragtag population of London's underclass. Ward was a well-known prostitute, who had been out on the streets the night before. A couple of years later she would find herself in the dock, found guilty and transported to North America for seven years, after a 'three in a bed' romp went disastrously wrong.[25] On this particular evening there was a waxing crescent moon low in the sky, which provided little light. Joseph Baretti, who was near blind with myopia after decades of close scholarship, probably could not see Ward or her companion as they sat on the step. He later claimed to have noticed only one woman, although everyone else claimed there were two.

What happened next was the nightmare feared by many people walking in the wrong place at the wrong time – a nightmare made more intense by Baretti's foreign accent combined with the xenophobia of many Londoners. In Ward's evidence at the Old Bailey she described how 'the other girl asked him to give her a glass of wine and put her hand towards him'. Baretti claimed that she had actually grabbed his genitals. Eighteenth-century men's breeches had wide slits on either side which made access to the crotch relatively easy and prostitutes frequently slipped a hand inside the breeches of a prospective client by way of encouragement.

In this instance, however, the gesture appears to have been executed in an overly enthusiastic manner and directed at the wrong person:

> She clapped her hands with such violence about my private parts, that it gave me great pain. This I instantly resented, by giving her a blow on the hand with a few angry words. The woman got up directly, raised her voice, and finding by my pronunciation I was a foreigner, she called me several bad names in a most consumelious strain; among which, French bugger, damned Frenchman, and a woman-hater, were the most audible.

The nature of the blow Baretti struck became a substantial point of issue at the later trial. Elizabeth Ward claimed that 'He went a little further on, and then turned back and struck me a great blow on the side of my face', after which she 'screamed out' for help. Others heard Ward cry out that 'he deserved a knock over his head with her patten'.

The altercation immediately attracted an ugly and dangerous crowd, several members of which later lay under suspicion of being Elizabeth Ward's confederates. Three men in particular came up and demanded how Baretti 'could strike a woman'. These were Evan Morgan, a ballad singer, John Clark, who Elizabeth Ward claimed had 'kissed' her 'the night before in the Haymarket' and who she recognised by virtue of his pronounced squint and, finally, Thomas Patman. These three young men were on their way from the pub:

> We drank three pints of beer together at a house that turns up on the left hand. We asked Morgan to give us a song; he said he would if we would go along with him to a house in Golden Square. We were going along the Haymarket all three together, and just at the corner of Panton Street there was a gentleman struck a woman. I saw him strike her on the head. She reeled and was near ready to fall.

What happened next is lost in confusion. In Thomas Patman's recollection:

> The other two men were behind me, and they immediately pushed me against the gentleman. I received a blow from him directly on my left side. The blood ran down into my shoe. I cried out that I was stabbed.
> The gentleman made off half way up Panton Street. Morgan ran after him, to take him, and just by the Hole in the Wall Morgan received a wound. I saw the gentleman strike at him as he was running up Panton Street. He struck him on the side of his body.

Joseph Baretti remembered the events slightly differently:

> I had not quite turned the corner before a man made me
> turn back by giving me a blow with his fist, and asking
> me how I dare strike a woman. Another pushed him
> against me, and pushed me off the pavement. Then three
> or four more joined them. I wonder I did not fall from the
> high step which is there. The pathway is much raised from
> the coachway. A great number of people surrounded me
> presently, many beating me, and all damning me on every
> side, in a most frightful manner. I was a Frenchman in
> their opinion, which made me apprehensive I must expect
> no favour nor protection, but all outrage and blows. There
> is generally a great puddle in the corner of Panton Street,
> even when the weather is fine; but that day it had rained
> incessantly, which made it very slippery. My assailants
> wanted to throw me into the puddle, where I might be
> trampled on; so I cried out murder. There was a space in
> the circle, from whence I ran into Panton Street and
> endeavoured to get into the footway. I was in the greatest
> horror lest I should run against some stones, as I have
> such bad eyes. I could not run so fast as my pursuers, so
> that they were upon me, continually beating and pushing
> me, some of them attempting to catch me by the hair-tail.
> If this had happened, I had been certainly a lost man.

Baretti was carrying a small knife and in his fear he used it.
Evan Morgan and Thomas Patman were taken to
Middlesex Hospital later that evening, accompanied by
John Clark, where the two wounded men were attended by
John Wyatt, the house surgeon. Morgan had been stabbed
three times, once in the abdomen and twice through the
lung. He died the next day.

Following the stabbing, and fearful for his life, Baretti
stumbled on in search of protection:

> I cannot absolutely fix the time and place where I first
> struck. I remember, somewhere in Panton Street, I gave a
> quick blow to one who beat off my hat with his fist. When
> I was in Oxendon Street, fifteen or sixteen yards from the

Haymarket, I stopped and faced about. My confusion was
great and seeing a shop open, I ran into it for protection,
quite spent with fatigue.

The shop was run by a grocer and was opposite the home of
John Lambert, a constable, who had just then sat down to
dinner. Lambert took up the story:

> I am a tallow chandler, and was then a constable. I was sat
> down to supper, when I heard the cry of murderer, or stop
> murderer, which alarmed me a good deal. I got to my
> door, and observed Baretti and two or three men pursuing
> him. He ran into a grocer's shop just opposite to me. I
> said, Sir, I beg you will surrender. One or two of my
> neighbours came in; Baretti said, 'Are you friends?' I said
> 'Yes, we were, and would protect him'. By that time a
> mob was gathered about the door, being between nine and
> ten. I did propose carrying him to the roundhouse, but Sir
> John Fielding's name being mentioned, Mr Barretti said
> he was very willing to go before him. He said he was a
> gentleman, and secretary to the Royal Academy in Pall
> Mall. I took him to Sir John, and he was committed.

Morgan had been immediately dispatched to hospital, but
Patman, Clark and Lambert accompanied Baretti to the
magistrate's office where the blind justice Sir John Fielding
committed Baretti to Tothill Fields Bridewell to await the
outcome of Morgan's struggle for life.

Had Baretti been a poor man, he would have been
marched through the streets to the prison, but instead a
coach was called, and the constable, along with two of
Baretti's friends (who had been summoned from the Royal
Academy), accompanied him through the now midnight
black streets of Westminster to the prison off Horse Ferry
Road. A few years later, the reformer John Howard claimed
that this particular house of correction had 'no straw, no
infirmary', but this hardly mattered to Baretti.[26] He paid for
a private room and food and drink to be brought and was

examined by his two companions, both of whom had medical experience, which allowed them later to describe in detail the bruises Baretti had suffered in the earlier altercation.

Following Morgan's death, a coroner's inquest was called and Baretti was charged with manslaughter. At the Old Bailey, however, the grand jury indicted him for murder. Facing a trial on this capital offence, Baretti immediately had two strikes against him. The first was his undoubted foreignness. It was one thing for an English gentleman to hit an English prostitute, but quite another for an Italian of whatever class to hit an Englishwoman, regardless of her profession. The second issue was the use of a knife.

Upper-class men had stopped regularly carrying a sword in the first half of the eighteenth century. By the 1770s most would have jauntily swung a stout walking stick, both as a means of protection and as a part of the performance of gentility. Such a stick could be swung with abandon, with little fear of attracting legal redress, wherever the blows fell. A knife was a different matter. It had none of the gentlemanly associations of a sword or the harmless uses that justified a stick. It was an offensive weapon of a sort that only a working man would normally carry.

Baretti's defence hung on two simple points; first, the normality of an educated foreigner carrying a small knife; and, second, his ability to create the impression that despite his foreignness, he was still a gentleman. At the trial, the first thing he did was to use flattery to defuse the ticking bomb of xenophobic prejudice that existed in the hearts of eighteenth-century Englishmen. As an Italian national, he had the right to be tried by a jury composed of half Englishman and half Italians, but he waived this right and, in a speech full of the sort of ringing pompous phrases geared to soothe an Englishman's ego, he turned to the Middlesex jury and explained:

> Equally confident of my own innocence and English
> discernment to trace out truth, I did resolve to waive the
> privilege granted to foreigners by the laws of this
> kingdom. Nor was my motive a compliment to this nation.
> My motive was my life and honour – that it should not be
> thought I received undeserved favour from a jury part
> from my own country. I chose to be tried by a jury of this
> country, for if my honour is not saved, I cannot much
> wish for the preservation of my life. I will wait for the
> determination of this awful court with that confidence, I
> hope, which innocence has a right to obtain. So God bless
> you all.

The knife required further explanation. It had a leather cover and silver case, which concealed a razor sharp steel blade within. It was described by Thomas Patman as a 'penknife' and was produced in court as evidence. But other witnesses, and Baretti himself, were keen that the jury understood precisely why a man such as himself would carry a knife like this. In Baretti's words:

> My knife was neither a weapon of offence nor defence. I
> wear it to carve fruit and sweetmeats and not to kill my
> fellow creature. It is a general custom in France not to put
> knives upon the table, so that even ladies wear them in
> their pockets for general use. I have continued to wear it
> after my return to England because I have found it
> occasionally convenient. Little did I think such an event
> would ever have happened. Let this trial turn out as
> favourable as my innocence may deserve, still my regret
> will endure as long as life shall last.

If Baretti's own affected words were not enough to explain the knife, others, including David Garrick, the well-travelled actor, were drafted in to reinforce the point. Having done all he could to establish the goodwill and admiration he felt for English justice and his sorrow at the death of Evan Morgan, it was left to Baretti to establish his character in order to support his plea of self-defence. Since the facts of this case were not clear, this was a trial where a good character had the potential to swing the case in his favour.

After all the evidence from prostitutes and their pimps, surgeons and constables had been rehearsed, the glitterati were called. First up was Topham Beauclerk, a wealthy book collector and intimate of Dr Johnson, but more importantly, a great grandson of Charles II and Nell Gwyn. As an aristocrat of unimpeachable social standing, whom Dr Johnson regarded as *the* expert on 'polite literature', Beauclerk was just the sort of witness to set the right tone. His evidence did not disappoint. He said of Baretti:

> I have known him ten years. I was acquainted with him
> before I went abroad. Some time after that I went to Italy,
> and he gave me letters of recommendation to some of the
> first people there, and to men of learning. I went to Italy
> the time the Duke of York did. Unless Mr Baretti had
> been a man of consequence, he could never have
> recommended me to such people as he did. He is a
> gentleman of letters, and a studious man.

Next came Baretti's old friend, the painter Sir Joshua Reynolds. He helped to place Baretti in a more conventional English context:

> He is a man of great humanity, and very active in
> endeavouring to help his friends. I have known many
> instances of it. He is a gentleman of a good temper. I
> never knew him quarrelsome in my life; he is of a sober
> disposition. This affair was on a club night of the Royal
> Academicians. We expected him there, and were
> enquiring about him, before we heard of this accident. Mr
> Baretti is secretary for foreign correspondents.

Next to take the stand was Dr Johnson, who testified to Baretti's studious and sober nature. According to Boswell, Johnson 'gave his evidence in a slow, deliberate, and distinct manner which was uncommonly impressive'.[27] Johnson answered questions about Baretti's eyesight, his tendency to anger and his relations with the women of the street. Johnson was followed by Edmund Burke the philosopher, David Garrick the actor and Oliver Goldsmith the playwright. Almost giving up and admitting that Baretti had effectively played the system, the *Proceedings* record:

> There were divers other gentlemen in court to speak for his character, but the court thought it needless to call them.

At the end of a long trial that seemed at the outset to be balanced on a knife's edge, Joseph Baretti was 'acquitted of the murder, of the manslaughter – self defence'.

A few days before the trial, James Boswell had been to Tyburn to see the execution of six men. What struck Boswell about the scene was 'that none seemed to be under any concern', an observation to which Johnson replied, 'Most of them, sir, have never thought at all'. Joseph Baretti's carefully deployed words, and carefully chosen friends, saved Dr Johnson the necessity of testing his jaundiced views of human nature with the experience of seeing this particular friend hang at Tyburn.[28]

Marrying by Whatever Name They Pleased

The introduction of lawyers changed the whole character of courtroom business. Confrontations between witnesses and the accused were supplemented, and often supplanted, by speeches and vigorous cross-examinations performed by lawyers. In this trial the victim and one of the two defendants never even spoke. Perhaps this is not surprising given the fact that central to the case was the nature of the evidence required to convict someone of conspiracy, a question of law, not fact. But the carefully marshalled arguments of both defence and prosecution counsel speak powerfully both to the changing nature of the criminal trial and the professionalisation of legal practice.

In October 1746 George Taylor and Mary Robinson, a widow, were tried for conspiring to impersonate Richard Holland, a gentleman. They were accused of marrying under a false name in order that the two could gain control of Holland's estate after his death. With the institution of marriage and the heredity of property at stake, this was a potentially serious crime. Despite the fact that as a misdemeanour the case would not normally have involved legal counsel, five lawyers participated in the trial, three for the prosecution and two for the defence. As was common in the published *Proceedings* in this period, the lawyers were not named.

The trial began with opening arguments from the counsel for the prosecution. In a long-winded statement one of the lawyers summarised the case. He explained that on 18 July, Mary Robinson, who lived in Richard Holland's house, arranged for some of his clothes to be placed in a box, which she then smuggled to a pub in Little Britain, just outside the City walls. She then sent George Taylor to Doctor's Commons to obtain a marriage licence (by purchasing a licence, they were able to marry immediately and avoid the publicity associated with posting banns). Taylor was refused the licence, however, because he was not one of the parties to the marriage (he was not yet claiming to be Holland). As a result, Mary Robinson had to go in person to obtain the licence. With George Taylor dressed up in Holland's clothes and with Mary Robinson in a white satin gown, they then went to the parish church of St Andrew Holborn where they were married under the names of Richard Holland and Mary Robinson. After dinner at the King's Head tavern, they arranged to return Richard Holland's clothes to his house in Hornsey. But they failed to return his wig and had also managed to disturb the papers in the pocket of his coat. As a result, when Holland next came to wear the coat, he became immediately suspicious and obtained a warrant for the arrest of Robinson and Taylor. When they were brought before Sir Thomas De Veil and examined, they confessed everything.

Prosecuting counsel were particularly keen to prove the defendants' intentions as a way of arguing that the purpose of the marriage had been to defraud Richard Holland – a much more serious charge than impersonation. Counsel noted that he was unlikely to be able to prove this directly, but set about constructing a case from inference. He pointed out that when the defendants were examined by De Veil and asked whether the marriage had been consummated, Taylor:

> Spoke plainly, that he had not lain with her. I mention this to show that there was no real marriage intended by these two persons, but a fraudulent marriage to another person. Tis not to be supposed that persons that had so much art and wickedness to conduct a scheme of this kind, should have so much honesty to declare their wicked intentions, therefore the fact must be gathered from circumstances.

Counsel went on to speculate on the likely ill effects of this spurious marriage:

> Let us consider what would be the natural consequence of this marriage. Suppose it could have been brought to take effect, between Mr Holland and the defendant, Robinson. If it took effect in his lifetime, it would have been the greatest injury imaginable, not only in point of fortune, in marrying a gentleman of fortune to a servant, a person worth nothing, and probably less than nothing, and binding him to a woman, whereas the very manner of his being bound to her, he must detest and abhor. If it was to take effect after his death, then it would be a great loss to the heirs of Mr Holland, who would lose so much of their own just rights. 'Tis not only a misdemeanour, but of such a heinous nature, that no punishment that the law can inflict for a misdemeanour is severe enough.

This was not so much evidence of a crime, but a construction on the evidence designed to convince the jury of the heinous nature of that crime.

The judge, conscious perhaps that prosecution counsel had already spent a substantial amount of time on their opening statements, urged that the evidence should be presented more quickly:

> Court.   I am not for going a round-about way when a
>   shorter is sufficient; you might go through all the
>   other evidence for the entertainment of the
>   audience, but if you prove the fact tis sufficient.

The first witness for the prosecution was James Wright, the man who married the two in St Andrew Holborn. This gave counsel for the defence their first chance to intervene. Wright was almost immediately challenged on the question of whether he could positively identify Taylor as the groom:

> Counsel.   Mr Wright, since you speak to the identity of the
>   man, do you know that you ever saw him before?
>   I suppose you marry a great many persons. Don't
>   you remember how you came to be so particular
>   as to take upon you to say that these are the
>   clothes that the man wore at that time?
>
> Wright.   The man was in so great confusion that the sweat
>   ran down his face. He seemed in the greatest
>   agony and confusion whatever.
>
> Q.   Sir, had you a suspicion that the man was doing
>   any thing wrong?
>
> Wright.   No, sir; but I saw the man in such a confusion that
>   I took particular notice of him. The man had a
>   whitish coat, and the wig as Mr Holland has now.
>
> Counsel.   So the only reason you judge them to be the same
>   clothes, is because he had a white coat and wig?
>
> Wright.   I saw them upon Mr Holland's back four or five
>   days after.

Counsel then suggested Wright's testimony had changed since the preliminary hearing:

Counsel.	Sir, was you before Sir Thomas De Veil? Did you not declare before the justice that you did not remember the man nor woman? Did you at that time say that you knew the man at all?
Wright.	I gave a description of the man as well as I could?

With the defence lawyer having completely undermined this witness's confidence in his own testimony, it is appropriate that his last response was reported in the form of a question.

A similar experience awaited Philip Moore, a young clerk in Doctor's Commons who had witnessed the issuing of the marriage licence. Referring to him patronisingly as 'my lad', defence counsel forcefully cross-examined his identification of Robinson as the bride.

Counsel.	I suppose you don't remember all the persons that come to your house for licences. If her face was covered with this bonnet, my lad, how came you to be so particular as to her face?
Moor.	It's a thing that seldom happens, for a woman to apply for a licence.
Counsel.	So then, when a woman applies for a licence, you more particularly remark her. Had you met this woman afterwards in the street should you have known her?
Moor.	Yes; because I believe I have seen her before, a considerable time before she lived in that neighbourhood.
Counsel.	Just now, if I understood you, you said you had not seen her before. If you had been accidentally in her company, should you have remarked that she was the same woman, if you had had no particular cause to have taken notice of her?
Moor.	I don't know whether I should or no.

The questioning then turned to whether he could remember her when he was asked about the case 9 or 10 days after the licence was issued.

Counsel.	Did you then presently recollect the circumstances of that woman?
Moor.	When they told me of the licence, I recollected then.
Counsel.	When you was first applied to, did you, or did you not recollect the person of the woman?
Moor.	The question that was put to me was, whether I did not remember there was such a licence, but I could not, at that instant, recollect that she was the woman, till they told me the circumstances more particular.
Q.	Now, before you recollected that she was the person of the woman, did any body remind you of any particular circumstance to put it into your memory? The first time you saw her, did you recollect her?
Moor.	Yes.
Counsel.	This Mrs Robinson is a pretty tall woman; therefore, though she had a bonnet upon her head, you might see her face much easier than another person, as you are such a short man.
Moor.	Yes.
Counsel.	Then you were very curious, my lad, and peeped very earnestly at it; then it pleased you very much.

This last statement was almost certainly delivered with lashings of irony.

When it came time to present the case for the defence, both counsel delivered long speeches. The first pointed out that it was not a crime to marry under an assumed name and claimed that the prosecution had not proven the charge of conspiracy, which required criminal intent. Although superficially polite to the 'gentlemen' counsel for the prosecution, he in fact tore their case to shreds:

> Please your lordship, and gentlemen of the jury, I am
> counsel in this cause for Mrs Robinson; against whom
> there is an indictment for conspiracy, etc. And the

gentlemen are extremely sensible, I find, on the other side,
if they had laid this fact without coupling it with a
conspiracy, that it would not have been at all criminal.
Our common law doesn't hinder any people from
marrying together by any name they please. Therefore,
this conspiracy only must appear to you to be some injury
to some person or another, and particularly this
gentleman, who says he is so injured. I never heard that
particular persons may not marry by whatsoever name
they please. By what law is any man injured by it? If they
could make out that there has been a combination on
purpose to affect the estate of a third person, or on
purpose to claim that estate in their lifetime; then it would
have amounted to a combination together; it would have
amounted to a conspiracy, to injure a third person. But, is
there any thing like it? Was there any discourse upon it?
What they might have in their heads, God knows! I never
knew any human judicature could reach the thoughts or
intentions, till facts were made plain and clear.

A second line of attack was to highlight the difficulty,
already exposed in cross-examination, witnesses had in
identifying Robinson as the bride in the marriage, because
she had been wearing a large bonnet which made it difficult
to see her face:

My lord there is a great stress laid upon this habit, this dress
of the lady's; she was dressed in satin, says the gentleman, a
pure white innocent satin; a very proper dress for a bride.
He would conclude from thence, that she was the person
actually married at this time. There is no positive evidence
she was married, tis only grounded on supposition. She was
dressed in a black bonnet. That is not conclusive evidence; a
hundred ladies may wear white satin and have black
bonnets, and the same day one of these ladies might be
married; and yet a young gentleman, says he, looked at her
very narrowly and could see her face. It was a wonderful
thing; I think it a great difficulty to distinguish one woman
from another when muffled up; therefore it was no wonder
if this young spark might be deceived, as his curiosity was
only led by the size of this bonnet.

Finally, counsel returned to the question of criminal intent, querying the significance of prosecution evidence that Robinson had secreted a suit of Holland's clothes out of the house to allow Taylor to wear it at the wedding:

> Why therefore this mighty matter, that a suit of clothes should go out of the house? How does this manifest an intention to do him any wrong? If I have another man's suit of clothes and am married in them, must it be inferred from thence that I intended to get his estate? They might also have said I intended to rob him, or cut his throat. This is saying a thing that I might never have had in my head; this intention ought to have been manifested by some overt open acts done. Is marrying in itself, by another name, an unlawful thing?

The other counsel for the defence repeated some of the same points, and then took upon himself to instruct the jury in a point of law, much as a judge might sum up a case:

> A conspiracy, in its nature, must be to do an injury to a third, in regard to his person or estate. Gentlemen, as to the fact, where a person is to be convicted as a criminal; where a person is subjected to a fine or imprisonment, there ought to be the clearest proof in the world. As to the marriage, I don't apprehend any one person has been capable to prove the fact, as to the identity of the woman; that is the fact that you are to try. If there is no evidence of it, in all cases of criminal prosecutions, we are to incline to the favourable side, which is mercy.

For the only time in the trial Mary Robinson then briefly addressed the court:

> My lord, I humbly beg this favour, though they prove my dress, that you would ask Mr Holland whether it was not my everyday dress; and I don't know, at this time, whether I had it on or not. Mr Holland invited me as a companion to himself; and I have it under his hand that I was not his servant.

It was not a particularly effective intervention, since she appeared to admit her presence at the marriage and called attention to a possible motive for the crime. Her counsel probably wished that she had remained quiet. Her fellow defendant, Taylor, did not testify at all.

As is sometimes the case when reading the *Proceedings*, the text of a trial seems to lead to the opposite conclusion to that reached by the jury. Despite the very strong defence made by counsel, both Mary Robinson and George Taylor were found guilty. Richard Holland, the victim, who had not testified in the trial, then 'recommended Taylor to the favour of the court, as believing him to be drawn in by the woman'. The court was in sympathy with this request:

> The judgment of the court upon Mary Robinson was as follows, that you be imprisoned for the space of two years in the gaol of Newgate; and after the expiration of that time to give security of 500 pounds and pay a fine of five marks.
>
> As to you, George Taylor, the sentence that the court thinks proper to pronounce upon you is that you be imprisoned for six months in the Poultry Compter; that you give security yourself in the sum of 40 pounds and two securities in 40 pounds each, and pay a fine of five marks. [A mark was 13s and 4d.]

The heavy punishments meted out demonstrate the significance the court accorded to the crime and help explain why both sides had chosen to be represented by lawyers at the trial.[29]

Mr Garrow for the Defence

The crime wave that followed the end of the American War in 1783 led to a dramatic increase in the number of cases coming to the Old Bailey. And just as the rhetoric of individual rights and liberties helped fuel that war, it also found a place in the

*repertory of arguments deployed by courtroom lawyers. The
1780s saw an ever growing number of defence lawyers seeking
to protect the rights of prisoners against the power of the state.
The most prominent of these was William Garrow, the son of a
clergyman, who was called to the bar at the precocious age of 23.
Having attended Old Bailey trials while studying law, he
immediately commenced a short but illustrious career as the
eighteenth century's most famous criminal lawyer. Between 1783
and 1793 he appeared as counsel no fewer than a thousand
times, acting for the defence in the vast majority of cases.[30]
Through aggressive and often sarcastic cross-examinations, and
by consistently undermining the motives of prosecutors, Garrow
famously managed to reduce witnesses to stuttering wrecks,
allegedly discouraging many victims from initiating prosecutions
in the first place. Well over half of his clients were acquitted,
which led prosecutors to start hiring Garrow as their counsel
simply in order to prevent him acting for the other side.[31]*

When three young men, William Eversall, William Roberts
and Joseph Barney, stood trial on the capital charge of
highway robbery on 7 May 1788, they must have feared the
worst. They had been arrested four weeks earlier by
watchmen on Golden Lane, just north of the City walls, and
accused of robbing John Troughton of his hat. On searching
Eversall, apparently irrefutable evidence against them was
found: the hat was hidden in his clothes, tucked between his
coat and his waistcoat. The prisoners' only grounds for
optimism was that they had secured the services of William
Garrow.

The prosecutor, John Troughton, did not have counsel
and testified first. Initially, the judge appears to have led the
questioning, prompting him to tell the story of the theft:

> I live in Cherry Tree Alley, Golden Lane, and on the 9th of
> April, a quarter before eleven o'clock at night, I was returning
> home. I was within fifty yards of home. I met the three prisoners

in a narrow alley, in company with two or three others. Being a
narrow place I made way for them to pass me. Seeing a number
of them I got close to the wall; and they collected themselves
into a body about two or three yards before me, and said
something, but I could not distinctly hear what they said. They
came towards me, and one of them, I believe Barney, had
something in his hand, which he threw into my eyes.

Court.   What was it he threw in your eyes?

Answer.   Snuff or tobacco dust. They said afterwards at the
                  watchhouse it was tobacco dust. I asked them
                  what they meant by that; and they said they would
                  let me know, or let me see; and I said I would
                  have one of them to the watchhouse, and I took
                  hold of one of them, but which I cannot positively
                  say, but I believe it was Barney. That is the man I
                  seized first; I held him some time, and struggled
                  to hold him till we got out of the alley into
                  Golden Lane, which might be eight or ten yards.
                  There was a lamp at the end of the alley where I
                  could discover them. I was rather come to my
                  sight and I know the faces of Barney and Roberts.

Court.   Had you known them before?

A.   No; we struggled till we got into Golden Lane,
                  then they all surrounded me, and I received some
                  blows about my face and head. I defended myself
                  as well as I could; one of the blows drove me
                  against the public house. I staggered against the
                  wall, I did not fall down; and in that position one
                  of them took off my hat and wig. I picked up my
                  wig, I suppose it fell out of my hat, and my hat
                  was gone almost instantly. I called out watch, and
                  stop thief, seeing they took different ways; but I
                  could see one of them, which was Joseph Barney.
                  He had something of an apron tied round him. I
                  pursued him by that particular mark through
                  what they call Basket Alley, and through a dark
                  passage, he was never out of my sight. I took him
                  in White Cross Street; he turned about, and said

> he was not the man. I took hold of him, and after
> some little struggle I brought him back with me.
> By the alarm of the watchman's rattle, a
> gentleman had stopped Roberts, and a watchman
> had taken Eversall.

By this point, Garrow seems to have taken over, and the questioning became more aggressive:

Mr Garrow.	You pursued Barney by the mark of something he had tied round him?
A.	Yes.
Q.	Did you know him before?
A.	No.
Q.	How came you to tell me he threw tobacco dust in your eyes?
A.	I cannot be positive who threw it; I thought it was him because he was the first man.
Q.	How do you know that the other men are the persons that were with Barney?
A.	I could only be positive to Roberts striking me; he attacked me in the face, he came under the light of the lamp.
Q.	Which is Roberts?
A.	The tall man in the middle; I cannot swear to Eversall.

Garrow proceeded now to exploit Troughton's uncertain identification of the culprits. By comparing Troughton's testimony in court to his original deposition given at the justice's preliminary examination, Garrow attempted to expose contradictions in his story:

Mr Garrow.	Did not you say before the justice that Eversall was the only one you could swear to?
A.	No.

Q.	Who was you examined before?
A.	Justice Blackborow.
Q.	Was it taken in writing?
A.	I believe it was.
Q.	Did you sign it?
A.	No.
Q.	This was a dark alley; the first thing before you observed the men, was something was thrown in your eyes?
A.	Yes.
Q.	How, having tobacco dust thrown in your eyes, can you swear to persons you had never seen before?
A.	I laid hold of Barney; and struggled with him, and said he should go to the watchhouse.
Q.	How is it that you with tobacco dust in your eyes, in a dark alley, knew these people?
A.	When I came to the bottom of the alley after the struggle, they all came round me. There was a lamp over my head; Barney and Roberts attacked me in front.

Garrow then questioned Troughton's motives in prosecuting the crime as a robbery (theft with violence), rather than a mere theft. Suggesting that 'thieftakers' had persuaded him to pursue this charge, Garrow implied that Troughton was acting solely in the hopes of receiving the £40 reward payable for the conviction of highway robbers:

Mr. Garrow.	You have cleared your eyes of the tobacco dust; and the thief-takers have thrown some gold dust in your eyes?
A.	There is no thief-takers in the business.
Q.	You know there is a reward of three times forty pounds, if the prisoners are convicted?
A.	To be sure, I know that, but I don't come here on that account.

Although Troughton denied the allegation, the ulterior motive had been skilfully planted in the minds of the jury. Garrow then returned to the alleged contradictions between his evidence in court and his original deposition. The question of whether his hat had fallen off or been *taken off* was vital, because the latter involved the violence necessary in order to secure a conviction for robbery:

Mr Garrow.	Did not you say before the justice that you did not know whether your hat fell off in the struggle, or was taken off?
A.	I don't know that I did.
Q.	Upon your oath, did not you tell the justice, that you did not know whether it fell off, or was taken off?
A.	I cannot tell, I don't know that I did, I might say so.
Q.	Don't you believe you said so?
A.	I believe I might, I cannot immediately recollect.
Q.	Who told you, if you should swear so here, these men could not be convicted so as to get the reward?
A.	Nobody.
Q.	Where do you live?
A.	No. 4 Atfield Street, St. Luke's; I have lived there many years.
Q.	You was sober?
A.	Perfectly sober; I am seldom otherwise.

At this point, Garrow appears to have secured the judge's interest:

Court.	You don't particularly recollect whether you told the justice you did not know whether your hat fell off, or was taken off; you believed you might say so?
A.	Yes.

Garrow continued his relentless, staccato cross-examination, in a voice dripping with ever increasing sarcasm. By the end of the exchange, Troughton was tripping over his own sentences, entirely uncertain what he knew and when he knew it.

Garrow.	I ask you then if you did say so before the justice; was what you said before the justice true?
A.	I don't recollect that I did say so.
Q.	When you was examined before the justice; did you know whether your hat fell off, or was taken off?
A.	Yes.
Q.	What did you know?
A.	That my hat was taken from me, and I am clear now it was taken off, and did not fall off.
Q.	Was you clear of that when you was before the justice?
A.	I don't know that I was so clear, I was a good deal confused and bruised.
Q.	When was you before the justice, the same night, or the next morning?
A.	The next morning.
Q.	Do you mean to say that you remember better now, what happened that night, than you did the next morning?
A.	I can recollect the circumstance very clear, and did then; if I made an error, it was not a wilful one.
Q.	You are sure it was taken off, and did not fall off?
A.	Yes, I verily believe it.
Q.	Are you sure of it?
A.	I am sure of it.
Q.	What makes you remember it better now than you did the day after?

A.   I was in a very bad state at the time; I had several
        wounds in my head, and was cut and bruised.

The activities of defence lawyers were severely limited in felony trials. They were not permitted to address the jury or to comment on the facts of a case (they could only speak to questions of law). But through aggressive cross-examinations such as this, Garrow was able to evade these restrictions and raise significant doubts about the evidence presented against his clients.

 When the watchmen and beadles who had apprehended the prisoners testified, Garrow did not even bother to cross-examine them. Neither did he allow the defendants to testify. Having essentially presented his case during the cross-examination of the prosecutor, the only testimony for the defence came from four character witnesses 'who gave Eversall and Roberts a good character. Barney did not call any witnesses to his character'. He did not need to. All three were acquitted, despite the apparently damning character of the evidence against them, which at the least seemed to prove that Eversall had committed a theft, with or without violence. Despite this lucky escape, each of the defendants returned to the Old Bailey in short order. Only four months later, Joseph Barney was convicted of grand larceny and sentenced to transportation. The following year, William Eversall was tried and acquitted of highway robbery, while five years after the original trial William Roberts, now aged 20, was convicted of grand larceny and sentenced 'to go for a soldier'.[32]

 Garrow's aggressive approach and commanding presence in the courtroom changed for ever the nature of the trials held at the Old Bailey. They became increasingly adversarial, where the skills of one's lawyer became as important as the facts of the case. Commentators, then and now, were not necessarily pleased with this change. One critic, in an open letter which sought to expose 'the licentiousness of the bar', described Garrow as 'a subtle, sagacious, bold, acute, and imperious advocate', whose merciless cross-examinations, regardless of the character and status of witnesses, were 'without a rival'.[33] But by querying unreliable evidence such as hearsay and that provided by accomplices, Garrow's penetrating critiques of prosecution evidence did much to extend the rights of the accused and to reform legal procedures, making trials fairer in the process. In an Old Bailey murder trial in 1791, he was even instrumental in articulating the belief, now enshrined in Anglo-American law, that 'every man is presumed to be innocent till proved guilty'.[34]

The Hanging Judge

In trials such as Joseph Baretti's, where the evidence was ambiguous, respectable character witnesses could make all the difference between a verdict of guilty and not guilty. But this strategy did not always work; there were times when pulling rank could be perceived as an attempt to bully the court, and some judges would not stand for it. Through their instructions to the jury, judges still exercised considerable power over trial outcomes. But what they could not control was the subsequent process of awarding royal pardons.

Richard Savage's life was so extraordinary that his friend, Samuel Johnson, was moved to write his biography, which has since become a classic of the genre. Savage's life was remarkable not only because he was a distinguished poet and playwright, as well as a notorious drunkard and libertine, but also because he was an extremely unlucky man. His mother was the Countess Macclesfield and his father the Earl Rivers, but their relationship was adulterous and he was born a bastard. Shortly after his birth his mother disowned him and placed him in the none too tender care of

a poor woman who was instructed to bring him up as a
pauper and hide the true identity of his parents. He
eventually discovered and proved his parentage, but his birth
mother continued to refuse to have anything to do with him
and when, on his death bed, the Earl Rivers sought to
include Savage in his will, he was dissuaded by the lie that
Savage himself was already dead. Nonetheless, having
received a grammar school education, Richard managed to
support himself by writing poetry and plays and through the
support and patronage of several aristocratic acquaintances.
But his fortunes once again turned for the worse on the
night of 20 November 1727.

Coming up to town on an errand, Savage ran into two
gentlemen acquaintances, James Gregory and William
Merchant. Together, they went to a nearby coffeehouse, and
stayed drinking till past midnight, 'It being in no time of Mr
Savage's life any part of his character to be the first of the
company that desired to separate'. Unable to find beds for
the night, they 'agreed to ramble about the streets, and divert
themselves with such amusements as should offer
themselves till morning'.[35] Happening to see a light in
Robinson's coffeehouse, near Charing Cross, they decided to
go in. Unknown to Savage and despite its respectable-
sounding name, Robinson's was a house of ill repute.

On this cold November evening, they demanded a room
with a fire and were told one would soon become available,
as a previous party of guests was just paying the bill in
preparation for departure. What happened next was
succinctly described by Samuel Johnson in his biography:

> Merchant, not satisfied with this answer, rushed into the
> room, and was followed by his companions. He then
> petulantly placed himself between the company and the
> fire, and soon after kicked down the table. This produced
> a quarrel, swords were drawn on both sides, and one Mr
> James Sinclair was killed.[36]

It was a classic early eighteenth-century swordfight between drunken gentlemen and in the chaos, Savage stabbed and mortally wounded Sinclair. In a state of shock, he escaped to a nearby courtyard where he and his two companions were apprehended. Following Sinclair's death the next day all three friends were committed to Newgate. Here, Johnson reported, they were 'treated with some distinction, exempted from the ignominy of chains, and confined, not among the common criminals, but in the press yard'.[37]

Although Savage and his friends would now almost certainly have to face trial, they could reassure themselves that they were unlikely to be charged or convicted of anything more serious than manslaughter, for clearly no malice or premeditation was involved. What they did not count on was the malice of Sinclair's friends and that of the employees of Robinson's coffeehouse. The coroner's inquest had to meet twice (each meeting characterised by intense debate) before a charge of manslaughter could finally be agreed. But when the three men stood trial in a packed courtroom at the Old Bailey two weeks later on 6 December, they were formally charged with murder. This was a relatively common practice and was almost certainly not unduly worrying to Savage and his friends. Most cases of this sort resulted in a verdict of manslaughter regardless of the initial charge.

Eight witnesses testified for the prosecution. At the request of the defendants, they were examined separately, resulting in several contradictions in the evidence heard by the court. Mr Nuttal, a companion of James Sinclair, took the stand first:

> On Monday the 20th of November, I, in company with Sinclair, Mr Limery and his brother, went to Robinson's Coffeehouse near Charing Cross, about 11 at night, where we stayed till one or two in the morning. We drank there two bowls of punch, which came to six shillings, and were

just concluding to go when the prisoners came into the
room. The first who came in was Mr Merchant, who,
setting his back to the fire, kicked down our table without
any provocation, upon which, I said, What do you mean?
Mr Gregory answered, What do you mean? Upon which
Mr Savage drew his sword. We retreated to the further end
of the room. I did not see Sinclair draw his sword, but Mr
Gregory drew, and I begged of Mr Savage and Mr Gregory
to put up their swords, which they refused, and Mr
Gregory turning to Sinclair, said, Villain deliver your
sword, and soon after took his sword from him. Mr
Gregory's sword was broke in the scuffle, but with
Sinclair's sword in his hand, and part of his own, he came
and demanded mine. I refused, he made a thrust at me, I
defended it; he endeavoured to get my sword, but he fell,
or I threw him, and took away the sword from him. Three
soldiers came into the room and secured him. I did not see
Mr Savage push at Sinclair, though I heard him say, I am a
dead man, soon after which the candles were put out. After
this I went up to Sinclair. I saw him in a chair, with
something hanging out of his belly, which I did believe to
be his caul, or fat. The maid servant of the house came in,
and kneeled on her knees to staunch the wound.

Nuttal had not seen Savage stab Sinclair, but he did suggest
that Sinclair had already surrendered his sword and was
defenceless when attacked.

The testimony of Mr Limery, another of James Sinclair's
friends, was both more and less damning than Nuttal's. On
the one hand, he had seen Savage inflict the wound, and
then struggle to escape:

I saw swords drawn, and Mr Savage made a thrust at the
deceased, who stooped and cried oh! at which Mr Savage
stood for some time astonished, and turned pale, then
endeavoured to get away. I held him, and the lights were
then put out. We struggled together, and the maid came to
my assistance, and pulling off his hat and wig, clung about
him, and striving to force himself from her he struck at
her, and cut her over the head with his sword and got away.

On the other hand, he reported that Sinclair still had his
sword at the time he was stabbed:

> When Mr Savage gave the wound the deceased had his
> sword drawn, but pointed downwards to the ground on the
> left side. As to Mr Merchant, I did not see he had a sword.

The employees at Robinson's then testified. Most important
was the testimony of Jane Leader, who was present at the
time of the fight:

> I was in the room and saw Mr Savage draw first, then Mr
> Gregory went up to Sinclair and Mr Savage stabbed him,
> and turning back he looked pale. Then Sinclair said, I am
> dead, I am dead, and would have gone out of the room,
> but I opened his coat and made the servant maid suck his
> wound, but no blood came. I, upon his death bed, asked
> him to tell how he was wounded. He said, the least in
> black gave the wound [which was Mr Savage, for Mr
> Merchant was in coloured clothes, and had no sword],
> that the tallest [which was Mr Gregory] passed or struck
> his sword, whilst Mr Savage stabbed him. I did not see
> Sinclair's sword at all, nor did he open his lips, or speak
> one word to the prisoners.

The words of a dying man were thought to possess a
distinctive truth. The Reverend Mr Taylor, who was
summoned to pray for Sinclair, told the court that Mr
Nuttal had asked him 'to ask the deceased a few questions',
but he refused. Nonetheless, Nuttal, keen to record the
words of a dying man:

> Persuaded Mr Taylor to stay whilst he himself should ask
> him a question, and turning to Sinclair, Mr Nuttal said,
> Do you know from which of the gentlemen you received
> the wound? To which Sinclair answered, From the shortest
> in black [which was Mr Savage], the tallest commanded
> my sword, and the other stabbed me.

Finally, two watchmen testified that Sinclair had told them
that 'he was stabbed barbarously before his sword was

drawn' and that he was 'stabbed cowardly'; and the surgeon told the court that Sinclair could not have been 'in a posture of defence' when he was stabbed, 'unless he was left handed'.

The evidence clearly identified Savage as the man responsible for Sinclair's death, but it was much less certain whether this was an accident, had occurred in a fair fight, or was a result of a one-sided assault. The defence argued that the killing was accidental. In order to establish this point, they tried to cast doubt on the character of the prosecution witnesses, to invalidate aspects of their evidence and to establish the trustworthiness and social standing of the defendants. First, James Gregory commented on the prosecution testimony:

> He endeavoured to bring the evidences for the king under the imputations of loose livers, and people that had no regard to justice or morality. He likewise insinuated to the court, that the house in which the disorder was committed bore a very infamous character.

This testimony was supported by that of Mary Stanley, who stated that 'she had seen Mr Nuttal and Mrs Leader, the owner of the coffeehouse, in bed together', and by that of John Pearce, who deposed that Leader 'was a woman of very ill reputation, and the coffeehouse had a bad character'. Even Sinclair's character was attacked:

> Daniel Boyle deposed, that the deceased had the character of an idle person, and had no place of residence. John Eaton said, he knew Sinclair for two months, and said, he had but an indifferent character, but yet he confessed he knew nothing of his character from other people.

Savage started his defence by attacking the evidence for the prosecution:

> He made some observations on the depositions of Mr Nuttal, Mr Limery, and Mrs Leader, in which he presumed there were some incoherencies; and then

proceeded to invalidate their evidence, and to prove, that
he, and the gentlemen of his company, were not of
inhumane or barbarous dispositions.

In testimony not reported in the *Proceedings*, he went on
to claim that he had acted in self-defence. As reported
by Johnson, he did not deny the fact:

> But endeavoured partly to extenuate it by urging the
> suddenness of the whole action, and the impossibility of
> any ill design or premeditated malice, and partly to justify
> it by the necessity of self-defence, and the hazard of his
> own life if he had lost that opportunity of giving the
> thrust. He observed that neither reason nor law obliged a
> man to wait for the blow which was threatened, and
> which, if he should suffer it, he might never be able to
> return; that it was always allowable to prevent an assault,
> and to preserve life by taking away that of the adversary
> by whom it was endangered.[38]

Savage concluded his testimony by seeking to explain away
his attempt to escape with the presumptuous claim that
prison was intolerable for a person of his status. He said:

> He should not have endeavoured to escape, but to avoid
> the inclemencies of a gaol, and the expences which must
> necessarily follow, which were too extravagant to be
> supported by a person in his circumstances.

Finally, the defendants attempted to establish their good
character:

> There appeared on behalf of the prisoners, several
> gentlemen and persons of honour, who gave each of them
> the character of being peaceable and quiet in their temper,
> and not given to quarrel; and the prisoners hoped, that
> their good character, and the suddenness of this
> unfortunate accident would entitle them to favour.

Johnson concluded his account of the case for the defence
with these words of praise.

> This defence, which took up more than an hour, was
> heard by the multitude that thronged the court with the
> most attentive and respectful silence. Those who thought
> he ought not to be acquitted owned that applause could
> not be refused him; and those who before pitied his
> misfortunes, now reverenced his abilities.[39]

The judge, Sir Francis Page, known as the 'hanging judge' following his zealous sentencing of deer stealers convicted on the notorious Black Act in 1723, was not so impressed. He appears to have been exasperated by the defendants' attempts to avoid conviction on the basis of their high social standing and good character. Unusually for an Old Bailey case in the 1720s, he delivered a lengthy summing up, letting the jury know precisely what verdict he expected them to deliver. Although judges were no longer allowed to coerce juries, they certainly retained the power to make their views known forcibly. As Page's speech was only partly recorded in the *Proceedings*, some of our knowledge of it comes from the unfavourable account in Johnson's biography. According to Johnson, Page started with these acid comments:

> Gentlemen of the jury, you are to consider that Mr Savage
> is a very great man, a much greater man than you or I,
> gentlemen of the jury; that he wears very fine clothes,
> much finer clothes than you or I, gentlemen of the jury;
> that he has abundance of money in his pocket, much more
> money than you or I, gentlemen of the jury; but,
> gentlemen of the jury, is it not a very hard case,
> gentlemen of the jury, that Mr Savage should therefore
> kill you or me, gentlemen of the jury?[40]

Page then summed up the evidence against Savage. As the *Proceedings* reported (in more measured tones):

> The court summed up the evidence, and took notice
> where there were any inconsistencies that might make for
> the prisoners, and directed the jury, that as the deceased

and his company were in possession of that part of the room where the fire was, that the prisoners were the aggressors, by kicking down the table and drawing their swords immediately upon it. That if they did believe that Sinclair retreated, was pursued, attacked and killed in the manner as is sworn, and declared by him on his death bed, without the least provocation on his part, that it was murder as well in him that gave the wound, as in the others who aided and abetted in this violence. That the jury had heard what had been objected to some of the evidence, and what had been replied on their behalf, and as they did credit them, they were to give a verdict accordingly.

Finally, returning to the character evidence, he told the jury that it could not invalidate the facts of the case:

> As to the character of the prisoner, that should influence a jury where the proof is doubtful, but not to defeat plain and positive evidence; the jury are to proceed according to the evidence and the rules of law.

Judge Page then explained how even in a sudden quarrel, one could be guilty of committing murder:

> As for the suddenness of this accident, where there is a sudden quarrel, and a provocation from one that is killed, or where on a sudden persons mutually attack each other and fight, and one is killed in the heat of blood, that is manslaughter; but where one is the aggressor, pursues his insult with his sword, and kills the person attacked without any provocation on his part, though on a sudden, the law implies malice, and this is murder.

The *Proceedings* report that the prisoners were given a chance to respond to Page's instructions:

> The court indulged the prisoners, to remind them if any thing that they thought material on their behalf, had been unobserved in summing up so long an evidence, and took notice accordingly to the jury of what they mentioned.

But according to Johnson's report, when Savage objected to some of the judge's comments about his attempts to escape, he was quickly slapped down:

> Mr Savage, hearing his defence thus misrepresented, and the men who were to decide his fate incited against him by invidious comparisons, resolutely asserted that his cause was not candidly explained, and began to recapitulate what he had before said with regard to his condition, and the necessity of endeavouring to escape the expences of imprisonment; but the judge, having ordered him to be silent, and repeated his orders without effect, commanded that he should be taken from the bar by force.[41]

Finally, after a trial lasting eight hours, the jury gave their verdict:

> That Richard Savage and James Gregory were guilty of murder, and that William Merchant was guilty of manslaughter.

Merchant, who had started the affair when he burst into the room, intruding himself in front of the fire and kicking over the table, had not been carrying a sword and so could not be found guilty of murder, but Gregory, although only an accomplice, could be. In cases involving murder, accessories to the crime were deemed equally culpable, and liable to the same punishments, as the principal.

Savage and Gregory were taken back to Newgate Prison, where as felons convicted of a capital offence they were closely confined and loaded with irons weighing 50 pounds. Four days later they returned to court to receive their inevitable death sentence. As was customary, the prisoners were first given the opportunity to address the court. Experienced writer that he was, Savage delivered the following finely worded oration:

> It is now, my Lord, too late to offer any thing by way of defence or vindication, nor can we expect from your

Lordships, in this court, but the sentence which the law requires you, as judges, to pronounce against men of our calamitous condition. But we are also persuaded that as mere men, and out of this seat of rigorous justice, you are susceptive of the tender passions, and too humane, not to commiserate the unhappy situation of those whom the law sometimes exacts from you to pronounce upon. No doubt you distinguish between offences which arise out of premeditation and a disposition habituated to vice or immorality and transgressions which are the unhappy and unforeseen effects of a casual absence of reason, and sudden impulse of passion. We therefore hope you will contribute all you can to an extension of that mercy, which the gentlemen of the jury have been pleased to show Mr Merchant, who (allowing facts as sworn against us by the evidence) has led us into this our calamity.[42]

Page, the 'hanging judge' was not moved, and the two were duly sentenced to hang.

There followed the usual attempts by their friends to solicit a pardon from the crown. Incredibly, these did not include Savage's mother, who maintained her lifelong hostility to her illegitimate son. Citing an earlier incident in which Savage had managed to find and enter his mother's house in order to seek a reconciliation, his mother spread the story that he had attempted to murder her in her own home. This led the queen to state that:

However unjustifiable might be the manner of his trial, or whatever extenuation the action for which he was condemned might admit, she could not think that man a proper object of the king's mercy, who had been capable of entering his mother's house in the night, with an intent to murder her.

Fortunately, Savage also had friends in high places. Only a week after the trial concluded, Charles Beckingham, a fellow poet and playwright, wrote a short six-penny pamphlet, *The Life of Mr. Richard Savage*. This included 'A

Letter to a Noble Lord on behalf of Mr Savage and Mr Gregory', a plea to this unidentified Lord (who turned out to be Lord Tyrconnel) to intercede for them. Not only was Savage described as 'a man of virtue and of honour, sufficient recommendation for your lordship to intercede for him', but some new evidence was presented about the witnesses who had testified against him:

> Blot out the unhappy moment which was the source of his present calamity, and Savage will appear unsullied in virtue and honour; nor will that appear so black, if murder in any case may be extenuated, when we consider the evidences who cast him; three women, my Lord, who have since contradicted what before they had sworn, the other evidence, a man, by report of no amiable character; but who are said to have most grossly misrepresented the fact, and to have industriously spread that misrepresentation. The reputations of Mr Savage and Mr Gregory have been always clear; nor are they in any action of their lives to be lamented by their friends but on this melancholy occasion. The first I have known and conversed with for several years, and can more fully speak of him. I have discovered in him a mind incapable of evil; I have beheld him sigh for the distressed, when more distressed himself.

The plea concluded:

> Since it is plain, the public may be a loser by the death of these gentlemen, and none but the grave can be a gainer, there is great reason to hope for a pardon, or an extensive reprieve.[43]

Lord Tyrconnel obliged and petitioned the king and queen, but according to Johnson, Savage's life was saved primarily by the intervention of the Countess of Hertford:

> Who engaged in his support with all the tenderness that is excited by pity, and all the zeal which is kindled by generosity; and, demanding an audience of the queen, laid before her the whole series of his mother's cruelty,

exposed the improbability of an accusation by which he was charged with an intent to commit a murder that could produce no advantage, and soon convinced her how little his former conduct could deserve to be mentioned as a reason for extraordinary severity. The interposition of this lady was so successful that he was soon after admitted to bail, and on the 9th of March 1728, pleaded the king's pardon.[44]

Gregory was also pardoned. Judge Page controlled his own court and, within limits, could effectively ensure that the sentence he wanted was passed, but even he could not overrule the collective influence of the English aristocracy.[45]

Conclusion

Readers were consistently drawn to the *Proceedings* because the trial reports they contained were full of drama and surprise. Defendant testimonies gave readers a rare opportunity to hear the genuine voices of criminals pleading for their lives. In the *Proceedings* they found the majesty of the court challenged by the defiance of highwaymen and murderers and read of elite men and women put on trial just like common criminals. But the drama of the Old Bailey courtroom was gradually eroded over the century as professional lawyers began to shape the trial to suit their own interests. Trials became increasingly stage managed. Prosecution lawyers read lengthy prepared speeches in opening and closing statements, and the pleadings of prisoners at the bar were ghost written by their counsel. Lawyers argued detailed points of law with the judge while the accused and accusers sat in silence. The most dramatic moment in any trial, the moment the defendant pleaded his case with his life on the line, was often erased altogether when his lawyer did not even permit him to speak. But some aspects of the drama remained. No one could completely dictate the decisions taken by the jury, which frequently remained independent minded and occasionally perverse, producing verdicts at odds with the evidence presented. Neither could the witnesses advanced on each side be counted on to toe the line. Character witnesses were sometimes all too honest in their assessments, such as the one who said of the defendant he was supposed to support, 'as for his character, I beg to be excused from saying anything about it'.[46] And the overwhelming significance of what was at stake was unchanged: an unlucky few would be convicted and hanged, while the majority of the accused escaped with lesser punishments or even walked free.

4

Crimes of Greed, Crimes of Lust

The offence most frequently prosecuted at the Old Bailey was theft. When fraud is included, over 90 percent of trials involved offences against property. But statute law did not see these crimes as occupying a single category. Instead, they were divided into an ever growing number of discrete capital offences, adding category after category to the common law offence of larceny to create the notorious 'Bloody Code'. Burglary, pickpocketing, robbery, shoplifting, theft from specified places (such as a warehouse), and forgery were all added to the range of crimes to be punished by hanging.

In the eyes of eighteenth-century men and women, this elaborate legal classification was necessary to combat an epidemic of theft that was in turn a product of loose morals. Many believed that minor sins such as profane swearing and cursing, Sabbath breaking, and getting drunk led inexorably down the slippery slope to the commission of more serious crimes including theft and murder. Although there is little evidence to support this theory of the causes of crime, there was some foundation to the contemporary belief that vice and theft were intimately associated. But, confounding eighteenth-century perceptions, it was generally the loose morals of the victims, rather than the perpetrators, of crime that did most to encourage theft. Men and women past caring, paralysed by the consumption of gin, staggered through the streets or lay unconscious in the gutters, making tempting targets for pickpockets. And the clients of prostitutes, preoccupied by lust and their wits frequently dulled by drink, were perfect marks for pilfering hands that pretended to other business in a man's breeches. It was difficult for the victims of such thefts to stand up in court and explain how they happened to lose their valuables. Drunkenness and prostitution were not crimes, but to many contemporaries the first was a sign of weakness and the second distinctly immoral. In an even more awkward position were men who engaged in sodomy (a capital offence until 1867). They were vulnerable to theft and extortion and their attempts to defend themselves could easily result in both prosecution and public humiliation. But regardless of these disincentives to prosecute, the *Proceedings* contain thousands of cases that arose out of awkward contexts such as these.

Despite the contemporary obsession with immorality, the motivation for most property crimes was simple poverty. Even a cursory exploration of the *Old Bailey Proceedings* reveals that many of the trials for theft involved the loss of goods valued at just a few pence – of handkerchiefs and items of clothing which were then immediately pawned or sold for small sums of money. A plain cotton handkerchief could be sold for six pence, while a silk one might fetch six shillings – enough to supply a hungry man or woman with hot dinners for a week. The same story of poverty and desperation that helps explain the motivation for most theft is also evident in the circumstances of many of the accused. They were from the vast body of London's poor: orphaned children, beggars, single women and the aged. Although in law, necessity gave no excuse for theft, many pleaded hunger and destitution in their defence, pleas that while unlikely to lead to an acquittal, often led at least to a lesser punishment.

The single most important cause of poverty was unemployment and prosecution rates shot up at the end of every war, as demobilised soldiers made their way back to the metropolis and war-related industries laid off workers. Although these 'crime waves' were at least as much a product of public fears of what desperate men accustomed to violence might do in the absence of a foreign enemy (preferably a Frenchman) to fight as of actual increases in theft, the difficulty of finding work in this volatile economy undoubtedly caused many to resort to theft, particularly since immigrants to the metropolis frequently had few family or friends to turn to and no right to claim poor relief from the parish.

Although hunger and real need explain most thefts, it does not explain them all. Many trials resulted from a different sort of greed: the desire to wear the latest fashions or follow the lifestyle of a higher social class. London's extensive upper and middle classes fuelled a boom in luxury goods (particularly clothes and jewellery) that had an impact on all classes of society. For the first time in English history, keeping up with the latest fashions became important to people beyond the narrow aristocracy. The commonplace theft of fashionable goods testifies not only to their intrinsic monetary value but sometimes also to the motivation behind the crime: occasionally the thief was caught actually parading the stolen clothes about the streets. The phenomenon of the gentleman highway robber – men (and very occasionally women) who purportedly treated their victims politely as they relieved them of their watches and pocketbooks – reflects the contemporary belief that even common thieves might have social aspirations and might commit crimes in order to achieve them. And even if in practice there is little evidence of 'polite' robbery of this sort, the behaviour of men such as James Maclaine, who used the substantial profits derived from his crimes to set himself up as a gentleman, suggests the possibilities of social mobility open to the successful criminal.

Other prosecutions for theft arose out of fundamental differences of opinion about the nature of property itself and who had the right to use it. In these trials the accused had no intention to commit a crime. The poor frequently borrowed from each other and from their employers and landlords, pawning their goods in order to make ends meet. Failure to obtain the consent of the owner in advance frequently led to disagreements over the terms of a loan, which in turn led to trials for theft, despite promises that the goods would be returned. Most poor Londoners, for instance, lived in furnished rooms rented out by the week. To the tenant, pawning the furniture for a few days (the use of which they had already paid for) often seemed a reasonable strategy to tide them over a rough patch; whereas to the landlord this same 'borrowing' could look like unadulterated theft. Disagreements between workers and their employers over the removal of scraps from the workplace, known as perquisites, also resulted in some prosecutions. The loose tobacco or sugar swept up after a ship was unloaded, for example, or the off-cuts of wood in a carpenter's shop, were often seen by workmen as a legitimate part of their wages. But as profits were squeezed towards the end of the century, employers increasingly attempted to stop these practices, relabelling them as 'pilfering' and 'embezzlement'. As a result, workplace conflicts between employers and employees over remuneration sometimes led to criminal prosecutions at the Old Bailey.

The eighteenth century witnessed the creation of a panoply of new forms of property and business that created in their turn new forms of theft. From the late seventeenth century, London's streets were increasingly lined with glass-fronted shops, which supplemented and gradually replaced traditional markets and hawkers. With their large bow windows filled with tempting goods, shops attracted thieves, often women dressed in large mantua gowns with plenty of space for secreting stolen goods. 'Shoplifting' became a separate capital offence in 1699. Later in the century the introduction of a postal service created the new crime of stealing letters from the post, a form of embezzlement defined by statute in 1767. Similarly, the growing use of paper credit, necessary in an expanding economy with limited hard currency, led to statutes against the embezzlement of notes, deeds and bills by officers or servants of a company (1742) and by employees of the Bank of England (1795 and 1797). More threatening still was the use of forgery to create false promissory notes as a way of obtaining lines of credit. Trust and credit, standing bond and surety for others, were the lubricants that allowed this economy to move; when these networks of trust turned out to be built on false foundations they could collapse with disastrous results for the entire business community. 'White-collar' crime of this sort frequently involved apparently respectable men and women from the upper classes and their trials attracted widespread attention as a result, raising difficult questions about the boundaries between acceptable and unacceptable business practices.

In principle all eighteenth-century Londoners agreed that theft was undesirable, but they could not always agree on what was meant by theft. Defendants, jurors and even judges struggled to clarify when a perquisite became embezzlement, a loan became stealing and an unsubstantiated promise became fraud. As difficult, they struggled to justify punishing a man or woman driven to theft by poverty, hunger and real need. With the death penalty looming behind almost every prosecution, the stakes were high.

Something Else Doing

Over 800 trials at the Old Bailey in the eighteenth century involved women accused of picking the pockets of men. The overwhelming majority of these alleged crimes occurred during acts of prostitution, leaving both prosecutors and defendants in a quandary about how much detail they should reveal at the trial. At least one of the parties, usually the defendant, normally found it advantageous to acknowledge that sex was in the air and in the first decades of the century, this did much to add titillating entertainment value to the Proceedings *(and profits to the publisher). But since these crimes and the sexual acts associated with them were normally committed in private, the resulting trials often became a direct contest for the truth between the two parties involved. As both prosecutor and defendant were often drunk and, almost by definition, not entirely respectable, juries were faced with the difficult prospect of deciding whether a crime had actually occurred at all. Despite the dubious character of the women accused in these cases, this ambiguity helps to explain why most (61 percent) were eventually acquitted.*

London possessed tens of thousands of drinking establishments. Alcohol was available everywhere and with the drink came almost ubiquitous prostitution. A ballad, 'The City Cheat Discovered, or, a New Coffee House Song', sung to the tune of Lillibulero, described how the keepers encouraged lewd women to prey on their male clientele:

> *Kissing, kissing, nothing but kissing;*
> *Kissing and billing is all that they do;*
> *There's kissing and wooing, and something else doing;*
> *And this is the ruin of Jack and Tom too.*
> Miss with all her delicate cider and mum,
> Can pick all their pockets before they well know.
> *Yes sir, pray sir, do sir, stay sir;*

What ye call, that ye shall, welcome sir.

Tho after his billing, he has not a shilling,

Which when he comes home makes a horrible stir.[1]

Men who lost their valuables in such situations had to choose between attempting to prosecute the culprit, thereby publicly exposing their own immoral behaviour, or refusing to prosecute and simply accepting the loss. Most men undoubtedly chose the latter. Of the minority who determined to prosecute, some tried to deny that there had been any sex involved. James Hughs prosecuted the unfortunately named Ann Hussey for picking his pocket of 8s and a piece of silver on the very dark night of 6 December 1724. As recorded in the third-person narrative published in the *Proceedings*, he told the court that Hussey propositioned him as he was going along Shoe Lane, but that he steadfastly resisted all her advances:

> The prisoner caught hold of his arm, and, my dear, says she, where are you going? Won't you give me a pint? You saucy bitch (says he) what should I give you a pint for? By God, says she, I will have a kiss then; and throwing one hand round his neck, he felt the other in his pocket. Rot your impudence for a corrupted toad, says he; do you want to pick my pocket? He pushed her from him, felt for his money, missed it, stopped her, and she cried out murder.

The jurors might well have found this story plausible, for London's prostitutes were notorious for aggressively accosting pedestrians on the streets. But the story told by Hussey was rather different:

> The prisoner in her defence said that as she was passing by Hughs, he threw his arm round her, and would needs go home with her. They went together to a neighbour's house, where he gave her 2 shillings to occupy her. He would have lain with her all night; but because she refused, he charged her with picking his pocket.

In this account James Hughs was the one seeking sex and Hussey argued that the prosecution arose from her refusal to satisfy all his demands. Faced with such contradictory accounts, the jury came to what amounted to a compromise, finding Hussey guilty on a partial verdict, of stealing goods but not privately, and only to the value of less than 5s. This meant that rather than being hanged, she was sentenced to transportation to North America.[2]

Although the trial report doesn't record this detail, it is likely that the missing money was found on Ann Hussey when she was searched. In such cases, the best defence was to say that the money had been freely given for services rendered. When James Lawson, for example, prosecuted Elizabeth Roberts, alias Bustock, for picking his pocket of two guineas in 1727, he was circumspect in his description of what the two had been doing together:

> On the 18th of December I was going along Cornhill between eleven and twelve o'clock at night and the prisoner desired me to go and drink with her. So we went to the Salutation Alehouse in Bell Yard, and going upstairs the prisoner sat down at the end of the table, and I sat down at the side, and my money was in my left pocket, for I had taken it out of my right side pocket and put it into the left after I came into the room, and had only some farthings in my right pocket. But after we had been drinking and I went to change a guinea to pay the reckoning, indeed I was in drink, but not so drunk neither but I can be sure the prisoner had picked my pocket, for my guineas were gone. I desired the prisoner to give me them back again, but she would not, so I stopped her, and spoke to the landlord to call a constable.

Elizabeth Roberts told a different story:

> I was going along Cornhill near the Royal Exchange, and the prosecutor asked me to go and drink with him. I denied him at first, but afterwards went along with him to this alehouse. I own I am an unfortunate woman, and live

by keeping company, but never wronged man, woman nor child in my life, but only what gentlemen please to give me (and what can be freer than a gift?) and when the constable came I offered to be searched, and told him if I had such money about me it was the prosecutor's, and that he must give it me among some half-pence which he gave me to buy a bunch of rods, for we were both drunk, and I did not mind what he gave me. I asked him what I was to do with the rods, and he said he wanted to be flogged, but the man of the house said he would not suffer any such doings in his house, and then the prosecutor sent for a constable, who carried us both to the compter.

Even though she confessed to the constable that she had 'cribbed' [pilfered] the money when it was found on her person, Robert's testimony, larded as it was with telling and titillating details that undermined Lawson's character, resulted in an acquittal.[3]

Other men, particularly in the first decades of the century, freely admitted that they had lost their valuables during a sexual encounter. Benjamin Gosling, for instance, seems to have felt little embarrassment when describing his encounter with Phillis Noble on a cold night in early January 1726:

I live in White Horse Alley in Drury Lane. I am a bricklayer's labourer, and it's well known that I work hard for my money, and so as I was saying, betwixt one and two a clock in the morning – and a mortal cold night it was – I am sure I have good cause to remember it, for as I was coming by the corner of Bennets Court, in Drury Lane; and who should I meet but the prisoner? And so says she, how d'ye do my dear, tis bloody cold weather, I wish you'd give me a dram. Whereof, says I again, I don't care if I do, if we can come to a good fire, and so – what signifies lying – we struck a bargain, and went to a gin shop, and I thought I had better do so than wander about the street all night, though I must needs say, I might as well have gone home to my wife – but that's neither here nor there. I was got a little in for it and when I am once

> in, I never mind which end goes foremost, and it's many a
> poor man's case as well as mine.

Following a round of drinks they appear to have decided to
go elsewhere:

> And so sir the reckoning came to 8 pence and I had got a
> brass box in my pocket, with 2 guineas in it, and a note
> upon command for 6 pounds 6 shillings, and some other
> odd matters. I takes out this box, in order to pay the shot.
> Now whether she saw the money in my box, or did not
> see it, I can't be positive, she might or she might not, but
> howsoever I gave my landlady a shilling to change, and
> put up my box again, and some other people came in to
> drink. And by and by my landlady brings me a groat, and
> so I went out with the groat in my hand, and Phillis along
> with me; and I goes to put my money up, and missed my
> box, and so I called the watch, and carried her to the
> round house.

Evidence for the prosecution was completed by testimony
from Benjamin Gosling's put-upon wife, who told the court
that she (of all people) had searched the prisoner and found
the box and the note upon her, but not the money.

Phillis Noble's defence suggested that something
altogether more disturbing happened once they left the gin
shop:

> It being a cold night, I went into a gin shop for a dram of
> aniseed, and there I saw this Gosling a drinking along
> with a parcel of bunters (whores), and he was got very
> drunk, and fain would have been rude with me. But never
> caring to make myself familiar with any such fellows, I
> went out, and he followed me, and thrust me up against
> the wall, and there he pulled out his pistol, and swore he'd
> let fly at me, if I would not let him ravish me.

Her account of assault and attempted rape did not wash
with the jury, however, and since at least some of the goods
were found on her, they declared her guilty, though once
again on a partial verdict.[4]

A few months later on a much warmer August evening, Alexander Watts lost several possessions during an open-air encounter with Isabel Lucky:

> I was got drunk, and was going home to Cats Hole in St Catherines. In my waistcoat pocket I had got a pound of hair in a bladder, and a pocketbook, a pair of gloves, and a handkerchief in the other pocket; and so coming under Aldgate, I saw Isabel Lucky before me, and I gave her a tap upon the shoulder, and asked her where she was going, and she said a little farther, and so she walked sometimes before me, and sometimes behind, till she came to Goodman's Yard, and there she turned down, and went into a porch, and I after her. Well, says she, what will you give me now. Why indeed my dear, says I again, I have got no money at present, but if you'll oblige me so and so, I'll make you amends the next time I see you, for I live but a little way off. Truly, says she, I can do nothing without ready money, for I can't afford to trust. – Indeed my dear you must for this once. – Will you be as good as your word then? – Yes indeed I will child. – Well then if I must, I must, and so, sir, I laid her upon the ground, for she was not afraid of daubing her clothes, because she was then in as dirty a pickle as she is in now. But however as foul as she was, I can't deny but that I did commit that filthy sin upon her, and just in the heat of action, she cried out, the watch, the watch is a coming, get away and shift for your self. So I got off, and turned my back upon her, and put up my breeches, but the watch not coming, I went to the porch and felt for her there, but she was gone. Then I felt in my pockets, and found that all was lost. Well, says I, to myself, the bitch has robbed me, she has taken away every thing that I had about me; my very hair and bladder and all, and I am an undone man! So having no body to make my apology to, I walked home in that condition.

Lucky was apprehended when another woman, Sarah Jones, tried to sell some of the hair to a barber. In this case, it was Lucky who denied any illicit sexual activity:

> Lucky in her defence said, that as she was going along
> Goodman's Yard, in the dark, she kicked something soft
> before her, and taking it up, found it to be hair.

Sarah Jones told a rather different story. She 'said that meeting Lucky, she asked her to drink, and desired her to sell the hair for her, telling her that she had the hair from a sailor of her acquaintance'. Perhaps because Watts had been so reckless in his behaviour, Lucky was found guilty on only a partial verdict and Jones, who denied knowing that the goods were stolen, was acquitted.[5]

The sexual activities of London's prostitutes and their clients were occasionally unconventional. Joseph Richmond, for instance, certainly seems to have developed a taste for flagellation and humiliation that he expected to be pandered to. One Sunday in early July 1725 he approached two women with a rather unusual request:

> About nine o'clock on Sunday night, Susan Brockway and
> Mary Gardner picked me up upon London Bridge. I went
> with them to the Cross Key Tavern upon Fish Street Hill,
> and there we stayed about an hour. I agreed to give them a
> crown apiece, to — to —, not to do them over, but for them
> to strip naked, and show me some tricks. And to satisfy them
> that I had money enough to be as good as my word, I took
> three broad pieces and three shillings out of my pocket.

Richmond went on to recount how:

> Susan Brockway said, she supposed it was not right gold,
> and so she took a piece to look upon it, whereupon she
> said it was very good, and gave it me again; and by and
> by she snatches all the money out of my hand, and put it
> into her bosom, and said, you shall never see it again. I'll
> keep it, to learn you more wit; that another time you may
> know an honest woman from a whore.

According to Joseph Richmond he immediately called in the tavern keeper and sent him to fetch a constable. At the subsequent trial, however, Susan Brockway and Mary

Gardner told a rather different and perhaps more believable story, implying that the prosecution arose because they had refused to satisfy all Richmond's requests.

> This man took us to the tavern, and offered us a crown a piece to strip ourselves naked, and show him postures. He gave Mary Gardner money to fetch a penny-worth of rods, for him to whip us across the room, and make us good girls; and then for us to whip him to make him a good boy. But we told him it was neither a proper time nor place for any such thing, for it was Sunday night, and others might overlook us in the room we were in, though the curtains were drawn. He bid us look to it; for it should be worse for us, if we would not do as he would have us; and so he called the tavern keeper, and said, we had got his money.

No money was found on the women when they were searched, and the jury, unsurprisingly, acquitted them.[6]

In 1725 when the publisher of the *Proceedings* was censured for 'lewd and indecent' reporting, the Court of Aldermen must have had cases like this (as well as that of the drunken Irish prosecutor) in mind. And as contemporary moral standards changed over the course of the century, not only did reports of this kind start to become more circumspect (this is already evident by the 1730s), but male victims and female defendants became less willing to admit their activities in open court. Reading between the lines, however, it is clear what was going on. Offering men sex for money continued to give poor women who were down on their luck easy opportunities to steal in circumstances where the victim was unlikely to prosecute. At the same time, though the number of prosecutions declined, some of the men who lost valuables in such seedy circumstances seem to have continued to believe (despite considerable evidence to the contrary) that the double standard, in combination with the poor character of the women involved, would make a conviction possible.

A Quiet Assignation in Chelsea Fields

The eighteenth-century world of commercial sex was not limited to heterosexual encounters, neither were the early eighteenth-century Proceedings *unwilling to report the details of less conventional sexual activity. As part of a vibrant 'molly house' culture, gay sex was also available for a price. Link boys and shoe blacks, children at the bottom of the economic pile, were frequently forced to sell sexual favours for a few pence, while the up-market masquerades and pleasure gardens of the capital played witness to more fortunate young men on the make. Despite the fact that sodomy was punishable by death, and despite the existence of virulent homophobia, many men and women seem to have taken a rather more relaxed attitude. Many Londoners agreed with John Bowes, who was caught sodomising Hugh Ryley up against the rails of the church yard at Covent Garden one early December evening in 1718. When challenged, Bowes replied 'Sirrah what's that to you, can't I make use of my own body?'[7]*

John Cooper was a male prostitute and transvestite who went by the nickname Princess Seraphina. On 7 June 1732 he strutted his stuff at the democratic pleasure garden at Vauxhall just south of the river. He was dressed in a woman's gown and mob hat and attended the *Ridotto al Fresco*, or open-air masquerade, that marked the triumphant reopening of Vauxhall Gardens. Everyone was there, including the Prince of Wales. Cooper's ability to live in this extraordinary way, to dress as a woman in public and to tout for trade as a male prostitute among the pleasure-seeking crowds at Vauxhall, reflects the 'double-think' practised by most Londoners. Until you were called a 'molly' or a sodomite, you were relatively safe in the unthinking tolerance of a great city, but once the finger of accusation was pointed, life could become very much more difficult very quickly. That summer, John Cooper certainly felt safe enough to prosecute Thomas

Gordon for the theft of his clothes, after a night on the tiles. Unfortunately for Cooper, what began as an attempt to gain recompense quickly degenerated into a mocking judgment of Cooper's lifestyle and sexuality. At Gordon's trial, Cooper described the events of the evening:

> On Whit Monday, May 29, I dressed myself and went abroad, and returning between 1 and 2 the next morning to my lodging at number 11 in Eagle Court, in the Strand, I knocked once, but finding nobody answered I went to a night cellar hard by. I called for a pint of beer and sitting down on a bench Thomas Gordon came and sat by me. He asked me if I did not know Mr Price and some other persons, and so we fell into discourse. We drank 3 hot pints together. I paid the reckoning, 9½ pence, and went up. I was got about 15 or 20 yards off when the prisoner came up to me, said it was a fine morning, and asked me to take a walk. I agreed, and we went into Chelsea Fields, and turned up to a private place among some trees.

According to Cooper, at this point what had been a pleasant interlude on a warm night turned suddenly dangerous:

> Gordon clapped his left hand to the right side of my coat, and tripped up my heels, and holding a knife to me, God damn you, says he, if you offer to speak or stir I'll kill you. Give me your ring. I gave it him and he put it on his own finger. Then he made me pull off my coat and waistcoat and breeches. I begged that he would not kill me, nor leave me naked. No, says he, I'll only change with you, come pull off your shirt, and put on mine. So he stripped and dressed himself in my clothes and I put on his.
>
> He asked me where I lived, and I told him. I suppose, says he, you intend to charge me with a robbery by and by, but if you do, I'll swear you are a sodomite and gave me the clothes to let you bugger me.

The threat of a charge of sodomy was very real. Just two years earlier, the Netherlands was rocked by the arrest of

over 250 men, dozens of whom were eventually executed in
the largest pogrom of its sort in European history prior to
the twentieth century. And in London six years earlier, the
Old Bailey and the lesser courts witnessed a spate of sodomy
trials that resulted in both hangings and the pillory. Cooper,
however, did not let the threat deter him from his attempts
to recover his clothes:

> Then Thomas Gordon bid me come along, and I followed
> him to Piccadilly, and so to Little Windmill Street, and
> there I called to 2 men, who took him into an alehouse. I
> told them he had robbed me, and he said that I had given
> him the clothes to let me bugger him. The men said they
> expected to be paid for their day's work, if they lost their
> time about my business. I promised them they should be
> satisfied.

The turning point came when the two men who had come
to Cooper's assistance heard Gordon's accusation:

> So we went toward Tyburn Road, into Marybone Fields,
> and there the men let the prisoner go. What do ye do?
> says I. Why what would you have us do? said they. He
> charges you with sodomy and says you gave him the
> clothes on that account. Another man coming by at the
> same time, I desired his assistance, but they telling him
> that I was a molly, he said I ought to be hanged, and he
> would have nothing to do with me.
>   Then Gordon began to run, and I after him; but one of
> the two men, who expected to be paid for their day's
> work, kicked up my heels, and as I was rising, he struck
> me down again. I was very much hurt, and spit blood, so
> that I could not follow them. And so they all got over a
> ditch and escaped.

Cooper did not give up easily. He discovered Gordon's name
from a neighbour and had him arrested for theft at the door
of a brandy shop in Drury Lane.

At Thomas Gordon's eventual trial, he gave a very
different account of the events in Chelsea Fields:

I was locked out and went to Mrs Holder's night cellar.
The prosecutor came and sat by me and asked me to
drink. I thought I had seen him before and we fell into
discourse, and had 3 hot pints of gin and ale between us.
About 4 in the morning he asked me to take a walk. We
went into Chelsea Fields and coming among some trees
and hedges, he kissed me and put his privy parts into my
hand. I asked him what he meant by that, and told him I
would expose him. He begged me not to do it, and said he
would make me amends. I asked him what amends? He
said he would give me all his clothes, and so we agreed,
and changed clothes.

At this point the trial took a significantly different turn.
Margaret Holder, the owner of the night cellar where the
two men had been drinking, was called. She confirmed that
Cooper and Gordon had been there, but ended her
testimony with a disastrous aside:

I keep the night cellar. Thomas Gordon came in about 10
at night and staid till 2 in the morning, and then John
Cooper came in and sat down by him, and said, Your
servant, sir, have you any company belonging to you, for I
don't love much company? Then they had 3 pints of
Huckle and Buss, as we call it, that's gin and ale made
hot. And so about 4 o'clock Gordon said he would go
home, for his mother would be up and he might get in
without his father's knowledge. And Cooper said, If you
go, I'll go too. So Gordon went up first and Cooper stayed
to change a shilling, and went out after him. I believe
Thomas Gordon is an honest man; but John Cooper and
Kitt Sandford too, use to come to my cellar with such sort
of people.

At this point the judge intervened:

Court.   What sort of people?
A.   Why, to tell you the truth, he is one of the
              runners that carries messages between gentlemen
              in that way.

Court.	In what way?
A.	Why he is one of them as you call molly culls. He gets his bread that way. To my certain knowledge he has got many a crown under some gentlemen.

For John Cooper the trial of Thomas Gordon might as well have ended here. There was no way that Gordon would be found guilty after Margaret Holder's revelation. And in due course the jury acquitted him, but not before John Cooper's lifestyle was paraded before the court. In testimony after testimony, his situation just got worse. Next to address the court (and to be interrogated by the bemused judge) was Jane Jones:

Jones.	I am a washer-woman in Drury-Lane. I went into Mr Poplet's, my next door neighbour, for a pint of beer, and said, there's the Princess Seraphina! So I looked at her, and Thomas Gordon was in the same box; and says he to the Princess, What a vile villain was you to –
Court.	What Princess?
Jones.	John Cooper, he goes by that name. What a villain was you, says Gordon, to offer so vile a thing? Did not you do so and so?
Court.	So and so; explain your self.
Jones.	Why in the way of sodomy, whatever that is! So says the Princess, If you don't give me my clothes again, I'll swear a robbery against you, but if you'll let me have them, I'll be easy. No, you villain, you shan't, says Gordon. Next day I went to Mr Stringer the pawnbroker's, facing Vinegar Yard in Drury Lane. I wash for him, and there I saw the Princess a pawning her shirt. O Princess! says I, are you there? You will be very fine by and by; you will have no occasion to pawn your linen when you get the reward for hanging Tom Gordon. But how can you be so

cruel to swear his life away, when you have owned that you
changed with him? What if I did, says he, I don't value
that, I shall do nothing but what I have been
advised to.

Next to give evidence was Mary Poplet:

I keep the Two Sugar Loaves in Drury Lane. Gordon and
the Princess came into my house, and the Princess
charged the prisoner with taking her clothes, and the
prisoner called her villain, and said she gave them to him.

I have known her Highness a pretty while. She used to
come to my house to enquire after some gentlemen of no
very good character. I have seen her several times in
woman's clothes. She commonly used to wear a white
gown and a scarlet cloak, with her hair frizzled and curled
all round her forehead, and then she would so flutter her
fan and make such fine curtsies that you would not have
known her from a woman. She takes great delight in balls
and masquerades, and always chooses to appear at them
in a female dress that she may have the satisfaction of
dancing with fine gentlemen. Her Highness lives with Mr
Tull in Eagle Court in the Strand, and calls him her master
because she was nurse to him and his wife when they
were both in a salivation for venereal disease. But the
Princess is rather Mr Tull's friend than his domestic
servant. I never heard that she had any other name than
the Princess Seraphina.

And finally, Mary Robinson:

I was trying on a suit of red damask at my mantua
maker's in the Strand when the Princess Seraphina came
up and told me the suit looked mighty pretty. I wish, says
he, you would lend them to me for a night to go to Mrs
Green's in Nottingham Court by the Seven Dials, for I am
to meet some fine gentlemen there. Why, says I, can't Mrs
Green furnish you? Yes, says he, she lends me a velvet
scarf and a gold watch sometimes. Another time he comes
to me, and says, Lord, Madam, I must ask your pardon. I
was at your mantua maker's yesterday and dressed my
head in your laced pinners, and I would fain have

borrowed them to have gone to the *Ridotto* at Vauxhall
last night, but I could not persuade her to lend them to
me. But however she lent me your calamanco gown and
Madam Nuttal's mob hat and one of her smocks. And so I
went thither to pick up some gentlemen to dance. And did
you make a good hand of it Princess? says I. No, Madam,
says he, I picked up two men who had no money, but
however they proved to be my old acquaintance, and very
good gentlewomen they were. One of them has been
transported for counterfeiting masquerade tickets; and the
other went to the masquerade in a velvet domino and
picked up an old gentleman, and went to bed with him.
But as soon as the old fellow found that he had got a man
by his side, he cried out, murder.

Princess Seraphina lived in a vibrant world of alcohol, sex
and cross-dressing, of the splendour of Vauxhall and the
squalor of Margaret Holder's night cellar. It was a world full
of contradictions. His female friends lent him clothes one
day, only to humiliate him in open court on the next. He
endeavoured to navigate the difficult waters of eighteenth-
century sexuality and was pulled under by their turbulence.
Put on trial for a capital offence, Thomas Gordon knew he
had a powerful weapon in the counter-accusation of sodomy
and he deployed it with devastating effect.[8]

The Gentleman Highwayman

*Even at the beginning of the eighteenth century, highwaymen
had a romantic reputation, but as new forms of popular
literature emerged, they became almost heroes in the public
imagination. For the men who stood trial for highway robbery,
this image, with its pretence to gentility and politeness, was
important. It allowed them to differentiate themselves, both in
the courtroom and in the court of public opinion, from the
maligned street robbers and footpads who were held responsible
for London's increasingly severe crime waves. But it did not*

necessarily spare them the ultimate penalty, since regardless of
public opinion, the courts treated highway robbery as a serious
offence.

The son of an Irish Presbyterian minister, James Maclaine showed an 'aversion to a mechanic employment' from an early age.[9] He squandered his own small inheritance, and came to London in 1743, attempting to recoup his fortune by courting rich women. He managed to marry one with a fortune of £500 in 1744 or 1745 and with this money set himself up as a grocer, while developing the expensive tastes suitable to a gentlemanly lifestyle. His economic security did not last long, however, and following his wife's death in 1748 he rapidly dissipated her wealth on luxuries and gambling. When down on his luck, he met William Plunket, an equally hard-up apothecary. Plunket told him he needed to take matters into his own hands:

> A brave man cannot want – he has a right to live, and
> need not want the conveniences of life, while the dull,
> plodding, busy knaves carry cash in their pockets. We
> must draw upon them to supply our wants. There needs
> only impudence, and getting the better of a few silly
> scruples. There is scarce courage necessary; all we have
> to deal with are such mere poltroons.

According to the Ordinary of Newgate, it did not take Maclaine long to understand the meaning of this suggestion:

> This discourse was soon understood by the unhappy
> Maclaine, who though at first shocked with the bare
> mention of it, yet the necessity of his pride and indolence
> suggested so strong, that he yielded to the temptation, and
> from that time, which might be about eight months after
> his wife's death, entered into a particular intimacy with
> Plunket, agreed to run all risks together, and, present or
> absent at any enterprise, to share all profits, of which, till
> the fatal discovery, they kept a fair and regular account.[10]

Figure 4.01 'The Ladies Hero, or the Unfortunate James McLeane Esq.' (1750). Note the Venetian mask (used in masquerades) lying on the ground next to his left foot. © Copyright The Trustees of The British Museum

Although their early crimes met with mixed success, with Maclaine often acting the coward, the pair soon amassed a considerable fortune, which allowed them to pursue their favourite vices:

> The money went as it came, for Plunket loved his bottle
> and a girl, and spent his share that way; and Maclaine was
> doatingly fond of gay clothes, balls, masquerades, etc., at
> all which places he made a very gay and impudent
> figure.[11]

According to the Ordinary, with the proceeds of a series of robberies on the highway, Maclaine:

> Lived in splendour, but to avoid impertinent questions,
> often shifted his lodgings; though he appeared in the
> greatest splendour in all public places, and kept company
> not only with the most noted ladies of the town, but some
> women of fortune and reputation were unguarded enough
> to admit him into their company, without any other
> recommendation than his appearing at all public places
> with great impudence, and a variety of rich clothes.[12]

The pair first acquired notoriety in November 1749 following their robbery in Hyde Park of Horace Walpole, author and son of the former prime minister, Robert Walpole. Horace Walpole later recorded the incident:

> One night in the beginning of November 1749 I was
> returning from Holland House by moonlight about ten at
> night. I was attacked by two highwaymen in Hyde Park,
> and the pistol of one of them going off accidentally razed
> the skin under my eye, and left some marks of shot on my
> face and stunned me. The ball went through the top of the
> chariot, and, if I had sat an inch nearer to the left side,
> must have gone through my head.

Walpole was not seriously injured and, following the robbery, he placed an advertisement offering a reward for the return of his watch. Shortly afterwards, in the first indication we have that Maclaine's social pretensions had begun to shape his criminal behaviour, he sent Walpole a letter. It was written on gilt-edged paper and, in spite of the poor spelling and grammatical errors, was full of polite and genteel phrases. The letter, transcribed literally, began:

> Sir,
> Seeing an advertisement in the papers of today giveing an account of your being robbed by two highwaymen on Wedensday night last in Hyde Parke and during that time a pistol being fired whether intended or accidentally was doubtfull. Oblidges us to take this method of assureing you that it was the latter. And by no means designed either to hurt or frighten you for tho we are reduced by the misfortunes of the world and obliged to have recourse to this method of getting money, yet we have humanity enough not to take any bodys life where there is not a nessecety for it.[13]

Maclaine tried (unsuccessfully) to extort double the reward offered by Walpole in his advertisement, but he also told him of his intention to repay the 'trifle' he had robbed from the footman who had attended the chariot. From this one robbery alone, Maclaine and Plunket secured 20 guineas, and it was only one of dozens committed by the pair over a period of several months.

When Maclaine was finally arrested on 27 July the following year after robbing the Salisbury Flying Coach on 26 June, he was described in the papers as a 'very genteel, tall young fellow, and very gay in his dress'.[14] The arrest made Maclaine the talk of the town. Writing to his friend Horace Mann a few days later, Walpole reported: 'I have been in town for a day or two, and heard no conversation but about Maclaine, a fashionable highwayman, who is just taken'. He and Plunket (who was not arrested) had certainly been living the high life:

> Maclaine had a lodging in St James's Street over against White's, and another at Chelsea; Plunket one in Jermyn Street, and their faces are as known about St James's as

any gentleman's who lives in that quarter, and who
perhaps goes upon the road too. There was a wardrobe of
clothes, three and twenty purses, and the celebrated
blunderbuss found at his lodgings, besides a famous kept
mistress.[15]

While imprisoned in the Gatehouse, Maclaine was visited
by many elite Londoners. After a few days, almost as if to
ensure that he retained his notoriety, he indicated that he
wished to make a confession. According to the *Gentleman's
Magazine*:

> Before a large company of lords and ladies, etc., he
> owned that he, with one Plunket, committed these
> robberies, also the robbing of Mr Walpole in Hyde Park,
> and appeared so concerned that some of the ladies shed
> tears.[16]

When Maclaine indicated he was in need of money, several
persons made him 'considerable presents'.[17] But when the
justice, Thomas Lediard, read him back his confession,
Maclaine prudently refused to sign it.

Such was the public sympathy for Maclaine that some of
his victims refused to testify against him at his trial. A 'Mr
L——r' was so impressed by his polite behaviour during the
robbery of the Salisbury Coach that he told the robbers at
the time:

> Gentlemen, as persons of your employ are very liable to
> come into trouble on these occasions, if it should so
> happen, for your civil treatment, I will do what lies in my
> power to serve you.[18]

Indeed, no person whose name matches this spelling
appeared at the trial. Similarly, Lord Eglington, who was
robbed of his purse and blunderbuss (and threatened with
having his brains blown out), refused to prosecute and
Walpole claimed he was 'honourably mentioned in a grub
street ballad' for not appearing at the trial.[19]

Nonetheless, one passenger on the Salisbury Coach, Josiah Higden, was willing to prosecute and Maclaine's trial went ahead on 12 September. At the Old Bailey, Higden described the robbery:

> On the 26th of June, I was passenger in the Salisbury Flying Coach, going thither. There were four gentlemen and one gentlewoman with me. Betwixt Turnham Green and Brentford, betwixt the five and six mile stone in the parish of Chiswick, between 1 and 2 o'clock in the morning, a man came up to the side of the coach and put his pistol in, demanding our money; at the same time calling to his companion who lagged behind to come up. Then came up another person. They were both armed and masked. The second acted but little; he rather sat on horseback as a guard. I gave about twelve or fourteen shillings to the man that came up first. They declared that should not do, and ordered us out of the coach into the highway. They took six shillings out of another pocket of mine, and four penny worth of halfpence out of my breeches pocket and threatened to blow my brains out for concealing it. He on horseback I believe threatened as much as the other. After this, the person who came up

Figure 4.02 'An Exact Representation of Maclaine the Highwayman Robbing Lord Eglington on Hounslow Heath' (1750). © Copyright The Trustees of The British Museum

first, declared he would see what was in the boot of the coach, and accordingly jumped up, and by the help of the coachman, took out two cloak bags; one of which was my property. They made the coachman help them up before them, and each rode off with one.

The robbers were sufficiently disguised (allegedly wearing Venetian masks) that Higden could not positively identify either of them: something that had become apparent when Maclaine cross-examined Josiah Higden at the preliminary hearing.

Q. Did not Mr Higden declare before the justice he never saw me before?

Higden. No, my Lord, I did not.

Q. Did not Mr Higden say, the man's voice that robbed him did not agree with mine?

Higden. I said, I could not say it was the prisoner's voice.

Q. Did he never declare he would have my life, and hoped on that account to be made a great man?

Higden. No, I never declared any such thing. I said I would go through with it in duty to my country.

But the trial did not rest entirely on this identification. Maclaine sold the stolen goods to a shopkeeper, William Loader, despite the fact that their theft had been advertised. Showing a remarkable lack of caution, Maclaine even left his name and address at the shop. The shopkeeper told the court:

The prisoner came himself to me, and desired I would come and look at some things he had to dispose of. I think this was the 19th of July. He lived with one Mr Dunn in St James's Street. He showed me a light coloured cloth coat and breeches, and a waistcoat with the lace ripped off. I bought them of him with other things. Mr Higden came to my shop some time after and found the things lying on the counter and owned them. I went and

> got a warrant for the prisoner in the name of Maclaine,
> the name he left with me of his own hand writing, for a
> direction for me to come to see the clothes. He was taken.

Josiah Hidgen described how other items were then found
in Maclaine's lodgings:

> I found there a light perriwig, three pair of stockings, a
> pair of double channel pumps, a handkerchief, and two
> canisters without tea. They were found on the 27th of July
> in his trunk, and they are my property, taken out of my
> cloakbag.

The portmanteau (or suitcase) in which Higden had been
carrying the goods was found three weeks later in the
Kensington Gravel Pits.

Since all this was circumstantial evidence, the trial
eventually turned on the confession Maclaine had made
before Justice Lediard and then repudiated. Maclaine
appears to have hoped he could turn king's evidence and win
a reprieve at the expense of Plunket's life, but Maclaine
himself was far too big a catch to be let off and Lediard
would not do a deal. In his testimony at the Old Bailey,
Lediard described their encounters:

> The prisoner and the things were brought before me. He
> denied the fact at first, he said if I would be of any service
> to him he would make a confession. I told him I could not
> admit him as an evidence, but if he had a mind to make a
> voluntary confession I would hear it, but I would not at all
> press him to it. I gave him an hour's time to do it. I went
> down stairs and up again, and then he told me he had
> committed this and several other robberies in company
> with one Plunket. I bid him recollect, as nearly as he
> could, all the robberies he had committed, and come again
> the next day. He brought it to me the next day in writing, I
> did not ask him to sign it, he gave it me to read, and said
> the contents of that paper were true. I left the paper in his
> hands and never asked it of him. He confessed the taking
> the two portmanteaus, and among the rest, the things that

lay then before him. He confessed this when I went to
him at the Gatehouse, and likewise when he was
examined by me the first of August.

For his defence, Maclaine read out a prepared written
statement, redolent of his social pretensions. Although it
was the jury that would determine his fate, he
presumptuously addressed the judge:

My Lord, I am persuaded from the candour and
indulgence shown me in the course of my trial, that your
lordship will hear me with patience, and make allowance
for the confusion I may show before an awful assembly,
upon so solemn an occasion.

Your lordship will not construe it vanity in me, at this
time, to say, that I am the son of a divine of the kingdom
of Ireland, well known for his zeal and affection to the
present royal family, and happy government; who
bestowed an education upon me becoming his character,
of which I have in my hand a certificate from a noble lord,
four members of parliament, and several justices of peace
for the country where I was born, and received my
education. About the beginning of the late French war, my
lord, I came to London, with a design to enter into the
military service of my king and country; but unexpected
disappointments obliged me to change my resolution; and
having married the daughter of a reputable tradesman, to
her fortune I added what little I had of my own, and
entered into trade in the grocery way, and continued
therein till my wife died. I very quickly after her death
found a decay in trade, arising from an unavoidable trust
reposed in servants; and fearing the consequence, I
candidly consulted some friends, and by their advice, sold
off my stock, and in the first place honestly discharged my
debts, and proposed to apply the residue of my fortune in
the purchase of some military employment, agreeable to
my first design.

Turning to the crime of which he was accused, he denied all,
blaming Plunket for supplying the stolen goods without his
knowledge:

During my application to trade, my lord, I unhappily
became acquainted with one Plunket, an apothecary, who,
by his account of himself, induced me to believe he had
travelled abroad, and was possessed of clothes and other
things suitable thereto, and prevailed on me to employ
him in attending on my family, and to lend him money to
the amount of 100 pounds and upwards.

When I left off trade, I pressed Plunket for payment,
and after receiving, by degrees, several sums, he
proposed, on my earnestly insisting that I must call in all
debts owing to me, to pay me part in goods and part in
money. These very clothes with which I am now charged,
my lord, were clothes he brought to me to make sale of,
towards payment of my debt, and accordingly, my lord, I
did sell them, very unfortunately, as it now appears; little
thinking they were come by in the manner Mr Higden
hath been pleased to express, whose word and honour are
too well known to doubt the truth.

He then explained why it would be unreasonable to expect
him to produce witnesses to these dealings with Plunket and
suggested how implausible it was that he would attempt to
dispose of stolen goods in such a reckless manner:

My lord, as the contracting this debt between Plunket and
myself was a matter of a private nature, so was the
payment of it; and therefore, it is impossible for me to
have the testimony of any one single witness to these
facts, which (as it is an unavoidable misfortune) I hope,
and doubt not, my lord, that your lordship and the
gentlemen of the jury will duly weigh.

My lord, I cannot avoid observing to your lordship, is it
probable, nay, is it possible, that if I had come by those
clothes by dishonest means, I should be so imprudent as
to bring a man to my lodgings at noon day to buy them,
and give him my name and place of residence, and even
write that name and residence myself in the salesman's
book? It seems to me, and I think must to every man, a
madness that no one, with the least share of sense, could
be capable of.

Finally, he tried to explain away the confession:

> My lord, it is very true, when I was first apprehended, the
> surprise confounded me, and gave me the most
> extraordinary shock. It caused a delirium and confusion in
> my brain, which rendered me incapable of being myself,
> or knowing what I said or did. I talked of robberies as
> another man would do in talking of stories; but, my lord,
> after my friends had visited me in the Gatehouse, and had
> given me some new spirits, and when I came to be
> reexamined before Justice Lediard, and then asked, if I
> could make any discovery of the robbery, I then recovered
> from my surprise.

He then produced a clever answer to anyone demanding an
alibi for the time of the robberies.

> It might be said, my lord, that I ought to show where I
> was at this time. To which, my lord, I answer, that I never
> heard the time, nor the day of the month, that Mr Higden
> was robbed; and, my lord, it is impossible for me, at this
> juncture, to recollect where I was, and much more to
> bring any testimony of it.

He concluded by calling evidence to his good character:

> My lord, I have lived in credit, and have had dealings with
> mankind, and therefore humbly beg leave, my lord, to call
> about a score to my character, or more, if your lordship
> pleases. And then, my lord, if in your lordship's opinion
> the evidence against me should be by law only
> circumstantial, and the character given of me by my
> witnesses should be so far satisfactory, as to have equal
> weight, I shall most willingly and readily submit to the
> jury's verdict.

In fact, the *Proceedings* report that 'He called nine
gentlemen of credit, who gave him a very good character'.
Playing on the romantic image of the gentleman
highwayman, one anonymous print suggested that a tenth
character witness had given evidence. In 'James Macleane,

Figure 4.03 'James Macleane, the Gentleman Highwayman at the Bar' (1750). © Copyright The Trustees of The British Museum

the Gentleman Highwayman at the Bar', the judge is depicted asking a well-dressed lady, 'What has your Ladyship to say in favour of the prisoner at the bar?', to which she replies with an undisguised *double entendre*: 'My Lord, I have had the pleasure to know him well, he has often been about my house and I never lost anything.'

Maclaine conducted a bold and legally clever defence, but in the view of the court he had to be held to account. Without leaving the room, the jury returned a verdict of guilty. When he was called to receive his sentence, he attempted to make an apology, but overwhelmed by grief, he was unable to speak. As was inevitable with such a notorious robber, he was sentenced to hang.

London in 1750 was in the midst of a serious crime wave, in which robberies were thought to be not only more numerous than ever before, but also more violent and audacious. The following year, Henry Fielding published his famous *Enquiry into the Causes of the Late Increase of Robbers*. Despite these inauspicious circumstances, Maclaine quickly became a celebrity. Several prints and pamphlets were published which depicted him as a gentleman who only robbed reluctantly, in opposition to the qualms of his conscience, and who always acted politely. There was, in fact, no evidence of polite behaviour in Higden's testimony at the Old Bailey, but in pamphlet accounts of the robbery, Plunket was described as having put away his pistol 'for fear of frightening the lady, and without forcing her out of the coach, they took what small matter she offered without further search'. As the robbers rode off, they allegedly bid a 'polite adieu to the passengers'. During the course of the robbery they took a bag of clothes belonging to a Catholic priest. When he 'expostulated with Plunket on the ungenteel treatment of taking a man's apparel from him', Plunket replied 'that it was necessity that forced them upon those hazardous enterprises; they did not rob through wantonness but they were forced to it for their immediate subsistence'.[20]

As implausible as these claims may seem, they worked, to the extent of securing Maclaine a good press. While he awaited his execution in Newgate, he was again visited frequently. Walpole reported that:

> The first Sunday after his condemnation, 3,000 people
> went to see him. You can't conceive of this ridiculous rage
> there is of going to Newgate; and the prints that are
> published of the malefactors, and the memoirs of their
> lives and deaths set forth with as much parade as – as –

Marshall Turenne's – we have no generals worth making a
parallel![21]

Turenne was a seventeenth-century French military hero.

But not everyone was taken in. Although Walpole
appears to have been bemused by all the publicity, he viewed
highway robbery as 'no joke'.[22] The Ordinary of Newgate
commented that although Maclaine:

> Has been called the gentleman highwayman, and in his
> dress and equipage very much affected the fine
> gentleman, yet to a man acquainted with good breeding,
> that can distinguish it from impudence and affectation,
> there was little in his address or behaviour, that could
> entitle him to that character.[23]

Over time, the pretensions of Maclaine and other gentleman
highwaymen were treated with increasing scepticism in print
as elite worries about crime trumped the celebration of
highway robbery's fashionable, polite and courageous
qualities. Ten years after Maclaine's death, the alleged
superiority of the gentleman highwayman over the street
robber was directly challenged in an exchange of letters in the
Public Advertiser. One, purportedly written by Maclaine to
'Ned Slinker, footpad, pickpocket and housebreaker', boasted
that:

> My irregularities were always conducted more with the
> spirit of a gentleman. There has not been for some years
> an instance in the papers of generosity, complaisance to
> ladies, or dexterity of contrivance, that I cannot justly
> claim the honour of. I was the person who obliged a
> couple of sneaking footpads to refund the week's wages
> they had taken from a poor labourer.

In reply, Slinker claimed:

> There is no great difference between us, either in point of
> honour, courage or genius. I confess I do not see the
> difference whether a man robs on horseback, or on foot;

with a pistol, or a dash of his pen. If you avoid robbing the poor, I cannot but fancy, if your motives were examined, 'tis not so much from a principle of generosity, as that you have not the spirit to venture your neck for sixpence. And as to dexterity, everyone must allow, that 'tis much easier to escape on horseback than on foot.

As to Maclaine's claim to gentility, Slinker wrote that although the appropriate clothing was easily acquired, it would not prevent a highwayman from being hanged: 'I doubt not with the assistance of a laced coat, bag wig, and white silk stockings, to make as captivating a figure, and swing as handsomely as the best gentleman of you all'.[24]

Fifteen years later, when Maclaine's crimes came to be written up in the first edition of the *Malefactor's Register*, they were presented as a case study in the folly of attempting to live beyond one's means. The account concluded:

The story speaks for itself. An immoderate attachment to what is falsely called pleasure, a turn for gaiety and dissipation, an idle and unwarrantable fondness of the graces of his own person, seem to have laid the foundation for his own ruin. From his unhappy fate, then, the doctrines of humility, and content with our station, will be better learnt than by a thousand sermons.[25]

Deprived of their glamour, highway robbers nonetheless continued to operate on the roads surrounding London until the early nineteenth century. They only disappeared as a result of the development of turnpikes and changes in policing and banking practices. The last mounted robbery in England took place in 1831, in Somerset.[26]

The Blackguard Children

Big cities have always attracted the homeless and the vagrant, some of whom drift into crime in order to survive. In the poverty-soaked neighbourhoods east of the Tower of London – in

Rosemary Lane, Glass House Yard and Salt Petre Bank –
orphans and runaways occasionally came together in bands of
mutual support. For the children involved, these gangs must have
provided a much needed surrogate family. But for more secure
Londoners, they were simply gangs of thieves and pickpockets led
into sin by the idleness and the corruption of their elders. From
the end of the seventeenth century they were known as the
'blackguard' and they quickly invaded the new world of the
novel. Daniel Defoe gave a blackguard boy the role of eponymous
hero in his History and Remarkable Life of the Truly
Honourable Col. Jack, *first published in 1722; and in the*
nineteenth century the criminal children of London's streets
found lasting literary fame in Charles Dickens's Oliver Twist.
The reality of the lives of abandoned and orphaned children was
in every way as tragic and colourful as those of their fictional
counterparts.

On 4 November 1730 two boys of perhaps 11 or 12 years,
Robert Shelton and Thomas Coleman, were out on Battersea
Common, near Clapham, south of the river. They were far
from their normal haunts around 'Rag Fair' and Glass House
Yard, but were looking for something to steal and this was an
occupation better practised away from home. Clean washing
was laid out on bushes on the common to dry in the sun and
Shelton and Coleman decided to take two dowlas shirts,
knowing that they could resell them for a good price. Dowlas
was a coarse linen cloth used to make the shirts and shifts
worn by most working Londoners. As is true of most
thieving, Shelton and Coleman's victims were people only
marginally better off than themselves. They were chased and
Shelton dropped the shirts and escaped. Thomas Coleman,
however, was not so lucky. He was taken up and frog-
marched to the home of the local magistrate, George
Wellham, who with the assistance of Thomas Coram, forced
a confession from the boy.

With every possibility that he would be tried for his life, Coleman turned king's evidence in the hope he would be spared prosecution. He gave a detailed statement that indicted a whole community of young thieves. Coleman explained:

> His father and mother being dead, he went to live with his aunt, Elizabeth Coleman, on Salt Petre Bank near Rag Fair where he became acquainted with Katherine Collins who lives there and harbours thieves and buys stolen goods.

Coleman moved from his aunt's house to Collins's in the autumn of 1729, and for the next year lived a life of constant danger. Every day he would 'go a thieving in company with Andrew Knowland, Daniel Smith, George Scott, Edward Perkins, Joseph Paternoster, Joseph Darvell, Nice Noddy, Little Tom, Dick Wools, Halfe Thumb, Abey Gibson, Robert Shelton and George the Sailor'. He explained that all these boys lodged with Katherine Collins and that 'she orders them to go out at night and steal any thing they could meet with'. Under pressure from the magistrates, Coleman detailed the items they had stolen:

> They brought home to her cheese and sold it for two pence a pound, likewise butter, bread, shoes and several other things which Katherine Collins bought of them. And when they came home without anything, she shut them out of doors and they went to the glass house near there and lay together.

Daniel Defoe described sleeping in the glass houses in *Colonel Jack*:

> Those who know the position of the glass houses, and the arches where they neal the bottles after they are made [allowing them to cool slowly], know that those places where the ashes are cast, and where the poor boys lie, are cavities in the brick-work, perfectly close, except at the entrance, and consequently warm as the dressing room of a bagnio [bathhouse].[27]

Once caught and examined, Thomas Coleman and all his friends were in real danger. The summer before, Katherine Collins's own 15-year-old son, John, along with 'Bristow Will' and 'Cow Cornish Cork Eye', had all been sentenced to transportation. John Collins, along with Robert Wheeler (whose colourful nickname was Bristow Will), had stolen two and a half yards of printed linen from a shop in Stepney. When challenged by a neighbour, Mary Richardson, 'they gave her saucy language, and she saw Wheeler take the cloth, and Collins standing a little distance from him'. Having run away, they were later taken up and one of them confessed that the cloth 'had been sold in Rag Fair'. And just a month later Charles Cornet, alias Cornish, had been tried for attempting to steal the cash drawer containing 14s from a shop he had mistakenly thought was empty. His nickname of 'cork eye' suggests that he was blind in one eye, which perhaps explains his incompetence as a thief. Like his friends before him, he was sentenced to transportation.[28]

To ensure that he did not suffer the same fate, Coleman confessed crime after crime:

> Last Monday night, I with Andrew Knowland and George Scott stole a pair of man's shoes and a pair of women's shoes out of a shoemaker's shop window in Leadenhall Street, which we sold to Mrs Collins for two shillings, and with Yarmouth the week before last, we stole out of a yard between White Chapel Turnpike and Hackney, two blew aprons and a dowlas shirt, and sold the same to Mrs Collins for eighteen pence. About a month ago Robert Shelton and I stole out of a yard in South Lambeth a linen printed gown and a striped blue and white waistcoat with a hole in the breast of it. We sold the same to Mrs Collins for eighteen pence.

And so he went on, claiming at one point to have averaged 'ten or a dozen' pocket handkerchiefs per day, stolen from the crowds at Bartholomew Fair.

The confession was rewritten and read back to Coleman, who signed it in a clear, schooled hand, before it was in turn signed by the magistrate. Like Charles Dickens's nineteenth-century fence and thief, Fagin and the Artful Dodger, Katherine Collins ran an organised criminal gang that was desperately vulnerable to any boy who turned king's evidence. With Thomas Coleman's arrest and confession, the fate of the 14 boys he named was largely sealed – even though the boys continued to steal, and in the chaotic world of eighteenth-century policing, it was months and even years before most of them finally stood at the bar at the Old Bailey.

The first to stand trial was Thomas Coleman himself. He could not be admitted as king's evidence because the crimes he had provided information about were not serious enough. On 15 January 1731 he was 'indicted for feloniously stealing two pair of shoes, the goods of Thomas Johnson, the 2nd of November last, but the evidence not being sufficient, he was acquitted'. His willingness to provide evidence against his fellows is the more likely explanation for this outcome. At the next sessions, in February 1731, Andrew Knowland or Noland, John Allright and Richard Collier were tried for 'stealing a piece of flannel'. Collier confessed to the offence in a last-ditch attempt to preserve his own liberty, but succeeded only in ensuring that all three boys were sentenced to transportation. John King testified:

> That he saw the prisoners standing at Seth Aylwing's door, and go into the shop and bring out the flannel, and they ran away together.[29]

Malachi Southy and George Beal were two of Collins's last boy clients. They stole a 'waterman's silver badge' – the symbol of the Watermen's Company and the licence that allowed boatmen to ply the river. In combination with 12 silver buttons, it was worth £7 and they sold it on to Katherine

Collins for 32s, a fraction of its value. This was within a week of Coleman's confession and at Southy and Beal's trial in February 1731, they reported that Collins 'is since run away'.[30]

By April 1732 George Scott was living in St Leonard's Foster Lane, and had garnered almost 18 months of freedom since he was named by Thomas Coleman. But in the early spring he too was indicted, along with Henry Whitesides, for the theft of 'a hat, value 10 shillings and a hatband, value 1 shilling, the goods of Paul Fellows'. Despite his protestations that he had only gone into the shop 'to ask what was a clock', he and Whitesides were both sentenced to transportation.[31]

Daniel Smith was luckier. In June 1731 he was named as an accomplice assisting Edward Perkins and a boy named Redding in the theft of a gold-headed cane worth four guineas. Samuel Sedgwick had set it casually on the counter of his shop on his return home, and the boys were caught a few hours later trying to sell it on 'at the sign of the George, in Rosemary Lane, for half a crown'. In this instance, the witnesses – perhaps by prior arrangement – did not appear for the trial: 'the proper evidences to fix the fact upon Edward Perkins not appearing in court, the jury acquitted him' and with that verdict effectively freed Smith of suspicion. Three years later, still at large, Smith was accused of involvement in the theft of '55 yards of printed linen, value ten pounds', but again escaped conviction.[32]

Perkins himself was not so lucky. Having been acquitted of stealing the cane, he was back at the bar within six weeks. In July 1731 he was accused of stealing two gold rings, worth some 23s, from the unconscious body of Dismore Brown. Brown told the court that going home, he:

> Fell down in the Minories [just west of Rag Fair and Rosemary Lane], and being stunned by the fall, when he was recovered, he felt somebody pulling of his hand, but could not say who it was. But soon after he found his

> rings were gone, and thereupon the next morning sent
> notice of their being lost to Mr Hardy, goldsmith, to stop
> them if offered to be sold, and that in an hour or two they
> were brought to him.

Perkins pleaded:

> That he had the rings to sell for two other boys that said
> they had found them in the Minories.

This plea 'appearing probable, by some circumstances deposed in court, the jury acquitted him' once again.[33]

But the list of crimes, trials and eventual punishments continued. Joseph Paterson, alias Peterson or Paternoster, and Joseph Darvan, who was listed as Durvell in Coleman's deposition, were tried for housebreaking in December 1731. Mary Callicant, alias Nowland, Noland or Knowland, was arrested for selling stolen goods, and while being held in the Surrey gaol, gave up Paternoster and Darvan to the authorities in an attempt to preserve her own life:

> Go, says she, to the Three Cranes in Castle Lane,
> Westminster, and enquire where Mrs Ram lives.
> Paternoster and Darvan lodge up one pair of stairs in her
> house. If you don't find them there, go to the Horse Shoe
> behind Green's Free School, and if you miss of them there
> too, desire the people of the house to tell you where Mr
> Morris the shoemaker lives, for they often meet at his
> house. Paternoster is a young man with a bald head, he
> wears a fair wig, an outside light drab coat, with a great
> cape. His under clothes are snuff colour, and sometimes
> blue grey turned up with black, and he has a silver watch
> with a crimson string. Darvan is a young lad near 19
> years of age, pretty well set. He wears a light wig, a new
> hat with a silver loop and button, a blue grey coat, and a
> worked waistcoat; and sometimes an olive coloured suit.
> Each of them wears a small diamond ring.

Paternoster and Darvan were arrested and their drawers and boxes ransacked. Among their goods, all the paraphernalia of thievery was discovered. The constables found a long wire with a hook on the end, designed to 'draw goods out at a window, when they lie too far within a room', and seven waistcoats marked with a 'GR' at the top, with the monograms partially picked out.[34] After three full trials for different crimes, including burglary, all conducted at the December 1731 sessions, after several failed attempts to pin the crimes on their landlady and to establish a credible alibi, Paternoster and Darvan were finally convicted and sentenced to transportation.[35]

In many respects Paternoster and Darvan represented the spectre of crime most feared by Londoners. Although many of the crimes committed by Coleman and his friends were relatively petty, Paternoster and Darvan had clearly progressed to more organised and financially rewarding activities. In the process they neatly confirmed contemporary beliefs that explained crime in terms of moral decay, beginning with the small depredations of children and growing into the fully fledged criminality of the professional thief. The flash clothing and specialised burglary equipment set them apart from most of the other boys named by Coleman.

Something peculiar also seems to have set apart Thomas Coleman's special partner in crime, nicknamed Yarmouth, an alias for John Crotch. Despite being named by Coleman, Yarmouth stayed away from the Old Bailey until April 1732, when, like almost all his companions from Salt Petre Bank, he was arrested for theft. His very presence on the street had aroused suspicion. On 9 April he and a friend were standing outside Pewterer's Hall Gate, humming a tune. John Maxey 'looked at them by the light of a lamp, and did not like them'. Maxey later testified that they followed him into Fenchurch Street, where 'one of them took hold of me, and clapped his hand to my mouth, and then snatched off my hat and wig and went off'. Yarmouth was found guilty and sentenced to be transported.[36]

As for Thomas Coleman himself, after having been acquitted of the theft of 'two pair of shoes' in January 1731, he seems to have avoided the law for a number of years. Someone of the same name was convicted and transported for the theft of two wrought iron boxes eight years later, but Coleman was a relatively common name and it is impossible to be sure that it was the same person.[37]

The boys who sheltered with Katherine Collins and accepted her harsh rules had few choices. Their options were limited and the alternatives unattractive. In Daniel Defoe's estimation:

> 'Tis scarce credible what a black throng they are. Many of them indeed perish young, and die miserable, before they may be said to look into life. Some are starved with hunger, some with cold, many are found frozen in the streets and fields, some drowned before they are old enough to be hanged.[38]

With Thomas Coleman's confession, however, some measure of change was perhaps set afoot. Sitting listening as Thomas Coleman gave up one friend after another was Captain Thomas Coram. In the decade before 1731, Coram had begun to militate for the foundation of a 'Foundling Hospital', motivated by the scenes of suffering he saw by the roadsides of London, 'young children exposed, sometimes alive, sometimes dead, and sometimes dying'.[39] The orphaned criminality of Thomas Coleman and his compatriots must have simply reinforced Coram's belief that something needed to be done.

Two Handkerchiefs upon the Counter

Eighteenth-century London witnessed a revolution in the way that Britons bought and sold the goods of everyday life. The bowed shop window, with its clear glass and elegant wares displayed on all sides, attracted the eyes of both rich and poor. One

French traveller marvelled at the shops at every turn, 'so richly
set out that they looked like a palace'.[40] *For those who could not*
afford the new fashions and imported trinkets, however, these
same displays presented a new opportunity for theft. With the
new shops came a new crime: shoplifting.

The pattern for eighteenth-century shoplifting was set early.
By the end of the previous century shopkeepers were being
warned about what to look out for:

> One who goes from shop to shop, pretending to buy. They
> will cheapen [haggle over] several sorts of goods as you
> sell till they have opportunity to convey away some of
> them into their coats, which are turned up on purpose for
> their design. They are most often women and commonly
> they go two together, and when the shop keeper turns his
> back, one of them conveys what she can get, and so goes
> away, so the other pretends there's nothing that pleases
> her.[41]

Two women who knew how to work this particular scam
were Mary Hudson and Hannah Hobbs. On 11 August
1790 the two of them, with Hudson's small child in tow,
went into a mercer's shop belonging to Samuel and
Alexander Sheen in Drury Lane. It was between 2 and 3
o'clock in the afternoon, and the Sheen brothers and the rest
of the family were at dinner, leaving only John Smith to look
after the customers.

Of all the new and fashionable items streaming into
London, cloth was the most important. Calicos and
calamancoes, brocades and silks, cotton, lace and linen, sold
in lengths and pieces, were the everyday commodities which
women, in particular, lusted after, and occasionally stole.
They could be sold on to a pawnbroker or used clothes
dealer, or made up into a new item of clothing. They could
also be secreted relatively easily within the folds and
flounces of a woman's dress.

John Charles Smith later described what happened that August afternoon:

> I am a shopman to Samuel and Alexander Sheen, in Drury Lane. On the 11th of August last, the two women came in together to the shop, and enquired the price of some printed cotton that hung over the counter, and after Hobbs had made many objections to the colours being dead, she said, she could not think of leaving the shop without buying something, and desired me to show her some cloth, and she bought a yard. She then desired me to show her some pieces of printed cotton. She objected to the pattern.

As was by now traditional for teams of female shoplifters, Hobbs was distracting Smith's attention, 'cheapening' the goods, and asking for one thing after another, while Hudson prepared to strike. Despite the innovative displays found in shop windows, most of the merchandise remained in drawers and cabinets, on high shelves and in back rooms, waiting to be fetched by the shopkeeper. If shoplifting today demands you avoid the attentions of the staff, in the eighteenth century the art was all in how to engage the shopkeeper's attention without arousing his suspicion. Rushing from drawer to cabinet to backroom, Smith had a hard time keeping an eye on both women:

> During this conversation between me and Hobbs, Hudson was at the opposite counter, with her child placed near a bundle of muslin on the counter.

Using her child as an excuse, Hudson then went into action. Smith later recounted that she:

> Requested me to show her some printed cotton for a child's frock. I showed her a few pieces; she fixed on one at twenty pence a yard, and desired me to cut a yard and a half off of it, and took out half a crown.

In many cases, teams of shoplifters would buy a small item to justify their visit to the shop, or even visit a shop three or four times, spending a few pence on each occasion, in order to create the impression that they were trustworthy, encouraging the shopkeeper to lower his guard and bring out more and better quality goods. At this stage in her life, Hudson was probably too poor to pursue this kind of strategy, and instead she did the next best thing. She offered Smith a bad shilling, and feigned shock when he refused to accept it, claiming:

> She knew where she had taken it, and would go and
> change it, and call for the cloth in the evening.

The bad shilling, almost certainly the only money Hudson possessed, was a master stroke. It forced Smith to examine it closely – taking his eyes off Hobbs and Hudson in the process – and created a perfect excuse for not actually purchasing anything. By this stage, the counter of the shop was groaning under the weight of the different types of cloth that Hobbs and Hudson had demanded to be shown and while Smith struggled to put away the goods, the two women quietly 'quitted the shop both together'.

It was only a few minutes later that Smith noticed that an item was missing. Five muslin handkerchiefs, 'put into a paper by the apprentice', had been carefully laid aside at one end of the counter earlier in the day. After Hobbs' and Hudson's departure, the package was gone. In response, Smith first informed the shop's owners, Samuel and Alexander Sheen, and then sent out notification to all the local pawnbrokers to be on their guard.

Mary Hudson and Hannah Hobbs must have been desperate for money. To safely dispose of the muslin handkerchiefs, all they needed to do was walk eastward to Rag Fair, where old clothes merchants paid a low price, but seldom asked any questions. Instead, they went west to a local pawnshop run by Richard Dozzell and James Collins at No. 5 Little Pultney Street. News of the theft had already reached Dozzell and Collins before the two women even walked through their door. Dozzell later recounted in court:

> I heard something was lost from Mr Sheen's. In about half an hour after, these two women came into the shop and Mary Hudson offered two muslin handkerchiefs to pledge. Upon questioning them, whose they were, she said, one was her own, and the other, the other woman's. I asked them, what they gave for them, she said, four shillings and sixpence for the two. I immediately got over the counter and bolted the shop door, and informed my master, and went to Mr Sheen's, and then to Bow Street, for the officer.

John Smith was the first to arrive:

> I went down to Mr Collins's shop, and found two handkerchiefs on the counter, one of which had my mark on, y | y, with a red pencil; I marked them myself. The prisoners were in the shop; I asked Hudson, if she had any more; she said she had one more, which she produced. Turning round from Hudson, I observed something white hanging from the pocket of Hobbs, which she observing, let fall from her pocket. I took up the handkerchiefs from the ground.

By this time John Shallard, an officer from Bow Street, had also arrived:

> On the 18th of August, I was sent for to Mr Collins's to take charge of the prisoners. I took this piece of cloth from the prisoner Hudson, and down her bosom I found this remnant. It appears to be a remnant of the handkerchiefs.

Hobbs and Hudson were caught and there was little they could do to avoid arrest and eventual trial. From prison, Mary Hudson tried to negotiate with the Sheen brothers. She wrote to them, offering to give evidence against Hannah Hobbs if they would drop the charge against her. It did not work but the strategy broke apart any friendship that may have existed between the two women. When the case came to court Hobbs asserted that Hudson alone was responsible, and that she was an innocent dupe, who had accepted Hudson's explanation that the handkerchiefs were a gift from John Smith, who Hobbs suggested was Mary Hudson's lover:

> That gentleman was very intimate with her, and often gave her things for the child, and he gave her these four handkerchiefs; and she told the gentleman, that he was her sweetheart some time back; and I really believe there was a great deal of intimacy between them.

Perhaps surprisingly, given the assiduity with which Smith pursued the two women, there was at least some truth in this claim. He grudgingly admitted:

> Some time ago, Mary Hudson had a remnant of muslin from me. The person whom I served my time with, about four years ago, was very intimate with her father-in-law. She came to town very frequently, and came to the shop to see Mr Coward, the person I served my time with. About three months ago she came to this shop. I had not seen her for three years and a half. She begged of me to show her some muslin, about three shillings a yard and I showed her some. She appeared to be in a very deplorable situation. She desired me to cut off two nails of this muslin; I believe it came to two-pence or three-pence. I told her, I was sorry to see her in such a situation, and I would make her a present of it.

Despite this previous encounter and the doubt it threw on Smith's account, both Mary Hudson and Hannah Hobbs were found guilty and sentenced to 12 months' imprisonment.[42]

The Macaroni Parson

The majority of crimes reported in the Proceedings *involved the theft of relatively low value goods perpetrated by the city's poorest inhabitants. But the rich committed crimes against property as well, the most serious of which was forgery. This could involve huge sums of money and could even threaten the stability of the entire financial system, which is why the crime was punishable by death. Paper credit fuelled the booming English economy in the second half of the eighteenth century. A simple promissory note, signed (apparently) with a flourish by a respectable man, could act as a form of legal tender, creating unsecured credit. As long as there was no occasion to redeem the bond prematurely, there appeared to be nothing wrong, but this practice was vulnerable to speculation and fraud. Sometimes the line between forgery and normal business practices was hard to draw.*

Ambitious, flamboyant and ever controversial, Dr William Dodd was a talented social climber, desperate to move beyond the limits of his Lincolnshire childhood and conquer the glittering world of London's elite. The son of a vicar (and a clergyman himself), he loved clothes and display and the company of the rich and famous. His extravagant lifestyle and fashionable dress led him to be called 'the macaroni parson'. According to one contemporary biographer, 'at no period of his life was he influenced by the rules of economy'.[43] Although he had many friends and supporters, his polemical writings and social pretensions also made him enemies. Like many social climbers then and now, he supported many charities, playing a key role in the establishment of the Society for the Relief and Discharge of Prisoners Imprisoned for Small Debts, the Royal Humane Society, and the Magdalen Hospital for penitent prostitutes. Ironically, given that his own life was to end on the scaffold, he also supported a campaign against the death penalty.

In the mid-1770s, Dodd's financial problems brought on by his extravagant lifestyle finally began to catch up with him. He was obliged 'to have recourse to almost any means to silence the importunities of creditors and to extricate himself from those difficulties which pressed upon him'.[44] In February 1777 Dodd devised a ruse which took advantage of his intimate knowledge of the affairs of Lord Chesterfield, his patron and a man whom he had tutored as a youth. He forged a bond between Lord Chesterfield and a Mr Fletcher, in which Fletcher purportedly promised to pay the enormous sum of £4,200 in return for Chesterfield's promise to pay him an annuity of £700 a year. Dodd forged Chesterfield's signature, both on the bond and on a receipt for the money. Using a broker, Lewis Robertson, Dodd then had the bond presented to Mr Fletcher through his agent, Mr Peach. Believing the bond to be genuine, Peach advanced this huge sum in the form of promissory notes, which were then redeemed at London banks. The scheme was not entirely foolish and he might have got away with it had he been able, as planned, to pay back the money before the forgery was detected or if, after it was detected, his prosecutors had not been so keen to see him punished.

The forgery, however, was soon discovered. As James Mansfield, prosecution counsel, later explained at the Old Bailey:

> After the money had been obtained, and the bond
> deposited with Mr John Manly, who acted as attorney for
> Mr Fletcher, he observed upon the bond a very
> remarkable blot. There was no particular effect, I think, in
> this blot, but it was in the letter e in the word seven. Mr
> Manly seeing this, it struck him as something singular; he
> spoke to Mr Fletcher about it, and told him that this bond
> had a very odd blot in it. There were some strokes both
> above and below the line of the bond, which had a very
> singular appearance; though they could not tell for what
> purpose any thing had been done with a pen, yet there
> appeared scratches with a pen as if something had been
> done. Mr Manly talking to Mr Fletcher about it, Mr
> Fletcher wished that another bond might be prepared,
> fairly and without any blot, and might be carried to Lord

Chesterfield to execute. This produced a meeting between
Mr Manly and my Lord Chesterfield: upon the 7th of
February, Lord Chesterfield seeing this bond said it was a
forgery, and not his bond.

Manly then went to see the Lord Mayor, reported the
alleged forgery and obtained warrants against Lewis
Robertson, the broker, and William Dodd. Robertson was
quickly arrested. Manly and two of the Lord Mayor's
officers took a coach to Dr Dodd's house in Argyll Street,
Westminster. Manly described the interview with Dodd:

> We were admitted into the house, and Dr Dodd soon after
> came down stairs to us. When we were in the parlour
> together, Mr Innis, myself, Dr Dodd, and the officers, and
> Robertson, I opened the occasion of our attending him. I
> told him I was very sorry to attend him upon such an
> unhappy occasion, it was upon a charge of forgery against
> him, and Robertson was then in custody for forging Lord
> Chesterfield's bond. The Doctor seemed very much
> struck, and was silent some time; I told him the broker
> laid the whole charge to him; and asked the Doctor what
> could induce him to do such an act. The Doctor said,
> urgent necessity, he was pressed to pay some tradesmen's
> bills; that he meant no injury to Lord Chesterfield, or any
> one, as he meant to pay the money back in three months.

Manly continued:

> I asked the Doctor, if he had the money to return as that
> would be the only means of saving him. He answered he
> had. I then desired him immediately to give it to me; he
> desired to go up stairs to fetch it, but my Lord Mayor's
> officer refused to let him go; upon which I desired leave
> of the officer to entrust him with me up stairs.
> Accordingly we went up stairs. Dr Dodd immediately
> returned me six notes of 500 pounds each of Sir Charles
> Raymond and Co.; these notes made 3000 pounds.

A further £600 was obtained, making a total of £3,600,
and then the parties went to the York coffeehouse in St

James's Street, where they were joined by Mr Fletcher and
Mr Corry, Chesterfield's solicitor:

> We ordered a room up stairs, and when we were all up
> stairs together in presence of all the gentlemen, I asked Dr
> Dodd if he could give any security for the remainder of
> the money. He immediately said he would give any
> security in his power, he was ready to make any
> restitution he could. I asked him if he would give a
> judgment upon his goods, he said he would, or any thing
> else; he was, in fact, desirous of doing it. He then
> executed a warrant of attorney to confess judgment as a
> security for the remaining 600 pounds and I believe that
> was attested by Mr Corry and myself. After he had given
> this judgment he said, I think I can draw for 200 pounds
> more upon my banker.

Dodd was now only £400 short of the amount required and
it was agreed that this amount could be recovered by the sale
of Dodd's goods. The following day all the parties involved,
including Lord Chesterfield, appeared before the Lord
Mayor.

At this point, with restitution having been made to the
injured parties, many of those involved did not wish to
pursue a formal prosecution. As a contemporary account of
the case sympathetic to Dodd reported:

> All the principals seemed so well satisfied with his
> behaviour, that no one of them was willing to prosecute
> him; he therefore earnestly begged to be dismissed.

Dodd said to the Lord Mayor:

> I cannot tell what to say in such a situation. I had no
> intention to defraud Lord Chesterfield. I hope his lordship
> will consider my case; I was pressed extremely for three
> or four hundred pounds to pay some tradesmen's bills. I
> meant it as a temporary resource. I should have repaid the
> money in half a year. I have made satisfaction, and I hope
> that will be considered. My Lord Chesterfield must have

some tenderness towards me; he knows I love him; he
knows I regard his honour as dearly as my own. I hope he
will, according to the mercy that is in his heart, show
clemency to me. There is nobody wishes to prosecute;
pray, my Lord Mayor, consider that, and dismiss me. Mr
Robertson is certainly innocent.

The Lord Mayor, apparently supported by Lord
Chesterfield, rejected this plea, and Dodd and Robertson
were committed to prison, with the others bound over to
prosecute. In a city whose financial system was based on the
security of paper credit, and where forgeries like the one
committed in this case were all too easy to carry out, the
crime had to be prosecuted and be seen to be prosecuted.
The news quickly spread, to the delight of Dodd's enemies
and the consternation of his friends.

Dodd stood trial at the Old Bailey on 19 February 1777,
only two weeks after the forgery was committed. Before the
trial began, a lengthy argument took place between Dodd's
three counsel, the judges, and prosecution counsel James
Mansfield, over the legality of the indictment. It turned out
that although he was implicated in the crime, Lewis
Robertson, Dodd's broker, had been allowed to testify to the
grand jury in support of the indictment and his evidence had
therefore formed part of the basis for the charge against
Dodd. This was highly irregular, for two reasons. First, in
the normal course of events only witnesses for the
prosecution were allowed to testify to the grand jury. As an
accomplice in the case, Robertson was clearly a potential
defendant and therefore had an interest in allocating all the
responsibility for the crime onto Dodd. Second, Robertson
had only appeared because an order to the keeper of
Newgate Prison to bring him to the courthouse had been
surreptitiously and improperly obtained. (The fact that
these irregularities took place suggests just how determined
the authorities were to prosecute Dodd.) While admitting

the improper order, the prosecution insisted that despite being an accomplice, Robertson could nevertheless legitimately testify before the grand jury. After listening to extensive arguments on both sides, the court ruled that the issue should be referred to the 12 senior judges of England for resolution and, in the meantime, the jury should hear the case as charged.

Mansfield introduced the case for the prosecution with a lengthy opening statement, which was followed by testimony from all the principal witnesses. Since Dodd had already confessed the forgery, this contained few surprises, but two problematic points did arise. The first concerned the circumstances under which Dodd had been promised that he would not be prosecuted if he made restitution of the funds. Manly was cross-examined by defence counsel on this point.

Question.	When the Doctor was first charged with the crime, before any offer or act towards restitution was done upon the part of Dr Dodd, it was I think you that said, that was the way to save him?
Answer.	Returning the money would be the means I told him I thought of saving him.
Q.	I need not ask your import of these words, saving him from the consequences of any prosecution?
A.	Yes; I so made use of these words.
Counsel for the Crown.	You said this subsequent to Dr Dodd's confession?
A.	Yes.

This exchange established that the confession had not been made in return for a promise not to prosecute (a promise which, in any case, Manly had no authority to make).

Second was the question of Robertson's complicity. Robertson effectively asserted his innocence of the forgery, but only at the price of admitting that he had signed the bond as a witness to Lord Chesterfield's signature when in fact the signature (which Dodd had forged) was already present on the bond when it was first presented to him. He was questioned about this first by prosecution counsel:

Q.   I perceive that your name is to that bond?

A.   Yes.

Q.   At whose desire did you put your name to it?

A.   I asked Dr Dodd if the bond had been regularly executed, when he presented it to me. I desired him to put his name as a witness to it.

Q.   When the bond was produced to you on Tuesday, was the name of Chesterfield subscribed to it?

A.   It was, and also to the receipt for the money.

Here the judge intervened to highlight this dishonest practice, which was clearly commonplace:

Court.   Is it your practice, in transacting the sale or loan of annuities, to subscribe your name as a witness to the execution of an instrument which you have not seen executed?

A.   No; it is not always the case, but I have done it.

Q.   Then you deceive the persons who place confidence in you; did you ever do it in any other instance?

A.   Yes; I have.

Finally, the court turned to Dodd, and asked him to state his case for the defence. An experienced and effective preacher, he delivered a polished speech:

My lords and gentlemen of the jury, upon the evidence which has been this day produced against me, I find it very difficult for me to address your lordships. There is no man in the world who has a deeper sense of the heinous nature of the crime for which I stand indicted than myself. I view it, my lords, in all its extent of malignancy towards a commercial state like ours; but, my lords, I humbly apprehend, though no lawyer, that the moral turpitude and malignity of the crime always, both in the eye of law, of reason, and of religion, consists in the intention. I am informed, my lords, that the act of parliament on this head runs perpetually in this style, with an intention to defraud. Such an intention, my lords, and gentlemen of the jury, I believe has not been attempted to be proved upon me, and the consequences that have happened, which have appeared before you, sufficiently prove that a perfect and ample restitution has been made. I leave it, my lords, to you, and the gentlemen of the jury, to consider, that if an unhappy man ever deviates from the law of right, yet, if in the single first moment of recollection, he does all he can to make a full and perfect amends, what, my lords, and gentlemen of the jury, can God and man desire further?

My lords, I solemnly protest that death of all blessings would be the most pleasant to me after this pain. I have yet, my lords, ties which call upon me; ties which render me desirous even to continue this miserable existence. I have a wife, my lords, who for 27 years has lived an unparalleled example of conjugal attachment and fidelity, and whose behaviour during this crying scene would draw tears of approbation; I am sure, even from the most inhuman. My lords, I have creditors, honest men, who will lose much by my death. I hope for the sake of justice towards them some mercy will be shown to me. If upon the whole these considerations at all avail with you, my lords, and you gentlemen of the jury, if upon the most partial survey of matters not the slightest intention of injury can appear to any one, and I solemnly declare, it was in my power to replace it in three months; and if no injury was done to any man upon the earth, I then hope, I trust, I fully confide myself in the tenderness, humanity, and protection of my country.

He called no witnesses in his defence, so the judge proceeded to the summing up. At the conclusion of his long speech, the judge's views on the case became clear:

> The whole is before you, with these observations. The
> facts seem to be clear, if you give credit to the witnesses,
> and if there is no foundation to discredit them; the fact
> has been supported by the evidence; and you have also the
> confession of the prisoner in corroboration of it. You are
> the judges of it.

These comments later occasioned some negative comment by Dodd's supporters, who felt the judge was directing the jury towards a guilty verdict:

> Judges should be more delicate in what they throw out on
> these occasions, since there are so few instances of a jury
> once in possession of a judge's opinion, returning a
> contrary verdict.[45]

The jury withdrew for between 10 and 30 minutes (accounts differ) and produced the expected verdict of guilty. However 'they at the same time presented a petition to the court, humbly recommending the prisoner to his majesty's mercy'.

Before the punishment could be determined, however, the question of the validity of the indictment had to be decided by the senior judges. Several weeks later they ruled unanimously that despite the illegitimate means by which Robertson's testimony to the grand jury had been obtained, he was a legal and competent witness and therefore the indictment, and the conviction, should stand.

Called to receive his sentence on the last day of the May sessions of the Old Bailey and given the chance 'to say why this court should not give you judgement to die according to law', Dodd delivered an even more eloquent speech, this time drafted by the noted lexicographer, Samuel Johnson. Although the two did not know each other, Dodd appealed to Johnson for help, seeking to take advantage of the Doctor's reputation for probity as well as his literary skills. Johnson, who found Dodd's activities distasteful (he once commented, 'his moral character is very bad'), agreed to support him primarily because of his principled opposition

to capital punishment.[46] The combination of Dodd's skills as
a preacher and Johnson's writing resulted in a fine speech.
With folded hands and tearful eyes, he began:

> My Lord, I now stand before you a dreadful example of
> human infirmity. I entered upon public life with the
> expectations common to young men whose education has
> been liberal, and whose abilities have been flattered; and
> when I became a clergyman, I considered myself as not
> impairing the dignity of the order. I was not an idle, or, I
> hope, a useless minister; I taught the truths of Christianity
> with the zeal of conviction and the authority of innocence.
> My labours were approved; my pulpit became popular;
> and, I have reason to believe, that of those who heard me,
> some have been preserved from sin, and some have been
> reclaimed. Condescend, my Lord, to think, if these
> considerations aggravate my crime, how much they must
> embitter my punishment!
>
> Being distinguished and elevated by the confidence of
> mankind, I had too much confidence in myself, and
> thinking my integrity – what others thought of it –
> established in sincerity, and fortified by religion, I did not
> consider the danger of vanity, nor suspect the
> deceitfulness of my own heart. The day of conflict came,
> in which temptation surprised and overwhelmed me! I
> committed the crime, which I entreat your Lordship to
> believe, that my conscience hourly represents to me in its
> full bulk of mischief and malignity. Many have been
> overpowered by temptation, who are now among the
> penitent in heaven!
>
> To an act now waiting the decision of vindictive justice,
> I will not presume to oppose the counterbalance of almost
> thirty years (a great part of the life of man) passed in
> exciting and exercising charity; in relieving such
> distresses as I now feel; in administering those
> consolations which I now want. I will not otherwise
> extenuate my offence, than by declaring that I did not
> intend finally to defraud. Nor will it become me to
> apportion my own punishment, by alledging, that my
> sufferings have been not much less than my guilt. I have
> fallen from reputation, which ought to have made me

cautious; and from a fortune which ought to have given
me content. I am sunk at once into poverty and scorn: my
name and my crime fill the ballads in the streets; the sport
of the thoughtless, and the triumph of the wicked!

According to a contemporary account, 'during this short
pathetic speech he was frequently interrupted by tears and
emotions too exquisite for description, and such as produced
a general sympathy':[47]

> The judges were seen to dab their cheeks, the clerks,
> lawyers, and tipstaves all wiped their eyes and blew their
> noses; Mr Akerman, the keeper of Newgate, joined in the
> universal tear, and there were moans of anguish and cries
> of dismay from the public gallery.[48]

Even the Recorder had tears in his eyes, but he steeled
himself to his task. He reminded Dodd when delivering his
sentence that the enormity of his offence, an offence which
was becoming all too prevalent, dictated that he must receive
the severest punishment:

> Dr William Dodd, you have been convicted of the offence
> of publishing a forged and counterfeit bond, knowing it to
> be forged and counterfeited, and you have had the
> advantage which the laws of this country afford to every
> man in that situation, a fair, an impartial, and an attentive
> trial.
>   You appear to entertain a very proper sense of the
> enormity of the offence which you have committed; you
> appear too in a state of contrition of mind, and I doubt not
> have duly reflected how far the dangerous tendency of the
> offence you have been guilty of, is increased by the
> influence of example, in being committed by a person of
> your character and of the sacred function of which you
> are a member. These sentiments seem to be yours; I
> would wish to cultivate such sentiments; but I would not
> wish to add to the anguish of a person in your situation by
> dwelling upon it.
>   Your application for mercy must be made elsewhere. It
> would be cruel in the court to flatter you; there is a power

of dispensing mercy where you may apply. Now having said this, I am obliged to pronounce the sentence of the law, which is,

That you, Doctor William Dodd, be carried from hence to the place from whence you came, that from thence you are to be carried to the place of execution, where you are to be hanged by the neck until you are dead.

Dodd 'then retired with trembling steps, groaning with unutterable anguish, and exclaiming in the most lamentable moanings, "Lord Jesus, receive my soul!"'[49]

Despite the Recorder's warning of the difficulty of obtaining a pardon, there followed a substantial campaign of appeals to the crown, 'unparalleled in the annals of this country in their number, the quality of the petitioners, and the earnestness of their requests'. This included petitions from the jurors in the case, his parishioners, Oxford and Cambridge Universities, and even the Common Council of the City of London, despite the serious threat forgeries like Dodd's posed to the city's businesses. One petition had 23,000 signatures. Even Manly, the attorney who had discovered the crime, wrote to Dodd volunteering to solicit mercy from the king on his behalf. Yet Dodd was not optimistic. In a letter to Manly written from Newgate, he thanked him for his offer but wrote: 'I have now only power to tell you, that I expect all is over with me in this world; and am looking only to that mercy, which I hope to receive from the judge of us all'.[50]

Indeed, the extraordinary pressure placed on the king seems to have backfired, and only resulted in the Chief Justice, Lord Mansfield, warning of the dangers of giving into public demands when he spoke to the case in Privy Council.[51] This, together with the need to be seen to punish forgery, meant that the sentence would be carried out. A last desperate attempt to save him was mounted by his wife and friends who attempted to bribe the keeper and turnkey of

Figure 4.06 'Dr Dodd and Joseph Harris at the Place of Execution' (1777). © British Library Board. All Rights Reserved. Shelfmark 6496.g.1(41), folio 114–115

Newgate with between £500 and £1,000 to allow Dodd to escape just before the execution – but to no avail.[52]

On 27 June a crowd of half a million people lined the streets in tearful silence as the procession carrying William Dodd and one other condemned man, a young highway robber named Joseph Harris, made its way to Tyburn. More than 40,000 people attended the execution itself, some paying a guinea apiece for a seat in the galleries. Dodd was dressed in a black suit and wore a full-bottomed wig:[53]

> When he arrived at the fatal tree, he ascended the cart, and spoke much to his fellow sufferer. He then prayed, not only for himself, but also for his wife, and for the unfortunate youth that suffered with him; and declaring that he died in the true faith of the gospel of Christ, in perfect love and charity with all mankind, and with thankfulness to his friends, he was launched into eternity.

Dodd's behaviour was widely praised:

> The behaviour of the divine, in his last moments, was penitent, manly, and resigned – the populace seemed universally affected at his fate, and even Jack Ketch [the hangman] himself shed a tear![54]

Dodd had intended to give a fuller speech, written by Johnson, but instead gave it to the Ordinary of Newgate in order to have it printed. In this 'last solemn declaration', he acknowledged his sins, but once again explained how he came to commit the offence in terms which suggest why this crime was so common:

> I was led astray from religious strictness by the delusion of show and the delights of voluptuousness. I never knew or attended to the calls of frugality, or the needful minuteness of painful economy. Vanity and pleasure, into which I plunged, required expence disproportionate to my income; expence brought distress upon me, and distress, importunate distress, urged me to temporary fraud.[55]

Conclusion

The values of a society can be measured by the offences that it defines as criminal and punishes in its courts. In medieval times, a man's honour was his most important possession and he protected his reputation with violence; consequently, court dockets were dominated by violent crimes (notably murder). By the eighteenth century English society had changed dramatically. The incidence of murder had declined significantly and would fall still further, while property crimes overwhelmingly dominated the list of offences tried at the Old Bailey. Money had become the most important social resource. Spent lavishly on the right clothes and combined with the right manners, you could even use it to achieve the status of a gentleman. The surfeit of prosecutions for theft at the Old Bailey reveals a city full of men and women who would do almost anything to acquire money, whether it was in order to purchase food to quell real hunger, to obtain clothes in order to follow the latest fashions or to acquire the accoutrements of an elite lifestyle. At the same time, prosecutions for theft illustrate the lengths to which those who lost property were willing to go in order to punish the men, women and children responsible. Even when it involved admitting to consorting with prostitutes or risking being labelled a 'molly cull', victims were willing to expose themselves in court in order to secure the punishment of those who stole their property. And they did so despite the fact that those whom they prosecuted, including both thieving children and gentlemen forgers, faced possible death for their crimes. Property was indeed more valuable than human life.

5

Retribution

All the felonies tried at the Old Bailey had at some point in the past been punishable by death. But there was never a desire to execute everyone found guilty (to do so would create a bloodbath); indeed, for the death penalty to achieve its intended purpose of deterrence, it was believed that only a fraction of those sentenced to death actually needed to be executed. For the rest, the magnanimous mercy of the king and his government could be demonstrated to the public by liberally doling out royal pardons and lesser punishments. In essence, the judicial process was as much an exercise in determining which unlucky convicts would be executed as it was a way of determining a more narrowly defined guilt. At the same time, the history of punishment in the eighteenth century is the story of the search for alternatives for those who were spared the noose.

The many dozens of capital convicts sentenced each year were whittled down to a manageable number to be hanged through connivance and artifice. Juries used partial verdicts ('pious perjury') to ensure that the lives of selected convicts were preserved. Many other lives were saved through 'benefit of clergy', which evolved from the medieval practice of handing over convicted clergymen to the church for punishment and asking them to demonstrate their clerical vocation through a reading test. As literacy rates improved, an increasing number of convicts were able to read the 'neck verse' (Psalm 51 from the Bible) and escape execution. In response, a series of statutes removed the most serious offences such as murder, rape and highway robbery from this benefit. In 1706 the reading test was abolished and benefit of clergy became automatic for those convicted of any offence that had not already been excluded. Those convicted of crimes for which benefit of clergy remained were branded on the thumb (with a 'T' for theft, 'F' for felon, or 'M' for murder). This ensured that benefit of clergy could only be claimed once.

Capital convicts ineligible for benefit of clergy still had the chance to claim that they were pregnant or to petition for a royal pardon. Women who 'pleaded their belly' (and there were many, some of whom had taken advantage of the loose living conditions in Newgate to become pregnant) were examined by a jury of matrons, chosen from women present in the courtroom. If the matrons determined you were 'quick with child' (if movement could be detected, signalling the beginning of life), your punishment was respited until after the baby was born. In principle, after the birth you would be put to death, but concern for the child and the cost of rearing it ensured that most new mothers escaped execution. This is one of the reasons why far fewer women than men were hanged.

All capital sentences from the Old Bailey were reviewed by the king and his cabinet following reports presented by the Recorder of London. In addition, the family and friends of convicts sentenced to death frequently petitioned the king for a pardon. In cases where evidence of good character could be produced, the accused was particularly young or the conviction was a first offence or the evidence was problematic, the king readily granted pardons, unless there was a compelling need for an 'example' to deter further crimes. Approximately 50–60 percent of those sentenced to death in the eighteenth century were pardoned. These took the form of either a free pardon or a conditional one. In the latter case, the convict had to accept branding or transportation in place of the noose. In some cases, messages bearing news of a pardon arrived at the very last minute, just as the convict mounted the scaffold.

Of the 33,000 defendants convicted at the Old Bailey in the eighteenth century, 1,600 were hanged. Performed in front of huge crowds, executions were a public spectacle, meant to act as a deterrent to crime. Convicts were drawn in a cart through the crowded streets from Newgate to Tyburn, where Marble Arch stands today. After they were given a chance to speak to the crowd (and, it was hoped, confess their sins), the condemned were blindfolded and placed in a horse-drawn cart. The noose was then placed around his or her neck and the cart pulled away. Until the introduction of a sharp drop in 1783, this caused a long and painful death by strangulation (friends of convicts often helped put them out of their misery by pulling on their legs). Those found guilty of treason and petty treason were subjected to more grue-some punishments: men were drawn and quartered while women were burned at the stake.

Regardless of the particular form of execution, it was a horrific death, rendered to a large extent pointless by the carnival atmosphere of the watching multitude. Pickpockets actively stalked the crowd, mocking the punishment's supposed deterrent effect. Even in the eighteenth century, few people actively praised the death penalty as a social good. Many were concerned at its failure to stop crime, while others pointed to the wholesale loss of lives needed to man ships and populate the colonies. But the alternatives were equally unsatisfactory: pardons provided no punishment at all and branding, which was often done with a cold iron, was felt to be both ineffectual and incommensurate with the severity of the offences being punished. In any case, decreasing tolerance of corporal punishments led to the abolition of branding in 1779.

Other existing punishments also seemed unsuitable substitutes for hanging. The pillory was used for some offences, notably notorious crimes such as sodomy, seditious words, fraud and perjury, where the public destruction of the reputation of the convict was deemed to be an appropriate punishment. But its reliance on the participation of the audience, which was expected to throw rotting fruit and vegetables and the odd dead cat at the culprit, meant that the pillory was alternately too severe and too trivial. For those who aroused intense popular anger, such as sodomites and thieftakers, the punishment could lead to a particularly gruesome death. In contrast, popular heroes such as Daniel Defoe, placed on the pillory in 1703 for seditious libel, were celebrated by the crowd and pelted with nothing more odoriferous than flowers. In many other cases, crowd apathy ensured that an hour in the pillory was passed in at least relative comfort, which is why the punishment for forgery was changed from the pillory to death in 1729. Owing to its perceived ineffectiveness and the cost of maintaining public order, from the last quarter of the century onwards the pillory was used by Old Bailey judges only for fraud and perjury.

Whipping, 'until his [or her] back be bloody', was traditionally carried out in public, with the convict stripped to the waist and bound to the back of a cart as it was drawn slowly through the public street nearest the scene of the crime. Although the courts frequently turned to whipping out of dissatisfaction with alternative punishments, particularly in cases of minor thefts, the character of this punishment changed during the century as more and more whippings were carried out in private. The disruption to traffic caused by the slow moving cart, as well as public apathy or hostility towards the punishment, led judges increasingly to insist that whipping, particularly of women, should be carried out behind closed doors, usually inside, or immediately outside, Newgate Prison, the Old Bailey, or a house of correction.

In frustration at the limitations of these traditional punishments, the eighteenth-century courts turned to two new punishments for felons: transportation and imprisonment. In 1718, confronted with political instability and rapidly rising crime rates, the insecure new Hanoverian monarchy and its Whig government passed the Transportation Act. This allowed the courts to sentence felons convicted of offences subject to the benefit of clergy to be sent to North America for seven years. Although the motives for the introduction of this new punishment included a desire to provide a labour force for the colonies and a belief that it might lead to the reformation of offenders, the act's primary purposes were deterrence and a desire to exile hardened offenders from the country. Almost immediately it became the punishment of choice at the Old Bailey: between 1718 and the outbreak of war with America in 1776, over two-thirds of those found guilty were sentenced to transportation.

Even before the outbreak of war with America, however, transportation began to fall out of favour. Too many convicts were returning from exile before the expiration of their sentences and the punishment's deterrent value declined as conditions in the rapidly growing American colonies improved. In any case, crime seemed to relentlessly increase despite the vast amount of money spent on transporting offenders to the other side of the world. As a result, when transportation came to an abrupt halt in 1776, a new punishment was already being contemplated:

imprisonment. Many were coming to believe that punishments should be graded according to the severity of the crime and that some convicts could be reformed and returned to society as productive members. Imprisonment at hard labour, with its tough discipline and severe regimen, came to seem an ever more attractive alternative. Between 1776 and the end of the century, over one-quarter of Old Bailey convicts were sentenced to imprisonment.

Nonetheless, transportation was still thought to be useful for the most hardened offenders. Despite the lack of a suitable destination, some convicts continued to be sentenced to transportation during the American War. While they awaited the execution of their sentence, male offenders were confined in the hulks and put to hard labour on the banks of the Thames, while women were imprisoned on land. By the time the war ended in 1783, Newgate Prison was seriously overcrowded and the hulks had acquired an unsavoury reputation for their unhealthy conditions and ease of escape. In a desperate attempt to restore a viable system of transportation, the government attempted to secretly send convicts to the now independent American colonies. Other destinations, including West Africa and Nova Scotia, were also tried (unsuccessfully), before the penal colony at New South Wales was settled on. The first fleet departed for Botany Bay in 1787.

Transportation never recovered the dominant position it enjoyed between 1718 and 1776, but even at the end of the century it remained the most frequently imposed sentence at the Old Bailey, accounting for just over one-third of all punishments. Despite the attractions of imprisonment, it was not yet thought to be sufficiently effective for more serious offenders, particularly those convicted of aggravated forms of theft such as theft from houses, who were still sentenced to transportation. Those convicted of the most serious offences, including murder, robbery and forgery, continued to be sentenced to death. But by 1800 the death penalty was in decline. Although it would survive for a further 165 years, the courts had finally found a sufficient array of acceptable alternative punishments for most convicts.

Tyburn Fair

The majority of men and women found guilty at the Old Bailey and sentenced to hang were subsequently pardoned and suffered some lesser punishment such as branding or transportation. For a minority, however, the black cap and awful words of the judge betokened their actual fate: 'That you, and each of you, be taken to the place of execution, there to be hanged by the neck until you are dead: and may the Lord have mercy upon your sinful souls'.[1] Until 1783 that place of execution was Tyburn and the rituals and emotions of the eight hanging days each year brought ordinary Londoners face to face with the awful power of the court. Despite the incontestable demonstration of the state's authority, executions were often marred by conflict, as the friends and relatives of the accused fought for possession of the corpse with surgeons and anatomists, keen to use the dead for their own purposes. Hanging days were also holidays, and the crowd found entertainment as well as conflict in the day's rituals.

Francis Place recalled the scene as condemned prisoners were hustled into carts and hauled three miles from Newgate Prison to Tyburn on the western edge of the city, at what is now the fashionable end of Oxford Street:

> Within my recollection a hanging day was to all intents and purposes a fair day. The streets from Newgate to Tyburn were thronged with people and all the windows of the houses were filled. The friends and acquaintance of those going to be hanged used to follow the carts in which the criminals were sealed, and if any one bore his fate with

> indifference or bravado he was occasionally applauded.
> People used to wait the coming of the carts in different
> places, some holding a pot of beer in their hands, others a
> measure of gin, to treat the criminals, for which purpose
> the cart occasionally made a stop. Others threw oranges
> and apples to them. Pie men and sellers of gingerbread nuts
> and other things bawled about. Songs were sung and the
> ballads sold at the corners of the streets all along Holborn,
> St Giles's and Oxford Street. Carts were placed along the
> middle of the street and the people paid a trifle for
> permission to sit or stand in them to see the culprits pass.[2]

The journey westward was eventful and full of ritual. The
muffled mourning bells rang out first from the spire of St
Sepulchre's church, as the condemned had their chains
struck off and their arms loosely bound in the press yard
before Newgate Prison, and later from the great bell as the
procession passed St Giles on its way to Tyburn. Along the
route the city marshals and constables struggled with the
crowds, which by all accounts were made up of a majority of
women and drawn from all classes of society. For the
condemned, the journey was a last performance. Some,
dressed in finery or their wedding outfits, played to the
galleries, preparing to die 'game' to the applause of an
audience that grew as the dismal procession travelled
westward. Others, clothed in shrouds, took refuge in drink
or religion or fainted with fear, knowing that the likelihood
of a last-minute pardon diminished with each cobble that
rumbled under the iron-clad wheels of the carts. Each
prisoner shared the cart with two or three others, as well as
the coffins intended to take their corpses. The procession
stopped at the Bowl Inn in the depths of St Giles and then
at the Mason's Arms, where the condemned were
anaesthetised with ever more strong liquor.

After a journey that could last up to three hours, the
murderous procession reached the execution ground. Most
of the year Tyburn was a muddy field by a busy road, home

to cows and milkmaids, but on hanging days it became an outdoor theatre. Stands were erected for those who could afford to pay for a seat and an unobstructed view. On their arrival the men and women set to hang were driven beneath the triple tree and their hands were secured, as the Ordinary of Newgate prayed furiously at their side. A desultory psalm was forced from their lips and each prisoner was given an opportunity to say a few last words. Some delivered long, prepared speeches, while others mumbled incoherently in their fear. The expectation was that the prisoner would admit their guilt and the justice of the sentence passed on them, before commending their own souls to God. Some went to their deaths asserting their innocence to the last, but the majority seem to have played the remorseful part expected of them. Finally, a coarse sack was placed over their heads and with the noose secured around their necks, the cart was driven from beneath their feet. Death came through slow strangulation and could take up to three-quarters of an hour – the condemned twisting and struggling as the noose tightened.

For the victim of this state-sponsored murder there was nothing worldly to hope for beyond a quick death and a Christian burial, but to achieve this second posthumous ambition they needed the help of their friends to keep their body out of the hands of the surgeons, ever hungry for a fresh corpse to anatomise.

Richard Shears made a meagre living from two horses, a cart and a lot of hard work. On hanging days, and in company with many Londoners, he earned a few pence from the crowds at Tyburn. On Monday 11 November 1751 he rose before dawn to secure a place near the gallows. His wife, Hannah, later told the court that:

> He went between five and six o'clock in the morning with his cart to Tyburn. He went to let his cart for people to get up upon to see the prisoners die.

Unfortunately for Richard Shears, on this occasion he came into conflict with the crowd at the base of the gallows as they struggled with the hangman and the surgeons to secure the bodies of the dead.

That particular Monday, nine men and one woman were set to hang. At the last minute, four of the accused, including the one woman, Elizabeth Davis, received a last-minute reprieve. This left only six men, in two carts, to make the long, slow journey to Tyburn. Among the six men were Alexander Byrne and Terence McCane. Both were 23 years old and had grown up in Dublin, before coming to London as teenagers. Their 'scene of action was generally at Spitalfields, Whitechapel and Rag Fair', just east of Tower Hill and the Tower of London. They had been convicted and sentenced to death for robbing Benjamin Smart on the highway of his hat, shoe buckles, tobacco box and 9s.[3] And even though nothing could be done to save their lives, their friends were determined to save their bodies from the desecration of the anatomists.

The City authorities were expecting trouble and the two carts 'were conveyed from Newgate to the place of execution, attended by a large number of constables and a multitude of people'. When they finally arrived at Tyburn, the men:

> Prayed very fervently while they were tying up to the fatal
> tree. After reading some prayers, recommending their
> souls to the Almighty's protection, they continued praying
> and calling on the Lord Jesus Christ to receive their souls,
> till the cart drew from under them.

A few minutes later, the battle for their bodies commenced. Michael Munday later recalled:

> There was such a mob. There were near a quarter of a
> hundred chairmen and milkmen, who seemed to be all
> concerned in taking away the bodies.

The crowd was made up mainly of Irishmen who worked the streets around the neighbourhoods of Rosemary Lane and Whitechapel. Most almost certainly knew Byrne and McCane, who came from the same neighbourhood and – like most of this particular crowd – were Irish.

In part, their determination to rescue the bodies was tied to a traditional understanding of the nature of the soul and the notion of resurrection and the afterlife. Most people believed in the physical existence of a corporeal soul. Philosophers such as Descartes believed that the soul could be found in the pineal gland at the centre of the brain, but for working-class Londoners in the eighteenth century it was enough to believe that one's soul had a physical existence and that the anatomists threatened its secure passage into the afterlife. The role of the body at the resurrection was also important, as regardless of the mechanism, a whole and consecrated corpse buried with Christian ceremony seemed to most people a more likely route to heaven than the messy reconstitution of the body from the bloody remains discarded in the bucket besides the anatomist's table. There was also a strong belief in ghosts and their ability to haunt the living. The anatomised corpse of a hanged man, not properly laid to rest, posed a threat even to his friends.

The intact corpse of a hanged man, even more than those of the everyday dead of this pre-modern world with its high levels of mortality, also had a particular meaning. The hand of a hanged man was thought to cure wens and cancers and, like the king's touch, could have a beneficial effect on scrofula. It was a common sight to see mothers lifting their children to allow the hand of a hanged man to brush against the child's cheek.

The crowd that rescued Byrne's and McCane's bodies was led by Michael MacGennis and Christopher Williams – known as Kit. But having fought off the surgeons and the hangman, who was keen to claim the dead men's clothes, they had no way of transporting the bodies away from the scene and quickly alighted on the cart and two horses Richard Shears had positioned just by the gallows. One witness at MacGennis's later trial recalled:

> I saw Michael MacGennis, and some more, put two
> bodies up in Richard Shears's cart, against the consent of

Figure 5.02 'The Reward of Cruelty', plate iv of 'The Four Stages of Cruelty', by William Hogarth (1751). © The Trustees of the Weston Park Foundation, UK/The Bridgeman Art Library

> Shears, who said, Gentlemen I hope you will be so good
> as not to throw these dead bodies up into my cart, for I
> am obliged to go home about some business.

Another witness recalled a rather less polite exchange:

> There was a sort of a skirmish, and Shears was striving to
> get his horses and cart from MacGennis, and two or three
> more, who had got them from him. MacGennis would not
> let him have them, and the man that drove the horses
> threatened to knock his brains out, if he did not go about
> his business.

With Kit Williams driving and Michael MacGennis at the
head of the two horses, and accompanied by 40 or 50 men,
they headed up the turnpike north of Hyde Park towards
Bayswater, Richard Shears's entreaties (polite or not) ringing
in their ears and two corpses secure in the back. The road
eastward, back to Tower Hill and East London, was still
blocked by the execution crowd, while the turnpike to the
west was clear.

Michael Munday recalled that:

> They drove the horses down to Bayswater, a place beyond
> Tyburn, about a quarter of a mile, where they stayed and
> drank, and from thence back by Tyburn with two of the
> dead bodies in the cart. I saw them use the horses very
> bad.

Heavy drinking had begun first thing that morning, and a
quick top-up at Bayswater was all that was required to keep
them going. The crowds having begun to disperse, Williams
and MacGennis turned back through Tyburn on their way
homeward, and, as Munday explained, they once more
encountered Richard Shears, now desperate to recover his
cart and horses:

> It was after they returned from Bayswater, about ten yards
> on this side of Tyburn. MacGennis had a hanger under his
> coat. I saw him pull it out when Shears came to him, and

cut him over the head. Shears went bare headed after his
cart, with the blood running down his ears. I saw him
following his cart almost by Nibs's Pound, and I saw him
no more.

A hanger is a short sword, like a cutlass, and a single blow
left Shears bleeding profusely, his skull fractured.

Edward Hilton was also there to witness the encounter
between Shears and MacGennis:

I saw them coming from Bayswater, swearing by their
maker very much, how they would serve Shears if he did
not lend them his horses and cart. He called them
Gentlemen, and begged and prayed to have them. They
used him very ill and called him thief. MacGennis was
riding on the top of the corpses. He had a hanger under
his clothes. He drew it out, he swore by God, and other
bitter oaths, if Shears did not get away and let go his
horses, he would jump off, and cut him down. Then he
jumped off and struck him on the right side of the head,
close to his ear, after which the cart went forwards.

William Latimore was one of the constables who had
attended the execution to maintain good order:

I did not follow the cart to Bayswater. I saw the cart come
back through the turnpike and Richard Shears came after
it with blood running down half an inch thick.

Eventually, having received the insults of the mob and the
blow from the hanger, Shears had to give up. Hannah,
Richard Shears's wife, heard the news of the fracas later that
afternoon:

I heard he was wounded, and gone to Hyde Park
Infirmary. I went there, and found him all in blood. I did
not see his wounds till after he was dead. On his dying
bed, he said, it was a short thick Irish milkman that gave
him his death wound, that he was wilfully murdered, and
that they ran away with his cart and horses, and that
murder will never be hid.

Ironically, George Hale, the surgeon who treated him, was well versed in anatomy. He described the cause of death in graphic detail:

> I am a surgeon, and dress under Mr Bromfield, at the hospital. Richard Shears was brought there on the eleventh of November, about two o'clock. He said he had received a large wound on his head. It had pierced through both tables of the scull on the right side, about the temple. It was judged necessary to trepan him [bore a hole in his skull], bad symptoms coming on. We found matter lodged between the membranes of the brain. He had several contusions from the wounds made, I suppose with sticks. He was hearty when he came.

Although a modern reader might suspect that Hale's own intervention was more likely to kill than cure, he had no hesitation in answering the court's question when asked:

Question.   What in your opinion was the occasion of his death?

Hale.   My opinion is that the wound on his head was.

In the meantime, MacGennis and Kit Williams drove the cart and horses eastward, back to Tower Hill in triumph, along much the same route Byrne and McCane had travelled just a few hours earlier. William Latimore followed, intent on making an arrest:

> I saw MacGennis with the rest of the mob at Tower Hill. I followed them. They put the bodies down on Tower Hill, and the constables came and took hold of MacGennis, and also another, named Kit Williams.

At Michael MacGennis's trial for murder, Kit Williams claimed complete innocence: 'They made me drive up one street and down another, just where they pleased. I was charged upon Tower Hill for bringing the dead bodies.' He also claimed to have solicited help for Shears: 'I saw the man all bloody. I said go and get your head dressed, I'll drive your horses as well as I can.'

In the end it was only Michael MacGennis who stood trial. He also protested his innocence: 'I know no more of it than the child in its mother's womb'. And he called a slew of character witnesses in his defence. Thomas Reed testified:

> I am a milkman. I have known MacGennis between five and six years. I never saw any thing amiss of him in my life. He has been a lodger of mine above a year and half.

And Mary Palace said:

> I have known him six years, he deals where I deal. I never heard he was quarrelsome in all my life, or to have such arms as he is accused with.

And so on. But to no avail. At the end of a long, cold trial in mid-January, he was found guilty of murder and was himself sentenced to hang.

Michael MacGennis was 32 years old, happily married and the father of several children. Like Byrne and McCane, he had grown up in Ireland, but unlike them the life story he recounted to the Ordinary of Newgate before his own execution seemed more sober and hardworking than sinful. According to the Ordinary, he was:

> Born in the Kingdom of Ireland, of parents whose circumstances would not admit of giving him any education; but they brought him up in a sober way, in the fear of God. He was esteemed a quiet, harmless youth by those who knew him in his early days. He scarce could give any account how his days had passed away, except that he had always worked hard for his living since he was sent into the world. Destitute of friends, and left to take care of himself, he came to England young, and whatever other business he might have followed, that of crying milk about the streets has been his chief employ. He has been married about nine years, and had several children, some of which are still alive. He has left a disconsolate widow, who follows the same calling for a livelihood.

To all intents and purposes MacGennis was typical of the men and women who crowded around Tyburn on hanging days. According to the Ordinary, 'He had been used to attend executions, and been often seen there'.

Many of his friends felt his conviction was unfair and a public meeting was called in an attempt to shift responsibility onto someone else and to secure a pardon. Even the Ordinary seemed a little uncertain about the justice of the case. There is a distinctly defensive note in his reaction to MacGennis' refusal to acknowledge his responsibility for Shears's death:

> Who did it? We have no authority yet to say, unless we accept the opinion of the court and jury who convicted MacGennis upon full evidence, unimpeached. And as the scheme set up to prove the contrary did not succeed, we can scarce believe, but that he was justly convicted and suffered accordingly.

On 23 March 1752, in company with 15 others, MacGennis journeyed from Newgate to Tyburn and was hanged. According to the Ordinary, 'for some days before his execution he became more hearty, and was in good health when he suffered, being as tight a little man as might swing on Tyburn tree'. This time, an accommodation was reached at Tyburn between the surgeons and the friends of the hanged:

> When there, some time was spent in recommending their souls to the Almighty's mercy; and then they were turned off, receiving the due reward of their deeds here. After they had hung a proper time, Hayes and Broughton's bodies were first cut down without the least stir and hurry, and delivered to be carried in a coach to the surgeon of the hospital in Lemon Street, Goodman's Fields, in order to be anatomised. The rest (including MacGennis's corpse) were delivered to their friends. And during the whole time of the execution, there was not the least disturbance.

That same spring of 1752 also saw the passage of the Murder Act, which was designed to deter crime by taking advantage of the popular fear of the anatomist's knife. It stipulated that anyone:

> Found guilty of wilful murder, be executed according to law on the day next but one after sentence passed, and that the body shall be dissected and anatomised by the surgeons and that in no case whatsoever, the body of any murderer shall be suffered to be buried, unless after such body shall have been dissected and anatomised.[4]

Although the state's use of anatomisation as a form of punishment might have exacerbated the struggle for the control of the bodies of the hanged at Tyburn, a fragile truce was negotiated, enforced by the sheriff and his officers. The bodies of those sentenced by the court to be anatomised were handed over to the surgeons, while those of all other convicts were handed over without a fight to their friends and families for a normal burial.

Exposed on the Pillory

Like other traditional punishments such as the stocks and penance, the pillory punished through humiliation. By publicly exposing the culprit, this punishment announced to the community that he or she could not be trusted. The audience were expected to contribute to the convict's shame by throwing polluting objects such as mud, rotten vegetables and eggs, dead cats, excrement and blood and guts from slaughterhouses. Although sometimes the crowd chose to applaud the convict instead, in other cases the missiles included bricks and stones and the damage done to the target was to more than just his reputation; at least seven died on London pillories during the century.

John Waller had 'a fruitful genius, which he applied to the wrong purposes', and his fraudulent use of the law made him many enemies:

He used to worm himself into the acquaintance of people who had but small fortunes, or such as they acquired by their daily labour, and particularly those who had families to maintain. He would cause such as these to be arrested at his suit, and would not scruple to swear that they were indebted to him in sums sufficient to have them committed to jail, and then under a specious show of compassion would bring them to a composition. He thought he could take advantage of the poorer sort, many of whose families were reduced to beggary by his illegal proceedings.

As a solicitor, he also took money from clients to pursue cases which he had no chance of winning.[5]

Worst of all, he was a corrupt thieftaker, who prosecuted men on trumped-up charges in order to secure a reward. His technique was to identify men whose reputations were poor and who were already considered suspicious and to manufacture charges against them. His most famous prosecution was of the well-known street robber James Dalton, whose gang terrorised London during the late 1720s. In April 1730 he enquired at the Wood Street Compter to determine when Dalton had been released from prison in the preceding year. He then used this information to choose the date for an accusation that Dalton had robbed him in the fields near Tottenham Court. There were no other witnesses to the alleged crime, but to confirm his accusation, Waller used inside knowledge to claim that the pistol used in the attack was the same one Dalton had brandished during his robbery of another man, Dr Mead, for which crime he had already been convicted.[6]

Dalton admitted his many crimes, but always denied that he had robbed Waller. As reported in the *Proceedings*, Dalton:

Denied the fact charged upon him by Waller, and exclaimed against him as a man of a vile character, that he was a common affidavit man, and was but lately,

before the time charged in the indictment, come out of
Newgate himself. That though he himself had done many
ill things, and had deserved death many times, yet not for
this fact, he being innocent of it; and said, Waller was as
great a rogue as himself, and there was never a barrel the
better herring.[7]

Despite his protestations of innocence, Dalton was
convicted, sentenced to death and executed on 17 April.
Waller's reward for the conviction was £80.

The following year, when Waller prosecuted Charles
Knowles and Sarah Harper at the assizes in Hertford for
robbing him near Newington, the court treated his evidence
much more sceptically. The judge observed:

Though the prisoner Harper was a person of bad
character, yet John Waller's being worse, rendered himself
notorious, and he having sworn robberies upon several
persons [probably only for the reward] who were
acquitted as innocent, and had hanged Dalton. The court
thought no regard was to be given to his evidence, and
thereupon the jury acquitted the prisoners.[8]

Justice finally caught up with Waller in May 1732 when
he was tried at the Old Bailey for perverting the course of
justice by falsely charging John Edlin with a highway
robbery in Hertfordshire. In his typical self-aggrandising
manner, Waller claimed:

That he called at the George at New Market, and that
either John Eldin or Uriah Davis came and begged alms
of him, and then he being moved with compassion, gave
him sixpence, and afterwards treated him on the road, as
they both travelled the same way, but at the bottom of
Botsam's Hill, this man having no sense of the kindness
that had been done to him, was so ungrateful as to assault
him. And the other man coming up at the same time, they
robbed him of three jacobuses, nine guineas, and a piece
of mechlin lace. And then they stripped him, and bound
him; and there he lay till he was relieved by a passenger.[9]

Waller, conscious that he was no longer trusted, made the accusation under a false name, John Trevor. As the justice of the peace, Justice Gifford, testified at Waller's trial:

> The prisoner, by the name of Trevor, charged John Edlin, and another, who was then in Newgate, with robbing him on the highway between Colney and St Albans. I thought that Edlin had an honester look than the prisoner, and that I had seen the prisoner before, but I could not recollect who he was. I sent to enquire after the prisoner's character, and was told that he was an honest man, and then I committed Edlin to Newgate. After this Waller came to me again, and told me, that I had made a mistake in committing Edlin on the information of Trevor, it should have been on the information of Waller, says he, for my name is Waller, and therefore must beg you to alter it. Oh, is it you Mr Waller? says I, I thought I had seen your face before. Had I known your name when you made this information, I had turned you out of doors, as I did five years ago, when you swore against two street robbers; but since it is so, I shall take a note of it.

When the case came up for trial on the Home Circuit Assizes, Waller, perhaps knowing that his evidence would not be trusted, failed to appear with his two witnesses and the defendants were acquitted. But he did not give up; he simply took his accusations to a different court, as the under-clerk of the Norfolk Circuit of the Assizes reported:

> John Waller having ill success at Hertford, came to Cambridge on the Tuesday following, and gave me an information against two men for robbing him, and they were both capitally convicted. The country was not satisfied and there were suspicions that Waller was a rogue. Baron Cummins ordered me to enquire into his character. I enquired of a gentleman at Thetford: Waller, says he, why, he's the vilest fellow living; he makes a trade of swearing away men's lives for the sake of the reward, granted for convicting robbers. This gentleman gave me direction to write to a gentleman for a

> description and character of the prisoner. I wrote, and
> received an answer at Bury. The answer described him
> exactly, and by good fortune it came just time enough to
> prevent the execution of the two men.

Waller was convicted at the Old Bailey of making a false accusation and was sentenced to a smorgasbord of punishments, reflecting the court's severe disapproval of his actions, and its wish to make the fact of his punishment known as widely as possible.

> John Waller is to stand once in the pillory at the Seven
> Dials, in St Giles in the Fields, and once in the pillory
> against Hicks Hall, for one hour each time. And to stand
> on the pillory at the same places, at two other different
> times, for one hour each time with his hat off, that he may
> be known by the people. An account of his offence to be
> written on a paper, and stuck on the pillory every time. To
> pay a fine of twenty marks; to be imprisoned for two
> years, and not to be discharged afterwards, till he has paid
> his fine, and given security for his good behaviour during
> his life.

Word that Waller would appear in the pillory soon spread and his many enemies looked forward to it with relish. About a week before he was to appear, Edward Dalton, the brother of James Dalton, told everyone he saw that:

> He would be revenged on Waller, because Waller had
> hanged his brother. By God, he said, he shall never come
> out alive, for I'll have his blood.

Similarly, Richard Griffith alias Sergeant told Thomas James 'that he would do his business'. Even the carman who was responsible for carrying the pillory to St Giles told a witness 'that he had carried almost a sack full of artichokes and cauliflower stalks in readiness; and swore that he would do Waller's business, and he should never live to stand at Hicks Hall'. The day before Waller's first stint on the pillory, William Belt alias Worrel, who had been employed to oversee the punishment, observed: 'He'll stand but once. He had better be hanged, for he shall never come back alive'.

On the morning of 13 June, a huge crowd gathered in Seven Dials. Spectators climbed lamp posts and fences and stood on carts in order to get a better view. At 11.00 William Belt brought Waller out of Redgate's alehouse in nearby King Street and placed his head and arms through the holes in the pillory. Immediately, 'the mob, which was very numerous, having been provided with large quantities of cabbage, cauliflower and artichoke stalks, began to pelt him in a most outrageous manner'.[10] These rotten, or not so rotten, vegetables and their stems clearly had the potential to cause serious injury, but some of the crowd were unwilling to leave it at that. After only a few minutes, Edward Dalton and Richard Griffith stepped onto the pillory and assaulted Waller. One of the spectators, Cartwright Richardson, described the attack:

> Griffith took hold of Waller's coat, and Dalton of the
> waistband of his breeches, and so they pulled his head out
> of the pillory, and he hung a little while by one hand, but
> pulling that hand out they threw him on to the pillory
> board.

Belt tried to put him back into the pillory:

> But Dalton and Griffith and a chimney sweeper laid hold
> of Waller, and stripped him as naked as he was born,
> except his feet, for they pulled his stockings over his
> shoes and so left them; then they beat him with
> cauliflower stalks, and threw him down upon the pillory
> board. The chimney sweeper put some soot into his
> mouth, and Griffith rammed it down his throat with a
> cauliflower stalk. Dalton and Griffith jumped and stamped
> upon his naked body and head, and kicked him and beat
> him with artichoke and cauliflower stalks, as he lay on the
> pillory board. They continued beating, kicking, and
> stamping upon him in this manner for above one quarter
> of an hour, and then the mob threw down the pillory, and

> all that were upon it. Waller then lay naked on the ground.
> Dalton got upon him, and stamping on his privy parts,
> Waller gave a dismal groan, and I believe it was his last;
> for after that I never heard him groan nor speak, nor saw
> him stir.

While they were stamping on Waller, 'Griffith said to Dalton, well played partner. And Dalton said, aye, damn him, I'll never leave him while he has a bit of life in him, for hanging my brother.'

After an hour, Waller was taken up and carried to St Giles's Roundhouse and then to Newgate Prison where his mother, Martha Smith, was waiting for him. But the turnkeys of Newgate Prison refused to accept his dead body, and instead it was placed in a coach with his mother:

> As soon as Dalton and Griffith saw her go in, they cried
> out here's the old bitch his mother, damn her, let's kill her
> too. So they went to the coach door, huzzaing and
> swearing that they had stood true to the stuff. Damn him,
> says Dalton, we have sent his soul half way to hell, and
> now we'll have his body to sell to the surgeons for money
> to pay the devil for his through passage. Then they tried to
> pull him out of the coach, but were prevented.

From the vantage point of the coach, Martha Smith described the same events as follows:

> My son had neither eyes, nor ears, nor nose to be seen;
> they had squeezed his head flat. Griffith pulled open the
> coach door, and struck me, pulled my son's head out of
> my lap, and his brains fell into my hand.

When Mr King, the coroner, saw the body the next day, he too was appalled:

> I never saw such a spectacle. I can't pretend to distinguish
> particularly in what part he was bruised most, for he was
> bruised all over. I could scarce perceive any part of his
> body free. His head was beat quite flat, no features could
> be seen in his face, and somebody had cut him quite
> down the back with a sharp instrument.

A jury was summoned, and 'hearing the depositions of several witnesses, brought in a verdict of wilful murder by persons unknown with unlawful weapons'.[11]

Although the inquest was inconclusive regarding the identity of those responsible, Dalton, Griffith and Belt were subsequently indicted for the murder of John Waller and stood trial at the Old Bailey on 6 September. There was substantial evidence that Dalton and Griffith had actively intended to kill Waller, but William Belt was able to successfully claim that he was powerless to stop Waller's attackers. As one witness testified:

> I was there, and neither saw nor heard of any hurt that Belt did to Waller, but so far from it, that he run the hazard of his own life, by endeavouring to put Waller's head in twice. It was not in his power to prevent the abuses the other prisoners committed, for he was forced to get off the pillory to save himself.

Other officers supported this testimony and Belt was acquitted by the jury, while Edward Dalton and Richard Griffith were found guilty and sentenced to death. The judge, Baron Thompson, condemned 'the liberty of the mob in presuming to insult a person defenceless in the pillory, under the sentence of the law, however great his crimes might be'.[12] Both were executed on 9 October at Tyburn, with Griffith maintaining that he was innocent of the murder to the end.[13]

Were Dalton and Griffith the only ones responsible for Waller's death? Although the sheriff claimed his usual fee of £1 10s for organising and supervising the punishment,[14] and while several soldiers were present, presumably to prevent any disorder, there is no evidence of any efforts on the part of the authorities to stop the killing. Indeed, when Dalton and Griffith began to attack Waller, all that Belt did was try to put him back into the pillory. In contrast, when John Middleton stood on the pillory nine years earlier, having been convicted of a similar crime, 20 constables and 104 assistants were employed to protect him – although even this did not prevent the crowd from smothering him to death with dirt. The authorities probably chose not to protect Waller because of disquiet at his corrupt attempts to manipulate the judicial system.

Despite these tragic lapses of order, the pillory was intended to be a much more constrained and ritualised punishment than was experienced by John Waller and John Middleton. Official policing was intended to regulate the actions of the crowd. In the memory of Francis Place, writing in the early nineteenth century:

> The constables who on these occasions are a numerous
> body, form a ring around the pillory, to keep the mob at a
> distance, and a considerable space is therefore left vacant
> between the cordon they form and the pillory.

Most pillories were designed to rotate around a central post, so two men could be punished at the same time by being forced to walk around in circles. A small number of women, as representatives of the community, were allowed to enter the space between the pillory and the ring of constables in order to administer the punishment:

> These women were supplied with the materials for
> offence from the baskets of those who brought them, the
> bystanders giving them money, for their 'wares'. Near the
> pillory were two stands for hackney coaches, under these
> there was a quantity of hay, dung and urine trampled into
> a mass by the feet of the horses. This was collected,
> soaked in the mud in the kennels and then handed to the
> women to pelt the men in the pillory, each of whom with
> her hands full of this stuff waited till one of the miserable
> wretches came close to her as she stood at the edge of the
> platform, to discharge the offensive matter at his face, and
> as the number of these vile women was considerable there
> was no intermission.

Despite the presence of the officers, a semblance of order could not always be maintained, and on occasion:

> The shouting of the mob exhilarated the pelters, and induced many who came as spectators to join in the mischief, and when the blackguardism had reached its height, it was no longer in the power of the constables to stay it, every sort of missile was thrown. A dead cat was a treat, a live one a still greater treat, and woe to the poor animal who fell into the hands of the miscreant. It was, however, soon killed and its carcase thrown about as long as any one could get hold of it. Stones and other hard substances frequently rebounded from the boards of the pillory and mingled the blood of the criminal with the mud which disfigured him, when struck by a stone or a penny piece many of which were thrown.[15]

The inability of the authorities to control this punishment, with the possibility either that the convict would be praised rather than punished or that standing on the pillory could be tantamount to a death sentence, greatly worried nineteenth-century observers. But in the wake of the French Revolution, perhaps their greatest worry was that the crowd would progress from punishment to uprising: 'Those whom you suffer to riot on the side of the laws may soon learn to oppose them with similar outrages'.[16] The use of the pillory was restricted to the punishment of perjury in 1816 and was finally abolished altogether in 1837.[17]

The Great Escape

From the passage of the Transportation Act in 1718 until the outbreak of the American Revolution, approximately 200 men, women and children were sentenced each year at the Old Bailey to be transported across the seas. For most this meant transportation to the colonies of North America to be sold for indentured labour for 7 or 14 years or for life. To return from transportation was to invite a sentence of death. As a form of punishment,

transportation provided a much needed labour force for colonies
such as Virginia and Maryland at the same time as it removed
undesirables from the streets of London. It also ensured that the
number of bodies hanging from the triple tree at Tyburn remained
at an acceptable level. But the outbreak of war in 1776 abruptly
cut off this convenient solution to the punishment of offenders. As
the war dragged on and the number of convicts held in Newgate
and on the 'hulks' floating at anchor on the Thames grew ever
larger, desperate measures were considered.

Thomas Limpus spent the summer of 1783 in the unhealthy
and overcrowded cells of Newgate Prison. He was blessed
with a remarkable constitution and, at the age of 20, had
already survived three years of imprisonment and a voyage
that had killed the majority of his fellows. Almost a year
earlier Limpus was convicted of stealing a cambric
handkerchief worth 10d and 'sentenced to be transported as
soon as conveniently might be, to some of his Majesty's
colonies and plantations in Africa, for the term of seven
years'. In a desperate attempt to find an alternative to
transporting felons to North America, the slave factories of
West Africa had been selected. At his later trial for
returning from transportation, Limpus explained how he
was unceremoniously landed at Gorée, on the coast of
modern Senegal, in the midst of an ongoing war between
the British and the French:

> I was landed with nineteen more. The soldiers were drawn
> up in a circle on the parade. The lieutenant of the island
> ordered us all into the middle of it, and told us we were
> all free men, and that we were to do the best we could, for
> he had no victuals. There was a ship lay in the bay; I went
> on shore several times and did work for the governor. I
> remained there till the time I came home.[18]

Gorée was the centre of the West African slave trade and
throughout the seventeenth and eighteenth centuries

witnessed both the brutal everyday horrors of slavery and
constant internecine fighting between colonial powers keen
to use the site as a base from which to dominate the trade.
To this day the 'house of slaves' at Gorée stands bitter
testimony to the millions of black Africans chained and
whipped and enslaved in the service of European expansion.
For the authorities in London, the idea of sending convicted
felons into servitude at Gorée must have appeared to possess
an ironic symmetry. But for the men sent to Africa it was
tantamount to a death sentence, with the vast majority
dying from disease and malnutrition. Thomas Limpus was
one of the few to survive and in the year after his arrival,
worked his passage back to Britain where he was once again
arrested on the streets of London. In a remarkable story of
crime and retribution, he was later clandestinely transported
to North America and then to Honduras, before finally
sailing to Australia as part of the First Fleet.

The importance of the summer he spent in Newgate
following his return from Gorée, however, lay in the seeds
of fear and desperation he sowed in the minds of his
fellow prisoners. Many of Limpus's wardmates had been
sentenced to transportation and that summer were
marched in irons down to the docks and transferred to a
ship in preparation for their journey. No one, however,
could assure them of their final destination. Having heard
Limpus's tale, many felt certain they were simply being
sent to their deaths. Certainly Charles Keeling, who was
sentenced to transportation for stealing a pair of pistols,
and his brother John, a sailor transported for stealing a
sword, worried that they were destined for Africa. Charles
brought up the possibility by way of mitigation at his later
trial for returning from transportation: 'Some of the men
informed us that our destination was for Africa; if they
could not dispose of us in America, they were to dispose
of us in Africa'.[19]

Figure 5.04 Convicts from Newgate being taken to Blackfriars for Transportation (c. 1760). Credit: Guildhall Library, City of London

In dribs and drabs over the course of that July and August, groups of five and six prisoners were delivered up in chains to the tender mercies of Thomas Bradbury, the mate of the *Swift*, moored in the Thames at Blackwall. It was put out in the papers that the *Swift* was bound for Halifax in Canada, where many loyalists and freed slaves, refugees from the American Revolution, were attempting to create a new colony, but this was not, in fact, true. The ship's real destination was Baltimore, Maryland, where it was hoped that a few last shiploads of convicts could be offloaded on an uncooperative United States. The plan was that the ship would claim to be short of supplies and in need of temporary shelter and that the prisoners would be sold as indentured servants to unsuspecting or complicit Americans. To maintain the subterfuge, and to ensure that the American authorities remained oblivious to the plan, the ship, which had up to then been called the *George*, was renamed the *Swift*.[20] The prisoners, however, were not told of the plan and their fear and uncertainty grew as the date of their departure approached.

On 16 August, the *Swift* left Blackwall:

> The next day down to the Galleons Reach, where we
> received the remainder on board from the ship *Censor* (a
> prison hulk). We left the Downs the 28th of August.

Under the command of Thomas Pamp and with a crew of
18, the ship sailed with 143 prisoners carefully secured
below decks, their legs in irons. Most of the prisoners were
landsmen and that first night, as the swells of the channel
rocked the vessel to a new and frightening rhythm, the fear
of the sea must have combined with a fear of Africa, with its
well-earned reputation as a killing field for Europeans. John
Harrower, who had made the same Atlantic crossing as an
indentured servant a few years earlier, described his
experience of being below decks on the first night at sea:

> I really think there was the oddest scene between decks
> that ever I heard or seen. There was some sleeping, some
> spewing, some pissing, some shitting, some farting, some
> fighting, some damning, some blasting their legs and
> thighs, some their liver, lungs, lights and eyes. And for to
> make the scene the odder, some cursed father, mother,
> sister, and brother.[21]

Unlike the indentured servants with whom Harrower
shared his earlier voyage, the men on the *Swift* were both
below decks and in irons. You could not, however, keep people
below forever. Good health and the running of the ship
demanded that the prisoners be allowed some exercise. They
also needed to wash the dirt of Newgate and the hulks from
their clothes and skin. And although the leg irons seemed to
promise security against a mutiny, they did not hold the
prisoners for long. On the evening of the 28th a group of men
wrote to the captain asking that he remove their leg irons and
threatening to take them off themselves when he refused.
According to Thomas Bradbury, 'They took them off
themselves with as much ease as if they had not any on.'

On the 29th, as the *Swift* sailed along the channel, the captain must have thought that the danger of a mutiny by the prisoners had passed since he allowed the men to come up on deck in groups, 'sometimes three messes, containing six in a mess, they were in irons'. Captain Pamp rationed out glasses of rum and began the arduous task of settling a frightened ship into the routines of a long transatlantic voyage.

But Pamp had miscalculated the mood of the prisoners. The prospect of being transported to Africa had given them a new determination. 'The reason for our first opposition' was 'reluctance that we were to go to Africa'. At ten in the morning, and still within sight of land, the prisoners 'rushed' the crew. David Hart, who was later accused of being a ringleader, explained what happened next:

> After I had done washing myself, I went down. The captain had just given me a glass of rum, and five or six of the convicts came down, who came from the *Censor*, and they said, is not your name Hart, and I said, yes. They insisted on me to help them to get their liberty, and that if I did not I was a coward.

The mate recalled that the:

> Captain was calling them up to give them a dram, those that were sick. And when the Captain gave Hart that dram, he bid him go below, and we did not know how to avoid it, but however he returned once or twice, and with the rest that were behind him, together made the rush.

John Kellan recollected that the captain:

> Permitted us to come upon deck in a great number, and seeing so fair an opportunity many of us were desirous of taking the ship. A man stood behind me and said, says he, if you do not endeavour to secure your liberty, I will knock you down.

The captain's cabin was soon taken: 'There were many in the cabin before me, seven or eight, some were with Mr

Bradbury, the mate, in his cabin'. With the captain and his mate secured, the ship was theirs.

Some of the men who took the *Swift* that day were hardened thieves. David Hart, for instance, had been tried for larceny on four occasions in the preceding three years. His *modus operandi* was to steal packages of goods from errand boys and coaches. On two occasions he was acquitted, and on a third committed to six months' imprisonment. His luck finally ran out in April 1783 when he was sentenced to transportation.[22] Thomas Millington was also a substantial thief; he was convicted of stealing 'four hundred and eight yards of muslin, and one hundred yards of muslin for handkerchiefs, and two linen wrappers', worth in total over £137. But most had committed much more petty crimes and were hapless victims of a system they were unable to navigate. Joseph Pentecross was transported for stealing the mattress from the room he shared with his lover. Charles Thomas received the same sentence for stealing a wooden tub full of butter, worth the princely sum of 5s.

Having secured the ship, the men then had to decide what to do next. Some were for robbing the captain and raping the female passengers and prisoners. Others were more controlled. John Kellan, or Keeling, was one of the few men on board with experience at sea. He seems to have quickly taken command. In his recollection:

> I took up a blunderbuss that laid by, and the keys of the bureau were there, and I threatened to shoot a man that was going to take the keys, and I immediately locked the bureau, and delivered the keys to the captain.

Several of the escaped prisoners were in favour of raping a passenger, Mrs Warwickshall, but Kellan stood in their way. Even Thomas Bradbury, the mate, had to admit, 'He protected her from the insult, for they would have behaved rudely to her, if it had not been for some of them that were there'. As for Captain Pamp, he seems to have been less concerned about Mrs Warwickshall than about his own position. His first action was to draw 'up a memorial in order to clear himself from any mean suspicion that might arise in the breast of his owner'. The captain's version did not meet with universal approval, and Kellan was asked to revise it. In the end, 'there were two or three of these papers drawn out', either because 'there was some word objected to' or else because the original was blotted with ink stains. John Kellan's name was the first on the list of signatures. Later in court he also claimed to have 'expressed my sorrow to the captain, at being at this time forced to get my liberty'.

With most of the crew locked below decks, the new masters of the ship had to bring it safely into harbour. By this time the *Swift* was off the south coast between Dungeness and Rye. According to Thomas Bradbury:

> After they had secured us, they bore away, and went a
> little to the east of Dungeness, between that and Rye.
> They let go the anchor and hoisted the boats out and went
> on shore. As many as could cleverly get into the boats got
> on shore, with the arms along with them. That was on the
> 29th, the same day they made the rush. It was six o'clock
> in the evening that they went on shore.

Samuel Read later claimed he was forced to escape: 'It was not my intent to come on board the boat, but being forced by the person that had the command of the vessel, as I had been at sea before, he insisted'. John White was also a reluctant escapee. He was quietly minding his own business below decks when 'a man came down to me, and said, Jack the ship is taken'. White's only reply was: 'I am sorry for it, I have no friends in England'. In total, 48 men escaped that evening.

In the meantime, the *Swift*, its crew secured below decks and the rest of the prisoners rapidly consuming the stores of rum, was in mortal danger on a lee shore. It was not until past midnight that the crew regained control:

> We told them what danger we were in, and they let the
> sailors up about half past three. They were many of them
> drunk, and went down below, and we drove the others
> down, and secured them there. The next morning we fell
> in with the *Perseverance* frigate, which conveyed us into
> Portsmouth.

The escaped prisoners landed on the coast road between the old port of Rye and the small village of Lydd. They soon broke up into small groups and spread across the Kent countryside. Some seem to have quickly lost enthusiasm for the venture, while others made rapid strides to ensure they would escape recapture. One group headed west towards Tunbridge Wells, while others took the road north through the villages of Snargate and Snave, towards Ashford and the road to London. They had perhaps a day before news of their escape spread through southern England and they needed to find a place of safety.

The coast they landed on was notorious for smuggling. In the same year of 1783, the Commission of the Excise estimated that 900 gallons of brandy and geneva were smuggled through Kent and Sussex every single day. It was a hugely profitable trade that relied on absolute secrecy and it occasionally resulted in acts of brutal violence. Just a few years earlier this same coast had witnessed the murder of two men, an excise officer and an informer, a crime that shocked the nation. They were tortured for days before being finally killed, their bodies thrown down a well. As a result the coasts of Kent and Sussex were perhaps the most carefully policed region in the country, but also a place where an escaped convict might hope to find a sympathetic hearing from people with no love for the authorities.[23]

Their first night on shore, the evening of the 29th, passed uneventfully, as the men found what shelter they could. Some used this time to put real distance between themselves and the shore. Within 48 hours, by the 31st when news of the escape finally reached the towns of Ashford and Rye, at least a few of the men were already in London. Abraham Hyam, who had stood trial the previous April for stealing five gowns, a shift and cloak from Elizabeth Nathan, and who had been a leading figure in the 'rush', had already reached the capital, 80 miles from their landfall. He was captured 'at a private house in Still Alley, near Devonshire Square'. Others had made less progress.

David Hart and Charles Keeling had journeyed less than 'half a dozen miles' by the same date. On that Sunday afternoon David Hindes, a local butcher, saw them on the road and became suspicious: 'I thought he and his mate were bad, and about half an hour after I had taken them up, we heard they were transports'. Hart claimed that he 'meant to go to town and surrender', while his partner, Charles Keeling, made no resistance and returned to custody 'very quietly'.

A couple of miles away, at Sandhurst, John Kellan and David Kilpack were also arrested around the same time. Kellan and Kilpack gave themselves up without a fight. At the later trials for returning from transportation, the judge repeatedly asked for an account of the prisoners' behaviour on arrest. Many of the escapees had lost the will to resist:

Question.   Did he make any resistance?

A.   Not in the least.

Q.   Surrendered himself quietly?

A.   Very much indeed sir, and very civilly.

John White, arrested that same day, 'behaved as well as any person could in his unhappy situation. He did not make the least resistance in the world'. And Thomas Bryant 'surrendered peaceably and quietly'.

31 August was a Sunday and concerted attempts to recapture the men only got properly underway on Monday.

At Hawkhurst, the home of a notorious smuggling gang in the 1730s and 1740s, still just a few miles from the coast, four men were captured. George Nash, Joseph Pentecross, Michael Gaffney and Andrew Dickson were confronted by Richard Taylor, who had helped to capture John White on the preceding evening. Taylor was the local innkeeper and clearly felt mixed emotions about his role in the recapture of the men. He repeatedly emphasised at the later trials the passivity and civility of the men when arrested: 'They stopped immediately, and gave themselves up, and confessed before the justice, that they were such people'. Taylor went on to confide to the court that, 'They behaved as well as could be expected from men in their unhappy situation, and I am very sorry for them'.

Nathaniel Collier and William Combes took the Canterbury Road north, but only travelled 30 miles before they too were arrested. They were surrounded by a group of men and quietly gave up their 'clubs and bludgeons'. Richard Partridge, John Birch and John Welch had struck out northwest and were captured at Tunbridge Wells. In total, 18 men were recaptured on that single Monday and all but four of them gave themselves up without a fight.

The few prisoners who did put up a fight were also the ones who made the most rapid progress towards London. Christopher Trusty had robbed a coach the previous spring – pistol in hand, a yellow scarf covering his face, and with the very real threat of 'I will blow your brains out' on his lips. He was also one of the most forward participants in the 'rush': 'He was the first that went into the cabin, and stole the Captain's buckles out of his shoes'. By Monday 1 September he was already holed up with two women in a private house in Sun Court, off Grub Street. Four marshals, getting wind of his location, descended on his hiding place and arrested him.

Three others had also reached London. William Matthews, Charles Thomas (alias Godby) and Thomas

Millington were hiding out in the house of the now dead
John Mills in Onslow Street, Saffron Hill – a poor and
violent corner of North London. Mills had been executed
the preceding spring for using a knife to slit open the nose
of Thomas Brazier in a vicious running street battle.[24] With
two other constables, Jonathan Redgrave tracked them
down. In this instance, the men were not taken easily:

> I am a constable belonging to St James's Clerkenwell. On
> the 1st of September we received an information that
> William Matthews with two others were at a house in
> Onslow Street. I and William Seasons and Thomas Isaacs
> went to this house, and we were met by a couple of
> women who endeavoured to prevent our going up.
> However, we got past them and when we entered the room
> Matthews stepped towards the bedstead with a poker in
> his hand. The others were armed, one with a large iron fire
> shovel, and the other with a large knife. I told the
> prisoner, knowing him perfectly (though I knew them all
> three), that it would be impossible to escape, but they
> might do us some mischief. Matthews, with the others,
> made a reply that they would sooner die than be taken.
> Matthews then struck Seasons on the head with a poker,
> which cut his head very much. He did not cut me.
> Seasons immediately closed on him, and they fell down
> on the bed together. Mr Isaacs and I were engaged with
> the other two men and two or three women, who fought as
> well as they could, and as much as the men. We had three
> cutlasses, and very happy it was for us that we had. The
> other two wounded me here on the head and cut me in the
> breast. At the same time one of the women struck me on
> the back of the head and stunned me. When I came to
> myself I found the blood running down. They said they
> were only sorry they had not cutlasses, for if they had we
> never should have gone away without murder.

Thomas Isaacs took up the story:

> I was at the house in Onslow Street, Saffron Hill. When
> we entered the room I observed Matthews with two
> others. He immediately seized a poker, and with very bad

> words, said that sooner than be taken they would lose
> their lives.
> I was beat and bruised over the head and shoulders by
> the women. Then we overpowered the prisoners and
> handcuffed them, and took them before a magistrate.

Some others had more luck or more sense. William Busby remained free for at least one day longer and was only discovered hiding in a ditch. He would not have been found 'if it had not been for a little dog'. William Blatherham and Francis Burke remained at large for two more weeks, and were only arrested on 15 September, while Charles Stoke kept out of harm's way three more weeks until 7 October and Thomas Wilson two weeks beyond that. He was arrested on 22 October. In total 39 of the 48 escapees were eventually arrested and 26 were once again tried for their lives at the Old Bailey. Most of the cases were heard at the September sessions and in the first instance, all the returned transportees were sentenced to hang. In the way of eighteenth-century justice, however, only seven were eventually executed and the rest were pardoned on condition of being transported once again. The broken spirit of the men who appeared at the bar, victims of imperial politics as much as anything else, is perhaps best summed up by Thomas Millington, who had fought for his freedom with the constables in Onslow Street. When asked to provide a defence, he said, 'I have nothing to say; my heart is quite broke'.

The recapture and retrial of the men did not, however, solve Britain's problems with transportation. The *Swift* was rapidly restocked with supplies of both food and prisoners and once again set out for Maryland, making landfall at Baltimore on Christmas Eve 1783. Captain Pamp informed the authorities that a shortage of supplies had prevented him from completing his fictitious journey to Halifax and he set about selling the prisoners' indentures as servants to local

landowners. Contractors taking transportees across the
Atlantic made their profit by retailing the prisoners' labour,
so their sale was crucial to the business success of the voyage.
In the end, it took months, until spring, to offload all but the
last half dozen men. As a result, and by every measure, the
voyage proved a disaster.[25]

Only one more attempt was made to send convicted
felons to North America. In April of 1784, the *Mercury* set
off with 179 prisoners with the intention of again selling
them as indentured servants to the planters of Virginia and
Maryland. Once again, however, there was a mutiny, this
time off the coast of the Scilly Isles and at least 108
prisoners, including Thomas Limpus, escaped. Most were
quickly recaptured and the *Mercury* sent on its way, but this
time the newly independent United States resolutely refused
permission for the convicts to land. The *Mercury* sailed on to
the recently established colony at Honduras, where the ship
received an equally unwelcoming reception – the settlers
fearing that accepting transportees 'would damage the credit
and character of the colony'.[26] In the end, in desperation,
Britain determined to create a new prison colony in
Australia. Among the 757 prisoners who formed the 'First
Fleet' in 1787, 10 had sailed on the *Swift* and a further 67
on the *Mercury*, and one, William Blatherhorn, had
participated in both mutinies.

Throughout the 1780s British judicial policy was in crisis.
A crime wave, crowded gaols and unhealthy 'hulks'
combined to put ever greater pressure on the courts and
judges. The chaos also had the effect of giving new
opportunities to those who found themselves in the none
too gentle embrace of the criminal justice system. At the
sessions at which the majority of the *Swift* mutineers were
tried, men (like Thomas Limpus) who had earlier been
sentenced to be transported either to Africa or the East
Indies were called before the bar. Most were offered the

opportunity of having their sentence commuted to transportation to America. Of the 10 men offered the opportunity to change their sentence, only one accepted. The rest calmly declared, in the words of Peter Airey, 'He would rather go to Africa'. In the certain knowledge that Britain no longer had any way of sending them there, these men confidently mocked Britain's imperial ambitions.[27]

To be Devoured by Savages

The 1780s witnessed a profound renegotiation of power in the courtroom. After the near anarchy of the Gordon riots and with the growing use of defence counsel and the chaos of the prisons and hulks caused by the disruption to transportation, the balance of power tipped significantly in the direction of the men and women who stood trial at the bar. To the discomfort of the judiciary, many defendants became increasingly bold in their attempts to manipulate the procedures of the court.

At the end of the first quarter of the nineteenth century, Francis Place could still recall the women in the 1780s who lived in Rosemary Lane, Wapping and Limehouse – the rough neighbourhoods around the docks in the East End:

> When I was an apprentice I went frequently among these girls and at that time spent many evenings at the dirty public houses frequented by them. At that time they wore long quartered shoes and large buckles. Many at that time wore no stays, their gowns were low round the neck and open in front. Those who wore handkerchiefs had theirs always open in front to expose their breasts. This was a fashion which the best dressed among them followed, but numbers wore no handkerchiefs at all in warm weather and the breasts of many hung down in a most disgusting manner. Their hair among the generality was straight and 'swung in rat tails' over their eyes and it was filled with lice. Drunkenness was common to them all, and at all

times when the means of drunkenness could be found,
fighting among themselves as well as with the men was
common and black eyes might be seen in a great many.[28]

Sarah Cowden, Sarah Storer and Martha Cutler inhabited
this world of drunkenness and violence. But in their case,
along with the ability to hold their gin, came an ability to
hold their own. Eventually they would challenge the very
authority of the Old Bailey itself.

As the three sat out together late on a Saturday night in
February 1788, Sarah Storer saw a man she knew going past
the entrance to Gun Court, just north of the river in
Wapping and called out his name – 'Solomons'. When he
turned to see who had called him, she rushed up and
according to Henry Solomons' later evidence:

> Took off my hat, and ran indoors with it. I said let me go
> about my business. Then there were two or three of them.
> Cowden was one of them. They made very bad
> expressions, which I would not choose to mention, and
> bid me go in and fetch my hat, and they immediately
> came round me and pushed me into the passage. Storer
> was in the parlour, and said, here is the hat, come in.
> Upon that, I went in. Cowden and Cutler immediately
> followed me in; they were in as soon as I. All three of
> them together threw me down upon the bed. It was a
> small room that would not hold above five or six when the
> bed was let down. Cowden laid upon me; Storer held my
> mouth fast; Cutler stood with her back against the door.
> Cowden took out of my pocket fourteen guineas and some
> silver, which was more than ten shillings. Storer took it
> from Cowden and gave it to Cutler, and she ran out with
> it. Cowden gave me my hat, and said, I might go about my
> business.

Unfortunately for the three women, Benjamin Ealing
who lived two doors down at No. 3 Gun Court, observed
the whole scene with vengeful eyes through the casement
window. He had sworn a warrant against Storer and Cutler

earlier that evening and was still smarting from the experience:

> I had taken up Cutler and Storer that night about seven
> o'clock, for abusing me. Storer had cut my hand with a
> knife, and Cutler had taken up a poker and struck me over
> the head, and cut my hat, but they were discharged, and
> were home again before eight o'clock.

At the Old Bailey he happily confirmed Solomons' evidence:

> I peeped into the room, it was a casement, and it was not
> quite shut. I saw Henry Solomons lying on the bed,
> struggling very much. I saw Cowden lying upon him.
> Storer had her hand on his mouth, and Cutler stood with
> her backside against the door. I sent my wife to call the
> watchman, but before the watchman came, Mr Solomons
> came out, and said, I am robbed, I am robbed.

At this juncture Martha Cutler made a rapid escape, but Storer and Cowden were arrested by Solomons, Ealing and John Addis and William Withering, two watchmen brought to the scene by Ealing's wife. Storer and Cowden were searched, but the 14 guineas Solomons claimed to have lost could not be located. Within half an hour, Martha Cutler was also under arrest and confined in the watchhouse, but again the money could not be found.

Two and a half weeks later all three stood trial together, charged with 'highway robbery'. Martha Cutler and Sarah Storer took the lead in cross-examining the witnesses produced against them. They questioned why Solomons was in the neighbourhood at all and implied that he had sought out their small and cramped room in search of sex. And Ealing's animosity and history of prosecution against them was highlighted. At the end of the trial, the defendants were offered the opportunity to present their defence. Sarah Cowden proclaimed her complete innocence, while

Cutler and Storer painted the prosecution as motivated by revenge visited on them by Benjamin Ealing in retribution for their earlier encounter. None of this washed with the court or the jury and all three were found guilty and sentenced to hang.

They were not, however, destined to die at the end of a rope. Royal pardons would be offered to all three, 'on condition of being transported for life'. By the spring of 1789 this meant a journey to the far side of the world, Australia and Botany Bay. With good luck this was a journey of almost a year, to an almost completely unknown continent. For many of the convicts, it must have seemed that they were being executed in a new and novel way. For all of them, there could have been little hope that they would ever see home again. Sarah Cowden, Martha Cutler and Sarah Storer were not going to be exiled in this way without a fight.

The first news of the progress of the settlement in Australia reached London in the last week of March 1789 and throughout April the newspapers were full of accounts of the landing at Botany Bay and the problems experienced by the new colony. The Royal Circus at St George's Fields put on a dance, staged just before the trick horsemanship, entitled 'The New Hollanders', representing every detail of the landing. But news of the real conditions in the colony was probably conveyed to the cells of Newgate by more direct means.[29] Storer, Cowden and Cutler had all lived on the docks and at least one of their fellow prisoners, Eleanor Kirvan, ran a bumboat, providing credit and comfort to returning seamen. Through friends and acquaintances they would have quickly heard stories of reduced rations and of the 'shy and ferocious' inhabitants who had reputedly already murdered several of the convicts.[30]

At the end of the April sessions, six weeks after Cowden, Storer and Cutler were convicted and sentenced to hang, they were among the 23 women brought before the bar at the Old Bailey and addressed by John William Rose, the presiding judge (who had also presided over the trial of Storer, Cowden and Cutler). All the women standing at the bar that day must have received news of their pardon on condition of 'transportation beyond the seas' as a mixed blessing. Sixteen 'accepted the conditions mentioned in his Majesty's pardon', but a further seven, including Cowden, Cutler and Storer, simply refused. Sarah Cowden was the first to speak:

> No, I will die by the laws of my country; I am innocent, and so is Sarah Storer. The people that had the money for which I was tried, are now at their liberty, therefore I will die by the laws of my country before ever I will go abroad for my life.

Next came Martha Cutler: 'Before I will go abroad for my natural life, I will sooner die'. And then Sarah Storer: 'I will not accept it. I am innocent.' In quick succession, four more women addressed the court. Sarah Mills, another East End woman convicted of stealing a watch from a sex-starved drunk in an alley behind an alehouse off Ratcliff Highway, declared, 'I will go to my former sentence. I had not power to speak on my trial'. And she concluded, 'I would rather die than go out of my own country to be devoured by savages'.

Mary Burgess, who had been in prison for over a year and a half, and who was convicted of stealing almost £4 worth of household goods from James Detheridge, replied in a similar vein:

> I had rather go to my former sentence. I had rather die than leave my child and husband behind me. I am very willing to die; I will die before I will leave my poor child in a strange place. I am satisfied I am a dying woman, and I will go to my former sentence. I will die an innocent death; I beg pardon for making so free.

By this time Judge Rose was growing increasingly restive.

> It is my duty to tell you if you refuse the pardon now, it
> will be too late ever to expect it afterwards. Consider
> what you are about. It is my duty to give you that notice,
> you certainly will be ordered immediately for execution.

Burgess's reply was swift and certain: 'Well, I am very glad
to hear it. I do not care how soon'.

Next came Jane Tyler and Eleanor Kirvan, who had both
appeared at the same sessions two years previously and had
spent the intervening years in Newgate. When addressed by
the court, Tyler said: 'My Lord, I will not accept it. I will go
to my former sentence. I will die first. I think I have suffered
hard enough to be in gaol three years for what I have done.'
And Eleanor Kirvan said:

> I hope this honorable court, or any of the gentlemen in
> company, will not object to what I shall say. I have lain in
> prison three years. I do not intend to object to my
> sentence, but I am not in a situation to go abroad; if I was
> I would go. The crime deserved death, it is an injury to
> the community, but I never was guilty of it. I have two
> small children. I have no objection to confinement for life,
> for I cannot live long.

At this point the judge tried to reason with the prisoners:

> If you do not accept it now I have no power. After you
> have accepted it you may apply further for mitigation, but
> if you do not accept of these terms, you stand as a person
> condemned to suffer death, and will be in the situation of
> those who are so condemned, and will certainly be
> ordered for execution, and it will be too late to recall your
> opinion. I recommend you to accept of that favour.

The 'Second Fleet' for Australia was already in preparation
and it is clear that part of the motivation behind this series of
refusals was a calculated and desperate hope that they could
avoid punishment altogether. At the very least, if they could

delay the process for just one or two sessions, there was every possibility that transportation as a punishment would be abandoned in light of the unpromising news trickling in from New South Wales. But their actions must also be seen as part of a more subtle power play between defendants and the court. Eleanor Kirvan had already escaped death once by claiming her 'belly'. After her trial in 1786 for forging a dead sailor's will in an attempt to collect his wages, she 'pleaded that she was with child; upon which a jury of matrons was empanelled, who withdrew with the prisoner, and returned with a verdict, that she was with quick child'. Her sentence 'was accordingly respited'. At a time when the court was anxious both to clear Newgate of prisoners and to avoid hanging too many of them in case the bloodbath led to public disorder; at a time, just a few years after the Gordon riots, when the uneasy relationship between defendants and the court seemed most vulnerable, women such as Cowden, Storer and Cutler represented a powerful threat to judicial authority. The last thing the court could afford was the sight of a large number of young women (Cowden was only 21) delivering speeches and dying 'game' before a massed London audience.

Transportation to Australia seemed to many lower class Londoners a punishment too far; an abnegation of the rights of true born Englishmen and a show of principled resistance would have rapidly garnered broader support. The spring and summer of 1789 witnessed the mutiny on the *Bounty*, the beginnings of the French Revolution and the final ratification of the Constitution of the United States. Rebellion was in the air in London as much as in Paris or on the South Seas. It was not the moment to provide a public platform, even if it was a scaffold, for the self-confident and pugnacious women of Limehouse and Wapping.

Having sent the women away, Judge Rose called them back at the end of the sessions. He was clearly frustrated by

their refusal to accept transportation and once again tried
both the offer of hope of mitigation, and the threat of
immediate execution:

> I find there are several of you who have refused his
> majesty's most gracious pardon on the present occasion.
> You have been convicted of very heinous offences, and
> you seem to forget that the king, in his great goodness has
> saved your lives; having saved your lives, your not being
> inclined to accept that pardon arises from a hope that you
> shall not be sent off so soon as the other prisoners. I think
> it my duty, who have not the power to alter the sentence at
> all, to tell you that this sort of conduct will be considered
> as an aggravation of your offences; and if you have any
> hopes that your sentence will be altered, you had much
> better accept of the king's pardon now, and try what
> interest you have to get that sentence mitigated; but if you
> go from the bar now, you will remain under sentence of
> death; and you may depend upon it, that you will suffer
> death with the first culprits, at the next execution. I hope
> you will take the advice of the court, and accept the
> pardon, if not it will certainly be too late hereafter.

But his pleas fell on self-confident ears. Burgess replied: 'I
am satisfied with what I hear about Australia. I will suffer
death before ever I will go abroad with them. I am very well
satisfied with the death that was ordered for me.' One after
the other, all seven women refused.

The court ordered them to 'be confined in separate cells
and fed on bread and water'. At first sight, the women had
won the reprieve they desired. Unfortunately, the 'Second
Fleet' had still not sailed when they were brought to the bar
again six weeks later on 9 June. The cells of Newgate were
unhealthy places and a diet of bread and water did not help.
Mary Burgess was too ill to appear and Eleanor Kirvan
disappears from the records, probably dead of gaol fever. In
the interval between the sessions, more detailed and official
accounts of the foundation of the new colony had reached a
wider public and it is possible that the women came to

believe that transportation need not be a certain sentence of death after all. Regardless of their motives, when at the end of the sessions the royal pardon was read out once more, one after another the women agreed to its conditions. Jane Tyler, 'Yes, I will'; Martha Cutler, 'Why, I must'; Sarah Mills, 'Yes'; Mary Burgess, 'I am sorry for the trouble I gave the court'.

That is, all except Sarah Cowden and Sarah Storer. Cowden's response was to bargain with her life:

> I will tell you what – I am willing to accept of whatever sentence the king passes upon me, but Sarah Storer is innocent. I would not care whatever sentence I went through, I will accept it if that woman's sentence is mitigated.

The judge was having none of it:

> Sarah Cowden, the only question you have to answer respects yourself. The king, after you had justly forfeited your life to the laws of your country, has been graciously pleased to extend his mercy to you, and to spare that life which has been so forfeited; but his majesty has thought fit to annex a condition to his pardon. You therefore have nothing to do with the case of any other person but yourself; and you are to choose, whether you will accept of the mercy of your sovereign, and preserve that life which he has put into your power to save, or whether you choose to be remanded to immediate execution?

Her answer did not please him: 'I will accept of my sentence willingly, if this woman's sentence is mitigated'.

In the argument with the judge that followed, Cowden more than held her own:

Judge.	Are you, or are you not willing to accept of your life on the condition your sovereign has offered?
Cowden.	I will never accept of it without this woman's sentence is mitigated.
Judge.	Remove all the women from the bar but Sarah Cowden.

Cowden.	Gentlemen, I hope you will excuse me for being so bold to speak in the court, but this woman is as innocent as a child unborn. She happened to come into the place where this robbery was done, she asked for the loan of a pair of bellows, and she was cast for death. And after being cast for death, I think to be cast for life is very hard. If this woman's sentence is not mitigated I will freely die with her. I am but a young girl, I am but one and twenty years of age.
Judge.	You will attend to this; the government of the country will not suffer the mercy of the king to be trifled with; if you continue to refuse his majesty's pardon, I think it right to tell you your fate, and also that of your companion, for whom you seem so much interested. I have offered the king's pardon to you; if you refuse it, I shall order you to be remanded; and you must prepare to die the day following; you shall be executed the day following.
Cowden.	I hope I shall have more mercy shown me than ever I had at this bar.
Judge.	If you are sufficiently prepared to die on Thursday next, the court will give orders accordingly?
Cowden.	That I am.
Judge.	Let her stand committed to the cells, and let the sheriffs prepare for an execution on Thursday morning. Take her away.

At this point, William Garrow intervened. He had had a good sessions and was clearly on a roll. He had represented 14 men accused of everything from perjury to murder. Nine out of the 14 had been declared innocent and walked free from the court and of the five found guilty, only one was sentenced to death. He volunteered to go and speak to Cowden and convince her of her mistake and reluctantly Judge Rose agreed.

While Garrow was trying to reason with Cowden, Judge Rose turned his attention to Sarah Storer. After Sarah Cowden had done so much to protest Storer's innocence, she could do no less than refuse: 'No, I will not'. But then her will broke:

Judge:	These women have done rashly, I meant in mercy to them to have given them further time, that by the death of one obstinate offender, sufficient warning might have been given to the rest. But you have voluntarily desired to be brought into court, for the purpose of insulting the court?
Storer:	I am willing to accept of it though I am innocent; I am willing to accept of it with all the felicity in life.

With one last show of passion, however, she added: 'I am willing to go, but not for my life, I never will'. Ignoring her caveat, the judge simply filled out the order and intoned to all the prisoners who had accepted the pardon: 'The court orders and adjudges you to be transported for your natural lives'.

By this time Garrow had convinced Cowden to change her mind, but he was then confronted with the necessity of begging Judge Rose to hear her speak one last time:

Garrow.	When I appeal to the court, and observe that the admonition your lordship has given has had that effect, which your lordship's admonitions seldom fail to produce, I humbly conceive your lordship will permit that unfortunate woman to be brought in once more.
Judge.	It is only subjecting the king's mercy to insult, to suffer her to be brought up again.
Garrow.	My lord, I shall have no objection to go into the gaol with her.
Judge.	I do not think that the king's mercy should go a begging, or be subjected to insult. The justice of

	the country is concerned, that the unhappy persons, who have forfeited their lives, should be made examples of; but I can show no indulgence to those who treat the mercy of the king with contempt, no application can be heard, that does not come from the prisoner, and an application, even coming from the prisoner, must be now received with great doubt.
Garrow.	I only ask the court, to consider the order not to be irrevocable.
Judge.	As to me it is irrevocable; I shall order the execution, unless the king otherwise directs; and the sheriffs will prepare accordingly.
Garrow.	My lord, I do not attend your lordship, nor address myself to the court, in the character of a counsel, but as a very humble supplicant, for a very miserable wretch, who desires now, having seen the folly of her behaviour, humbly to entreat that she may be permitted to accept that pardon of his majesty, which she has dared contumaciously to refuse.

Finally, Judge Rose agreed, and 'Sarah Cowden was brought in once more'. Perhaps because her friend, Sarah Storer, had finally submitted to her sentence, or perhaps because William Garrow was as eloquent outside the courtroom as within, Cowden finally agreed:

Judge.	Sarah Cowden, you stand attainted of felony; his majesty has been graciously pleased, to extend his royal mercy to you, on condition of your being transported for life, are you willing to accept his majesty's mercy on that condition?
Cowden.	Yes sir, I am.

For Sarah Cowden, however, the story was not yet finished. At least two of the 'refusers' were put aboard the *Lady Juliana*, which was scheduled to leave British waters with 226 female convicts on 29 July. While at anchor in Portsmouth harbour on the night of the 28th, four of the female convicts quietly escaped. Among them were Sarah Cowden and Mary Burgess. John Nicol, the ship's steward, later recounted the incident:

> Others did all in their power to make their escape. These were such as had left their associates in rapine on shore, and were hardened to every feeling but the abandoned enjoyments of their companions. Four of these made their escape on the evening before we left England, through the assistance of their confederates on shore. They gave the man on watch gin to drink, as he sat on the quarterdeck, the others singing and making fun. These four slipped over her bows into a boat provided for their escape. I never heard if they were retaken. We sailed without them.[31]

Of these four women, three were eventually recaptured and retried. Mary Burgess remained free for over three years until August 1792, supporting herself by selling old clothes around Petticoat Lane. Still complaining of poor health, she was arrested in her bed and once more tried at the Old Bailey. Again found guilty and sentenced to hang, she was eventually pardoned and transported for life, finally arriving in Australia on 25 October 1794. Sarah Cowden fared rather better. She was arrested at the end of September 1792, a little over a month after Mary Burgess. By this time she was making a living in Spitalfields in the silk industry and was able to call a string of witnesses to her reformed character. Although found guilty and sentenced to death, the jury 'recommended her to mercy', and the presiding judge, Lord Kenyon, added his own recommendation and admonishment: 'If you are let loose, I hope you will pursue the same line of industry which you have done according to the character you have had given you this day'. But, Cowden did not have to wait on the king in this instance. Instead, she pleaded her belly:

> A jury of matrons were empanelled on Sarah Cowden's
> application to the court that she was pregnant, and they
> returned a verdict that she was with quick child, upon
> which the execution was stayed.

She was never transported and was soon once again free on the streets of London.

For the court, its problems were not finished by the apparent capitulation of Cowden and her colleagues in June 1789. At the September sessions that year, as the 'Second Fleet' continued its preparations for departure, a further 12 men also refused the king's pardon. Some claimed innocence, questioning their treatment at the hands of the court. John Durham complained bitterly of his conviction on the basis of uncollaborated evidence and declared: 'I think I ought to suffer as a man; I am very sorry I must refuse it'. In this instance, it was not until the October sessions that all the men could be convinced to accept transportation and it was only when the colony in New South Wales became more established and secure that men and women stopped challenging the authority of the court in this way.[32]

Tools for a Breakout

Towards the end of the eighteenth century the judges at the Old Bailey turned for the first time to imprisonment on a large scale as a punishment for convicted felons. In the last two decades of the century over one-quarter of convicts were sentenced to a period of incarceration, often at hard labour. Imprisonment had become attractive owing both to dissatisfaction with the main alternative punishments (death, transportation and whipping), and because it promised to reform offenders. In order for London's prisons to realise that ambition, however, prison buildings and disciplinary regimes needed to be radically overhauled. That process would take time and the thousands of convicts sentenced

*to imprisonment in the late eighteenth century experienced a
regime little changed from the traditional system of open wards
and loose governance.*

The passage of the Penitentiary Act in 1779 heralded the
beginning of a new era in the history of imprisonment.
Authorising the construction of two new prisons in the
metropolis, the statute prescribed an entirely new type of
incarceration for felons. By following a strict regime,
prisoners were to be reformed through a combination of
hard labour, religious instruction and solitary confinement.
Rather than focusing on retribution and deterrence through
inflicting pain on the body, punishment would for the first
time concentrate on reforming the convict from within.
Everything from the prisoners' uniforms to their sustenance
was designed to humiliate them and force them to reflect on
the errors of their ways: their food and drink were to consist
only of 'bread, and any coarse meat, or other inferior food,
and water, or small beer'.[33]
Fortunately for the convicts, the two prisons were never
built, largely because the government was unwilling to pay
for them. Nonetheless, the aspirations of prison reformers
were gradually achieved through the piecemeal
reconstruction of existing prisons and the occasional
building of locally funded new ones. In London, a new
house of correction was built at Coldbath Fields, where
convicted felons were subjected to the controversial system
of solitary confinement. But London's primary prison for
felons, Newgate, remained largely unchanged. Rebuilt to the
same design in a fortress-like neo-classical style in 1780–83
following its destruction during the Gordon riots, Newgate
was an imposing structure when seen from the street, with
its 300 foot long rusticated stone walls, with no exterior
windows. Nonetheless, prisoners continued to be kept in
large open wards rather than individual cells. And although

the prison was divided into three main quadrangles, for male felons, female felons and debtors, in practice the different categories of prisoners were able to intermingle in parts of the prison such as the tap room. These included the accused awaiting their trials at the Old Bailey and convicts held awaiting the execution of sentences such as transportation and the death penalty, as well as the essentially new category of those convicts imprisoned as a form of punishment. Among the last was Renwick Williams, the 'Monster', who was imprisoned in 1790 for six years for his knife attacks on young women.

In 1799 one prisoner awaiting the execution of his sentence was William Harper, convicted in February and sentenced to death for impersonating a sailor in order to collect the prize money owed to the crew of the ship *The Powerful*, in reward for the capture of *The Countess of Rochmandorff* at St Helena in 1797. Unfortunately for Harper, when he presented his forged certificate it turned out that the real William Harper had already collected his prize several months before.[34] Another prisoner awaiting his execution was John Tate, who had been convicted of robbing a sailor in East Smithfield of his knife and 6s in company with John Connoway – also known as Irish Jack.[35]

Prisoners in Newgate were still allowed to have visitors and those visitors were allowed to bring food and drink, but, in a sign that prison life was changing, they were no longer allowed to have hard liquor. A regular visitor to the prison in the spring of 1799 was Elizabeth Willoughby, the common law wife of John Tate. According to John Pitt, one of the prison turnkeys, Willoughby 'was every day in the prison, backwards and forwards, to a man that she called her husband'. On 25 March:

> I let her in; she had been there some little time, about half
> an hour, and went out to get some refreshment for the
> prisoners. She returned again in about twenty minutes. I

Figure 5.05 Newgate Prison, rebuilt 1780–83. Credit: General
Photographic Agency/Hulton Archive/Getty Images

> was walking backwards and forwards in the passage, and
> I said to her, what have you been after. I thought she
> might have been out for spirits, or something of that sort.
> I asked her what she had got; says I, give me the bottle
> that you have got.

Pitt then proceeded to search her:

> I put my hand down her side, and felt something in her
> pocket; then I took her into the tap room and searched
> her, and in her pocket I found three spring saws, and four
> gimblets. Then I said, you have got more things about
> you; I then felt her breast, and found something concealed
> down her bosom; then I sent for Mr Kirby, and I saw
> these two chisels, and handles, taken from her bosom.

Rather than alcohol, Pitt had discovered a complete set of
tools calculated to engineer an escape from Newgate, despite
the prison's formidable construction. As Pitt explained:

> The spring saws would cut any iron in the world, the
> fetters, or the bars of the prison; and the chisels would
> break the walls for them to get out. The gimblets would
> make holes in the door, one after another, round, and
> would take any panel out of a door, with a saw.

Believing that Willoughby had more tools hidden about her
person, he sent for a woman, Ann Sells, to search her 'more
privately than a man in decency ought to do'. According to
Sells, 'I searched the prisoner, and found nothing upon her,
any further than in her pocket, a paper, and the money that
was out of the change'. On the paper was written, 'three
spring saws, four spike gimblets, two strong chisels, the saws
with frames' and there was a sketch of what the saws should
look like.

At this point the keeper of Newgate Prison, John Kirby,
was summoned (the long-serving former keeper, Richard
Akerman, died in 1789). Kirby asked Willoughby to explain
why she had these tools:

> She said, she was sent out by a man with a bushy head. I
> knew by that she meant Harper, a man who is under
> sentence of death, and has a very bushy head; and she
> told me he had given her a paper. I can swear that it is
> Harper's handwriting.

Joseph Russell, a shopman to an ironmonger's in Foster
Lane, off Newgate Street, a few blocks away from the
prison, had sold her the tools:

> I served her with those articles, three saws, two chisels,
> four gimblets, and two handles. There was a model of the
> pattern of the saw upon the paper which she produced;
> she said to me, I come from Saffron Hill, and presented
> me with that paper. I wrote what the articles came to upon
> that paper, and signed it with my name; they came to nine
> shillings and three pence. She smelt very strong of liquor.
> We had many different kinds of chisels, and I asked her
> what sort she wanted; she said, she did not know. I asked

her what trade the person was that they were for; and she
said a carpenter. She gave me a guinea, and one of my
masters gave her the change.

The fact Willoughby had been drinking helps explain
why the turnkey simply assumed she was concealing a
bottle. But regardless of her state of mind, she had been
caught red handed. Her defence at her eventual trial at the
Old Bailey seemed more an explanation, than an attempt to
escape punishment:

I came to John Tate, as I used to do every day, I used to
take him his dinner. As I was coming away, Harper
followed me, and asked me if I would go of an errand for
him. I said I would; he told me to go to Saffron Hill, and I
went there, and they told me to go to this gentleman's
house for the goods.

Unsurprisingly, the jury found her guilty. Her sentence, ironically given how well she knew the prison, was to be confined
in Newgate for two years, and to pay a 1s fine. Elizabeth
Willoughby was thus given more time to spend with her
pretended husband, at least until John Tate's sentence was
carried out.[36]

Conclusion

Each of the punishments imposed by the judges at the Old
Bailey proved to be problematic. The disorder of 'Tyburn
Fair' subverted the supposed deterrent effect of the death
penalty. Crowds transformed the pillory according to their
whim into either a celebration of the convict or a scene of
chaos and death. Transportation was subverted by the
extraordinary ability of convicts to find their way back to
England, not to mention the difficulty of finding a colony
wishing to serve as a receptacle for Britain's undesirables.
And imprisonment failed to live up to its promise of
reforming offenders. But most crucially, each new

experiment in penal policy failed to stop the apparently ever rising tide of crime. Punishments that were supposed to deter others from committing crime or reform offenders manifestly failed to do either.

Yet the judges soldiered on. Corporal and capital punishments increasingly fell out of favour owing to changing cultural attitudes towards violence and the growing faith in reform, and so transportation and imprisonment grew in popularity despite evidence that not only were they costly but they did not work. There was simply no alternative. What the eighteenth-century judicial system bequeathed to modern Britain is not only the punishment of imprisonment, now long established as our primary method of dealing with felons, but also the stubborn belief, in the face of all the evidence, that this punishment has the potential successfully to reform convicts and prevent crime.

Epilogue

London's first crime wave occurred long before the eighteenth century, but it was in the 1700s, with the advent of a popular press, that panic about crime became endemic. Although there were many innovative responses to this perceived threat (notably thief taking and the Bow Street runners), the government's first reaction was deeply traditional: to pass statute after statute mandating the death penalty for ever more narrowly defined crimes (such as embezzling banknotes by employees of the Bank of England). The rapid accumulation of these statutes created what became known as the 'Bloody Code', a body of law prescribing the death penalty for over 200 separate offences.

But this accumulation of laws, this apparently ever greater reliance on state-sponsored murder, was a strategy that could not last. The eighteenth century marked a turning point in the history of capital punishment. Reluctance to execute more than a small number of 'examples' meant that the 'Bloody Code' was never fully implemented and, as a proportion of total punishments, the number of convicts actually executed declined. At the same time, concern about the disorder and holiday-like atmosphere of public executions led to the abolition of the traditional procession from Newgate Prison to Tyburn. From 1783 executions took place immediately outside Newgate, eliminating the many traditions associated with the journey, while the introduction of 'the drop' expedited the deaths of the condemned, cutting short the minutes during which men

and women 'danced' for the execution crowd as they slowly
strangled. The power of the state was more forcefully
expressed and the crowd more easily controlled as
executions, acted out against the sober backdrop of
Newgate's impenetrable stone walls, became, though
proportionally fewer, considerably more efficient.

Capital punishment was further curbed in the next
century. The proportion of those pardoned after being
sentenced to death increased to over 90 percent.
Rationalisation of the criminal laws between the 1820s and
the 1840s led to a substantial reduction in the number of
capital offences and from the late 1830s it was rare for
anyone to be executed for anything other than murder. In
1861 the death penalty was abolished for all crimes except
murder, high treason, piracy with violence and arson in the
royal dockyards. This statutory limitation on capital
punishment was followed in 1868 by the abolition of public
executions. The small number that continued to be
performed were moved inside prison buildings and enacted
in front of only a handful of witnesses. It was not until 1965,
however, that the death penalty was abolished for murder;
and only in 2003, following the incorporation of the
European Convention on Human Rights, that it was totally
eliminated from British law. Peter Anthony Allen and John
Robson Walby were executed in Liverpool and Manchester
respectively on 13 August 1964 and became the last people
to suffer this punishment in Britain.

The death penalty worked (in theory) by deterrence, and
it could only be abolished when alternative strategies were
developed to convince prospective criminals that
punishment was both likely and unpleasant. The first
substantial alternative to hanging, transportation, flourished
into the early nineteenth century. By virtue of the long
voyage and the harsh conditions in a strange land that
convicts could expect, transportation was believed to act as a

deterrent to crime just like hanging, with the added virtue that jurors and judges had little hesitation in imposing it. At its peak in the 1830s, over 3,000 convicts a year were sent to Australia. But the growing belief that prisoners should be reformed rather than exiled, not to mention opposition from within the rapidly developing colony, led to the effective end of transportation in 1857. Over the course of the first half of the nineteenth century, and despite its frequently noted limitations, imprisonment became the primary method of punishing felons. Efforts to reform prisoners through either the 'silent system', in which all communication was forbidden, or solitary confinement, both of which were enforced through a disciplinary regime of the whip, treadmills and electric shock, failed as they proved both unenforceable and led to psychological illnesses. Faith in the reformative potential of hard labour also waned. Instead, like transportation before it, imprisonment's primary function gradually became the simple removal of individual criminals from society. With the Gaol Fees Abolition Act of 1815 and the establishment of a prison inspectorate in 1835, the state accepted the responsibility for living standards in prison and at least basic conditions improved.

The establishment of the Metropolitan Police in 1829 was an essential prerequisite to the reduction in the scope of the death penalty. The purpose of the 3,000 uniformed police, deployed in regular and frequent patrols through every street in London, was explicitly preventive: detection and punishment would be rendered redundant if no crimes were allowed to occur in the first place. Reflecting this optimistic premise, the Metropolitan Police did not even have a detective force until 1842. While many aspects of the new police were actually invented in the eighteenth century, such as the use of salaried officers, uniforms and prescribed beats, both the complete reliance on surveillance and the centralisation of control by the Home Office were nineteenth-century innovations. Prevention, of course, did not work, but the presence of so many officers on the streets did lead to greater enforcement of the laws against public order offences and a crackdown on begging, public drunkenness and illegal street selling.

The new police also fundamentally changed the relationship between the public and the law. With a professional body of men responsible for enforcement, ordinary citizens ceased to feel obliged to respond to cries of 'stop thief!' Although private prosecution remained, the police also played an increasingly important role in the courtroom both as witnesses and prosecutors, where their uniform accorded them a level of credibility not always available to other witnesses. In 1879 the shift towards a system of publicly funded and directed prosecutions was signalled by the appointment of the first director of public prosecutions.

The establishment of the new police also changed perceptions of crime. The line between legitimate and illegitimate behaviour was more firmly drawn and those on the wrong side of the law came to be seen as members of a separate 'criminal class', with their own amoral culture and distinctive lifestyle, living in separate slums or 'rookeries'. In the fourth volume of his *London Labour and the London Poor* (1861), Henry Mayhew depicted the lives of thieves, prostitutes and beggars as if they belonged to a different race. Epitomised in the concept of the 'habitual criminal', these Londoners came to be seen as innately lawless and inferior. Owing to the disproportionate attention the men and women identified in this way received from the police, these labels became essentially self-fulfilling.

But crime itself was also changing. The decline in violence, reflected since the Middle Ages in falling homicide rates, continued past the end of World War I. In contrast to the public swordfights of early eighteenth-century London, frequently played out between strangers, by the twentieth century most murderers were related to their victims and killings and other violent offences increasingly took place in the home, out of the sight of the police. As is evident in the decline of both state-inflicted corporal punishments and blood sports, public violence became ever more culturally unacceptable. Perhaps more surprising, there was also a significant decline in prosecutions for theft in the second half of the nineteenth century, as improving economic conditions and increased police surveillance reduced levels of petty and opportunistic crime, leaving a recalcitrant core of more professional criminal activity. Nonetheless, the relentless growth of newspapers meant that public awareness and concern about crime reached new heights. It is this combination of relatively low actual crime and intense press interest which forms the context for the media-induced panic over the Jack the Ripper murders in 1888 and any number of sensationalised murders in more recent times.

And what of the hanging court itself and its *Proceedings*? In 1834 the Old Bailey was renamed the Central Criminal Court and its jurisdiction was expanded geographically to reflect the growth of London and legally to include the most serious crimes from across the country. With the growing role of lawyers, trials became both longer and less entertaining. Nonetheless, accounts of trials continued to be published in the *Proceedings of the Central Criminal Court* throughout the nineteenth century and up until 1913. Almost as suddenly as it had started back in 1674, publication ceased in April 1913, bringing an extraordinary periodical run to an abrupt end. Over the course of its 240-year history, the *Proceedings* reported over 200,000 trials in almost 1 billion words, telling stories by turns sensational and mundane in their accounts of intense emotions and heartbreaking losses. After the final number, the public would have to rely on the newspaper press and, increasingly, the electronic media for their knowledge of the trials that took place in the world's most famous courthouse.

Further Reading

There is a substantial body of historical writing on eighteenth-century London, on the history of crime and punishment, and on the history of the Old Bailey and the *Old Bailey Proceedings*. For general background information on many of the topics covered in this book see the historical background pages of the *Old Bailey Proceedings Online* (www.oldbaileyonline.org/history/). The suggestions for further reading below concentrate on books available in print, although a rich body of periodical literature on all these topics also exists (see, for example, the *London Journal*). For a comprehensive bibliography relating to the Old Bailey and the history of criminal justice, see the bibliography in the *Old Bailey Proceedings Online* and for London more generally, *London's Past Online* (www.rhs.ac.uk/bibl/london.asp). All works listed below were published in London unless otherwise indicated.

Despite having been written over 80 years ago, the most authoritative history of eighteenth-century London remains Dorothy George, *London Life in the Eighteenth Century* (1925; 2nd edn, 1966, and still in print). In the last few decades this work has been supplemented by George Rudé, *Hanoverian London 1714–1808* (1971); Peter Earle, *A City Full of People: Men and Women of London 1650–1750* (1994) and *The Making of the English Middle Class: Business, Society and Family Life in London 1660–1730* (1989); Margaret Hunt, *The Middling Sort: Commerce, Gender and the Family in England, 1680–1780* (Berkeley, California, 1996); and Leonard Schwarz, *London in the Age of Industrialization:*

Entrepreneurs, Labour Force and Living Conditions, 1700–1850 (Cambridge, 1992). Two accessible recent collections of essays on eighteenth-century London history are Paul Griffiths and Mark S. R. Jenner, eds, *Londinopolis: Essays in the Cultural and Social History of Early Modern London* (Manchester, 2000); and Tim Hitchcock and Heather Shore, eds, *The Streets of London from the Great Fire to the Great Stink* (2003). For eighteenth-century histories addressed to a more popular audience, see Liza Picard, *Restoration London* (1997) and *Dr Johnson's London: Everyday Life in London in the Mid Eighteenth Century* (2001); and Maureen Waller, *1700: Scenes from London Life* (2001). Two excellent general histories of London are Roy Porter, *London: A Social History* (1994); and Peter Ackroyd, *London: The Biography* (2001).

The all-important desk reference work for the history of London is Ben Weinreb and Christopher Hibbert, eds, *The London Encyclopaedia* (1993).

More specialised studies that address the field in a useful, thematic way include Sheila O'Connell, *London 1753* (2003); Miles Ogborn, *Spaces of Modernity: London's Geographies, 1680–1780* (Guildford, 1998); Dan Cruickshank and Neil Burton, *Life in the Georgian City* (1990); Peter Guillery, *The Small House in Eighteenth-Century London* (New Haven and London, 2004); and Gretchen Gerzina, *Black London: Life Before Emancipation* (New Jersey, 1995). For the lives of the poor, see Tim Hitchcock, *Down and Out in Eighteenth-Century London* (2004); and Tanya Evans, *Unfortunate Objects: Lone Mothers in Eighteenth-Century London* (2005). Donna Andrew, *Philanthropy and Police: London Charity in the Eighteenth Century* (Princeton, New Jersey, 1989) examines the new charitable institutions of the metropolis.

General works on crime and criminal justice in this period include Clive Emsley, *Crime and Society in England,*

1750–1900 (3rd edn, 2004); J. A. Sharpe, *Crime in Early Modern England, 1550–1750* (2nd edn, 1999); Malcolm Gaskill, *Crime and Mentalities in Early Modern England* (Cambridge, 2000); and Garthine Walker, *Crime, Gender and Social Order in Early Modern England* (Cambridge, 2003). For two excellent recent surveys of crime and justice in London published for a wider audience, see Mark Herber, *Legal London: A Pictorial History* (Chichester, 1999) and *Criminal London: A Pictorial History from Medieval Times to 1939* (Chichester, 2002). For the key judicial institutions in London, see Donald Rumbelow, *The Triple Tree: Newgate, Tyburn, and the Old Bailey* (1982).

The starting point for any detailed history of criminal justice in England remains Leon Radzinowicz, *History of English Criminal Law and its Administration from 1750* (5 vols, London and Oxford, 1948–90); but for the eighteenth century this has now been supplemented by J. M. Beattie, *Crime and the Courts in England 1660–1800* (Princeton, 1986); Peter King, *Crime, Justice and Discretion in England, 1740–1820* (Oxford, 2000); Douglas Hay and Francis Snyder, eds, *Policing and Prosecution in Britain, 1750–1850* (Oxford, 1989); Douglas Hay et al., eds, *Albion's Fatal Tree: Crime and Society in Eighteenth-Century England* (1976); and John Brewer and John Styles, eds, *An Ungovernable People: The English and their Law in the Seventeenth and Eighteenth Centuries* (1980). For volumes specifically on the administration of justice in London in this period, see J. M. Beattie, *Policing and Punishment in London, 1660–1750: Urban Crime and the Limits of Terror* (Oxford, 2001); and R. B. Shoemaker, *Prosecution and Punishment: Petty Crime and the Law in London and Rural Middlesex*, c.1660–1725 (Cambridge, 1991).

More specialised works on policing include Clive Emsley, *The English Police: A Political and Social History* (Harlow, Essex, 1991); Elaine Reynolds, *Before the Bobbies: The Night*

Watch and Police Reform in Metropolitan London, 1720–1830 (Basingstoke, 1998); and Andrew Harris, *Policing the City: Crime and Legal Authority in London, 1780–1840* (Columbus, Ohio, 2004). For the activities of Henry and John Fielding at Bow Street, see Anthony Babbington, *A House in Bow Street: Crime and the Magistracy in London, 1740–1881* (1969; 2000); and Martin C. Battestin with Ruthe R. Battestin, *Henry Fielding: A Life* (1989). On the introduction of lawyers into the Old Bailey, see J. H. Langbein, *The Origins of Adversary Criminal Trial* (Oxford, 2003); and Allyson May, *The Bar and the Old Bailey, 1750–1850* (North Carolina, 2003).

The history of punishment has also generated a series of important works. For executions, see V. A. C. Gatrell, *The Hanging Tree: Execution and the English People 1770–1868* (Oxford, 1994). For transportation, see Roger Ekirch, *Bound for America: The Transportation of British Convicts to the Colonies 1718–1775* (Oxford, 1987); Gwenda Morgan and Peter Rushton, *Eighteenth-Century Criminal Transportation: The Formation of the Criminal Atlantic* (Basingstoke, 2004); Robert Hughes, *The Fatal Shore: A History of the Transportation of Convicts to Australia 1787–1868* (1987); and Siân Rees, *The Floating Brothel: The Extraordinary True Story of an Eighteenth-Century Ship and its Cargo of Female Convicts* (2002). For the rise of imprisonment, see Michael Ignatieff, *A Just Measure of Pain: The Penitentiary in the Industrial Revolution, 1750–1850* (1978; Harmondsworth, 1989).

There are several books about specific types of crime and social disorder. For theft, see Peter Linebaugh, *The London Hanged: Crime and Civil Society in the Eighteenth Century* (1991). For riot and public violence, see Robert Shoemaker, *The London Mob: Violence and Disorder in Eighteenth-Century England* (2004); Nicholas Rogers, *Crowds, Culture and Politics in Georgian Britain* (Oxford, 1998); George

Rudé, *Paris and London in the Eighteenth Century: Studies in Popular Protest* (1970); John Stevenson, *Popular Disturbances in England 1700–1870* (2nd edn, 1992), chapter 4; and Jennine Hurl-Eamon, *Gender and Petty Violence in London, 1680–1720* (Columbus, Ohio, 2005). For prostitution, the best works are by Tony Henderson, *Disorderly Women in Eighteenth-Century London: Prostitution and Control in the Metropolis, 1730–1830* (1999); and Randolph Trumbach, *Sex and the Gender Revolution. Volume 1, Heterosexuality and the Third Gender in Enlightenment London* (Chicago, 1998). For homosexuality, see Netta Goldsmith, *Worst of Crimes: Homosexuality and the Law in Eighteenth-Century London* (Aldershot, 1998); and Rictor Norton, *Mother Clap's Molly House: The Gay Subculture in England, 1700–1830* (1992). For the gin craze, see Jessica Warner, *Craze: Gin and Debauchery in the Age of Reason* (2003).

Individual criminals and thieftakers have also found their biographers. The best biography of this sort remains Gerald Howson's, *Thief-Taker General: The Rise and Fall of Jonathan Wild* (1970), but this has been supplemented by a number of engaging volumes including Donna Andrew and Randall McGowen, *The Perreaus and Mrs Rudd: Forgery and Betrayal in Eighteenth-Century London* (Berkeley, California, 2001); John Brewer, *Sentimental Murder: Love and Madness in the Eighteenth Century* (2004) (about the murder of Martha Ray by James Hackman); James Sharpe, *Dick Turpin: The Myth of the English Highwayman* (2004); and Jan Bondeson, *The London Monster* (2000). Lucy Moore has pioneered a new form of popular collective criminal biography with her *The Thieves' Opera: The Remarkable Lives and Deaths of Jonathan Wild, Thief-Taker, and Jack Sheppard, House-Breaker* (London, 1997) and *Con Men and Cutpurses: Scenes from the Hogarthian Underworld* (2000).

Finally, eighteenth-century criminal narratives of the sort on which this book is based are the subject of a growing literature including Hal Gladfelder, *Criminality and Narrative in Eighteenth-Century England: Beyond the Law* (2001); Gillian Spraggs, *Outlaws and Highwaymen: The Cult of the Robber in England from the Middle Ages to the Nineteenth Century* (2001); Philip Rawlings, *Drunks, Whores and Idle Apprentices: Criminal Biographies of the Eighteenth Century* (1992); and Lincoln B. Faller, *Turned to Account: The Forms and Functions of Criminal Biography in Late Seventeenth- and Early Eighteenth-Century England* (Cambridge, 1987).

Notes

Prologue

[1] John Strype, *A Survey of the Cities of London and Westminster ... Written at First in ... 1598 by John Stow ... Now ... Brought Down from the Year 1633 ... to the Present Time*, 2 vols (1720); quoted in Ben Weinreb and Christopher Hibbert, eds, *The London Encyclopedia* (1983), p. 144.

[2] V. A. C. Gatrell, *The Hanging Tree: Execution and the English people, 1770–1868* (Oxford, 1994), p. 616.

[3] *Old Bailey Proceedings Online* (www.oldbaileyonline.org, 1 May 2006; henceforth *OBP*), January 1742, Eleanor Brown (t17420115-9); London Metropolitan Archives (henceforth LMA), CLA/047/LJ/01/0784-7; CLA/047/LJ/04/109 (SM/109), Dec 1741–Oct 1742.

Introduction

[1] Thomas Brown, *Amusements Serious and Comical, Calculated for the Meridian of London* (2nd edn 1702), p. 22.

[2] James Dawson Burn, *The Autobiography of a Beggar Boy*, ed. with an introduction by David Vincent (1978), p. 57.

[3] Henry Fielding, *An Enquiry into the Causes of the Late Increase of Robbers, etc., With some Proposals for Remedying this Growing Evil* (1751), pp. 142–3.

[4] Robert Southey, *Letters from England* (2nd edn, 1808), i, pp. 122–3.

[5] N. Bailey, *Dictionarium Britannicum* (1730), under gentleman.

[6] *The Cheats of London Exposed: or The Tricks of the Town Laid Open to Both Sexes* (1770), pp. 87–8.

Chapter 1

[1]   *London Evening Post*, 13–15 May 1735.

[2]   *London Evening Post*, 22–24 May 1735.

[3]   OBP, December 1734, John Sutton (t17341204-54).

[4]   *London Evening Post*, 3–5 June 1735.

[5]   OBP, May 1735, John Sutton (t17350522-19).

[6]   British Library (henceforth BL), Add. MS, 27826, 'Place Papers, vol. xxxviii', fol.159.

[7]   For the trial of Catherine Hayes, see Chapter 2, 'He was None the Best of Husbands'.

[8]   *London Journal*, 30 July 1726; *Weekly Journal, Or British Gazetteer*, 30 July 1726; both quoted at 'Homosexuality in Eighteenth-Century Britain, A Source Book Compiled by Rictor Norton', www.infopt.demon.co.uk, consulted on 1 May 2006; OBP, July 1726, Margaret Clap (t17260711-54), and April 1726, Gabriel Lawrence (t17260420-64).

[9]   For the warrant, see Lucy Moore, ed., *Con Men and Cutpurses: Scenes from the Hogarthian Underworld* (2000), pp. 261–2.

[10] *London Journal*, 29 May 1725.

[11] [Daniel Defoe], *The Life of Jonathan Wilde, Thief-Taker General of Great Britain and Ireland, from his Birth to his Death* (1725).

[12] OBP, May 1725, Jonathan Wild (t17250513-55).

[13] LMA, OB/SP/1774/12/036.

[14] *Public Advertiser*, 20 December 1754.

[15] OBP, September 1774, John Viner (t17740907-1).

[16] OBP, October 1774, Edward Parker (t17741019-33).

[17] OBP, December 1774, William Pritchard, Peter Thane, and Edward Parker (t17741207-36).

[18] OBP, September 1742, William Bird (t17420909-37) and October 1742, William Bird (t17421013-19).

[19] OBP, July 1735, John Dun (t17350702-36).

[20] *Memoirs of the Life and Times of Sir Thomas Deveil* (1748), p. 55.

[21] *Select Trials at the Sessions-House in the Old-Bailey*, 4 vols (Dublin, 1742), iv, pp. 131–2.

[22] OBP, July 1735, John Dun (t17350702-36); and September 1735, Patrick Gaffney and James Barthelemi (t17350911-14).

23 Ben Weinreb and Christopher Hibbert, eds, *The London Encyclopedia* (1983), pp. 451–3.
24 Sunset that evening was 6.22 pm.
25 BL, Add. MS, 27825, 'Place Papers, vol. xxxvii', fol. 147.
26 *The Ordinary of Newgate, His Account of the Behaviour, Confession, and Dying Words, of the Malefactors, Who were Executed at Tyburn, on Friday the 7th of June, 1745* (1745), p. 8.
27 Charles Dickens, *Sketches by Boz* (1836; Wordsworth Edition, 1999), p. 73.
28 *The Ordinary of Newgate, His Account ... 7th of June 1745* (1745), pp. 8, 10; *OBP*, April 1745, Mary Cut-and-Come-Again (t17450424-31).
29 *OBP*, September 1748, John Kates (t17480907-17).
30 *OBP*, January 1756, William Thornton (t17560115-29).
31 *OBP*, July 1741, Mary Smith, alias Rouse (t17410701-13).
32 *OBP*, April 1742, Elizabeth Bennet (t17420428-11); and April 1742, Elizabeth Newbury (t17420428-12).

Chapter 2

1 The National Archives (henceforth TNA), SP 44/87, fols 69, 76–7 (26 October 1761).
2 *The Affecting Case of the Unfortunate Thomas Daniels* (1761).
3 *OBP*, September 1761, Thomas Daniels (t17610916-44).
4 *British Journal*, 14 May 1727.
5 For the trials of the sodomites, see Chapter 1, 'Mother Clap's Molly House'.
6 *The Ordinary of Newgate, His Account... 9th of this instant May, 1726* (1726), pp. 2–3.
7 *A Narrative of the Barbarous and Unheard of Murder of Mr John Hayes, by Catherine his Wife, Thomas Billings, and Thomas Wood, on the 1st of March at Night* (1726).
8 *A New Miscellany* (1730), pp. 34–6.
9 *OBP*, April 1726, Katharine Hays (note alternative spelling of 'Catherine Hayes'), (t17260420-42).
10 Charles Fearne, *Minutes of the Proceedings at the Trial of Rear Admiral Knowles, Before a Court-Martial, held on board his Majesty's Yacht the Charlotte... on the 1st of October 1748* (1750).

11 *The Trial of Capt. Edward Clark, Commander of His Majesty's Ship the Canterbury, for the Murder of Capt. Tho. Innes, Commander of His Majesty's Ship the Warwick; in a Duel in Hyde Park* (1750), p. 11.

12 *Trial of Capt. Edward Clark*, p. 9.

13 *Trial of Capt. Edward Clark*, pp. 4–5.

14 *Trial of Capt. Edward Clark*, p. 12.

15 *Trial of Capt. Edward Clark*, p. 15.

16 *Trial of Capt. Edward Clark*, p. 18.

17 *OBP*, April 1750, Edward Clark (t17500425-19).

18 LMA, LSP/1751/5 (July).

19 *OBP*, July 1751, Charles Troop (t17510703-39).

20 Cited in George Rudé, *Paris and London in the Eighteenth Century: Studies in Popular Protest* (1970), p. 220.

21 *Spittlefields and Shoreditch in an Uproar OR the Devil to Pay with the English and Irish* [1736].

22 *London Evening Post*, 27–29 July 1730.

23 Rudé, *Paris and London*, p. 207.

24 *OBP*, October 1736, Robert Page, William Orman Rod, and Thomas Putrode (t17361013-5), and Robert Mickey and Joshua Hall (t17361013-6).

25 Henry Fielding, *A Charge Delivered to the Grand Jury... the 29th of June 1749* (1749), in *An Enquiry into the Causes of the Late Increase of Robbers and Related Writings*, ed. Malvin R. Zirker (1988), p. 23.

26 *London Evening Post*, 1–4 July 1749.

27 *London Evening Post*, 1–4 July 1749.

28 Henry Fielding, *A True State of the Case of Bosavern Penlez* (1749), in *Enquiry into the Causes*, ed. Zirker, pp. 55–6.

29 LMA, MJ/SP/1749/07/096.

30 Fielding, *True State of the Case*, p. 50.

31 Malvin R. Zirker, 'General Introduction', in *Enquiry into the Causes*, ed. Zirker, p. xl.

32 Peter Linebaugh, 'The Tyburn Riot Against the Surgeons' in Douglas Hay et al., eds, *Albion's Fatal Tree* (1975), p. 94, citing TNA, SP 35/29, pt 2, fol. 52.

33 *The Ordinary of Newgate, His Account ... 18th of October, 1749* (1749), p. 91.

[34] *London Evening Post*, 17–19 October 1749.

[35] Zirker, 'General Introduction', in *Enquiry into the Causes*, ed. Zirker, p. xli.

[36] *T—t—m and V—d—t. A Collection of the Advertisements and Hand-Bills, Serious, Satyrical and Humorous, Published on Both Sides During the Election for the City and Liberty of Westminster* (Dublin, 1749), pp. 47–8.

[37] Cited in Nicholas Rogers, 'Aristocratic Clientage, Trade and Dependency: Popular Politics in Pre-Radical Westminster', *Past and Present* 61 (1973), p. 100.

[38] *The Case of the Unfortunate Bosavern Penlez* (1749), pp. 27, 39, 43, 54.

[39] Fielding, *A True State of the Case of Bosavern Penlez*, in *Enquiry into the Causes*, ed. Zirker, pp. 57–9.

[40] Linebaugh, 'The Tyburn Riot', pp. 89–102; Rogers, 'Aristocratic Clientage', pp. 98–100; Zirker, 'General Introduction', in *Enquiry into the Causes*, ed. Zirker, p. 1; *OBP*, September 1749, John Willson, Bosavern Pen Lez, and Benjamin Launder (t17490906-4).

[41] Samuel Romilly, *Memoirs of the Life of Sir S. Romilly, Written by Himself; With a Selection from his Correspondence. Edited by his Sons* (1840), i, p. 114.

[42] *Memoirs of the Life of Sir S. Romilly*, i, p. 115.

[43] *Memoirs of the Life of Sir S. Romilly*, i, p. 116.

[44] Ann Candler, *Poetical Attempts by Ann Candler, a Suffolk Cottager with a Short Narrative of Her Life* (Ipswich, 1803), p. 10.

[45] *OBP*, June 1780, James Jackson (t17800628-112).

[46] *OBP*, June 1780, Richard Hyde (t17800628-111).

[47] *OBP*, June 1780, Benjamin Bowsey (t17800628-33).

[48] Ben Weinreb and Christopher Hibbert, eds, *The London Encyclopedia* (1983), p. 546.

[49] 'The Gordon Riots', www.nationalarchives.gov.uk/pathways/blackhistory/rights/gordon.htm (4 May 2006).

[50] Quoted in Christopher Hibbert, *King Mob: The Story of Lord George Gordon and the Riots of 1780* (1959), p. 86.

[51] René Huchon, *George Crabbe and His Times, 1754–1832* (1968), p. 103.

[52] Hibbert, *King Mob*, p. 86.

53 *OBP*, June 1780, Francis Mockford (t17800628-92).
54 *Memoirs of the Life of Sir S. Romilly*, i, p. 124.
55 *Memoirs of the Life of Sir S. Romilly*, i, p. 122.
56 *The Autobiography of Francis Place (1771–1854)*, ed. Mary Thale (1972), p. 34.
57 Huchon, *George Crabbe*, p. 103.
58 BL, Add. MS, 27,825, 'Place Papers, vol. xxxvii', fol. 146.
59 *OBP*, September 1796, William Clark (t17960914-22).
60 Georg Forster, *Werke*, xii, *Tagebücher* (Berlin, 1973), pp. 297–8, quoted in Jan Bondeson, *The London Monster* (2000), p. 51. This book provides the most comprehensive secondary account of these events.
61 Bondeson, *Monster*, pp. 113–14.
62 Bondeson, *Monster*, p. 137.
63 Bondeson, *Monster*, p. 162.
64 *OBP*, July 1790, Renwick Williams (t17900708-1); and December 1790, Renwick Williams (t17901208-54).

Chapter 3

1 *OBP*, December 1739, Elizabeth Bradshaw (t17391205-52).
2 César de Saussure, *A Foreign View of England in 1725–1729: The Letters of Monsieur César De Saussure to His Family*, trans. and ed. Mme Van Muyden (1995), p. 74.
3 Andrea McKenzie, '"This death some strong and stout hearted man doth choose": The practice of *peine forte et dure* in seventeenth- and eighteenth-century England', *Law and History Review*, 23 (June 2005), p. 283.
4 Gerald Howson, *Thief-taker General: The Rise and Fall of Jonathan Wild* (1970), p. 313.
5 *The Ordinary of Newgate, His Account ... 8th of February 1720–21* (1721), pp. 4–5.
6 *The Ordinary of Newgate, His Account ... 8th of February 1720–21*, p. 5.
7 *The Ordinary of Newgate, His Account ... 8th of February 1720–21*, p. 5.

8   *The Ordinary of Newgate, His Account ... 8th of February 1720–21*, pp. 2–3.

9   McKenzie, "'This death some strong and stout hearted man doth choose"'; Andrea McKenzie, 'Martyrs in Low Life? Dying "Game" in Augustan England', *Journal of British Studies*, 42 (2003), pp. 167–205.

10   *OBP*, January 1721, William Spigget alias Spiggot, Thomas Phillips alias Cross, and William Heater (t17210113-43).

11   LMA, Repertories of the Court of Aldermen, cxxix, pp. 368, 376–7 (29 September and 7 October 1725).

12   *OBP*, April 1725, Susan Grimes (t17250407-66).

13   *London Evening Post*, 3–6 February 1733.

14   LMA, City Sessions Papers, February 1733.

15   *London Magazine*, 8–10 February 1733, pp. 95–6.

16   Amy Masciola, "'I can see by the woman's features that she is capable of any wickedness": Images of Sarah Malcolm in Court Records and Popular Literature', conference paper presented at 'Tales from the Old Bailey: Writing a New History from Below', University of Hertfordshire, 5 July 2004.

17   *The Ordinary of Newgate, His Account ... 5th of this instant March, 1733* (1733), p. 16.

18   *A True Copy of the Paper, Delivered the Night before her Execution by Sarah Malcolm to the Rev. Mr Piddington* (1733).

19   *London Magazine*, 10 February 1733, p. 96.

20   *The Ordinary of Newgate, His Account ... 5th of this instant March, 1733*, pp. 22–3.

21   John Ireland, *Hogarth Illustrated* (1806), ii, p. 313.

22   Paul Langford, *A Polite and Commercial People: England 1727–1783* (Oxford, 1989), p. 31.

23   Henry Fielding, *Amelia* (Dublin, 1752), i, p. 31. For Hayes's trial, see Chapter 2, Crimes of Blood.

24   *OBP*, February 1733, Sarah Malcolm (t17330221-52).

25   *OBP*, September 1771, Ann Thomas, Elizabeth Ward and Thomas Ward (t17710911-85).

26   John Howard, *The State of the Prisons in England and Wales, with Preliminary Observations, and an Account of Some Foreign Prisons* (1777), p. 193.

[27] James Boswell, *Life of Samuel Johnson* (1791; 1979), ed. Christopher Hibbert, p. 146, 20 October 1769.

[28] *OBP*, October 1769, Joseph Baretti (t17691018-9).

[29] *OBP*, October 1746, George Taylor and Mary Robinson (t17461015-20).

[30] J.M. Beattie, 'Scales of Justice: Defence Counsel and the English Criminal Trial in the Eighteenth and Nineteenth Centuries', *Law and History Review*, 9 (1991), p. 264, n. 54.

[31] John Beattie, 'Garrow for the Defence', *History Today*, 41 (February 1991), p. 51; John H. Langbein, *The Origins of Adversary Criminal Trial* (Oxford, 2003), p. 315.

[32] *OBP*, September 1788, Joseph Barney (t17880910-67); January 1789, William Eversal and John Hathaway (t17890114-19); and May 1793, William Roberts (t17930529-43).

[33] Thomas Hague, *A Letter to William Garrow, Esq., in which the Conduct of Counsel in the Cross-Examination of Witnesses, and Commenting on their Testimony, is Fully Discussed, and the Licentiousness of the Bar Exposed* [c. 1808], p. 45.

[34] *OBP*, September 1791, George Dingler (t17910914-1); Langbein, *Origins of Adversary Criminal Trial*, p. 265.

[35] Samuel Johnson, *An Account of the Life of Mr Richard Savage* (1744), pp. 35–6.

[36] Johnson, *Savage*, p. 36.

[37] Johnson, *Savage*, p. 37.

[38] Johnson, *Savage*, p. 38.

[39] Johnson, *Savage*, p. 39.

[40] Johnson, *Savage*, pp. 39–40.

[41] Johnson, *Savage*, p. 40.

[42] [Charles Beckingham and Thomas Cooke (?)], *The Life of Mr. Richard Savage* (1727), pp. 23–4.

[43] [Beckingham and Cooke], *Life*, pp. 25–8.

[44] Johnson, *Savage*, p. 45.

[45] *OBP*, December 1727, Richard Savage, James Gregory and William Merchant (t17271206-24).

[46] *OBP*, April 1732, Edward Wentland alias Winkland (t17320419-9).

Chapter 4

1 *The City Cheat Discovered, or, a New Coffee House Song* (1691), Pepys Ballads, 5.102, consulted at http://emc.english.vcsb.edu/ballad_project (10 May 2006).

2 *OBP*, January 1725, Ann Hussey (t17250115-21).

3 *OBP*, January 1727, Elizabeth Roberts alias Bustock (t17270113-11).

4 *OBP*, January 1726, Phillis Noble (t17260114-5).

5 *OBP*, August 1726, Isabel Lucky and Sarah Jones (t17260831-27).

6 *OBP*, August 1725, Susan Brockway and Mary Gardner (t17250827-2).

7 *OBP*, December 1718, John Bowes and Hugh Ryly (t17181205-24).

8 *OBP*, July 1732, Thomas Gordon (t17320705-30).

9 *A Complete History of James Maclaine, the Gentleman Highwayman* (1750), p. 5.

10 *The Ordinary of Newgate, His Account … 3 October, 1750* (1750), p. 87, *OBP*, October 1750 (oa17501003).

11 *Complete History of James Maclaine*, p. 21.

12 *Ordinary of Newgate, His Account … 3 October, 1750*, p. 88.

13 *Horace Walpole's Correspondence*, ed. W. S. Lewis, 48 vols (London, New Haven, and Oxford, 1937–1983), xiii, p. 23, xl, pp. 63–5.

14 *Whitehall Evening Post*, 26–28 July 1750.

15 *Horace Walpole's Correspondence*, xx, pp. 168–9.

16 *Gentleman's Magazine*, 20 (1750), p. 390.

17 *A Genuine Account of the Life and Actions of James Maclaine, Highwayman* [1750?], p. 22.

18 *Genuine Account of the Life and Actions of James Maclaine*, p. 12.

19 *Genuine Account of the Life and Actions of James Maclaine*, p. 14; *Horace Walpole's Correspondence*, xx, p. 188.

20 *Genuine Account of the Life and Actions of James Maclaine*, pp. 11, 13; *Complete History of James Maclaine*, p. 52.

21 *Horace Walpole's Correspondence*, xx, p. 199.

22 *Horace Walpole's Correspondence*, xx, p. 188.

[23] *Ordinary of Newgate, His Account ... 3 October, 1750,* pp. 85, 88.

[24] *Public Advertiser,* 29 February and 1 March 1764.

[25] *The Malefactor's Register; or the Newgate and Tyburn Calendar,* 5 vols (1779), iii, p. 276.

[26] *OBP,* September 1750, James Macleane (t17500912-22).

[27] Daniel Defoe, *The History and Remarkable Life of the Truly Honourable Col. Jacque, Commonly Called Col. Jack* (1722; Oxford, 1970), p. 9.

[28] *OBP,* August 1730, Charles Cornet alias Cornish (t17300828-45).

[29] *OBP,* February 1731, Andrew Noland and John Allright (t17310224-19).

[30] *OBP,* February 1731, Malachy Southy and George Beal (t17310224-31).

[31] *OBP,* April 1732, Henry Whitesides and George Scott (t17320419-22).

[32] *OBP,* June 1731, Edward Perkins (t17310602-9), and July 1734, John Fossey (t17340710-38).

[33] *OBP,* July 1731, Edward Perkins (t17310714-14).

[34] *OBP,* December 1731, Joseph Paterson alias Paternoster and Joseph Darvan (t17311208-26).

[35] *OBP,* December 1731, Joseph Paterson alias Peterson alias Paternoster and Joseph Darvan (t17311208-26, t17311208-27 and t17311208-74).

[36] *OBP,* May 1732, John Crotch alias Yarmouth (t17320525-22).

[37] *OBP,* January 1731, Thomas Coleman alias John Haynes (t17310115-59), and May 1739, Thomas Coleman (t17390502-42).

[38] Daniel Defoe, *Some Considerations upon Street-Walkers* (1726); quoted in Sean Shesgreen, *Images of the Outcast: The Urban Poor in the Cries of London* (Manchester, 2002), pp. 114–15.

[39] Quoted in Ruth McClure, *Coram's Children: The London Foundling Hospital in the Eighteenth Century* (New Haven, Connecticut, 1981), p. 19.

[40] Quoted in Hoh-Cheung and Lorna H. Mui, *Shops and Shopkeeping in Eighteenth-Century England* (1989), p. 222.

[41] *A Warning for House Keepers, or, A Discovery of all Sorts of Thieves and Robbers* (1676), pp. 6–7.

[42] *OBP*, September 1790, Mary Hudson and Hannah Hobbs (t17900915-36).

[43] *An Authentic Account of the Late Unfortunate Doctor William Dodd* (Rochester, 1777), p. 16.

[44] *An Authentic Account of the Late Unfortunate Doctor William Dodd*, p. 16.

[45] *A Full and Circumstantial Account of the Trial of the Reverend Doctor Dodd* (1777), pp. 41, 55.

[46] *The Letters of Samuel Johnson*, ed. R. W. Chapman, 3 vols (Oxford, 1952), ii, p. 180 (no. 524). See also John J. Burke, Jr., 'Crime and Punishment in 1777: The Execution of Dr William Dodd and its Impact upon his Contemporaries', in W. B. Thesing, ed., *Executions and the British Experience from the Seventeenth to the Twentieth Century* (1990), pp. 59–75.

[47] *Morning Post and Daily Advertiser*, 17 May 1777.

[48] Gerald Howson, *The Macaroni Parson* (1973), pp. 178–9.

[49] *Morning Chronicle and London Advertiser*, 17 May 1777.

[50] BL, Add. MS, 24419, fol. 6 (16 May 1777).

[51] Philip Rawlings, 'William Dodd', *Oxford Dictionary of National Biography* (www.oxforddnb.com, 12 February 2006).

[52] John Hawkins, *The Life of Samuel Johnson* (1787), pp. 528–9.

[53] *Morning Post and Daily Advertiser*, 28 June 1777; *Morning Chronicle and London Advertiser*, 28 June 1777.

[54] *Morning Post and Daily Advertiser*, 28 June 1777.

[55] *An Authentic Account of the Late Unfortunate Doctor William Dodd*, pp. 25, 27; *OBP*, February 1777, William Dodd (t17770219-1) and May 1777, William Dodd (o17770514-1).

Chapter 5

[1] *OBP*, August 1786, punishment summary (s17860830-1).

[2] BL, Add. MS, 27826, 'Place Papers, vol. xxxviii', Manners and Morals, ii, fol. 97.

382 Notes

3   *OBP*, October 1751, Alexander Byrne, James Mallone and
Terence McCane (t17511016-13).
4   *The Ordinary of Newgate's Account ... 2 July 1752* (1752), *OBP*,
July 1752 (oa17520702); *The Ordinary of Newgate's Account ...
23 March 1752* (1752), *OBP*, March 1752 (oa17520323); *The
Ordinary of Newgate's Account ... 11th of November 1751* (1751),
OBP, November 1751 (oa17511111); *OBP*, January 1752,
Michael Magennis (t17520116-28); and June 1752,
supplementary material (o17520625-2).
5   *The Life and Infamous Actions of that Perjured Villain John
Waller* (1732), pp. 7, 10, 29.
6   *OBP*, January 1730, James Dalton (t17300116-13).
7   *OBP*, April 1730, James Dalton (t17300408-61).
8   *OBP*, October 1731, Charles Knowles and Sarah Harper
(t17311013-47).
9   *Infamous Actions*, p. 21.
10 *Infamous Actions*, p. 29.
11 *Infamous Actions*, p. 30.
12 Edward Umfreville, *Lex Coronatoria: Or, the Office and Duty of
Coroners*, 2 vols (1761), i, p. 43.
13 *London Evening Post*, 7–10 October 1732.
14 TNA, 'Bills of Sheriff's Craving', E197/33, fol. 337.
15 BL, Add. MS, 27826, 'Place Papers, vol. xxxviii', Manners and
Morals, ii, fols. 173–5.
16 [Thomas Talfourd], 'Brief Observations on the Punishment
of the Pillory', in *The Pamphleteer: Respectfully Dedicated to both
Houses of Punishment* (1814), p. 548.
17 *OBP*, May 1732, John Waller (t17320525-69); May 1732,
punishment summary (s17320525-1); and September 1732,
Edward Dalton, Richard Griffith alias Sergeant and William
Belt alias Worrel (t17320906-69).
18 *OBP*, September 1783, Thomas Limpus (t17830910-41). For
a fuller treatment of Limpus's career, see Emma Christopher,
'Steal a handkerchief, see the world: The trans-oceanic voyaging
of Thomas Limpus', ANU EPress – Different Modes of Trans-
National History, http://epress.anu.edu.au/cw/ pdf/cw_part2.pdf
(consulted on 17 May 2006).
19 *OBP*, September 1783, Charles Keeling (t17830910-20).

[20] A. Roger Ekirch, 'Great Britain's Secret Convict Trade to America, 1783–1784', *American Historical Review*, 89, 5 (Dec., 1984), pp. 1285–91.

[21] Edward Miles Riley, ed., *The Journal of John Harrower: An Indentured Servant in the Colony of Virginia, 1773–1776* (Williamsburg, Virginia, 1963), pp. 24–5.

[22] *OBP*, September 1780, David Hart (t17800913-34); January 1782, David Hart (t17820109-62); February 1783, Charles Stokes, David Hart and Philip Gibson (t17830226-5); and April 1783, David Hart (t17830430-65).

[23] Carl Winslow, 'Sussex Smugglers' in Douglas Hay et al., eds, *Albion's Fatal Tree: Crime and Society in Eighteenth-Century England* (1975), pp. 119–66.

[24] *OBP*, April 1783, John Mills (t17830430-70).

[25] Ekirch, 'Secret Convict Trade'.

[26] Quoted in Emma Christopher, 'Steal a handkerchief', p. 84.

[27] *OBP*, September 1783, supplementary material (s17830910-1).

[28] BL, Add. MS, 27828, 'Place Papers, vol. xl', Manners and Morals, iv, fol. 119.

[29] *The Times*, 27 March 1789 and 13 April 1789.

[30] *The Times*, 6 June 1789.

[31] Tim Flannery, ed., *The Life and Adventures of John Nicol, Mariner* (1822; Melbourne, 1997), p. 119.

[32] *OBP*, October 1787, Mary wife of William Burgess (t17871024-30); February 1788, Martha Cutler, Sarah Cowden and Sarah Storer (t17880227-25); April 1789, supplementary material: Sarah Cowden and Eleanor Kirvan otherwise Caravan (o17890422-1); June 1789, supplementary material: Martha Cutler, Sarah Cowden, Sarah Storer, Sarah Mills, Jane Tyler and Mary Burgess (o17890603-1); September 1789, supplementary material (s17890909-1); September 1792, Mary Burgess (t17920912-18); October 1792, Sarah Cowden (t17921031-7); October 1792, punishment summary (s17921031-1); and June 1794, supplementary material (o17940604-2). See also Lynn MacKay, 'Refusing the Royal Pardon: London Capital Convicts and the Reactions of the Courts and Press, 1789', *London Journal*, 28, 2 (2003), pp. 21–40; and Siân Rees, *The Floating*

Brothel: The Extraordinary True Story of an Eighteenth-Century Ship and its Cargo of Female Convicts (2001).

[33] Quoted by J. M. Beattie, *Crime and the Courts in England 1660–1800* (Princeton, 1986), p. 575.

[34] *OBP*, February 1799, William Harper (t17990220-57).

[35] *OBP*, February 1799, John Tate and John Connoway otherwise Irish Jack (t17990220-56).

[36] *OBP*, May 1799, Elizabeth Willoughby (t17990508-53).

Index

Note: page numbers in **bold** refer to illustrations.